A FIELD GUIDE TO THE

BIRDS

—— OF ——

THAILAND

CRAIG ROBSON

ILLUSTRATED BY RICHARD ALLEN, TIM WORFOLK, STEPHEN MESSAGE,
JAN WILCZUR, CLIVE BYERS, MIKE LANGMAN,
IAN LEWINGTON, CHRISTOPHER SCHMIDT, ANDREW MACKAY,
JOHN COX, ANTHONY DISLEY, HILARY BURN,
DANIEL COLE AND MARTIN ELLIOTT.

ASIA BOOKS

Published and Distributed by
Asia Books Co., Ltd.
5 Sukhumvit Road Soi 61,
P.O. Box 40,
Bangkok 10110, Thailand
Tel: (66 2) 715-9000 ext. 3202–4
Fax: (66 2) 714-2799
E-mail: information@asiabooks.com
Website: www.asiabooks.com

10 9 8 7 6 5 4 3 2 1

ISBN 1 84330 058 3

Publishing Manager: Jo Hemmings
Project Editor: Lorna Sharrock
Editor: Nigel Collar
Editorial Assistant: Daniela Filippin
Preliminary editorial liaison: Mike Unwin
Design and plate make-up: D & N Publishing, Marlborough, Wiltshire
Cartography: Carte Blanche and Shane O'Dwyer
Production: Joan Woodroffe

Reproduction by Modern Age Repro Co. Ltd, Hong Kong
Printed and bound in Singapore by Tien Wah Press (Pte) Ltd

CONTENTS

INTRODUCTION

This guide is a condensed version of *A Field Guide to the Birds of South-East Asia* (Robson 2000), tailored specifically for Thailand, and intended to be as portable as possible, for use in the field. Obviously, in order to save space and, therefore, weight, the species accounts are relatively short and are intended to be as concise as possible within the publisher's brief. For more detailed information on a given species, the above-mentioned guide should be consulted.

Taxonomy and nomenclature follow *A Field Guide to the Birds of South-East Asia*, with two exceptions; **Slender-billed Vulture** *Gyps tenuirostris* is split from **Long-billed (Indian) Vulture** *G. indicus*, following Rasmussen and Parry (2001), and the very distinctive **Green-backed Flycatcher** *Ficedula elisae* is split from **Narcissus Flycatcher** *F. narcissina,* following Philip Round's *Field Check-list of Thai Birds* (Round 2000).

Unfortunately, however, in order to balance out the plates, and compare some similar species, it has not been possible to follow the exact (correct) species order.

A small number of additional illustrations, depicting recently recorded species in Thailand and certain races found in Thailand, have been executed for this book.

All species recorded in Thailand up to mid-February 2001 are dealt with and illustrated. Two new species for Thailand have been recorded between this date and the book going to press: **Pallid Harrier** *Circus macrourus* at Thale Noi, S Thailand, in late February 2001, and **Long-tailed Wren Babbler** *Spelaeornis chocolatinus* on a high mountain near Umphang, W Thailand, in late April 2001.

If readers find any errors or omissions, the author (c/o the publishers, New Holland) would be pleased to receive any information which updates or corrects that presented herein, in the hope that an improved edition may appear in the future.

SPECIES ACCOUNT/PLATE INFORMATION

◆ The **total length** of each species appears after the species name.

◆ A comparative approach has been adopted with species descriptions, where scarcer species are generally compared to commoner or more widespread species. In general, those species considered to be easily identifiable have been afforded less coverage than the more difficult species.

◆ **Comparisons between similar species** are dealt with directly and separately under the various sex/age or other headings.

◆ **Males** are described first (except in polyandrous species) and female plumage compared directly to the male plumage.

◆ Names of illustrated **subspecies** are given only after the first sex/age class dealt with. It can be assumed that the following illustrations are of the same race, until another one is mentioned. The regions of Thailand (see end paper) where a given subspecies has been recorded (NW, S etc.) appear in brackets after its name, though generally not in the case of the first subspecies dealt with, the range of which can be deduced by consulting the map and then subtracting the ranges of other subspecies. Subspecies given as '*ssp.*' are in the process of being described. See for example White Wagtail *Motacilla alba ssp./sp.*, which is likely to be described as a new species shortly.

Details of **non-illustrated** sex/age classes refer to the first subspecies illustrated, unless stated. Apart from a few exceptions, the subspecies listed under '**Other subspecies**' are not considered to differ markedly from the first subspecies mentioned.

◆ **Altitude ranges** refer to Thailand only.

◆ Species depicted on any one plate have been illustrated to the same **scale** (smaller in the case of flight figures) unless stated otherwise.

◆ Readers may notice that the **generic names** of a few species have been abbreviated. This was a necessary space-saving measure.

MAP KEY

The maps are based on those produced by Philip Round in his ground-breaking *A Guide to the Birds of Thailand* (Boonsong Lekagul and Philip D. Round 1991), but have been updated where recent information was available to the author. They represent real (known) distribution only.

■ resident

■ breeding visitor

■ winter/non-breeding visitor

□ passage migrant

E = extirpated

E? = possibly extirpated

B? = possible breeding visitor

I = introduced

I? = possibly introduced

○ vagrant/rare

⊙ formerly recorded

USEFUL ADDRESSES

Local

Bird Conservation Society of Thailand
69/12 Ramindra 24
Jarakheebua, Lardprao
Bangkok 10230
Email: bcst@box1.a-net.net.th

Conservation Data Centre
Institute of Science and Technology for Research and
    Development
Mahidol University
Salaya
Nakhon Pathom 73170

Hornbill Research Foundation
c/o Department of Microbiology, Faculty of Science
Mahidol University
Rama 6 Road
Bangkok 10400
Tel: 02 246 0063 ext. 4606, Fax: 02 246 3026

Royal Forest Department
61 Phaholyothin Road
Ladprao, Chatuchak
Bangkok 10900
Tel: 02 579 5734, Fax: 02 579 9576

Wildlife Fund Thailand
251/88-90 Phaholyothin Road
Bangkhen
Bangkok 10220
Tel: 02 521 3435, Fax: 02 552 6083
Email: WILDLIFE@mozart.inet.co.th

World Wide Fund for Nature Thailand Programme
104 Outreach Building
AIT
PO Box 4 Klong Luang
Pathumtani 12120
Tel: 02 524 6128-9, Fax: 02 524 6134

International

BirdLife International
Wellbrook Court
Girton Road
Cambridge CB3 0NA
U.K.
Email: birdlife@birdlife.org.uk

Oriental Bird Club
c/o The Lodge
Sandy
Bedfordshire SG19 2DL
U.K.
Email: mail@orientalbirdclub.org

Traffic Southeast Asia
Locked bag no. 911
Jln. Sultan PO
46990 Petaling Jaya
Malaysia

Wetlands International–Asia Pacific
Institute of Advanced Studies
University of Malaya
Lembah Pantai
50603 Kuala Lumpur
Malaysia

AVIAN TOPOGRAPHY

The figures below illustrate the main plumage tracts and bare-part features. This terminology for bird topography has been used extensively in the species descriptions, and a full understanding of these terms is important if the reader is to make full use of this book; they are a starting point in putting together a description.

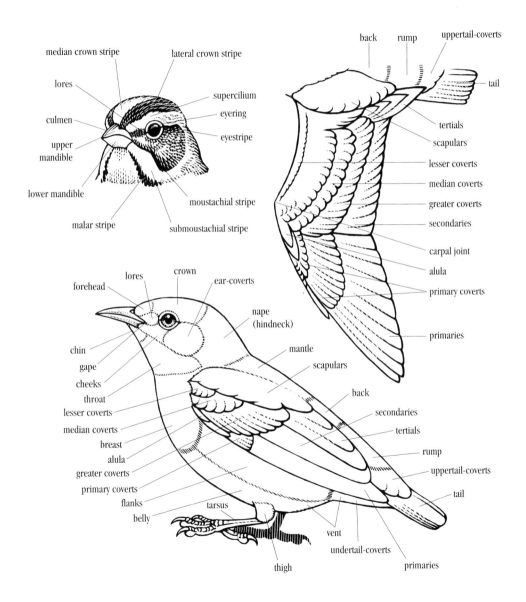

PLATE 1 CHINESE FRANCOLIN, PARTRIDGES, QUAILS & BUTTONQUAILS

CHINESE FRANCOLIN *Francolinus pintadeanus* 30.5–33.5 cm

(1) **Male** *phayrei*: Black body boldly spotted and barred whitish to buffy-white, bold black, chestnut and white head pattern, chestnut scapulars. (2) **Female**: Duller than male, chestnut areas washed brown, facial pattern softer, underparts barred. (3) **Juvenile**: Duller than female, less rufous on crown-sides, pale-streaked upperparts. **VOICE** Male territorial call is a loud harsh metallic *wi-ta-tak-takaa*, repeated after rather long intervals. **HABITAT** Open forest and woodland, grass and scrub; up to 1,500 m.

LONG-BILLED PARTRIDGE *Rhizothera longirostris* 36–40.5 cm

(4) **Male** *longirostris*: Long stout bill, dark chestnut crown, light chestnut head-sides and throat and lower breast/flanks, grey foreneck and upper breast to upper mantle, mostly buffish wing-coverts, yellow legs. (5) **Female**: Lacks grey on breast/mantle; throat/breast light chestnut; back to uppertail-coverts warmer buffish. (6) **Juvenile**: As female but warmer above, dark spots/bars on breast, buff-streaked throat/breast/neck/mantle. **VOICE** Territorial call is a far-carrying double whistle with distinctly higher second note; usually given in duet, producing a rising repetitive four-note sequence. **HABITAT** Broadleaved evergreen forest, bamboo; up to 300 m.

CRESTED PARTRIDGE *Rollulus rouloul* 24–29.5 cm

(7) **Male**: Glossy blue-black above and below (usually bluer on mantle, greener towards tail), large fan-shaped chestnut-maroon crest, long wire-like forehead plumes, red orbital skin, bill-base and legs, dark brownish wings. (8) **Female**: Green with grey hood, blackish nape, chestnut/rusty wings with darker markings, red eyering/legs. (9) **Juvenile**: Warm brown crown-sides, duller mantle and breast, dull greyish belly/vent; pale wing-covert spots. **VOICE** Persistently uttered melancholy, upslurring, whistled *su-il*. **HABITAT & BEHAVIOUR** Lowland broadleaved evergreen forest. Usually in flocks, sometimes quite large.

JAPANESE QUAIL *Coturnix japonica* 19 cm

(10) **Male non-breeding**: Dark centre/transverse band on white throat, richer buff/chestnut breast than female. (11) **Male breeding** *japonica*: Uniform pale pinkish-chestnut head-sides and throat. (12,13) **Female**: Greyish-brown above with dark marks and pale streaks, pale ear-coverts, white throat with dark bars at side, rufescent breast/flanks with dark markings and whitish streaks. Plain upperwing, barred primaries. **First winter**: Similar to female. **VOICE** Male territorial call is a loud *choo-peet-trrr* or *guku kr-r-r-r-r*. **HABITAT** Grassy areas, cultivation; up to 400 m.

RAIN QUAIL *Coturnix coromandelica* 16.5–18.5 cm

(14) **Male**: Large black breast-patch, black flank-streaks. (15) **Female**: Washed-out (often greyish-tinged) breast with irregular dark spots; unbarred primaries. **Juvenile**: Similar to female (both sexes) but perhaps initially more heavily speckled on breast. **VOICE** Male territorial call is a loud sharp

metallic *whit-whit* or *which-which*, repeated every 0.5–1 s, in series of 3–5. **HABITAT** Dry grassland and scrub, dry cultivation; lowlands.

BLUE-BREASTED QUAIL *Coturnix chinensis* 13–15 cm

(16) **Male** *chinensis*: Relatively unstreaked upperparts; slaty-blue face, breast and flanks, black-and-white markings on throat and upper breast, chestnut lower breast to vent. (17,18) **Female**: Smaller than other quail with less streaked upperparts, long buff supercilium, barring on breast and flanks, yellowish legs; uniform brown upperwing. **Juvenile**: Similar to female but initially (at least when very small) lacks rufous on head and neck and has dense blackish-brown mottling and whitish streaks on breast and flanks. Males soon attain patches of adult plumage. **VOICE** Male territorial call is sweet whistled *ti-yu ti-yu*. **HABITAT** Dry/slightly marshy grassland, scrub, cultivation; up to 1,300 m.

SMALL BUTTONQUAIL *Turnix sylvatica* 13–14 cm

(19,20) **Female** *mikado*: Like Yellow-legged Buttonquail but smaller, with pale chestnut wing-coverts (contrast less with flight feathers than in other buttonquail), strong buff stripes on mantle and tertials, paler buff and sharply defined breast-patch, slaty-blue to blackish bill, fleshy-greyish legs. (21) **Juvenile**: Less distinct buff breast-patch, blackish spots across breast. **Male**: Mantle duller. **VOICE** Female territorial call is far-carrying series of booming *booooooo* notes (each 1 s long, after 1–3 s intervals). **HABITAT** Dry grassland, scrub and grass bordering cultivation; up to 400 m.

YELLOW-LEGGED BUTTONQUAIL *Turnix tanki* 16.5–18 cm

(22,23) **Female** *blanfordii*: Sandy-buff wing-coverts (more contrasting with flight feathers than in other buttonquail) with large black spots, deep buff breast-band, round black spots on upper flanks (otherwise rather plain below), rufous nuchal collar (lacking on male), extensive yellowish bill, yellow legs. (24) **Juvenile**: Duller; less distinct breast-patch, faint narrow bars on throat/breast, indistinct wing-covert spots. **Male**: Lacks female's rufous nuchal collar. **VOICE** Female territorial call is described as series of low-pitched hooting notes, gradually increasing in strength and turning into a human-like moan. **HABITAT** Grassy areas, slightly marshy grassland, scrub, cultivation, secondary growth; up to 2,000 m.

BARRED BUTTONQUAIL *Turnix suscitator* 15–17.5 cm

(25,26) **Female** *thai*: Bold, dense pattern on head/breast/flanks/wing-coverts, whitish-buff speckled head, black throat/upper breast, black-and-whitish bars on lower throat to flanks, black-and-buff barred coverts, rufous vent. (27) **Male**: Like female but no black patch on throat and breast. (28) **Female** *blakistoni* (recorded NW): More rufous-chestnut above, buffier below (both sexes). **Juvenile**: As male. **Other subspecies** *T.s.atrogularis* (S): Richer belly/vent. **VOICE** Females give soft reverberating booming notes, which gradually get louder. **HABITAT** Dry grassland, cultivation, secondary growth; up to 1,500 m.

PLATE 2 PARTRIDGES & RED JUNGLEFOWL

RUFOUS-THROATED PARTRIDGE *Arborophila rufogularis* 25.5–29 cm

(1) **Adult** *tickelli*: Dark-streaked brown crown, plain olive-brown mantle, whitish lores, supercilium and ear-coverts with dark streaks, orange-rufous throat, grey breast to belly, chestnut flank-markings. (2) **Juvenile**: Plain buffish supercilium and throat, underparts spotted and streaked white. **VOICE** Territorial call is a long clear plaintive whistle leading into repeated series of double whistles: ***whu-whu whu-whu***..., gradually ascending scale and increasing in pitch. Partner may join in with more rapid, monotonous ***kew-kew-kew-kew***... **HABITAT** Broadleaved evergreen forest; 1,200–2,565 m.

BAR-BACKED PARTRIDGE *Arborophila brunneopectus* 26.5–29.5 cm

(3) **Adult** *brunneopectus*: Pale buff face, dark eyestripe and crown, black bars on mantle, black foreneck with buff streaks, warm brown breast to upper belly, black-and-white flank-markings. **Juvenile**: May differ by broken blackish bars on breast. **VOICE** Territorial call is series of loud ***brr*** notes, becoming louder and leading to series of ***WI-wu*** couplets, which also become louder before ending abruptly: ***brr-brr-brr-brr-brr-brr WI-wu WI-wu WI-wu WI-wu***... Partner often gives rapid ***chew-chew-chew-chew-chew***... at same time. Sibilant ***wu-wirr wu-wirr wu-wirr***... in alarm. **HABITAT** Broadleaved evergreen forest; 500–1,480 m.

MALAYAN PARTRIDGE *Arborophila campbelli* 28 cm

(4) **Adult**: Mostly black hood, white forehead-sides (sometimes faint supercilium) and cheek/ear-covert patch, a few white streaks on neck, slaty-greyish upper mantle and breast, pale rufous and black flank markings. **Juvenile**: More chestnut-tinged above, breast darker with blackish, grey and dull rufous bars, heavier chestnut, blackish and buffish flank markings. **VOICE** Like Bar-backed: whistled *oii* notes (c. 13 times in 10 s), usually followed by loud shrill ***pi-hor*** couplets. Subdued ***wut-wit wut-wit wut-wit***... when alarmed. **HABITAT** Broadleaved evergreen forest; 1,000–1,600 m. **NOTE** Formerly lumped in **Grey-breasted Partridge** *A. orientalis*.

SIAMESE PARTRIDGE *Arborophila diversa* 28 cm

(5) **Adult**: From Bar-backed by chestnut patch on breast, more extensive black-and-white markings on flanks and belly, and less contrasting head pattern. (6) **Adult**: Less well-marked individual. **Juvenile**: Chestnut of breast paler and washed-out, head pattern less contrasting. **VOICE** Said to recall Bar-backed. **HABITAT** Broadleaved evergreen forest; 700–1,500 m.

CHESTNUT-NECKLACED PARTRIDGE *Arborophila charltonii* 26–32 cm

(7) **Adult** *charltonii*: Chestnut breast-band, pale chestnut ear-covert patch, heavy breast/flank markings. **Juvenile**: Undescribed. **VOICE** Possibly not distinguishable from Scaly-breasted. **HABITAT** Broadleaved evergreen forest; below 200 m.

SCALY-BREASTED PARTRIDGE *Arborophila chloropus* 27–31.5 cm

(8) **Adult** *chloropus*: Rather plain; upperparts/breast olive-brown with blackish vermiculations, foreneck, lower breast/upper belly orange-buff; blackish flank markings, greenish legs, reddish bill with dull greenish-yellow tip. **Juvenile**: Whitish feather-shafts/tips on breast/flanks. **Other subspecies** *A.c.peninsularis* (south W): Much duller below. **VOICE** 20–90 clear notes, leading to 5–7 loud shrill, undulating couplets: ***tu-tu....tu-tu...tu-tu-tu..tu-tu.tu-tu-tu-tutututututu TCHIRRA-TCHWIU-TCHIRRA-TCHWIU-TCHIRRA-TCHWIU-TCHIRRA-TCHWIU-TCHIRRA-TCHWIU***. **HABITAT** Various broadleaved forests, secondary growth, bamboo; up to 1,000 m.

FERRUGINOUS PARTRIDGE *Caloperdix oculea* 27.5–32 cm

(9) **Male** *oculea*: Chestnut head and breast, black-and-whitish scaled mantle and flanks, black-and-rufous back to tail, black spots on pale wing-coverts. **Female**: Lacks leg spurs or shows single short one. See Long-billed and Black Partridges. **Juvenile**: Has black bars on nape and irregular blackish spots and bars on breast. **VOICE** Territorial call is an ascending, gradually accelerating series of high-pitched notes, terminating abruptly with harsher couplets: ***p-pi-pi-pipipip-ipipi dit-duit dit-duit***. **HABITAT** Broadleaved evergreen forest, bamboo, freshwater swamp forest; up to 915 m.

MOUNTAIN BAMBOO PARTRIDGE *Bambusicola fytchii* 32–37 cm

(10) **Male** *fytchii*: Rather long neck and tail; buffish head-sides and throat with blackish stripe behind eye, greyish-brown above with distinct dark spots, chestnut streaks on neck and breast and bold black markings on flanks. (11) **Female**: Like male but eyestripe brown. **Juvenile**: Like female but more rufescent crown, duller hindneck, more buffy-grey above with dark greyish vermiculations and larger/darker markings, greyer breast with some darker bars. **VOICE** Very loud bouts of explosive shrill chattering (two notes rapidly repeated), which slows then dies away. Hoarse ***tch-hherrrr*** call notes. **HABITAT & BEHAVIOUR** Grass, scrub, bamboo, secondary growth; 1,200–2,135 m. Usually in small flocks, easily flushed.

RED JUNGLEFOWL *Gallus gallus* Male 65–78 cm (includes tail up to 28 cm), female 41–46 cm

(12) **Male** *spadiceus*: Long rufous/yellow hackles, blackish below, green arched tail, red comb/face skin/lappets. (13) **Male eclipse**: No hackles, leaving all-blackish crown and neck; smaller comb and lappets. (14) **Female**: Smaller; short blackish/golden-buff hackles, drab brown above with fine dark vermiculations and buffy-white shaft-streaks, paler below, plain greyish-brown vent, rather short/blunt dark tail, bare pinkish face. (15) **Male** *gallus* (eastern NE, SE): Conspicuous white 'ear-patch' (smaller on female). **Juvenile**: Similar to female (both sexes). **VOICE** Territorial call is similar to domestic fowl but higher-pitched, with last syllable cut short. **HABITAT** Forest edge, open woodland, overgrown clearings, scrub and grass; up to 1,830 m.

12–15 to different scale

PLATE 3 PHEASANTS

SILVER PHEASANT *Lophura nycthemera* Male c.80–127 cm (includes tail to 76 cm), female 56–71 cm

(1) **Male** *nycthemera*: White above with black chevron/lines, blue-black below, red facial skin/legs. (2) **Female**: Plain mid-brown above (sometimes warm-tinged) with faint vermiculations, broad white and blackish scales below, blackish-and-whitish barring on outertail. (3) **Male** *lineata* (W, western NW)/*crawfurdii* (south W): Much denser black markings above; legs/feet often dark grey or greyish-brown to pinkish-brown (particularly *lineata*). (4) **Female**: Light scaling above, sharp black-and-white V-shapes on hindneck, largely dull chestnut breast/belly (blackish on *crawfurdii*) with white streaks, paler creamier central tail. (5) **Male** *lewisi* (SE): Like *lineata* but upperpart markings bolder, legs/feet red. (6) **Female**: Chestnut-tinged above with greyish scaling, greyer and relatively plain below. **Juvenile**: As female but may have black spots/bars on scapulars/coverts; males soon distinguishable. **voice** Grunting **WWERK** notes, running to **WWERK wuk-uk-uk-uk-uk** and sharp high **HSSiik**. Similar, rising **hwii-ieeik**. **HABITAT & BEHAVIOUR** Broadleaved evergreen and mixed deciduous forest; 700–2,000 m. In small flocks; usually shy.

CRESTED FIREBACK *Lophura ignita* Male 65–73.5 cm (includes tail to 26.5 cm), female 56–59 cm

(7) **Male** *rufa*: Blue facial skin, purplish blue-black body, golden-rufous upper back grading to maroon shorter uppertail-coverts, white streaks on flanks, arched white central tail feathers, reddish legs. (8) **Female**: Dull rufous-chestnut, with white-streaked breast and white-scaled belly/vent. **Juvenile female**: No crest, may have black-barred nape to scapulars/coverts. **Subadult male** As adult but tail has chestnut centre, rufous flank-streaks. **voice** Guttural **UKHH-UKHH-UKHH**... (**HH** more metallic) and low **uur** notes. **HABITAT & BEHAVIOUR** Broadleaved evergreen forest; below 200 m. Loud wing-whirrs during display.

SIAMESE FIREBACK *Lophura diardi* Male c. 70–80 cm (includes tail to 39 cm), female 53–60 cm

(9) **Male**: Pendant-tipped crest, mostly grey body, black-and-white bars on scapulars/coverts, golden-buff back-patch, bluish bars on maroon rump to uppertail-coverts and on glossy purplish-black belly, blackish-green tail. (10) **Female**: Boldly barred wings/tail, largely rufous-chestnut body and outertail, white-scaled belly/flanks. **Juvenile**: As female but may have duller mantle with dark vermiculations and duller base colour to underparts; males lack rufous/chestnut tones and soon attain adult plumage patches. **voice** Metallic *tsik tik-tik tik tik tik*... and guttural grunting **UKHT' UKHT' UKHT'**... and **UKHT hewer UKHT** (**hewer** thin, rather metallic-ended), in alarm. Low **yurk-yurk** when flushed. **HABITAT** Broadleaved evergreen and semi-evergreen forest, secondary growth; up to 800 m.

MRS HUME'S PHEASANT *Syrmaticus humiae* Male 90–92 cm (includes tail to 53.5 cm), female c.60–61 cm

(11) **Male** *burmanicus*: Dark greyish-purple hood, chestnut body, white wing-bars, dark-barred greyish tail. (12) **Female**: White-tipped tail; generally warm brown, with blackish markings above and whitish wing-bars, warmer below with whitish scales on lower breast to vent. **Subadult male**

Some female-like wing feathers (April). **voice** Male territorial call is crowing **cher-a-per cher-a-per cher cher cheria cheria**. Cackling **waaak** notes. Sharp **tuk tuk** when alarmed. **HABITAT** More open broadleaved evergreen forest (mainly oak and mixed oak/pine), grass and scrub; 1,200–2,285 m.

GREY PEACOCK PHEASANT *Polyplectron bicalcaratum* Male 56–76 cm (includes tail to 42 cm), female 48.5–53 cm

(13) **Male** *bicalcaratum*: Greyish; whitish throat, green/purplish ocelli, short crest, pink facial skin. (14) **Female**: Darker and plainer with less distinct ocelli, duller facial skin. **Juvenile**: Like female. Male develops more defined and colourful ocelli during first winter and assumes adult plumage by second winter. **voice** Territorial call is loud, airy **PU PWOI** or **POI PWOI** (latterly drawn/rising). Also low growling rattles, becoming louder and running into much louder and harsher notes: **uhrrrrr....uhrrrrruk....orrokbokbokbokb....OKH-OKH-OKH-OKH-OKH...ORKH-ORKH-ORKH...ORKH-ORKH-ORKH**... **HABITAT** Broadleaved evergreen forest; 300–1,800 m.

MALAYAN PEACOCK PHEASANT *Polyplectron malacense* Male 50–53.5 cm (includes tail to 25.5 cm), female 40–45 cm

(15) **Male**: Warmer brown than Grey, ocelli greener, long dark crest, pale orange face-skin, darker ear-coverts. (16) **Female**: Smaller, shorter-tailed, less distinct/more pointed ocelli, little crest, indistinct paler scales above. **Juvenile**: Both sexes as female. **voice** Territorial call (dawn/dusk) is a repeated loud slow melancholy **PUU PWOII** or **PUU PWORR** (second note more drawn-out/rising). Also a harsh explosive cackle, running into throaty clucks: **TCHI-TCHI-TCHAO-TCHAO wuk-wuk-wuk-wuk-wuk**... Repeated loud harsh grating **TCHOW** or **KAAOW**. **HABITAT & BEHAVIOUR** Broadleaved evergreen forest; up to 305 m. Holds crest forwards over bill during display.

GREAT ARGUS *Argusianus argus* Male 160–203 cm (includes tail to 145 cm, secondaries to 102 cm), female 72–76 cm

(17) **Male** *argus*: Brown/chestnut; blue face-/neck-skin, pale-marked upperparts/tail, very long secondaries/tail. (18) **Female**: Rufous-chestnut collar, less distinct markings above, much shorter secondaries/tail (latter barred). **Juvenile**: As female; males soon develop longer tail with tiny pale spots. **voice** Male territorial call is a very loud **KWAH-WAU** (louder, longer second note). Female gives series of 25–35 **WAU** notes, the last longer, more upward-inflected. **HABITAT & BEHAVIOUR** Broadleaved evergreen forest; up to 900 m. Very shy. Male's secondaries raised/fanned towards female during display on dancing-ground.

GREEN PEAFOWL *Pavo muticus* Male 180–250 cm (includes 'train' to 162 cm), female 100–110 cm

(19) **Male** *imperator*: Mostly glossy green; tall crest, long broad train with large ocelli. (20) **Female**: Like male but duller, no train. **Juvenile**: Duller than female. **Other subspecies** *P.m.muticus* (S). **voice** Territorial males utter very loud **KI-WAO** or **YEE-OW** notes: **YEE-OW..KI-WAO KI-WAO KI-WAO**... etc.; females a loud **AOW-AA** (**AOW** stressed), often repeated. **HABITAT & BEHAVIOUR** Open broadleaved forest, mainly bordering rivers/wetlands, secondary growth, bamboo; up to 915 m. Shy but males call from trees in early morning.

1–10, 11–12 and 13–20 to different scales

PLATE 4 WHISTLING-DUCKS, GEESE, SHELDUCKS, WHITE-WINGED DUCK & COMB DUCK

LESSER WHISTLING-DUCK *Dendrocygna javanica* 38–41 cm
(1,2) **Adult**: Rather long neck, relatively plain plumage, darker cap, rufous-fringed mantle feathers and scapulars, reddish-chestnut uppertail-coverts, thin whitish flank-streaks; broad, rounded dark wings with reddish-chestnut lesser and median upperwing-coverts. **Juvenile**: Somewhat duller overall, crown often paler and more greyish-brown. **VOICE** Incessantly repeated, clear, low whistled *whi-whee*, usually when flying. Wings also make whistling sound in flight. **HABITAT & BEHAVIOUR** Lakes, marshes, sometimes mangroves, various wetlands; up to 800 m. Very gregarious, often in large flocks.

SWAN GOOSE *Anser cygnoides* 81–94 cm
(3,4) **Adult**: Resembles Greylag but bill thicker-based and blackish; crown and nape/hindneck uniform dark brown, contrasting strongly with very pale lower head-sides and throat/foreneck; darker wing-coverts in flight. (5) **Juvenile**: Crown, nape and hindneck duller, no whitish face-band. **VOICE** Prolonged resounding honks, ending at higher pitch. Short harsh note repeated 2–3 times in alarm. **HABITAT** Banks of large rivers, marshy edges of freshwater wetlands; recorded at c.400 m.

GREYLAG GOOSE *Anser anser* 78–90 cm
(6,7) **Adult** *rubrirostris*: Relatively uniform pale brownish-grey plumage, plain head/neck, pinkish bill and legs/feet; pale wing-coverts contrast with dark flight feathers above and below. **Juvenile**: Bill and legs somewhat duller, lacks dark speckling on belly. **VOICE** Noisy. In flight, utters loud series of clanging honking notes: *aahng-ahng-ung*, deeper than other geese. **HABITAT & BEHAVIOUR** Lakes, rivers, estuaries, arable fields, grassy areas; lowlands. Gregarious, usually found in flocks, may associate with other geese.

BAR-HEADED GOOSE *Anser indicus* 71–76 cm
(8,9) **Adult**: Two black bands on back of white head, white line down neck-side, dark-tipped yellow bill, orange-yellow legs/feet. Upper foreneck/upper hindneck blacker than lower neck. In flight, wings like Greylag but upperwing-coverts/bases of outer primaries more uniform pale grey (sharp contrast with blackish remainder of wing). (10) **Juvenile**: Hindcrown/hindneck dark grey-brown, dusky loral line, rest of neck more uniform pale greyish. **VOICE** Soft, nasal, repeated honking: *oh-wa*, *aah-aah* and *ooh-ah* etc. Notes somewhat lower, more nasal and wider-spaced than other geese. **HABITAT & BEHAVIOUR** Large rivers, lakes, arable fields, grassy areas; up to 400 m. Usually in small flocks.

RUDDY SHELDUCK *Tadorna ferruginea* 61–67 cm
(11,12) **Male breeding**: Relatively large size and predominantly orange-rufous plumage with mostly creamy-buff head diagnostic. Has narrow black collar. In flight, shows distinctive blackish wings with contrasting whitish coverts (above and below); bottle-green gloss on secondaries. (13) **Female**: Lacks black collar, face extensively white, head buffier. **Male non-**

breeding Black neck-collar faint or lacking. **Juvenile**: Like female but head and upperparts strongly washed greyish-brown, underparts duller. **VOICE** Rather vocal. Typically utters a rolling, honking *aakh* and trumpeted *pok-pok-pok-pok*... **HABITAT & BEHAVIOUR** Large rivers, lakes; up to 400 m. Normally in flocks.

COMMON SHELDUCK *Tadorna tadorna* 58–67 cm
(14,15) **Male**: White body, contrasting black hood (glossed green), scapular and ventral stripes, and broad chestnut breast-/mantle-band. Bill red with prominent knob at base. In flight, wing pattern very similar to Ruddy. (16) **Female**: Smaller, bill duller (no knob), hood duller, head markings white, breast-band narrower/duller. **Male eclipse**: Smaller bill-knob, whitish mottling on face, less defined breast-band, fine greyish bars on body. **Female eclipse** Somewhat duller/greyer; more white face markings, even less distinct breast-band (may closely resemble juvenile). **Juvenile**: Head, neck and upperparts mostly sooty-brownish, face, eyering and foreneck whitish, no breast-band, all whitish below, white-tipped secondaries/inner primaries, dull pinkish bill. **VOICE** Female utters rapid chattering *gag-ag-ag-ag-ag*...; male calls with thin low whistles. **HABITAT** Large rivers, lakes, coastal mudflats etc.; up to 400 m.

WHITE-WINGED DUCK *Cairina scutulata* 66–81 cm
(17,18) **Male**: All-dark body, contrasting whitish head and upper neck and mostly dull yellowish to orange-yellowish bill distinctive. Head and upper neck variably mottled blackish (can be mainly white), lesser and median upperwing-coverts and inner edges of tertials white, secondaries bluish-grey. In flight, white wing-coverts (above and below) contrast sharply with rest of wings. **Female**: Smaller and slightly duller, usually with more densely mottled head and upper neck. **Juvenile**: Duller and browner, initially with pale brownish head and neck. **VOICE** Flight call is a prolonged, vibrant series of honks, often ending with a nasal whistle; mainly at dawn and dusk. Also single short harsh honks. **HABITAT & BEHAVIOUR** Pools and rivers in forest, freshwater swamp forest; up to 900 m. Usually encountered singly or in pairs. Feeds mostly at night, flying to and from roosting sites at dawn and dusk.

COMB DUCK *Sarkidiornis melanotos* 56–76 cm
(19) **Male non-breeding** *melanotis*: Black-speckled head and neck, rest of underparts whitish with grey-washed flanks, dark bill with broad knob (comb); wings appear all blackish, contrasting with pale underparts. (20,21) **Female**: Much smaller, upperside duller and less glossy, lacks knob on bill. (22) **Juvenile**: Crown/eyestripe dark brown, dark brown above with warm buff feather fringes, rest of head, neck and underparts strongly washed brownish-buff with some dark brown markings on sides of breast and flanks. **Male breeding**: Much larger knob on top of bill, rich buffish wash to sides of head and neck. **VOICE** Occasionally utters low croaking sounds. Also wheezy whistles and grunts during breeding season. **HABITAT & BEHAVIOUR** Freshwater lakes and marshes; lowlands. Found singly, in pairs or small flocks, often associating with other ducks. Feeds on land and in water.

PLATE 5 DABBLING DUCKS

GADWALL *Anas strepera* 46–56 cm

(1) **Male**: Greyish overall, black vent, blackish bill. Square white patch on inner secondaries contrasts with dark outer secondaries/inner greater coverts; maroon on median coverts. (2,3) **Female**: Like Mallard but more compact with squarer head; head pattern less contrasting, bill finer and blackish with orange sides. White patch on inner secondaries (often visible at rest). **Male eclipse**: Like female but greyer, more uniform above; retains tertial/upperwing colour/pattern below. Bill can be all dark (see female Falcated Duck). **Juvenile**: Like female but richer brown below with more distinctly streaked breast. White patch on secondaries may be very indistinct on females. **VOICE** Usually silent. Courting males utter a short *nheck* and low whistle; females a repeated *gag-ag-ag-ag-ag*... **HABITAT** Freshwater lakes and marshes; up to 400 m.

FALCATED DUCK *Anas falcata* 48–54 cm

(4) **Male**: Head glossy green with long 'mane' and purple crown and cheeks; throat and upper foreneck white, bisected by black band; has long curved black-and-whitish tertials, black-bordered yellowish-white patch on vent-sides; rather pale grey upperwing-coverts contrast with green-glossed black secondaries. (5,6) **Female**: From Gadwall/Eurasian Wigeon by combination of longish, narrow, dark grey bill, rather plain greyish-brown head, rather full nape feathers, dark-scaled rich brown breast/flanks, all-dark secondaries, white bar across greater upperwing-covert tips, contrasting white underwing-coverts. **Male eclipse**: Like female but crown, hindneck and upperparts darker, breast and flanks richer brown; wing pattern retained but tertials shorter. **Juvenile**: Like female but bufflier, with greyer tips to greater upperwing-coverts. **VOICE** Deep nasal *bep* (male). In flight may give distinctive short low whistle followed by wavering *uit-trr*. **HABITAT** Lakes and marshes; up to 400 m.

EURASIAN WIGEON *Anas penelope* 45–51 cm

(7,8) **Male**: Bright chestnut head with broad yellowish median stripe, pinkish breast, black vent. Bill pale grey with black tip, centre of abdomen and rear flanks white. Large white patch on upperwing-coverts, greyish underwing with whiter greater/primary coverts. (9,10) **Female**: Rounded head, shortish pale grey bill with black tip, rather plain dark brownish head, neck, breast and flanks. Breast and flanks more chestnut-tinged. In flight, underside appears uniform brownish with sharply contrasting white belly/vent; upperwing-coverts paler and greyer than rest of wing. **Male eclipse**: Similar to female but head and breast richer brown; retains white patch on upperwing-coverts (often visible at rest). **Juvenile**: Like female but has almost glossless secondaries and some brown mottling on belly. **VOICE** Male utters piercing, whistled *wheeooo* and more subdued *whut-whittoo*; female gives low growling *krrr* or *karr*. **HABITAT** Lakes, large rivers, various wetlands; up to 400 m.

MALLARD *Anas platyrhynchos* 50–65 cm

(11) **Male** *platyrhynchos*: Mostly pale brownish-grey, yellowish bill, glossy green head with purple sheen, white collar, purplish-brown breast. Tail-coverts/lower scapulars black. In flight, shows glossy dark bluish secondaries, bordered at front/rear by defined white band, dark

underwing with contrasting white coverts/secondary bases. (12) **Male eclipse**: Like female but breast more chestnut, bill dull yellowish. (13,14) **Female**: Similar to several other female *Anas* ducks. Distinguished by combination of relatively large size, elongated shape, dull orange to dull reddish bill with dark brown markings (not distinctly bicoloured), contrasting dark crown and eyestripe and, in flight, wing colour and pattern (like male but upperwing-coverts browner). **Juvenile**: As female but crown/eyestripe blackish, breast neatly streaked, flanks more streaked (less scaled), bill initially mostly dull reddish to dull orange. **VOICE** Male utters a rasping *kreep*; female gives series of mocking quacks, descending towards end: *QUACK-QUACK-QUACK-quack-quack-quack*... **HABITAT** Lakes, large rivers, various wetlands; up to 400 m.

NORTHERN SHOVELER *Anas clypeata* 43–52 cm

(15,16) **Male**: Long, wide, spatula-shaped bill, glossy green hood, white breast, mostly chestnut sides. Has yellow eyes, white patch on sides of vent and black tail-coverts. In flight, shows distinctive blue median/lesser upperwing-coverts, broadly white-tipped secondaries, glossy green secondaries and contrasting white underwing-coverts. (17) **Male eclipse**: Like female but flanks/belly more rufous, body markings blacker, upperwing-coverts bluer. (18,19) **Female**: From other scaly brown *Anas* ducks by distinctive bill, greyish-blue median and lesser upperwing-coverts and broadly white-tipped greater coverts. Eyes usually brown. **Juvenile male**: Like juvenile female but upperwing similar to adult. Immatures can resemble sub-eclipse adults. **Juvenile female**: Like adult but crown and nape darker, underparts paler and more spotted, greater covert bar indistinct, lacks obvious gloss on secondaries. **VOICE** Courting male utters a repeated, liquid, hollow *sluk-uk* or *g'dunk*; female gives a descending *gak-gak-gak-ga-ga*. **HABITAT** Lakes, large rivers, marshes, various wetlands; up to 400 m.

NORTHERN PINTAIL *Anas acuta* 51–56 cm (male's tail up to 10 cm more)

(20,21) **Male**: Slender and long-necked, predominantly grey; dark chocolate-brown hood, white line from head-sides down neck to whitish lower foreneck/upper breast, yellowish-white patch on rear flanks, black tail-coverts. Has relatively long slender grey bill with blackish median stripe and distinctive elongated central tail feathers. In flight, shows grey upperwing-coverts, rufous-buff tips to greater coverts, glossy blackish-green secondaries with broad white tips and mostly greyish underwing with blackish median and lesser coverts. (22,23) **Female**: Slender proportions, longish neck, long darkish grey bill, rather plain head, distinctly pointed tail. In flight shows distinctive greyish underwing with dark median/lesser coverts and white-tipped secondaries. Upperwing-coverts duller than male, secondaries much duller/browner, tips of greater coverts whiter. **Male eclipse**: Like female but greyer above, has grey tertials; retains bill and wing colour and pattern. **Juvenile**: Like female but upperparts darker, flanks more boldly patterned. **VOICE** Male gives a low *preep-preep*; female utters weak descending quacks and low growling croaks when flushed. **HABITAT** Lakes, large rivers, marshes, various wetlands; up to 400 m.

PLATE 6 COTTON PYGMY-GOOSE, DABBLING DUCKS & SCALY-SIDED MERGANSER

COTTON PYGMY-GOOSE *Nettapus coromandelianus* 36 cm

 (1,2) **Male** *coromandelianus*: Small; blackish cap, breast-band/collar, upperparts (glossed green) and vent, white head-sides/neck and underparts, grey-washed flanks; rounded wings with broad white band. (3,4) **Female**: Black eyestripe, duller/browner above, duller neck/underparts, with darker mottling (particularly breast), no defined breast-band/collar, pale vent; dark wings with narrow white trailing edge to secondaries. **Male eclipse**: Greyish-washed head-sides/neck, darker eyestripe, greyish-mottled breast and flanks, no obvious breast-band/collar. Retains distinctive wing pattern. **Juvenile**: Like female but sides of head less white, eyestripe broader, lacks any obvious gloss on upperparts. **VOICE** Male has a staccato cackling *WUK-wirrarrak-WUK-wirrarrak-WUK-wirrarrak*..., usually in flight; female gives a weak *quack*. **HABITAT** Lakes, marshes and other freshwater wetlands; up to 800 m.

MANDARIN DUCK *Aix galericulata* 41–49 cm

 (5) **Male**: Big head, pinkish-red bill (tip pale), broad whitish supercilium, orange-rufous fan of pale-streaked 'hackles' on lower head-sides, erect pale-tipped orange-rufous wing 'sails', white bands on sides of black breast. (6,7) **Female**: Greyish head, white 'spectacles', rather full nape/hindneck, dark greenish-brown above, white throat, belly centre and vent, dark brown breast/flanks with heavy whitish streaks/mottling, pink-tinged dark greyish bill with pale tip. In flight, upperwing quite uniform with white-tipped greenish secondaries. (8) **Juvenile**: Duller and browner overall than female, particularly head, with less pronounced 'spectacles' (sometimes lacking) and more diffuse markings on breast and flanks. **Male eclipse**: Similar to female but bill reddish, 'spectacles' less pronounced, neck feathers shaggier, upperparts glossier. **VOICE** Usually silent. **HABITAT** Freshwater lakes and pools; up to 400 m.

SPOT-BILLED DUCK *Anas poecilorhyncha* 55–63 cm

 (9,10) **Male** *haringtoni*: Recalls some female *Anas* ducks but has pale, rather plain head/neck, contrasting blackish crown/eyestripe, blackish bill with broad yellow tip, red loral spot at bill-base, mostly whitish outer webs of longest two tertials. Much of body prominently scaled/mottled. In flight, shows green secondaries, bordered at front/rear by black and white band, sharply contrasting white tertials/underwing-coverts. **Female**: Somewhat smaller; red loral spot indistinct (or absent), usually smaller and less distinct breast and flank markings. **Juvenile**: As female but browner and less distinctly marked below, no red on lores. **VOICE** Descending series of *quark* notes. **HABITAT** Lakes, large rivers, marshes; up to 400 m.

GARGANEY *Anas querquedula* 36–41 cm

 (11,12) **Male**: Relatively small; mostly dark brownish head and neck with blacker crown and pronounced long white supercilium. Rest of plumage brownish-grey with distinctly pale grey, dark-vermiculated flanks and elongated, grey scapulars with long black and white streaks. In flight shows mostly bluish-grey upperwing-coverts and glossy blackish-green secondaries, bordered at front and rear by broad white band. (13,14) **Female**: Relatively small with bold head pattern. Has dark crown,

narrow whitish supercilium, bold dark eyestripe, large whitish loral patch continuing in narrow line below blackish eyestripe, dark cheek-bar and whitish throat. Centre of belly extensively whitish. In flight, shows grey tinge to upperwing-coverts, mostly dark brownish secondaries (little green gloss), bordered at front and rear by narrow white band and distinctly dark leading edge to underwing-coverts. (15) **Juvenile**: Darker than female with less defined head pattern; dark markings on belly. **Male eclipse**: As female but no defined white line below blackish eyestripe, throat whiter; retains wing colour and pattern. **VOICE** Male utters rattling *knerek*, female a short high *quack*. **HABITAT** Lakes, marshes, various wetlands; up to 400 m.

BAIKAL TEAL *Anas formosa* 39–43 cm

 (16) **Male**: Striking buff, green, white and black head pattern, dark-spotted pinkish breast, grey flanks with vertical white band at front and rear, black undertail-coverts. In flight, from Common Teal as female. (17) **Male eclipse**: As female but darker/warmer mantle fringing, breast/flanks warmer, loral spot less distinct. (18,19) **Female**: From Garganey by isolated round white loral spot, vertical whitish band from below/behind eye to throat, broken supercilium (more buffish behind eye), buffish-white line at side of undertail-coverts. In flight, from Common Teal by rufescent-tipped greater coverts (often hard to see), blacker leading edge to underwing-coverts. (20) **Juvenile**: As female but buffier and slightly larger loral spot; dark mottling on whitish belly (plain-centred on adult female). **VOICE** Male gives chuckling *wot-wot-wot*..., female has a low *quack*. **HABITAT** Freshwater lakes; up to 400 m.

COMMON TEAL *Anas crecca* 34–38 cm

 (21) **Male** *crecca*: Small; chestnut head with buff-edged dark green eye-/nape-patch, buffish patch on blackish vent; horizontal white scapular line. Wing pattern like female but upperwing-coverts greyer. (22,23) **Female**: Like Garganey but smaller/smaller-billed (often some dull flesh/orange at base), head rather plain, apart from darker crown/eyestripe; has narrow buffish-white line along side of undertail-coverts, and more restricted whitish belly-centre. In flight, broad white tips to greater coverts, narrow white tips to dark green secondaries, greyish underwing with somewhat darker leading edge and dark axillaries/band across coverts. **Male eclipse**: As female but darker/more uniform above, larger dark markings below, eyestripe faint/absent. **Juvenile**: As female but somewhat plainer above, belly speckled dark; may show darker area on ear-coverts. **VOICE** Male utters soft, liquid *preep-preep*...; female may give sharp high *quack* when flushed. **HABITAT** Lakes, large rivers, marshes, various wetlands; up to 400 m.

SCALY-SIDED MERGANSER *Mergus squamatus* 52–58 cm

 (24,25) **Male**: Spiky crest, flanks white with pointed dark grey scales, greater coverts tipped black; large white upperwing-patch is bisected by two black lines. (26,27) **Female**: Spiky crest, ill-defined whitish throat, dark grey scaling on white sides of breast/flanks; white wing-patch bisected by single dark line. **Male eclipse**: Similar to female but darker above; retains wing pattern. **Juvenile**: As female but flanks may be more uniformly grey. **VOICE** Usually silent. **HABITAT** Large rivers, lakes; up to 500 m.

PLATE 7 DIVING DUCKS & GREBES

RED-CRESTED POCHARD *Rhodonessa rufina* 53–57 cm

(1) **Male**: Red bill, bulky orange-rufous head, black breast, tail-coverts and vent, broad white flank-patch. (2,3) **Female**: Plain brownish with dark crown (extending round eye), contrasting whitish head-sides to upper foreneck, pink-tipped dark bill; relatively pale brown upperwing-coverts, broad whitish band across flight feathers, largely whitish underwing (male's wing pattern similar but upperwing-coverts darker brown). **Male eclipse**: Like female but bill red, eyes reddish. **Juvenile**: Like female but bill all dark. **VOICE** Usually silent. Courting male gives a rasping wheeze; female has a grating chatter. **HABITAT & BEHAVIOUR** Freshwater lakes and marshes, large rivers; up to 400 m. Primarily feeds by diving, sometimes by up-ending and head-dipping.

COMMON POCHARD *Aythya ferina* 42–49 cm

(4) **Male**: Plain chestnut head and upper neck, rather plain grey remainder of plumage with contrasting black lower neck, breast and tail-coverts. Bill blackish with broad pale bluish-grey central band. In flight, upperwing like female but coverts purer grey. (5) **Male eclipse**: Duller and browner-tinged overall. (6,7) **Female non-breeding**: Told by combination of peaked head, pale spectacles and facial/throat markings, dark eyes, mottled greyish-brown body, dark undertail-coverts; distinctive greyish upperwing, without white band. **Female breeding** Body somewhat plainer and browner, sides of head somewhat plainer. **Juvenile**: Generally duller than female with more uniform upperparts, all-dark bill and much plainer head (may lack obvious spectacles). **VOICE** Female sometimes utters a harsh *krrr* or *krrah*; courting male may give a repeated soft wheezy whistled *pee*. **HABITAT** Freshwater lakes; up to 400 m.

FERRUGINOUS POCHARD *Aythya nyroca* 38–42 cm

(8) **Male**: White eyes, rich chestnut (domed) head, neck, breast and flanks, blackish upperparts and sharply demarcated white undertail-coverts diagnostic. In flight, upperwing has more extensive white bar across flight feathers than other *Aythya* ducks, white belly-centre sharply defined. (9,10) **Female**: Duller, more chestnut-brown, eyes dark. **Male eclipse**: Like female but head, neck and breast somewhat brighter; retains white eyes. **Juvenile**: Like female but sides of head, foreneck, flanks and upperparts somewhat paler, belly and sides of undertail-coverts mottled brown. **VOICE** Usually silent. Courting male has a short *chuk* and soft *wheeoo*; female utters a snoring *err err err*... and harsh *gaaa*. **HABITAT** Freshwater lakes and marshes, large rivers; up to 400 m.

BAER'S POCHARD *Aythya baeri* 41–46 cm

(11) **Male**: Told by combination of glossy greenish-black hood, whitish eyes, blackish upperparts, rich chestnut-brown lower neck/breast, chestnut-brown sides with large white patch on foreflanks, white undertail-coverts. In flight, wing pattern like Ferruginous but white upperwing-band extends less onto outer primaries. (12,13) **Female**: Similar to male but hood dark brown, typically has large diffuse dark chestnut loral patch, eyes dark, often has some whitish mottling on throat, duller breast/flanks, smaller white patch on foreflanks (may not

be visible when swimming). Combination of domed head without nuchal tuft, contrast between dark head and warm brown breast, and presence of white on foreflanks rule out Ferruginous and Tufted Duck. **Male eclipse**: Similar to female but eyes whitish. **Juvenile**: Similar to female but head tinged more chestnut with darker crown and hindneck; no defined loral patch. **VOICE** Usually silent. **HABITAT** Lakes, large rivers and their deltas; up to 400 m.

TUFTED DUCK *Aythya fuligula* 40–47 cm

(14) **Male**: Blackish plumage, contrasting white flanks, drooping crest. Bill grey with whitish subterminal band and black tip, eyes yellow, head glossed dark purplish. In flight, upperwing has less extensive white bar across flight feathers than other *Aythya* ducks. (15) **Male eclipse**: Crest reduced; head/breast and upperparts more brownish-black, flanks greyish, bill duller. (16–18) **Female**: Told by rather uniform dull dark brownish plumage with paler lower neck/breast and particularly flanks, squarish head, usually with suggestion of crest (short tuft/bump), yellow eyes and upperwing pattern (like male). May have white undertail-coverts, recalling Ferruginous/Baer's Pochards, or white face-patches. Bill duller than male. **Juvenile**: Similar to female but head and upperparts somewhat lighter brown (crown dark), has pale area on lores, little or no sign of crest and browner-tinged eyes (particularly female). **VOICE** Female sometimes gives a low gruff growling *err err err*...; courting male utters a low vibrant whistled *wheep-wee-whew*. **HABITAT** Lakes, large rivers; up to 400 m.

LITTLE GREBE *Tachybaptus ruficollis* 25–29 cm

(19,20) **Adult non-breeding** *poggei*: Small, stocky and duck-like, puffed-up rear end, rather narrow, mostly pale bill. Brownish-buff head-sides/underparts (throat and vent whiter) contrast with dark brown crown, hindneck and upperside. Eyes dark. In flight, upperwing all dark with narrow whitish trailing edge to secondaries. (21) **Adult breeding**: Sides of head, throat and foreneck dark rufous-chestnut, flanks rich dark brown, eyes yellow, bill blackish with prominent yellow gapeskin. **Juvenile**: Similar to adult non-breeding but sides of head have dark brown stripes, neck and breast often tinged rufous. **VOICE** Territorial call is a shrill whinnying trill, recalling some *Porzana* crakes. Sharp *wit* notes when alarmed. **HABITAT & BEHAVIOUR** Lakes, pools, well-watered marshes; up to 800 m. Swims buoyantly, dives frequently.

GREAT CRESTED GREBE *Podiceps cristatus* 46–51 cm

(22,23) **Adult non-breeding** *cristatus*: Relatively large/long-necked, bill rather long/slender and pinkish, crown, hindneck and upperside blackish-brown, head-sides/neck and underparts white, black loral stripe, greyish-brown flanks. In flight, long neck extends forwards, legs/feet protrude beyond short rear end, wings rather long/narrow, upperwing with contrasting white leading edge, scapular band and secondaries. (24) **Adult breeding**: Blackish crest, rufous-chestnut and blackish 'frills' on rear head-sides, rufescent flanks. **Juvenile**: Similar to adult non-breeding but has brown stripes across head-sides. **VOICE** Usually silent. Gives harsh, rolling *aooorrr* and chattering *kek-kek-kek*... on breeding grounds. **HABITAT** Lakes, large rivers, coastal waters; up to 400 m.

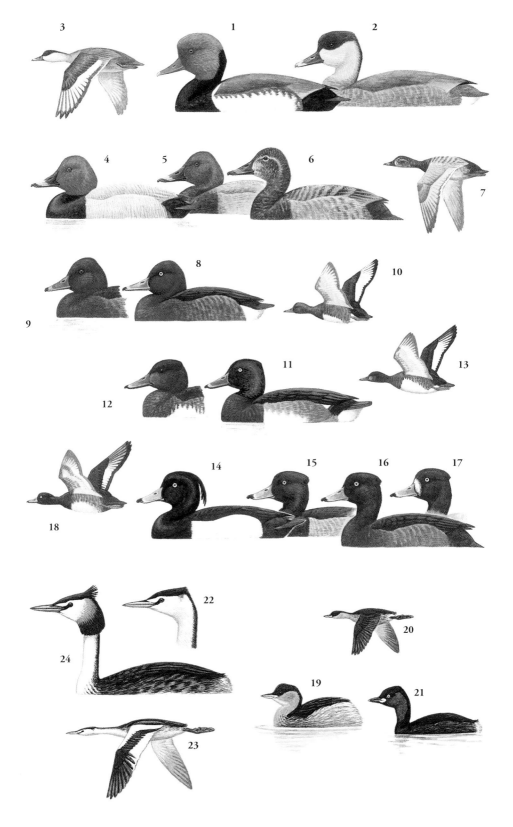

PLATE 8 MALAYSIAN HONEYGUIDE & PIED & SMALLER TYPICAL WOODPECKERS

MALAYSIAN HONEYGUIDE *Indicator archipelagicus* 18 cm

(1) **Male**: Lemon-yellow shoulder-patch (often hidden; lacked by female), thick bill with paler lower mandible, deep red eye, dirty whitish underparts, greyish wash across breast, dark-streaked lower flanks. **Female**: Lacks shoulder-patch. **Juvenile**: Like female but underparts indistinctly streaked, eyes brown. **VOICE** Song is a mewing note followed by a nasal ascending rattle: *miaw-krrrruuu* or *miaw-miaw-krrwuu*. **HABITAT & BEHAVIOUR** Broadleaved evergreen forest; up to 800 m. Sits motionless for long periods; visits bee nests.

GREY-CAPPED PYGMY WOODPECKER *Dendrocopos canicapillus* 13–15.5 cm

(2) **Male** *canicapillus*: Small; brownish-grey (black-bordered) crown, ear-covert band and washed-out submoustachial stripe; blackish above with white bars, dark-streaked below, short red streak on rear crown-side. (3) **Female**: No red on crown. **Juvenile**: Darker; heavier streaks below. Male often has more orange-red (not red) on nape/rear crown-sides. **Other subspecies** *D.c.delacouri* (south-eastern), *auritus* (S). **VOICE** Male territorial call is a rattling *tit-tit-erb-r-r-r-r-b*, usually introduced by call. Drumming fairly subdued. Short *kik* or *pit* and squeaky *kweek-kweek-kweek*. **HABITAT** Various broadleaved forests, coastal scrub; up to 1,830 m.

FULVOUS-BREASTED WOODPECKER *D. macei* 17–18 cm

(4) **Male** *longipennis*: Red crown, black nape, barred above, whitish below with streaks/bars, pinkish vent. (5) **Female**: Crown and nape all black. **Juvenile**: Duller, pink/red of undertail-coverts paler/more restricted, both sexes have some red on crown-centre (particularly male). **VOICE** Male territorial call is rapid *pik pipipipipipipipipi*. Drumming short and weak. Call is a loud *tchik* or *pik* (sharper than Grey-capped Pygmy), soft *chik-a-chik-a-chit* and sometimes *pik-pik*. **HABITAT** Deciduous woodland, scattered trees in open country, gardens, plantations; up to 600 m.

STRIPE-BREASTED WOODPECKER *D. atratus* 21 cm

(6) **Male**: Upper mantle unbarred, uniformly and distinctly streaked below, base colour of belly dusky buffish golden-brown. Note habitat and range. (7) **Female**: Like male but crown and nape black. **Juvenile**: Much paler and greyer below with less distinct streaks on belly and paler, more flame-red undertail-coverts. Male has paler red on crown, female some red on centre of crown. **VOICE** Male territorial call is a whinnying rattle. Call is a loud *tchik*. **HABITAT** Broadleaved evergreen forest; 800–2,200 m.

YELLOW-CROWNED WOODPECKER *Dendrocopos mahrattensis* 17–19 cm

(8) **Male** *aurocristatus*: Brownish-yellow forecrown grades to red hindcrown, dense white bars/spots above, no blackish head markings, brown streaking on underparts, red belly-centre, no red on undertail-coverts. (9) **Female**: Yellowish-brown hindcrown. **Juvenile**: Browner above, diffuse streaks below, pinker belly-patch. Male has some orange-red on hindcrown, female some on crown-centre. **VOICE** Rapid *kik-kik-kik-r-r-r-r-b* territorial call. Drums. Calls with sharp *click-click* and weak *peek* notes. **HABITAT** Deciduous woodland, scattered trees in open country; lowlands.

RUFOUS-BELLIED WOODPECKER *Dendrocopos hyperythrus* 19–23 cm

(10) **Male** *hyperythrus*: Red crown and nape, whitish face, deep rufous underparts, red undertail-coverts. (11) **Female**: Crown and nape black with white speckles, vent paler red. **Juvenile**: Dark streaks on head-sides, duller/paler below with heavy blackish bars. Both sexes have orange-red tips to crown feathers (less on female); subadults have blackish bars and whitish mottling on throat/breast. **Other subspecies** *D.h.annamensis* (NE): Paler rufous head-sides/underparts, less red on nape. **VOICE** Male territorial call is a rattling *ki-i-i-i-i-i-i* or *chit-chit-chit-r-r-r-r-b*. Both sexes drum. Calls with fast *ptikitititit...* and *tik-tik-tik-tik...* **HABITAT** Open oak and pine forest, mixed broadleaved evergreen/coniferous forest, locally deciduous forest; 600–1,200 m.

CRIMSON-BREASTED WOODPECKER *Dendrocopos cathpharius* 17–17.5 cm

(12) **Male** *tenebrosus*: All-black mantle and scapulars, large white wing-patch, red hindcrown and nape, heavy dark underpart-streaks, red breast-patch and undertail-coverts. (13) **Female**: Black hindcrown and nape, red breast-patch duller and smaller. **Juvenile**: Duller above, whiter below with diffuse streaks, no red on breast, red of undertail-coverts paler/lacking, orange-red on hindcrown/nape (less on female). **VOICE** Male territorial call is a fast, descending rattle. Also drums. Calls are loud *chip* or *tchik* and shrill *kee-kee-kee*. **HABITAT** Broadleaved evergreen forest; 1,600–1,800 m.

PALE-HEADED WOODPECKER *Gecinulus grantia* 25 cm

(14) **Male** *indochinensis*: Mainly maroon-chestnut above, pinkish-red crown-centre, bars on wings and tail. (15) **Female**: No red crown-patch. **Juvenile**: As female but mostly dark brown above, very dark brown/grey-brown below. **VOICE** Territorial call recalls Bay: loud laughing *yi wee-wee-wee*. Drums in loud, even bursts. Harsh high *grrrit-grrrit-grrrit* and *grridit grrit-grrit...* etc. **HABITAT** Bamboo, broadleaved and semi-deciduous forest; recorded at c.400 m.

BAMBOO WOODPECKER *Gecinulus viridis* 25–26 cm

(16) **Male** *viridis*: Greyish-olive above, red mid-crown/nape, red on rump/uppertail-coverts, olive-brown below. (17) **Female**: Pale yellowish-green head. **Juvenile**: Like female but darker/browner above, very dark, often grey-tinged below. **Other subspecies** *G.v.robinsoni* (S). **VOICE** Territorial call is a shrill monotone *kyeek-kyeek-kyeek-kyeek*; *keep-kee-kee-kee-kee-kee* or *kwi-kwi-kwi-kweek-kweek*. Drums in short loud bursts. Also, similar cackling to Bay, but slower and occasional *bik* notes. **HABITAT** Bamboo, broadleaved evergreen and deciduous forest; up to 1,400 m.

PLATE 9 EURASIAN WRYNECK, PICULETS & SMALLER TYPICAL WOODPECKERS

EURASIAN WRYNECK *Jynx torquilla* 16–18 cm
(1) **Adult** *chinensis*: Cryptically patterned; upperparts greyish-brown with broad dark stripe down centre, underparts buffish-white, barred blackish, wings and tail heavily barred and vermiculated. **Juvenile**: Duller, darker and more barred above, less distinctly barred below. **VOICE** Male territorial call is a repeated series of clear, ringing notes, each falling in pitch at end: *quee-quee-quee-quee-quee*... Otherwise gives repeated *tak* or *kek* notes. **HABITAT & BEHAVIOUR** Open dry country, secondary growth, scrub and grass, cultivation; up to 2,000 m. Often feeds on ground, sits motionless for long periods, particularly when disturbed.

SPECKLED PICULET *Picumnus innominatus* 9–10.5 cm
(2) **Male** *malayorum*: Tiny and short-tailed, with bold olive-slate and white marking on head, rufous-buff forehead with black barring, olive-green upperparts, whitish underparts with bold blackish spots and bars. (3) **Female**: Forehead concolorous with crown. **Juvenile**: Resembles respective adults but has pale bill. **VOICE** Territorial call is a high *ti-ti-ti-ti-ti*. Also produces loud tinny drumming. Calls include sharp *tsit* and squeaky *sik-sik-sik*. **HABITAT & BEHAVIOUR** Broadleaved evergreen and mixed deciduous forest, secondary growth, bamboo; up to 1,830 m. Often joins bird-waves.

RUFOUS PICULET *Sasia abnormis* 8–9.5 cm
(4) **Male** *abnormis*: Like White-browed but lacks supercilium; darker olive above, darker rufous below. Eyering dull pinkish-red, forehead yellowish. (5) **Female**: Forehead dark rufous. (6) **Juvenile**: Upperparts duller olive (washed slaty on mantle), head and underparts dull brownish-slate, may show a little dull rufous on chin, belly and vent. Bill all dark. **VOICE** Male territorial call is a high-pitched *kik-ik-ik-ik-ik-ik*. Also drums like White-browed. Call is a sharp *tic* or *tsit*. **HABITAT & BEHAVIOUR** Bamboo, broadleaved evergreen forest, secondary growth; up to 1,300 m. Often joins bird-waves.

WHITE-BROWED PICULET *Sasia ochracea* 8–9.5 cm
(7) **Male** *reichenowi*: White supercilium behind eye, rufescent-olive mantle/scapulars, buffish-rufous underparts. (8) **Female**: Forehead rufous. (9) **Male** *hasbroucki* (S): Blackish eyering. **Juvenile**: Similar to Rufous. **Other subspecies** *S.o.ochracea* (NW,NE; syn. *querulivox, kinneari*): Darker crown, dark olive wash on mantle, rufous-collared appearance, deeper rufous head-sides/underparts. **VOICE** Territorial call is a rapid high trill preceded by call note: *chi rrrrrrrrra*. Loud tinny drumming on bamboo: *tit..trrrrrrrrrrit*. Call is a sharp *chi*. **HABITAT & BEHAVIOUR** Bamboo, broadleaved evergreen and mixed deciduous forest; up to 1,830 m. Joins bird-waves.

BUFF-RUMPED WOODPECKER *Meiglyptes tristis* 17 cm
(10) **Male** *grammithorax*: Small; dense pale barring on blackish plumage, plain whitish-buff lower back/rump. (11) **Female**: Lacks red submoustachial stripe. **Juvenile**: Somewhat darker with narrower pale body-barring and more obscurely marked underparts. **VOICE** Male territorial call is a rapid trilled *ki-i-i-i-i-i*. Drums in weak bursts. Calls with a single sharp *pit* (sometimes repeated) and longer *pee* notes. **HABITAT** Broadleaved evergreen forest, forest edge, secondary growth, sometimes plantations; up to 600 m.

BLACK-AND-BUFF WOODPECKER *Meiglyptes jugularis* 17–19.5 cm
(12) **Male**: From Heart-spotted by white hind-neck, mostly blackish malar area/throat, black-and-white barred tertials, short reddish submoustachial stripe, fine whitish bars/speckles on blackish forecrown/head-sides/throat. (13) **Female**: No reddish submoustachial stripe. Otherwise from Heart-spotted as male; also by dark forecrown. **Juvenile**: Duller, head more clearly barred. **VOICE** Male territorial call is a high rattling *titititititit'weerk'weerk'weerk*..., sometimes interspersed with nasal *ki'yew* notes. **HABITAT** Relatively open broadleaved evergreen and semi-evergreen forest, bamboo; up to 915 m.

BUFF-NECKED WOODPECKER *Meiglyptes tukki* 21 cm
(14) **Male** *tukki*: Recalls Buff-rumped but larger, with narrower pale barring, plain head, pale buff neck-patch. (15) **Female**: Lacks red submoustachial stripe. **Juvenile**: Pale barring broader, upper breast less contrastingly dark. Male may show some red on forehead and crown. **VOICE** Male territorial call is a high-pitched, monotone, trilled *kirr-r-r*, recalling Buff-rumped. Both sexes drum. Other calls include a high-pitched *ti ti ti ti*..., *ki-ti ti ti ti*... and single *pee* notes, like Buff-rumped. **HABITAT** Broadleaved evergreen forest; up to 600 m.

GREY-AND-BUFF WOODPECKER *Hemicircus concretus* 14 cm
(16) **Male** *sordidus*: Small and very short-tailed, with prominent triangular crest. Sooty-greyish with red crown, bold whitish-buff scales above and on vent, and whitish rump. Tertials boldly patterned whitish-buff and black. (17) **Female**: Greyish crown. **Juvenile**: Scaling buffier and more prominent, crown feathers cinnamon-rufous with narrow black tips; both sexes show some red on crown. **VOICE** Drums weakly. Calls include a high-pitched drawn-out *ki-yow* or *kee-yew*, sharp *pit* notes and vibrating *chitterr*. **HABITAT** Broadleaved evergreen forest; up to 900 m.

HEART-SPOTTED WOODPECKER *Hemicircus canente* 15.5–17 cm
(18) **Male**: Relatively small/short-tailed with prominent triangular crest. Mostly blackish with white throat, malar area and sides/front of neck and white lower scapulars and tertials with prominent black heart-shaped markings. (19) **Female**: Whitish forecrown. **Juvenile**: As female but whitish parts buffier; forehead often black-barred. **VOICE** Drumming weak. Calls with nasal *ki-yew* (*yew* stressed), high *kee-kee-kee-kee*, drawn-out grating *chur-r* and squeaky *chirrick* (often in flight). **HABITAT** Deciduous, broadleaved evergreen and semi-evergreen forest, forest edge, bamboo; up to 915 m.

10–19 to different scale

PLATE 10 LARGER TYPICAL WOODPECKERS

BANDED WOODPECKER *Picus mineaceus* 25.5–27 cm

(1) **Male** *malaccensis*: Largely reddish/rufous head, scaled mantle/scapulars, barred underparts and primaries. (2) **Female**: No reddish tinge on ear-coverts; whitish speckled forehead and face. **Juvenile**: Duller; initially has dull brown forehead and crown (red at rear), mantle plainer, less obviously barred below. **Other subspecies** *P.m.perlutus* (W): Narrower dark bars below. **VOICE** Male gives 1–7 mournful, falling *peew* or *kwee* notes. Call is a short *keek*. **HABITAT** Broadleaved evergreen forest, secondary growth, plantations; up to 915 m.

LESSER YELLOWNAPE *Picus chlorolophus* 25–28 cm

(3) **Male** *chlorolophus*: Narrowly red crown-sides, red submoustachial stripe, barred lower breast to undertail-coverts, yellow nuchal crest, plain primaries. (4) **Female**: Red on side of rear crown only. **Juvenile**: Crown/nape duller than respective adults; breast-barring more distinct; male lacks red submoustachial stripe. **Other subspecies** *P.c.laotianus* (east NW, north NE) and *annamensis* (NE[south-west],SE): More red on crown; *annamensis* darker above, whiter on lower underparts. **VOICE** Male utters plaintive *peee-uu* or *pee-a*. Also slightly descending series of *kwee* or *kee* notes. Occasionally drums. Call is a short *chak*. **HABITAT** Broadleaved evergreen and deciduous forest; up to 1,800 m.

CRIMSON-WINGED WOODPECKER *Picus puniceus* 24–28 cm

(5) **Male** *observandus*: Red crown, submoustachial stripe and wings, olive-greenish head-sides, mantle and breast. (6) **Female**: Lacks red submoustachial stripe. **Juvenile**: Duller/greyer; red of head on hindcrown only, head-/neck-sides and underparts speckled whitish. Male has smaller/no submoustachial stripe. **VOICE** Clear *pee-bee* or *pee-bee-bee-bee*; sometimes *peep* or falling *pi-eew*. Drums weakly. **HABITAT** Broadleaved evergreen forest, secondary growth; up to 600 m.

GREATER YELLOWNAPE *Picus flavinucha* 31.5–35 cm

(7) **Male** *lylei*: Rufescent crown, yellow throat, dark-streaked lower throat/uppermost breast, barred primaries. (8) **Female**: Olive-tinged hindcrown, dull chestnut submoustachial stripe, upper throat striped blackish and whitish. (9) **Male** *flavinucha* (W): Olive hindcrown, darker sides of neck and breast. **Juvenile**: Duller below; belly may have faint bars. Male initially has olive-scaled crown, yellow of throat more buffy-whitish. **Other subspecies** *P.f.archon* (east NW, north NE) and *pierrei* (NE[south],SE): Black streaks go further up throat. **VOICE** Male gives accelerating *kwee-kwee-kwee-kwee-kwee-kwee-kwee-kwi-kwi-kwi-wi-wi-wi-wi-wik*. Rarely drums. Call is loud *kyaa* or *kiyaep*. **HABITAT** Broadleaved evergreen and deciduous forest, native pine forest; up to 2,000 m.

CHECKER-THROATED WOODPECKER *Picus mentalis* 26.5–29.5 cm

(10) **Male** *humii*: No red on head, olive crown, chestnut neck-sides/upper breast, plain belly, barred primaries. (11) **Female**: Neck-sides, upper breast and submoustachial stripe dull chestnut. **Juvenile**: Crown and underparts browner, wings duller. **VOICE** Territorial male utters a long series of *wi* notes, similar to Greater Yellownape. Drums in short bursts. Calls include a single *kyick* and *kiyee..kiyee..kiyee...*, with stressed first syllable. **HABITAT** Broadleaved evergreen forest; up to 1,300 m.

STREAK-BREASTED WOODPECKER *Picus viridanus* 30.5–32.5 cm

(12) **Male** *viridanus*: Red crown/nape. From Laced by duller olive neck-sides/throat, streaked throat/upper breast. (13) **Female**: Black crown and nape. **Juvenile**: Duller; underpart markings less distinct (particularly on throat/breast), flanks/belly appear more scaled; male's crown more orange-red. **Other subspecies** *P.v.weberi* (S): 28–31 cm; body rather darker. **VOICE** Explosive *kirrr* and series of *tcheu* notes. **HABITAT** Broadleaved evergreen forest, coastal scrub, mangroves; lowlands.

LACED WOODPECKER *Picus vittatus* 27–33 cm

(14) **Male**: Red crown/nape, plain buffy yellowish-olive neck/throat/breast, dark streaks/loops on olive-whitish belly. (15) **Female**: Black crown and nape. **Juvenile**: Belly scalier; lower throat/breast may be faintly streaked; red on male's crown paler/less extensive. **VOICE** Territorial call like Grey-headed but faster, notes shorter/lower-pitched. Drums in steady rolls. Call is a loud *ik*. **HABITAT** Broadleaved evergreen and deciduous forest, secondary growth, gardens, plantations, bamboo; up to 1,525 m.

STREAK-THROATED WOODPECKER *Picus xanthopygaeus* 27.5–30 cm

(16) **Male**: Pale eye, white supercilium, vague submoustachial stripe, streaked head-/neck-sides, throat and breast. (17) **Female**: Greyish streaks on black crown, white supercilium. **Juvenile**: Duller than respective adult with less distinct underpart markings; appears somewhat more scaled/barred on belly. Male has less red on crown and nape, female less distinct crown-streaks. **VOICE** Drums. Call is a sharp *queemp*. **HABITAT** Deciduous forest, scattered trees in open areas; up to 500 m.

BLACK-HEADED WOODPECKER *P.erythropygius* 31–35 cm

(18) **Male** *nigrigenis*: Black head and central nape-line, red-centred crown, yellow throat/nape-sides, red rump. (19) **Female**: All-black crown. **Juvenile**: Duller; throat paler, upper breast buffier, diffuse scales below. Red on male's crown faint. **Other subspecies** *P.e.erythropygius* (NE): Less red on crown. **VOICE** Yelping *ka-tek-a-tek-a-tek...*; rapid *cha-cha-cha...cha-cha-cha* (stressed first notes). Loud double call note. **HABITAT** Dry dipterocarp, deciduous and pine forest; up to 900 m.

GREY-HEADED WOODPECKER *Picus canus* 30.5–34.5 cm

(20) **Male** *hessei* (syn. *gyldenstolpei*): Red forecrown, black hindcrown and nape-centre, plain grey head-sides, black loral and submoustachial stripes, unmarked greyish-olive underparts. (21) **Female**: Crown all black with grey streaks. **Juvenile**: Duller; mantle/scapulars slightly mottled; submoustachial stripe less defined, belly may be barred/mottled; less red on male's forecrown. **VOICE** Male utters loud, descending *kieu... kieu...kieu...kieu* (3–4 or more notes). Drums in long rolls. Calls are *kik* and *keek..kak-kak-kak*. **HABITAT** Open forest of various types; up to 1,800 m.

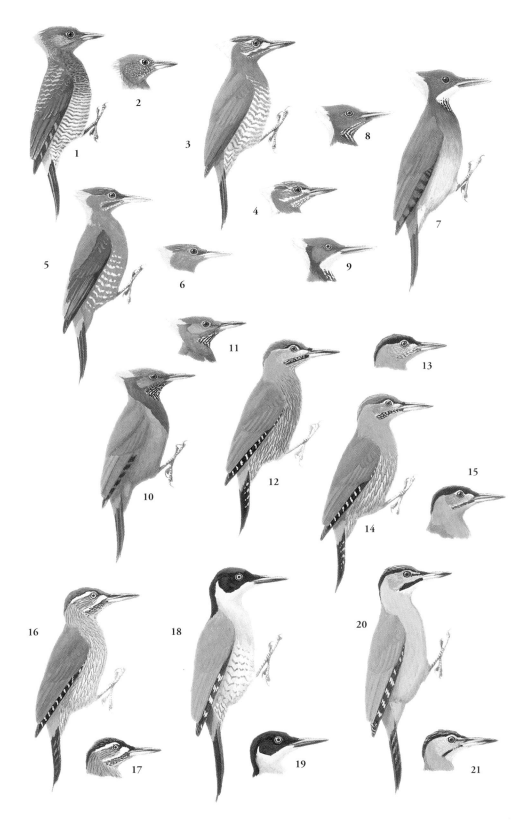

PLATE 11 TYPICAL WOODPECKERS & FLAMEBACKS

OLIVE-BACKED WOODPECKER *Dinopium rafflesii* 28 cm

(1) **Male** *rafflesii*: Like flamebacks but olive-green above, breast to vent plain dull olive. Red crown and crest. (2) **Female**: Black crown and crest. **Juvenile**: Duller. Male has red of head restricted to crest, forehead sometimes spotted red. **VOICE** Male territorial call is a slow, variable *chak chak chak chak chak-chak* (6–30 or more notes) or faster, more regular series of 10–50 notes. Drumming unrecorded. Calls include a single *chak*, soft trilling *ti-i-i-i-i* and squeaky *tiririt*. **HABITAT** Broadleaved evergreen forest; up to 800 m.

COMMON FLAMEBACK *Dinopium javanense* 28–30 cm

(3,4) **Male** *intermedium*: Single black submoustachial stripe, black hindneck, no black on lores/crown-sides. (5) **Female**: Black crown and crest with white streaks. **Juvenile**: Breast more blackish-brown with white spots, lower underparts more obscurely marked; male's forehead/crown mostly black, crest red, female's crown more spotted than streaked. **Other subspecies** *D.j.javanense* (S). **VOICE** A long, trilled *ka-di-di-di-di-di-di*..., recalling some *Porzana* crakes; faster and less metallic than Greater. Drumming softer than Greater. Calls include a single or double *kow* note and *kowp-owp-owp-owp*, uttered in flight. **HABITAT** Open deciduous forest, scrub, gardens, plantations, sometimes mangroves; up to 800 m.

GREATER FLAMEBACK *Chrysocolaptes lucidus* 29–32 cm

(6,7) **Male** *guttacristatus*: Largish, long-billed; black lores, crown-edge, mask and looped submoustachial stripe, red rump/uppertail-coverts, blackish-scaled white underparts/upper mantle, white centre of hindneck. (8) **Female**: Black crown and crest with white spots. **Juvenile**: More olive above, duller, more obscurely marked below; male has less red on crown, variable pale spots on forehead/crown. **VOICE** Sharp, metallic, monotone *tibititititit*... Drums loudly. Also single *kik* notes. **HABITAT** Deciduous and broadleaved evergreen forest, forest edge, mangroves, old plantations; up to 1,200 m.

MAROON WOODPECKER *Blythipicus rubiginosus* 23–24 cm

(9) **Male**: Like Bay but smaller, upperparts and wings unbarred maroon-chestnut (except flight feathers and tertials), tail blackish with faint pale bars. Prominent red neck-patch, often some red on submoustachial area. (10) **Female**: Lacks red on head. **Juvenile**: More rufescent above, sometimes some red on crown. **VOICE** Male territorial call is a shrill, descending *keek-eek-eek-eek-eek-eek*, higher-pitched than Bay. Calls include a wavering high-pitched *kik-kik-kik-kik-kik-kik-kik-kik*... (slows somewhat towards end) and nervously repeated *kik* notes. **HABITAT** Broadleaved evergreen forest, secondary growth, bamboo; up to 1,200 m.

BAY WOODPECKER *Blythipicus pyrrhotis* 26.5–29 cm

(11) **Male** *pyrrhotis*: Long pale bill; dull rufescent-brown with paler head, black bars above, red neck-patch. (12) **Female**: Lacks red on neck. **Juvenile**: Darker crown with paler streaks, bolder bars above, darker below with faint rufous bars; male has less red on neck. **VOICE** Loud descending laughter: *keek*

keek-keek-keek-keek-keek. Calls with undulating cackling *dit-d-d-di-di-di-di-dit-d-d-di-di*...; squirrel-like *keker-rak-keker-rak*...; chattering *kerer-kerer-kerer*... **HABITAT** Broadleaved evergreen and sometimes semi-evergreen and mixed deciduous forest; 300–2,200 m.

RUFOUS WOODPECKER *Celeus brachyurus* 25 cm

(13) **Male** *phaioceps*: Rufescent; blackish bars above, red cheek-patch; shortish black bill, speckled throat. (14) **Female**: Lacks red cheek-patch. (15) **Male** *squamigularis* (S): More heavily marked throat, barred belly. **VOICE** Male territorial call is a nasal laughing *kweep-kweep-kweep*. Also utters a long, slightly descending and accelerating series of notes. Drumming (both sexes) diagnostic, grinding slowly to a halt: *bdddddd d d d dt*. **HABITAT** Broadleaved evergreen and deciduous forest, forest edge, secondary growth; up to 900 m.

ORANGE-BACKED WOODPECKER *Reinwardtipicus validus* 30 cm

(16) **Male** *xanthopygius*: Long-necked; red crown and underparts, broad whitish to orange-buff stripe down centre of upperparts. (17) **Female**: Blackish crown and crest, whitish back and rump, dull greyish-brown underparts. **Juvenile**: Both sexes like female. Male may show some red on crown and orange-buff on rump. **VOICE** Rapid trilled *ki-i-i-i-i-ik*. Drumming quite weak, in short bursts. Also squeaky anxious *kit kit kit kit kit-it* (with sharply rising last note) in alarm. **HABITAT** Broadleaved evergreen forest; up to 730 m.

GREAT SLATY WOODPECKER *Mulleripicus pulverulentus* 45–51 cm

(18) **Male** *harterti*: Large size, long thin neck, grey plumage, red submoustachial patch, buff throat/foreneck. (19) **Female**: Lacks red submoustachial patch. **Juvenile**: Duller; indistinct head speckling, throat/foreneck whitish; larger red submoustachial stripe on male (may show red on crown). **Other subspecies** *M.p.pulverulentus* (southern S): More blackish-slate overall. **VOICE** Loud, rapid 2–5 note whinny: *woi-kwoi-kwoi-kwoik*...*woi-kwoi-kwoikwoik*... (often in flight). Calls with a single *dwot* and soft *whu-ick*. **HABITAT** Various broadleaved forests, forest edge, mangroves; up to 1,000 m.

WHITE-BELLIED WOODPECKER *Dryocopus javensis* 37.5–43 cm

(20) **Male** *feddeni*: Large size, black and white plumage, red crown, crest and submoustachial band. (21) **Female**: Black forecrown, no red submoustachial band. **Juvenile**: Duller with paler throat; male has black mottling on forecrown, much smaller red submoustachial patch. **Other subspecies** *D.j.javensis* (S): Black rump (juvenile may show some white). **VOICE** Staccato *kek-ek-ek-ek-ek* and *kiau-kiau-kiau*. Loud accelerating drumming (both sexes). Typical call is a loud explosive *keer* or *kyab*. **HABITAT** Deciduous and broadleaved evergreen forest, sometimes coniferous forest, mangroves; up to 915 m.

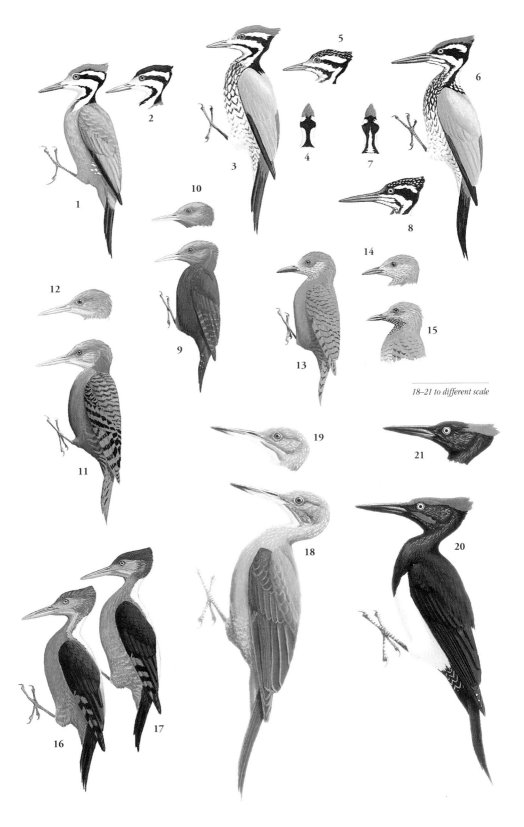

18–21 to different scale

PLATE 12 BARBETS

FIRE-TUFTED BARBET *Psilopogon pyrolophus* 28 cm

(1) **Adult**: Green with brownish-maroon hind-crown and nape, whitish band across forecrown, pale yellowish-green bill with vertical dark band, short green supercilium, grey ear-coverts, yellow and blackish breast-bands. (2) **Juvenile**: Dull olive-brown hindcrown and nape, dull supercilium. **VOICE** Male territorial call is an unusual cicada-like buzzing, starting with spaced notes, then speeding up and rising in pitch towards end. Recalls some broadbills. **HABITAT** Broadleaved evergreen forest; mountains (recorded at c.700 m).

GREAT BARBET *Megalaima virens* 32–33 cm

(3) **Adult** *virens*: Relatively large and long-tailed, large yellowish bill, dark bluish head, brownish mantle and breast, dark greenish-blue streaks on yellow belly, red undertail-coverts. **Juvenile**: Similar to adult. **VOICE** Male territorial call is a very loud strident *kay-oh*, repeated about once a second. Also (by female?) a more rapid, continuous *piou-piou-piou-piou*..., often given with former in duet by pair. Alarm call is a harsh grating *keeab*. **HABITAT** Broadleaved evergreen and occasionally deciduous forest; 600–2,565 m.

LINEATED BARBET *Megalaima lineata* 27–28 cm

(4) **Adult** *hodgsoni*: Thick yellowish bill, dark brown head and breast with broad whitish streaks, yellow orbital skin. **Juvenile**: Similar to adult. **VOICE** Male territorial call is a very loud, mellow *poo-pob*, with higher second note, repeated about once a second. Also a rapid, dry, bubbling *koh-koh-koh-koh-koh*... **HABITAT** Deciduous forest, scattered trees in open areas, coastal scrub, plantations; up to 800 m.

GREEN-EARED BARBET *Megalaima faiostricta* 24.5–27 cm

(5) **Adult** *faiostricta*: Like Lineated Barbet but smaller, bill mostly dark, dark orbital skin, green ear-coverts, all-green mantle, red spot on breast-side. **Juvenile**: Like adult. **VOICE** Male territorial call is a loud throaty *took-a-prruk*, rapidly repeated more than once per second. Also a mellow, fluty, rising *pooouk*. **HABITAT** Broadleaved evergreen and semi-evergreen forest, mixed deciduous forest, scattered trees in more open areas; up to 900 m.

GOLD-WHISKERED BARBET *Megalaima chrysopogon* 30 cm

(6) **Adult** *laeta*: Blackish bill, broad eyestripe above large yellow patch on lower head-side, pale greyish-buff throat. **Juvenile**: Has duller yellow patch on lower sides of head. **VOICE** Male territorial call is a very loud, rather deep, rapid *teboop-teboop-teboop-teboop-teboop*... Also a repeated, long, low-pitched trill on one note, gradually slowing and eventually breaking up into 3–4 note phrases. **HABITAT** Broadleaved evergreen forest; up to 1,000 m.

GOLDEN-THROATED BARBET *Megalaima franklinii* 20.5–23.5 cm

(7) **Adult** *ramsayi*: Red and yellow crown, yellow upper, grey lower throat, grey-streaked blackish ear-coverts. (8) **Juvenile**: Duller, with less distinct head pattern. (9) **Adult** *franklinii* (east NW,NE): Plain black eyestripe, deeper yellow upper throat. **Other subspecies** *M.f.trangensis* (S). *M.f.minor* (presumably in extreme S): Differs as *franklinii* and also has some blue behind ear-coverts. **VOICE** Male territorial call is a very loud, ringing *pukwowk*, repeated about once a second. **HABITAT** Broadleaved evergreen forest; 900–2,565 m.

BLACK-BROWED BARBET *Megalaima oorti* 21.5–23.5 cm

(10) **Adult** *oorti*: Recalls Golden-throated, with blue ear-coverts, blue-bordered yellow throat, red spot on breast-side. (11) **Juvenile**: Duller with less distinct head pattern. **VOICE** Male territorial call is a loud, throaty *toka-r'ut*, repeated about once a second. **HABITAT** Broadleaved evergreen forest; 1,200–1,400 m (likely to occur down to at least 900 m).

BLUE-THROATED BARBET *Megalaima asiatica* 23 cm

(12) **Adult** *davisoni*: All-blue head-sides and throat, red crown with blue mid-band, red spot on breast-side. (13) **Juvenile**: Duller with ill-defined head pattern. (14) **Adult** *chersonesus* (S): More extensively blue crown. **VOICE** Male territorial call is a very loud, quickly repeated *took-arook*. **HABITAT** Broadleaved evergreen forest, secondary growth; 600–1,830 m.

MOUSTACHED BARBET *Megalaima incognita* 23 cm

(15) **Adult** *elbeli*: Small red patch on rear crown, blue cheeks and throat, black eye- and submoustachial stripe. (16) **Juvenile**: Duller, greener sides of head and throat, narrower submoustachial stripe. **Other subspecies** *M.i.incognita* (W), *euroa* (SE). **VOICE** Male territorial call similar to Blue-throated but notes more spaced and deliberate: *u'ik-a-ruk u'ik-a-ruk u'ik-a-ruk*... **HABITAT** Broadleaved evergreen forest; 600–1,700 m.

BLUE-EARED BARBET *Megalaima australis* 17–18 cm

(17) **Male** *cyanotis*: Small; black front of head, blue midcrown, ear-coverts and throat, red patches above and below ear-coverts, orange-red cheek-patch. (18) **Female**: Head pattern duller. (19) **Juvenile**: Rather uniform dull green with blue-tinged ear-coverts and throat. (20) **Male** *duvaucelii* (possibly occurs in extreme S): Black ear-coverts and broad band across lower throat/upper breast, red cheek-patch, larger red patches by ear-coverts. Intergrades with *stuarti* may also occur. **Other subspecies** *M.a.stuarti* (W,S): Like *cyanotis* but tends to have more black on lower throat/upper breast. **VOICE** Male territorial call is a loud, monotonous, rapidly repeated *ko-tek*. Also a series of shrill whistled *pleow* notes, about one per second. **HABITAT** Open broadleaved evergreen and semi-evergreen forest, mixed deciduous forest, secondary growth; up to 1,525 m.

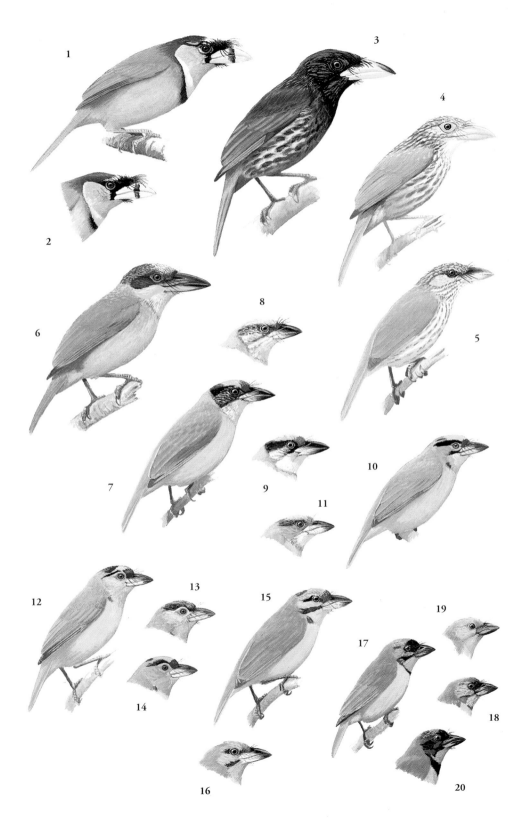

PLATE 13 BARBETS & HORNBILLS

RED-CROWNED BARBET *Megalaima rafflesii* 25–27 cm

(1) **Adult** *malayensis*: All-red crown, blue throat, blue supercilium, smallish yellow neck-patch, small red patch on side of upper breast. (2) **Juvenile**: Much duller, with less defined head pattern. **VOICE** Male territorial call is a loud series of 1–2 **took** notes followed, after a pause, by up to 20 rapidly repeated, shorter **tuk** notes. **HABITAT** Broadleaved evergreen forest; below 200 m.

RED-THROATED BARBET *Megalaima mystacophanos* 23 cm

(3) **Male** *mystacophanos*: Red throat and crown, yellow forehead, broad black line through eye, blue cheeks and band across uppermost breast, prominent red patch on side of upper breast. (4) **Female**: Mostly greenish head without black, red patches on lores, hindcrown and upper breast-side. (5) **Juvenile**: Head all green with yellower-tinged forehead and throat. **VOICE** Territorial call is 1–2 (sometimes 3) deep notes at uneven intervals: **chok..chok-chok chok...chok-chok..chok**... etc. Also a high trill, gradually shortening. **HABITAT** Broadleaved evergreen forest; up to 760 m.

YELLOW-CROWNED BARBET *Megalaima henricii* 22–23 cm

(6) **Adult** *henricii*: Smallish; yellow forecrown and sides of crown, green sides of head, blue throat, black lores and short eyestripe, blue centre of hindcrown, small red patches on foreneck and neck-sides. (7) **Juvenile**: Duller, with more washed-out head pattern. **VOICE** Male territorial call consists of 4–6 loud **tok** notes introduced by short trill: **trrok....tok-tok-tok-tok**..., with one phrase about every 2 s. **HABITAT** Broadleaved evergreen forest; up to 800 m.

COPPERSMITH BARBET *Megalaima haemacephala* 17 cm

(8) **Adult** *indica*: Small; yellow head-sides/throat, black eyestripe and submoustachial stripe, pale greenish underparts with broad dark green streaks. Crown red at front, black towards rear; red breast-band. (9) **Juvenile**: Dark parts of head duller, yellow of sides of head and throat paler, no red on crown or breast. **VOICE** Male territorial call is series of up to 100 or more loud, quickly repeated **tonk** notes. **HABITAT** Deciduous forest, forest edge, mangroves, scattered trees in open areas, parks and gardens, plantations; up to 800 m.

BROWN BARBET *Calorhamphus fuliginosus* 20 cm

(10) **Adult** *hayii*: Brown plumage with paler, more whitish breast to vent. Legs and feet pinkish-orange. **Juvenile**: Similar to adult. **VOICE** Thin, forced **pseeoo** notes. **HABITAT & BEHAVIOUR** Broadleaved evergreen forest, secondary growth, scattered trees in more open areas; up to 1,000 m. Often forages in small parties.

ORIENTAL PIED HORNBILL *Anthracoceros albirostris* 68–70 cm

(11,12) **Male** *albirostris*: Relatively small; white belly/vent, white facial markings, pale yellowish bill/casque with dark markings; black wings with broad white trailing edge, black tail with broadly white-tipped outer feathers. (13) **Female**: Bill and casque smaller and more extensively dark distally. (14) **Male** *convexus* (extreme S): Mostly white outertail feathers (tail often appears white from below). **Juvenile**: Plain bill/casque (latter very small), less white on tail. **VOICE** Loud yelping **kleng-keng kek-kek-kek-kek-kek** and **ayip-yip-yip-yip**... etc. **HABITAT & BEHAVIOUR** Broadleaved evergreen and mixed deciduous forest, island forest, secondary growth, plantations/gardens; up to 1,400 m (*convexus* below 150 m). Usually in flocks, may be quite large.

RHINOCEROS HORNBILL *Buceros rhinoceros* 91–122 cm

(15) **Male** *rhinoceros*: Huge; red and yellow upcurved casque, all-black head, neck and wings, reddish eyes. (16) **Female**: Whitish eyes. **Juvenile**: Bill-base orange, casque very small, eyes/eye-ring bluish-grey. **VOICE** Male utters deep, forceful **hok** notes, female a higher **hak**, often in duet: **hok-hak hok-hak hok-hak**... Loud throaty **ger-ronk** (both sexes). **HABITAT & BEHAVIOUR** Broadleaved evergreen forest; up to 1,220 m. In pairs or small groups, sometimes flocks of up to 25.

GREAT HORNBILL *Buceros bicornis* 119–122 cm (birds in S average smaller)

(17) **Male** *homrai*: Very large; black and yellowish-white head pattern, large yellowish bill and casque, white tail with broad black central band, reddish eye; double broad yellowish-white and white bands across wings. (18) **Female**: Whitish eye; shows less black on casque than male. **Juvenile**: Bill much smaller, casque barely developed, eyes pale blue-grey, eyering pinkish. **VOICE** Very loud, deep **gok** or **kok** notes (by duetting pairs), leading to loud harsh roaring/barking. Also, deep coarse **who** by male and **whaa** by female; double **who-whaa** at take-off/in flight is duet of these calls. **HABITAT & BEHAVIOUR** Broadleaved evergreen and mixed deciduous forest, forest on some larger islands; up to 1,525 m. Usually found in pairs or small groups.

HELMETED HORNBILL *Buceros vigil* 127 cm (central tail feathers up to 50 cm more)

(19,20) **Male**: Huge; white tail with black central band and elongated central feathers, bare red head-sides, throat and neck, short straight bill, short, rounded reddish casque with yellow tip; broad white trailing edge to wing. **Female**: Smaller, bill speckled black at tip, face/neck-skin tinged pale lilac. **Juvenile**: Bill yellowish-olive, casque very small, head/neck-skin pale greenish-blue, central tail feathers shorter. **VOICE** Loud, long series of spaced **hoop** notes, slowly quickening to **ke-hoop** and ending with manic, comical laughter. Also loud clanking **ka-hank ka-hank**... **HABITAT & BEHAVIOUR** Broadleaved evergreen forest; up to 1,200 m. Usually singly or in pairs.

11–20 to different scale

PLATE 14 HORNBILLS

BLACK HORNBILL *Anthracoceros malayanus* 76 cm

(1,2) **Male**: Relatively small, all black; yellowish-white bill/casque, broad white outertail-tips, dark orbital skin. (3) **Male variant**: Broad white supercilium. (4) **Female**: Bill and casque smaller and blackish, orbital skin and submoustachial patch pinkish. **Juvenile**: Bill pale greenish-yellow (darker on very young birds) with undeveloped casque, facial skin dull yellowish with orange around eye, white tail-tips flecked black. **VOICE** Unusual and distinctive loud harsh retching sounds and grating growls. **HABITAT & BEHAVIOUR** Broadleaved evergreen forest; below 215 m. Usually found in pairs or small flocks, occasionally larger flocks of up to 30 or more.

BROWN HORNBILL *Anorrhinus tickelli* 73–74 cm

(5,6) **Male** *austeni*: Relatively small, mostly brownish; whitish throat and upper breast, brownish-rufous lower breast and belly, pale yellowish bill with small casque; white tips to outer primaries and outertail feathers. (7) **Female**: Dark brownish throat/underparts, smaller casque (*A.t.tickelli* has horn-coloured to blackish bill). (8) **Male** *tickelli* (W) Bright brownish-rufous throat and underparts. **Juvenile**: As female but dull greyish-brown below, no white primary tips, smaller bill, pinkish orbital skin. **VOICE** Loud, piercing, airy yelps and squeals. Loud, yelping, upward-inflected **klee-ah**. **HABITAT & BEHAVIOUR** Broadleaved evergreen forest, sometimes adjacent mixed deciduous forest, secondary forest; up to 1,500 m. Usually found in flocks, sometimes quite large.

BUSHY-CRESTED HORNBILL *Anorrhinus galeritus* 89 cm

(9,10) **Male**: All dark; thick drooping crest, somewhat paler and greyer vent, paler dirty brownish-grey basal two-thirds of tail. Bill and small casque blackish, bare orbital and gular skin pale bluish. (11) **Female**: Casque smaller, often has extensively dull yellowish to ivory-coloured bill. **Juvenile**: Belly whiter, bill pale olive, head-skin pale yellowish (eyering pink). **VOICE** Rising and falling yelps, **klia-klia-klia kliu-kliu**...; **wah wah wohawaha** etc.; often by all flock members, building to crescendo. High **aak aak aak** in alarm. **HABITAT & BEHAVIOUR** Broadleaved evergreen forest; up to 1,220 m. Flocks of 5–15.

WHITE-CROWNED HORNBILL *Aceros comatus* 90–101 cm

(12) **Male**: All-whitish head, neck, breast and tail, long shaggy whitish crest. Upperparts, lower belly, vent and wings black, primaries broadly tipped white, bill blackish with paler base and small casque, facial skin pale blue. (13,14) **Female**: Black neck and underparts. **Juvenile**: Similar to female but somewhat browner with blackish bases and shafts to crest feathers, base of tail black, bill yellowish-brown with dark patches; may show whitish tips to greater coverts. Male gradually attains white patches on underparts. **VOICE** Deep, resonant hooting with lower first note: **boo hu-hu-hu hu-hu-hu**...; often dying away. **HABITAT & BEHAVIOUR** Broadleaved evergreen forest; up to 800 m. Usually found in small flocks, often low down in forest. Less frugivorous than other hornbills.

RUFOUS-NECKED HORNBILL *Aceros nipalensis* 117 cm

(15) **Male**: Very large, bright rufous head, neck and underparts, white tail with black basal third/half, pale yellowish bill with virtually no casque, bright red gular skin; black wings with white-tipped outer primaries. (16,17) **Female**: Head, neck and underparts black, orbital skin a little duller. **Juvenile**: Both sexes like male but bill smaller with no dark ridges, tail feathers may be narrowly dark-tipped. **VOICE** Barking **kup** notes; less deep than similar calls of Great Hornbill. **HABITAT & BEHAVIOUR** Broadleaved evergreen forest; 600–1,800 m. Usually in pairs, sometimes small groups.

WRINKLED HORNBILL *Aceros corrugatus* 81–82 cm

(18,19) **Male**: Resembles Wreathed Hornbill but smaller, has smaller yellow bill with reddish base, somewhat squarer-looking reddish casque, blue orbital skin, unmarked and less bulging gular pouch, blacker crown-centre and nape and black base of tail (often difficult to see). White of tail usually strongly stained buffish to yellowish. (20) **Female**: From Wreathed by smaller size, smaller plain yellowish bill, shorter/squarer casque, blue orbital skin, plain and less bulging gular pouch, less pronounced crest and black base of tail. Note habitat/range. **Juvenile**: Like male (both sexes) but bill unridged and pale yellow with orange wash at base, casque undeveloped, orbital skin pale yellow; may have blackish base to upper mandible. **VOICE** Sharp, barking **kak kak-kak** etc. **HABITAT & BEHAVIOUR** Broadleaved evergreen forest, freshwater swamp forest; lowlands. Usually found in pairs or small flocks.

WREATHED HORNBILL *Aceros undulatus* Male 100.5–115 cm; female 84–98 cm (smaller in S)

(21,22) **Male**: Mostly blackish with brownish-white head-sides/neck/breast and white tail (often stained yellowish or brownish). Dark streak on yellow gular pouch, shaggy warm dark brown crown-centre/hind-neck, pale yellowish bill with darker corrugated base (not always obvious), dark-ridged small/short casque, reddish orbital skin. (23) **Female**: Blue gular pouch, all-black head, neck and underparts. **Juvenile**: Both sexes like male but casque undeveloped, bill uncorrugated, dark streak on gular pouch fainter. **VOICE** A loud, rather breathless **kuk-kwehk**, with emphasis on higher second note. **HABITAT & BEHAVIOUR** Broadleaved evergreen and mixed deciduous forest, forest on islands; up to 1,800 m. Usually found in pairs or small flocks. May be seen in very large flocks flying to and from roosts; even over deforested areas.

PLAIN-POUCHED HORNBILL *Aceros subruficollis* Male 86.5–89.5 cm; female 76–84 cm

(24,25) **Male**: Very like Wreathed Hornbill but somewhat smaller, bill shorter with warm brownish base and no corrugations, casque slightly more peaked with more dark ridges, lacks blackish streak on gular pouch. (26) **Female**: Very similar to Wreathed, differing as male. **Juvenile**: As male but casque undeveloped, bill plain pale yellowish. Only differs from Wreathed by plain gular pouch? **VOICE** Loud **keb-kek-kehk**, higher-pitched and more quacking than Wreathed. **HABITAT & BEHAVIOUR** Broadleaved evergreen and mixed deciduous forest; up to 915 m. Usually found in pairs, sometimes small groups.

PLATE 15 TROGONS & KINGFISHERS

RED-NAPED TROGON *Harpactes kasumba* 31.5–34.5 cm
(1) **Male** *kasumba*: Like Diard's but crown all black, has broad red nuchal patch meeting broad cobalt-blue facial skin, well-demarcated narrow white breast-band, dull golden-buffish upperparts, usually redder underparts and unmarked white on undertail. (2) **Female**: Brownish-buff lower breast to vent, unmarked white on underside of tail. **Juvenile**: Similar to female; males soon attain patches of adult plumage. **VOICE** Male territorial call is a subdued but rather harsh, evenly pitched, 3–6 note *kau kau kau kau*..., lower-pitched and more spaced than that of Diard's. Female gives a quiet whirring rattle. **HABITAT** Broadleaved evergreen and freshwater swamp forest, bamboo; up to 550 m.

DIARD'S TROGON *Harpactes diardii* 32.5–35 cm
(3) **Male** *sumatranus*: Black head and upper breast with maroon-washed hindneck and narrow pink nuchal band; pale pink breast-band, reddish-pink belly/vent. Orbital skin violet/violet-blue, undertail as female. (4) **Female**: Told by combination of rather uniform dull brown head, upper breast and mantle, contrasting reddish-pink to pink belly and dark vermiculations/speckles on white of undertail. Back to uppertail-coverts more rufescent, lower breast more buffish-brown, undertail-coverts buffish-brown mixed with pink. **Juvenile**: Both sexes similar to female. Male soon attains patches of adult plumage. **VOICE** Male territorial call is a series of 10–12 *kau* notes, either with the second somewhat higher than the first and the rest descending, with the last few slower, or else all evenly spaced. **HABITAT & BEHAVIOUR**. Middle storey of broadleaved evergreen forest; up to 600 m. Very unobtrusive.

CINNAMON-RUMPED TROGON *Harpactes orrhophaeus* 25.5–28 cm

(5) **Male** *orrhophaeus*: Larger than Scarlet-rumped, thicker bill, brown rump/uppertail-coverts, pinker below. (6) **Female**: From Scarlet-rumped by lack of pink in plumage, darker/richer brown head, with contrasting deep rufous lores/around eye, blackish-brown throat with dull rufous centre; slightly duller, less rufescent above. **Juvenile**: Like female but pale wing vermiculations much broader; duller/greyer and more uniform above, more extensive deep rufous on lores, head-sides and throat. From Scarlet-rumped by extensive, contrasting deep rufous on head-sides, more uniform upperparts (including rump and uppertail-coverts), darker, less buffish breast. **VOICE** Territorial call of male is a weak, descending, 3–4 note *taup taup taup*... or *ta'up ta'up ta'up ta'up*, with each note inflected downwards. **HABITAT & BEHAVIOUR** Broadleaved evergreen forest; below 200 m. Frequents lower to middle storey, very shy.

SCARLET-RUMPED TROGON *Harpactes duvaucelii* 23.5–26.5 cm

(7) **Male**: Black head, blue 'eye-brow', bill and gape skin, bright red rump, uppertail-coverts and underparts. (8) **Female**: Drab dark brown head, paler/slightly warmer lores, around eye and throat, mostly buffy-brown rump and uppertail-coverts (mixed with pink), deep buffy-brown breast, pinkish/reddish-pink belly and vent. (9) **Juvenile female**: Lacks obvious pink in plumage; rump and uppertail-coverts rufescent, underparts rufous-buff with pale buff centrally (males show some pink below and soon attain patches of adult plumage).

VOICE Male territorial call is unusual accelerating, descending *teuk teuk teuk-euk-euk-euk-euk-euk-euk-euk-euk-euk-euk*... Female gives quiet whirring rattle. **HABITAT** Middle to lower storey of broadleaved evergreen forest; up to 400 m.

ORANGE-BREASTED TROGON *Harpactes oreskios* 26.5–31.5 cm

(10) **Male** *stellae*: Head and upper breast greenish-olive (throat and central breast more yellowish-tinged), upperparts chestnut-maroon, underparts yellowish-orange with paler, yellower vent. (11) **Female**: Head to back uniform drab olive-brownish, rump and uppertail-coverts duller/paler, throat and upper breast distinctly grey-washed, rest of underparts paler and yellower, broader pale bars on wings. **Juvenile**: Head, upperparts and breast tinged rufous-chestnut, pale wing-barring broader, belly/vent paler/whitish; males have chestnut mantle, scapulars and back. **Other subspecies** *H.o.uniformis* (S). **VOICE** Territorial call is a subdued, rather rapid 3–5 note *teu-teu-teu*... or *tu-tau-tau-tau*... Female may utter slower, lower-pitched version. **HABITAT** Middle to upper storey of broadleaved evergreen, semi-evergreen and mixed deciduous forest, bamboo; up to 1,100 m.

RED-HEADED TROGON *Harpactes erythrocephalus* 31–35.5 cm

(12) **Male** *erythrocephalus*: Dark red head/breast, white breast-band, pinkish-red belly, whitish wing-barring. (13) **Female**: Brown head/breast, warmish brown wing-barring, white undertail with black border (both sexes). **Juvenile**: Like female but head, breast and upperparts rufescent; has less red on underparts. Male has broad buff bars on wings and attains red on head and upper breast. **Other subspecies** *H.e.klossi* (SE), *annamensis* (NE). *H.e.chaseni* (S): Smaller than other races. **VOICE** Male territorial call is a deep, well-spaced, descending 4–5 note *taup taup taup taup taup*... Call is a coarse, rattling *tewirr*. **HABITAT & BEHAVIOUR** Broadleaved evergreen forest, 400–2,000 m. Frequents middle to upper storey; unobtrusive, spending long periods sitting motionless.

BROWN-WINGED KINGFISHER *Halcyon amauroptera* 36–37 cm

(14) **Adult**: Orange-buff head and underparts, dark brown mantle, wings and tail. **Juvenile**: Nape, neck, breast and flanks vermiculated dusky brown, wing-coverts with narrow pale fringes. **VOICE** A loud, tremulous, descending *tree treew-treew* etc., and a loud deep *cha-cha-cha-cha*.... **HABITAT** Mangroves, particularly old growth.

STORK-BILLED KINGFISHER *Halcyon capensis* 37.5–41 cm

(15) **Male** *burmanica*: Large; huge red bill, pale brown crown/head-sides, greenish-blue above, buffish below. (16) **Male**: *malaccensis* (S): Darker crown and head-sides, bluer (less turquoise) upperparts, wings and tail. **Female**: Typically duller above. **Juvenile**: Dusky-brown barring on nape/neck and breast/flanks (broader/denser on breast). **VOICE** Territorial call is a melancholy whistled *iuu-iuu iuu-iuu iuu-iuu iuu-iuu iuu-iuu*.. (*i* higher); often in duet with rasping calls. Loud *tree-trew* (*trew* lower) and explosive cackling *kek-ek-ek-ek*... **HABITAT** Rivers/large waterbodies in or near broadleaved forest/woodland, occasionally mangroves; up to 800 m.

14–16 to different scale

PLATE 16 KINGFISHERS

BLYTH'S KINGFISHER *Alcedo hercules* 22–23 cm

(1) **Male**: Like Blue-eared (*A.m.verreauxii*) but much larger with longer, heavier, all-black bill, darker lores, darker crown, ear-coverts and wings. **Female**: Base of lower mandible reddish. **VOICE** Call is hoarser than that of Common, closer to Blue-eared but much louder. **HABITAT** Larger streams or smaller rivers in broadleaved evergreen forest, secondary growth; up to 400 m.

COMMON KINGFISHER *Alcedo atthis* 16–18 cm

(2) **Male** *bengalensis*: Small; rufous ear-coverts, turquoise stripe down upperparts, pale rufous below with whitish throat, mostly blackish bill. (3) **Juvenile**: Duller, paler below with dusky wash across breast, orange-reddish base to lower mandible. **Female**: Base/most of lower mandible orange-reddish. **VOICE** Sharp *zii* (mainly in flight), sometimes *zii-ti* (*ti* softer). **HABITAT** Streams in open and wooded areas (usually avoids denser forest), various wetlands; up to 1,830 m.

BLUE-EARED KINGFISHER *Alcedo meninting* 15.5–16.5 cm

(4) **Female** *verreauxii*: Like Common but slightly smaller, with blue ear-coverts, deeper blue crown, upperparts and wings (without turquoise), deeper orange-rufous below. Male bill mostly blackish. (5) **Juvenile**: Rufous on cheeks and ear-coverts, dark scales on duller breast, initially mostly reddish bill. (6) **Female** *coltarti* (NW, north-west NE): Pale turquoise crown-bars, wing-covert spots and stripe down upperparts. **Other subspecies** *A.m.scintillans* (W,SE, south-west NE): Roughly intermediate between *verreauxii* and *coltarti*. **VOICE** Typical call is higher-pitched and shorter than in Common, and often given singly. **HABITAT** Streams, smaller rivers and pools in broadleaved evergreen and mixed deciduous forest, mangroves; up to 915 m.

BLUE-BANDED KINGFISHER *Alcedo euryzona* 20–20.5 cm

(7) **Male** *peninsulae*: Mostly dull dark brownish wings, blue breast-band, blackish bill. (8) **Female**: Like Common but larger and bulkier, with much duller, browner crown, scapulars and wings, dark ear-coverts, paler blue stripe down upperparts. Mostly dull reddish lower mandible. **Juvenile male**: Shows more rufous on belly than adult. **VOICE** Similar to Common but less shrill. **HABITAT** Medium-sized and larger streams in broadleaved evergreen forest, sometimes smaller streams; up to 825 m.

BANDED KINGFISHER *Lacedo pulchella* 21.5–24.5 cm

(9) **Male** *amabilis*: Long tail, chestnut forehead/mask, blue hindcrown/nape, blue bars above, warm buffish breast-band. (10) **Female**: Rufous-and-black bars on head and upperside, white below with blackish scales on breast and flanks. **Juvenile male**: Dusky scales/bars on ear-coverts and breast, bill mainly brown, with orange lower mandible and pale tip. **Juvenile female**: Heavy blackish scales/bars above; bill as juvenile male. **Other subspecies** *L.p.deignani* (S), *pulchella* (extreme S). **VOICE** Long whistle, followed by up to 15 slow double whistles: *wheeeoo chi-wiu chi-wiu chi-wiu chi-wiu*... (gradually dies away). Also sharp *wiak wiak*... **HABITAT & BEHAVIOUR** Broadleaved evergreen and mixed deciduous forest, bamboo, often away from water; up to 1,100 m. Slowly raises/lowers crown/nape feathers when alarmed.

RUDDY KINGFISHER *Halcyon coromanda* 26.5–27 cm

(11) **Adult** *coromanda*: Bright rufous, violet-tinged above, bluish-white lower back and rump-patch, red bill. (12) **Juvenile**: Much browner above, narrow dark bars below, browner bill; back/rump brilliant blue (less whitish). **Other subspecies** *H.c.minor* (resident S): Darker above, much darker below, breast violet-tinged, rump-patch larger. **VOICE** Territorial call is a soft, rather hoarse, tremulous *tyuur-rrrr* or *quirrr-r-r-r-r*, repeated after short intervals. **HABITAT** Mangroves, forest on islands, broadleaved evergreen forest near water; up to 900 m.

WHITE-THROATED KINGFISHER *Halcyon smyrnensis* 27.5–29.5 cm

(13,14) **Adult** *perpulchra*: Dark chestnut head and belly, white throat and breast, turquoise above with chestnut and black on wing-coverts, dark red bill; whitish patch on primaries. **Juvenile**: Upperparts, wings and tail duller, with dark vermiculations on throat and breast, browner bill. **VOICE** Territorial call is a loud whinnying *klilililili*. Also utters shrill staccato descending laughter: *chake ake ake-ake-ake-ake*... **HABITAT** Open areas, secondary growth, cultivation; up to 1,525 m.

BLACK-CAPPED KINGFISHER *Halcyon pileata* 29–31.5 cm

(15,16) **Adult**: Black crown and head-sides, white collar, throat and breast, purple-blue above with mostly black wing-coverts, red bill; whitish patch on primaries. **Juvenile**: Blue parts duller, with small rufous-buff loral spot, collar buff-tinged; has dark vermiculations on sides of throat and breast (throat-sides sometimes streaked) and brownish-orange bill. **VOICE** Ringing, cackling *kikikikikiki*... **HABITAT** Mangroves, sea coasts, various inland and coastal wetlands, gardens; up to 900 m (mostly lowlands).

COLLARED KINGFISHER *Todiramphus chloris* 24–26 cm

(17) **Adult** *armstrongi*: Blue above with variable turquoise wash, whitish collar/underparts, mostly dark bill. **Juvenile**: Duller/greener above, narrow buff wing-covert fringes, dark vermiculations on collar/breast; collar and breast-sides/flanks often tinged buffish-brown. **Other subspecies** *T.c.humii* (S): Bluer above. **VOICE** Deliberate loud nasal shrieking *kick kyew, kick kyew*... (*kick* rising, *kyew* falling). Loud shrill *krerk krerk krerk*... or *kek-kek-kek-kek*..., often followed by characteristic *jee-jaw* notes. **HABITAT** Mangroves, coastal wetlands, cultivation, parks, sometimes large rivers, marshes; lowlands.

RUFOUS-COLLARED KINGFISHER *Actenoides concretus* 24–25 cm

(18) **Male**: *concretus*: Green crown, blue above, paler back/rump, black/blue head-stripes, rufous collar/breast. (19) **Female**: Mostly dull green above, pale buffish speckling on scapulars and wing-coverts. **Other subspecies** *A.c.peristephes* (north of Trang). **Juvenile**: Bill brownish with yellowish tip/base; male has heavy mantle spotting. **VOICE** Rising whistles: *kwi-i kwi-i kwi-i kwi-i kwi-i*... (c.1 per s). Also softer *kwi-irr kwi-irr kwi-irr*... **HABITAT & BEHAVIOUR** Broadleaved evergreen forest, up to 760 m. Sits motionless for long spells.

PLATE 17 KINGFISHERS & BEE-EATERS

BLACK-BACKED KINGFISHER *Ceyx erithacus* 12.5–14 cm

(1) **Adult** *erithacus*: Rufous, lilac and yellowish; red bill, blackish-blue mantle/scapulars, dark wings, blue patches on forehead and nape-sides. **Juvenile**: Duller/more whitish below, breast often washed brownish, bill duller. **voice** Sharp piping, weaker/higher than Blue-eared. Contact calls are a weak, shrill *tit-sreet* and *tit-tit*. **habitat** Vicinity of small streams and pools in broadleaved evergreen forest, sometimes gardens and mangroves on migration; up to 915 m.

RUFOUS-BACKED KINGFISHER *Ceyx rufidorsa* 12.5–14.5 cm

(2) **Adult** *rufidorsa*: Like Black-backed but mantle and scapulars all rufous, no blue head-patches. **Juvenile**: Underparts duller, more whitish, often with brownish wash across breast; bill duller. **voice** Similar to Black-backed. A soft high insect-like *tjie-tjie-tjie*, usually in flight, and a shrill *tsriet-siet*. **habitat** Vicinity of small streams and pools in broadleaved evergreen forest, sometimes mangroves; up to 455 m.

CRESTED KINGFISHER *Megaceryle lugubris* 38–41.5 cm

(3) **Male** *guttulata*: Very large; uneven spiky crest, blackish speckles and pale chestnut flecks on malar area/breast. (4) **Female**: Usually no chestnut flecking but pale rufous underwing-coverts (white on male). **Juvenile**: As female but neck-sides, breast, flanks and undertail-coverts washed pale rufous. **voice** Loud squeaky *aick* or indignant *kek*; rapidly repeated raucous grating notes. **habitat** Large streams, medium-sized rivers, lakes, in/near forested areas; up to 1,200 m.

PIED KINGFISHER *Ceryle rudis* 27–30.5 cm

(5,6) **Adult** *leucomelanura*: More distinct areas of black and white than on larger Crested; flattish crest, two black bands on side of breast; contrasting upperwing and tail pattern. (7) **Female**: Single breast-band. **Juvenile**: As female but brownish fringing on lores, throat and breast, greyer breast-band, shorter bill. **voice** Irregularly repeated high chattering, squeaky *kwik* or *kik*, loud shrill *chirruk chirruk*... and high *TREEtiti TREEtiti*... **habitat & behaviour** Rivers, canals and lakes in open country, flooded fields; lowlands. Hovers over water.

RED-BEARDED BEE-EATER *Nyctyornis amictus* 32–34.5 cm

(8) **Male**: Red on throat/breast, purplish-pink forecrown, broad black terminal band on undertail. (9) **Female**: Forehead usually red. (10) **Juvenile**: Mostly green head/body. **voice** Loud gruff *chachachacha*..., *quo-qua-qua-qua*. Slightly descending, chattering *kak kak-ka-ka-ka-ka*... Deep croaking *aark* and *kwow* or *kwok* and rattling *kwak-wakoogoogoo*. **habitat & behaviour** Broadleaved evergreen forest; up to 1,525 m. Often in lower canopy.

BLUE-BEARDED BEE-EATER *Nyctyornis athertoni* 33–37 cm

(11) **Adult** *athertoni*: Green upperparts with light blue wash, blue forecrown and shaggy throat and breast feathers, pale buffish-yellow belly with broad green streaks, golden-yellowish undertail with indistinct terminal band. **Juvenile**: Apparently shows some brown markings on

crown and centre of throat, undertail more golden-brown. **voice** A loud deep guttural croaking and harsh cackling, including a purring *grrew-grrew-grrew*..., harsh *kow kow-kow kowkowkow*... and repeated *gikhu* and *gikh* notes. **habitat & behaviour** Broadleaved evergreen, semi-evergreen and mixed deciduous forest, freshwater swamp forest, rarely wooded gardens; up to 2,200 m. Usually in lower canopy.

GREEN BEE-EATER *Merops orientalis* 19–20 cm (tail-prongs extend up to 6 cm more)

(12) **Adult** *ferrugeiceps*: Small; coppery-rufous crown to mantle, green throat, light blue chin and cheeks, black gorget, mostly green uppertail. (13) **Juvenile**: Mostly green crown and mantle, mostly yellowish throat, no gorget. **voice** A pleasant, rather monotonous trilling *tree-tree-tree-tree*... and staccato *ti-ic* or *ti-ti-ti* when alarmed. **habitat** Drier open country and cultivation, beach slacks; up to 1,500 m.

BLUE-THROATED BEE-EATER *Merops viridis* 22.5–23.5 cm (tail-prongs extend up to 9 cm more)

(14,15) **Adult** *viridis*: Dark chestnut crown to mantle, blue throat, distinctly pale blue rump and uppertail-coverts. (16) **Juvenile**: Green crown and mantle, pale chin. **voice** Typical contact calls (richer than similar calls of Blue-tailed) include a liquid *terrip-terrip-terrip*..., faster *terrip-rrip-rrip* and deeper *trrurrip*; sharp *chip* when alarmed. **habitat & behaviour** Open country, borders of large rivers, cultivation, sometimes parks and gardens; also forest clearings and edge, and mangroves (mainly non-breeders); up 800 m. Usually in flocks; often roosts in large numbers.

BLUE-TAILED BEE-EATER *Merops philippinus* 23–24 cm (tail-prongs up to 7.5 cm more)

(17,18) **Adult**: Bronze-green crown/mantle, yellowish upper throat, dull chestnut-washed lower throat/upper breast. (19) **Juvenile**: Washed-out chestnut on lower throat and upper breast, more bluish-green crown and mantle. **voice** Typical contact calls (particularly in flight) are a loud *rillip rillip rillip*..., shorter *trrrit trrrit trrrit*... and rapid *tri-tri-trip*, sometimes interspersed with stressed *chip* notes; sharp *pit* notes when perched. **habitat & behaviour** Open country, cultivation, beach slacks, dunes, borders of large rivers, mangroves; up to 800 m (breeds in lowlands). Gregarious, often in large flocks at traditional roosting sites and during migration (when may occur over forest).

CHESTNUT-HEADED BEE-EATER *Merops leschenaulti* 21–22.5 cm

(20) **Adult** *leschenaulti*: Chestnut crown/mantle, pale yellow throat, chestnut and black gorget, no tail-prongs. (21) **Juvenile**: Crown and mantle mostly green, some dull chestnut on hindcrown/nape, washed-out gorget. **voice** In flight a repeated soft bubbling *prruuip*, *pruik*, *churit* or *djewy*; a soft airy *chewy-chewy-chewy* when perched. **habitat** Open broadleaved evergreen, semi-evergreen and mixed deciduous forest and bamboo (often along rivers), coastal scrub, mangroves, island forest, sometimes plantations; up to 1,830 m.

PLATE 18 HAWK CUCKOOS & COUCALS

LARGE HAWK CUCKOO *Hierococcyx sparverioides*
38–41.5 cm

(1) Adult *sparverioides*: Relatively large; slaty-grey crown/nape and head-sides, contrasting brownish-grey mantle and wings, extensively dark chin, deep rufous breast-patch (extent variable), prominent darker streaks on lower throat/breast, dark-barred whitish lower breast to flanks, greyish tail with broad dark bands and buffish tip. **(2) Juvenile**: Dark brown upperparts with rufous bars, buffy-white underparts with bold drop-like streaks. **(3) Immature/subadult**: Greyish-brown crown, dull rufous bars above; similar to juvenile below but rufous on breast. From nominate adult Hodgson's by size, more dark on chin, heavy throat-streaks; flanks tend to be barred. **voice** Territorial call is a very loud, shrill, spaced, stressed *pwi pwee-wru*, steadily repeated on rising pitch to screaming crescendo. **habitat & behaviour** Broadleaved evergreen and deciduous forest, more open habitats, gardens, mangroves etc. on migration; up to 2,565 m (mainly breeds above 650 m). Secretive and often difficult to observe.

COMMON HAWK CUCKOO *Hierococcyx varius* 33–37 cm

(4) Adult: Like Large but smaller, upperparts usually ashier-grey (no contrast with crown), has less black on chin, often paler and more extensive rufous below (reaching belly/flanks), faintly streaked or unstreaked lower throat and breast, less distinct barring below, narrower dark tail-bands. **(5) Juvenile**: Best separated from Large by smaller size, less distinct underpart markings, narrower tail-bands. **(6) Immature/subadult**: Best separated from Large by same characters as juvenile. **voice** Territorial call is 4–6 loud, high *wee-piwhit* phrases (*piw* stressed), progressing to frantic shrillness and ending abruptly. Strident screaming trill from female. **habitat** Open deciduous forest, secondary growth; lowlands.

MOUSTACHED HAWK CUCKOO *Hierococcyx vagans*
28–30 cm

(7) Adult: Relatively small and long-tailed, slaty crown and nape, conspicuous dark moustachial/cheek-bar separating whitish upper throat from whitish ear-coverts, creamy-whitish underparts with blackish-brown streaks on lower throat to belly and flanks, white tail-tip. **Juvenile**: Poorly documented. Probably like adult but with brownish crown and nape. **voice** Territorial call is a loud, well-spaced *chu-chu*, repeated monotonously (c.1 call every 2 s). Secondary call is an ascending sequence of mellow notes, first singly after short intervals, then paired and accelerating to fever-pitch, ending abruptly. **habitat** Broadleaved evergreen forest, secondary growth; up to 915 m.

HODGSON'S HAWK CUCKOO *Hierococcyx fugax* 27–31 cm

(8) Adult *fugax*: (resident S): From Moustached by all-dark head-sides, dark chin, mostly pale chestnut tail-tip (extreme tip narrowly whitish). From Large by size, underpart colour/pattern, even tail-barring, tail-tip colour. **(9) Juvenile**: Dark brown above with faint pale fringing, white patch on nape-side, spot-like streaking below. **(10) Adult** *nisicolor* (rest of range): Greyer above, no rufous bars on flight feathers, inner tertial usually whiter than rest (plain or barred/notched darker), dark underpart-streaks often split with whitish, pinkish-rufous on breast/upper belly (quite uniform if dark streaks very fine, as in

plate); penultimate dark tail-band is narrowest. **(11) Juvenile**: Warmer, buffier fringes on upperparts; usually shows paler innermost tertial. **voice** Territorial call is loud, shrill, very high *pi-pwik* or *pi-pwit* phrases (c.8 every 10 s), often followed by rapid *ti-tu-tu* phrases, accelerating/ascending to shrill crescendo climax/climaxes; followed by slower *tu-tu-tu-tu*... before tailing of or (in *H.f.nisicolor*) by rapid *trrrrr-titititititrrrtrrr*... **habitat** Broadleaved evergreen and mixed deciduous forest; up to 250 m. *H.f.nisicolor* occurs up to 1,300 m, sometimes 1,550 m (mainly breeds above 500 m). Typically secretive and difficult to observe.

SHORT-TOED COUCAL *Centropus rectunguis* 37 cm

(12) Adult: Resembles Greater but considerably smaller and relatively shorter-tailed. Underwing-coverts black. **(13) Juvenile**: Chestnut-brown crown and mantle with blackish bars, narrow blackish bars on tertials and wing-coverts, dark brown underparts with whitish to buff bars and shaft-streaks, browner bill. **voice** Territorial call is a series of 4–5 slow, deep, melancholy, resonant notes: *whu huup-huup-huup-huup*, descending somewhat towards end and repeated every 6–7 s. Sometimes more rapid series on rising scale. **habitat & behaviour** Broadleaved evergreen forest; up to 600 m (mainly lowlands). Shy and skulking, usually on ground.

GREATER COUCAL *Centropus sinensis* 48–52 cm

(14) Adult *intermedius*: Relatively large; glossy purplish blue-black with uniform chestnut back and wings. **(15) Juvenile**: Back and wings duller with heavy blackish bars; rest of plumage blackish with small whitish streaks and flecks turning to buffier bars on lower body, tail barred brownish- to greyish-white, browner bill. **voice** Territorial call is a series of loud, deep, far-carrying, mournful notes: *puup puup puup puup*... or *wuup-uup-uup-uup-uupuupuupuupuup*, speeding up and ascending scale, before becoming lower and more even; sometimes ascends scale again during longer sequence. Also a more spaced, even 3–4 note series, introduced by a higher note: *hi huup-huup-huup*... Alarm call is a scolding, hissing *shaeoooo* or *scheeeoh*. **habitat** Open forest, forest edge, secondary growth, scrub, grassland, mangroves; up to 1,525 m.

LESSER COUCAL *Centropus bengalensis* 38 cm

(16) Adult breeding *chamnongi*: Like Short-toed Coucal but with duller back and darker wing-tips. **(17) Adult non-breeding**: Dark brown head, mantle and scapulars with whitish-buff streaks, dull buff below with some blackish-brown bars and whitish-buff shaft-streaks; pale bill. **(18) Juvenile**: As adult non-breeding but very rufous above, blackish-brown streaks on crown, blackish bars on rest of upperside, warmer below with broader dark bars; very long uppertail-coverts (also adult non-breeding). **Other subspecies** *C.b.javanensis* (S). **voice** Territorial call is 3–5 jolly, hollow notes, followed by 2–5 staccato phrases: *huup huup huup-uup tokalok-tokalok* or *huup huup huup-uup-uup tokaruk-tokaruk-tokaruk*... etc. Also metallic clucking notes, repeated quickly, then slowing/falling slightly before speeding up again and tailing off: *thicthic-thicthicthicthicthic-thuc-thuc-thuc-thuc-thucthucthucucucucuc*... **habitat & behaviour** Grassland, including marshy areas, scrub; up to 1,830 m. Secretive but often ascends grass stems or perches in bushes to sun itself.

12–18 to different scale

PLATE 19 *CLAMATOR* CUCKOOS & TYPICAL CUCKOOS

PIED CUCKOO *Clamator jacobinus* 31.5–33 cm

(1) **Adult** *jacobinus*: Recalls Chestnut-winged but somewhat smaller, with glossy black hindneck and wings, all-white underparts. Has distinctive short white bar across base of primaries and broad white outertail-tips. (2) **Juvenile**: Upperparts and wings drab brown (crown and uppertail darker), throat and breast initially dull greyish, rest of underparts tinged buff, crest shorter, bill browner with yellow-based lower mandible, has narrow whitish tips to wing feathers and scapulars. **VOICE** Frequently repeated loud metallic, ringing ***kleeuw*** or ***keeu*** notes: ***kleeuw kleeuw kleeuw kleeuw***... (both sexes); sometimes preceded by shrill ***kiu-kewkew...kiu-kewkewkew...kiu-kewkew***... Male often adds fast series of short, rising notes: ***kwik-kwik-kweek***. Also, an abrupt ***kweek***. **HABITAT** Open deciduous woodland, scrub, cultivation; lowlands.

CHESTNUT-WINGED CUCKOO *Clamator coromandus* 38–41.5 cm

(3) **Adult**: Slender and long-tailed, with glossy blackish upperparts and crest, white hind-collar, largely rufous-chestnut wings, whitish underparts with buffy-rufous throat, blackish vent and narrowly white-tipped outer tail feathers. Could be confused with Lesser Coucal in flight. (4) **Juvenile**: Upperparts dark greenish-brown with pale chestnut to buff tips, wings similar to adult but feathers tipped pale chestnut to buff, hind-collar buffish, underparts all whitish, crest much shorter, bill paler. Gradually attains patches of adult plumage. **VOICE** Territorial call is a series of metallic whistled paired-notes: ***thu-thu...thu-thu...thu-thu***..., very similar to Moustached Hawk Cuckoo but each couplet has less well-spaced notes. Also a rapid grating woodpecker-like ***crititititit***. **HABITAT** Secondary growth, scrub, bamboo thickets, broadleaved evergreen forest and mangroves in winter and on migration; up to 1,300 m.

INDIAN CUCKOO *Cuculus micropterus* 31–33 cm

(5) **Male** *micropterus*: From other *Cuculus* cuckoos by distinctive brownish tinge to mantle, wings and tail (contrasts with grey head), prominent broad dark subterminal tail-band and dull yellowish to greyish-green eyering. (6) **Female**: Rufescent wash across breast. (7) **Juvenile**: Crown and head-sides browner than adult with distinctive very broad buffish-white tips, upperparts and wings with prominent rufous or buffish to whitish tips, underparts buffish with broken dark bars, particularly on throat, breast and flanks; may have rufous wash on throat and breast. **Other subspecies** *C.m.concretus* (resident extreme S): Somewhat smaller/darker-toned. **VOICE** Male territorial call is a loud ***whi-whi-whi-wu*** or ***wa-wa-wa-wu***, either with a lower last note or alternating high and low (may omit last note). Also a loud hurried bubbling (probably female only). **HABITAT** Broadleaved evergreen and deciduous forest, secondary growth; up to 1,830 m.

EURASIAN CUCKOO *Cuculus canorus* 32.5–34.5 cm

(8) **Male** *bakeri*: Difficult to separate from Oriental Cuckoo but usually slightly larger, with cleaner white underparts, often with somewhat fainter (less blackish) and sometimes narrower bars, has grey bars on white leading edge of wing (difficult to see in field); typically shows whitish undertail-coverts

with prominent blackish bars. (9) **Female hepatic morph**: Rufescent-brown head/upperparts, buffy-rufous throat/breast, white lower underparts, strong blackish-brown bars overall; narrower than on Oriental (particularly back to uppertail and breast). (10) **Juvenile**: Dark head and upperside with whitish fringing, white nuchal patch (fresh plumage). Usually more narrowly barred below than Oriental. (11) **Juvenile female hepatic morph**: Whitish fringing on upperside, white nuchal patch (fresh plumage). More narrowly barred above than Oriental, and less warm buffish below with less prominent dark bars. **Female**: If present, rufous-buff wash across grey of upper breast usually less extensive than on Oriental. **VOICE** Male territorial call is a loud, mellow ***cuc-coo***, with lower-pitched second note. Both sexes also give a loud bubbling trill. **HABITAT** Open broadleaved evergreen forest, secondary growth, more open habitats on migration; up to 2,195 m (probably only breeds above 600 m).

ORIENTAL CUCKOO *Cuculus saturatus* 29.5–32.5 cm

(12) **Male** *saturatus* (incl. *horsfieldi*): Very similar to Eurasian but usually slightly smaller, underparts typically buff-tinged, often with somewhat blacker and sometimes slightly broader bars; has plain buffish-white/whitish leading edge of wing (difficult to see in field), typically less obvious/no blackish bars on undertail-coverts. (13) **Female hepatic morph**: Very similar to Eurasian (see that species). (14) **Juvenile**: Like Eurasian but usually has broader dark bars below. (15) **Juvenile female hepatic morph**: Like Eurasian but warmer buffish below, broader dark barring overall. **Female**: Similar to male but usually has rufous-buff wash across grey of upper breast, typically more extensive than on female Eurasian. **VOICE** Male territorial call is a loud series of 2–4 mellow notes preceded by softer, shorter note: ***kuk PUP-PUP-PUP*** or ***kuk HU-HU-HU***. Also, nervous rapid uneven ***wuk-wuk-wuk-wuk-wuk-wuk-uk***... (female only?). **HABITAT** Broadleaved evergreen forest, open wooded country, secondary growth; breeds 800–2,030 m, down to sea level on passage and in winter.

LESSER CUCKOO *Cuculus poliocephalus* 26–26.5 cm

(16) **Male**: Like Oriental but smaller, with finer bill, usually darker rump and uppertail-coverts, contrasting less with blackish tail, usually more buffish underparts with wider-spaced and bolder black bars. (17) **Female hepatic morph**: Typically occurs in this plumage but sometimes similar to male. Like Oriental but usually more rufous, sometimes with almost no bars on crown, nape, rump and uppertail-coverts. (18) **Juvenile**: Dark grey-brown above with variable narrow whitish/rufous bars and a few whitish spots on nape. Crown/head-sides and mantle darker/more uniform than Oriental, underparts whiter with bolder dark bars. (19) **Juvenile female hepatic morph**: More prominent dark bars on crown and mantle and whitish nuchal patch. **VOICE** Male territorial call is a very loud, quite shrill series of 5–6 whistled notes (third prolonged/stressed): rather even ***wit-wit-witi-wit wit-wit-witi-wit wit-wit-witi-wit***... or rising and falling ***wit it-iti-witu wit it-iti-witu wit it-iti-witu***... Repeated up to 7 times or more, high-pitched at first, gradually becoming slower/lower-pitched. **HABITAT** Broadleaved evergreen forest, secondary growth, also deciduous forest on migration; 1,300–1,600 m; sometimes lower on migration.

PLATE 20 SMALLER CUCKOOS & ASIAN KOEL

BANDED BAY CUCKOO *Cacomantis sonneratii* 23–24 cm

(1) **Adult** *sonneratii*: Like hepatic female Plaintive but dark mask isolated by broad whitish supercilium; whiter underparts with narrower dark bars. (2) **Juvenile**: Whitish to pale buff bars on sides of head and upperparts (particularly crown and mantle), weaker mask, coarser and more spaced dark barring. **Other subspecies** *C.s.malayanus* (S): A little smaller/more rufescent. **VOICE** Territorial call is a loud descending hurried series of *bee bew-bew-bew* or *pibu-bibu* phrases. Secondary call is a rapid rising *pi pi pi pi-bi-bi-bi pi-bi-bi-bi pi-bi-bi-bi* (variable). **HABITAT** Broadleaved evergreen and deciduous forest, secondary growth; to 1,500 m.

PLAINTIVE CUCKOO *Cacomantis merulinus* 21.5–23.5 cm

(3) **Male** *querulus*: Relatively small; grey head, throat and upper breast, peachy-rufous remainder of underparts. (4) **Female hepatic morph**: Usually occurs in this plumage but sometimes similar to male. Rufescent above with even blackish barring, pale below with less pronounced barring, slightly paler supercilium, completely barred tail. (5) **Female hepatic morph variant**: Whiter below and more evenly barred. (6) **Juvenile**: Resembles female hepatic morph but paler rufous to more buffish (whiter below), with prominent blackish streaks on crown to upper mantle, throat and upper breast, indistinct barring on rest of underparts. **VOICE** Male territorial call is a plaintive series of high whistles: *phi phi phi phi phi-pipipi* or *pi pi pi pi pi-bibibi*, hurried and fading at end. Secondary call is an ascending *pii-pi-pui pii-pi-pui pii-pi-pui...*, gradually accelerating and sounding more agitated. **HABITAT** Secondary growth, open woodlands, scrub, grassland, cultivated areas, parks and gardens; up to 1,830 m.

RUSTY-BREASTED CUCKOO *Cacomantis sepulcralis* 21.5–24 cm

(7) **Adult** *sepulcralis*: Slightly slatier-grey than male Plaintive, entirely peachy-rufous underparts, yellow eyering. (8) **Adult hepatic morph**: Rare and probably only occurs among females. Difficult to separate from hepatic female Plaintive but slightly larger and proportionately longer-tailed, much broader blackish bars on upperside, throat and breast, distinctive uppertail pattern with rufous bars restricted to notches along outer fringes. (9) **Juvenile**: More uniformly dark above than hepatic adult, with narrow/rather broken buffish/rufous barring. **VOICE** Male territorial call is a series of 6–15 even melancholy whistled notes, gradually descending scale: *whi whi whi whi whi...* Secondary call is a gradually accelerating series of *whi-wibu* or *whi-w'bu* phrases. **HABITAT** Broadleaved evergreen forest, forest edge, secondary growth, mangroves, sometimes gardens; up to 600 m.

LITTLE BRONZE CUCKOO *Chrysococcyx minutillus* 16 cm

(10) **Male** *peninsularis*: Like female Violet but bill black, eyering red, has pale forehead, dark ear-covert patch, more uniform upperparts, glossy bottle-green crown, bronzy-green mantle, little rufescent coloration on outertail. (11) **Female**: Crown pale and less glossy, mantle less bronzy; less conspicuous pale forehead, eyering duller. (12) **Juvenile**: Like female but duller and browner above, almost uniform greyish- to brownish-white underparts. **VOICE** Territorial call is a descending

thin tremulous 3–5 note *rhew rhew rhew rhew*... or *eug eug eug eug*...; sometimes interrupted by rising, screeching *wireeg-reeg-reeg*. Secondary call is a high, drawn-out descending trill. **HABITAT & BEHAVIOUR** Mangroves, coastal scrub, secondary growth, forest edge; locally parks/gardens; up to 250 m. Very unobtrusive.

ASIAN EMERALD CUCKOO *Chrysococcyx maculatus* 17 cm

(13) **Male**: Small; glossy gold-tinged emerald-green; white-barred lower breast to vent, dark-tipped yellowish bill. (14) **Female**: Plain rufous crown/nape (fades to mantle/ear-coverts), coppery-green above, all-barred below. (15) **Juvenile**: Less green above than female, with rufous tips and dark and buff bars on crown to mantle, dark tail with more rufous/no white on outer feathers and less white at tip; darker bill, rufous throat/breast wash. **VOICE** Loud descending 3–4 note *kee-kee-kee*... Sharp *chut-week* flight-call. **HABITAT** Broadleaved evergreen forest, second growth; 600–1,800 m. To sea-level in swamp forest, plantations, gardens etc., on passage/in winter.

VIOLET CUCKOO *Chrysococcyx xanthorhynchus* 16.5–17 cm

(16) **Male** *xanthorhynchus*: Glossy violet-purple, white bars on lower breast to vent, orange bill with red base. (17) **Female**: Browner above than Asian Emerald, mostly bronzy-brown crown/nape, yellowish bill (red at base). (18) **Juvenile**: Like Asian Emerald but darker, more rufous-chestnut base colour of crown/nape, bold rufous-chestnut and dark greenish bars above, rufous-chestnut fringes to flight feathers, no rufous wash on throat/breast. **VOICE** Loud, sharp *tee-wit*, during undulating flight. Also, shrill accelerating/descending trill preceded by triple note: *seer-se-seer, seeseeseesee*. **HABITAT** Various broadleaved forests; up to 600 m. Sometimes parks/gardens to 1,100 m during non-breeding movements. Often in canopy of tall trees.

DRONGO CUCKOO *Surniculus lugubris* 24.5 cm

(19) **Adult** *dicruroides*: Glossy greenish-black, longish, slightly forked tail (like some drongos), slender, slightly downcurved bill, white bars on undertail-coverts/underside of outertail; white feathers on nape (often concealed). (20) **Juvenile**: Browner, less glossy, with distinct white spots on body, wing-coverts and tail-tips. **Other subspecies** *S.l.brachyurus* (south S). **VOICE** Slowly rising 5–7 note *pi pi pi pi pi*. Also shrill *phew phew phewphewphewphewphew phew phew*... (quickens and rises, then falls away). **HABITAT** Broadleaved evergreen and deciduous forest, secondary growth; parks, gardens, mangroves etc. on migration. Up to 1,300 m.

ASIAN KOEL *Eudynamys scolopacea* 40–44 cm

(21) **Male** *chinensis*: Fairly large, long-tailed; glossy blue-black, stout greenish bill, red eyes. (22) **Female**: Blackish-brown, predominantly streaked, spotted and barred whitish. (23) **Juvenile**: White/buff tips on brownish-black upperside, warm brown tail-bars, white/buff belly/vent barring. (24) **Female** *malayana* (resident W[south],C,SE,S): Predominantly spotted and barred buff to rufous. **VOICE** Male's territorial call is loud *ko-el* (*el* stressed), repeated with increasing emphasis. Secondary call is loud, descending, bubbling *wreep-wreep-wreep-wreep-wreepwreepwreep*... **HABITAT & BEHAVIOUR** Open woodland, secondary growth, scrub, cultivated areas, parks and gardens; up to 400 m. Noisy but surprisingly skulking.

21–24 to different scale

PLATE 21 MALKOHAS, CORAL-BILLED GROUND CUCKOO & ROLLERS

BLACK-BELLIED MALKOHA *Phaenicophaeus diardi*
35.5–38 cm (including 23 cm tail)

(1) **Adult** *diardi*: Smaller and shorter-tailed than Green-billed, throat/breast darker with fainter streaks, no whitish border to facial skin, narrower white tail-tips. Eyes pale blue or dark brown. **Juvenile**: Browner above, throat paler with no shaft-streaks, bill smaller and darker, eyes brown. **VOICE** A gruff *gwaup*, more hurried *gwagaup* and louder, more emphatic *pauk*. **HABITAT** Broadleaved evergreen forest, forest edge, secondary growth, sometimes plantations; below 200 m.

CHESTNUT-BELLIED MALKOHA *Phaenicophaeus sumatranus* 40–40.5 cm (including 23 cm tail)

(2) **Adult** *sumatranus*: Like Black-bellied but has chestnut belly and undertail-coverts (may appear blackish in field), somewhat thicker bill and more orange facial skin. Eyes whitish, pale blue, brown or red (any difference between sexes not yet documented). **Juvenile**: Like adult but tail feathers narrower with less white at tip. **VOICE** Low *tok tok*... Also thin high-pitched mewing. **HABITAT** Mangroves, broadleaved evergreen forest, sometimes secondary growth and mature plantations; below 200 m.

GREEN-BILLED MALKOHA *Phaenicophaeus tristis*
52–59.5 cm (including 38 cm tail)

(3) **Adult** *longicaudatus*: Large and longer-tailed than other malkohas, greyish head/underparts with dark shaft-streaks, dark vent, white-edged red facial skin, green bill. Tail feathers broadly tipped white. (4) **Juvenile**: Browner-tinged above, browner vent, blacker bill, duller face skin with less defined border. **Other subspecies** *P.t.saliens* (east NW). **VOICE** Mellow, slightly nasal *oh oh oh oh*... (probably territorial call). Typical call is a clucking, croaking *ko ko ko*..., sometimes with added gruff flurry: *co-co-co-co*... Harsh chuckles when agitated. **HABITAT & BEHAVIOUR** Broadleaved forest, freshwater swamp and peat swamp forest, secondary growth, coastal scrub, bamboo, sometimes plantations; up to 1,600 m. Forages in dense foliage.

RAFFLES'S MALKOHA *Phaenicophaeus chlorophaeus* 35 cm (including 19 cm tail)

(5) **Male** *chlorophaeus*: Rufescent head/breast, rufous-chestnut mantle/wings, blackish tail with white tip. Bill green, facial skin turquoise, back/rump and tail-coverts blackish, dull bronze tail-bars. (6) **Female**: Greyish head/breast, buffish belly, rufous-chestnut tail with black subterminal band and white tip. **VOICE** 3–6 slow descending, strained mewing notes: *kiau kiau kiau*... Hoarse strained *beeah* or *baaeew* (singly or doubled) and harsh, strained croaking. **HABITAT & BEHAVIOUR** Mid-storey of broadleaved evergreen forest, forest edge, sometimes plantations; up to 900 m. Forages in dense foliage.

RED-BILLED MALKOHA *Phaenicophaeus javanicus*
45–45.5 cm (including 26 cm tail)

(7) **Adult** *pallidus*: Red bill, pale blue orbital skin, mostly greyish above, mostly rufescent below. Throat/upper breast rusty-rufous, belly/undertail-coverts chestnut, rest of underparts pale greyish, wings and tail glossed green (latter broadly tipped white), eyes whitish, brown or red (any difference

between sexes not yet documented). **Juvenile**: Tail feathers narrower with less white at tip, primary coverts washed rufous, with pale fringes. **VOICE** An even, hard, frog-like *uc uc uc uc uc uc*..., sometimes ending in a flurry: *uc-uc-uc*... **HABITAT** Broadleaved evergreen forest, forest edge, secondary growth; up to 1,000 m.

CHESTNUT-BREASTED MALKOHA *Phaenicophaeus curvirostris* 45.5–46 cm (including 26 cm tail)

(8) **Male** *singularis*: Dark chestnut throat/breast and tail-tip, pale bill with red lower mandible, pale blue eyes. **Female**: Golden-yellow to whitish eyes. **Juvenile**: Similar to adult but facial skin reduced, bill mostly blackish on lower mandible and nasal area (initially all dark), eyes brown to grey, tail feathers narrower and shorter with little chestnut. **VOICE** Low, clucking *kuk kuk kuk*..., faster *kok-kok-kok*... when disturbed, and harsh, cat-like *miaou* when foraging. **HABITAT & BEHAVIOUR** Broadleaved evergreen forest, secondary growth, sometimes mangroves, plantations, gardens; up to 900 m. Forages in dense mid-storey foliage.

CORAL-BILLED GROUND CUCKOO *Carpococcyx renauldi*
68.5–69 cm (including 36 cm tail)

(9) **Adult**: Large and greyish with blackish hood/upper breast, primaries and tail. Fine blackish vermiculations on pale of underside, stout red bill, legs and feet, violet and red facial skin. (10) **Juvenile**: Browner hood/upper breast, greenish- and purple-tinged dull brown above, rufescent-tipped scapulars/wing feathers, drab rufous-chestnut throat and breast. Facial skin greyish, legs/feet dark brownish. **VOICE** Territorial call is a loud, moaning *woaaaah* or *wohaaau*, repeated every 5–10 s. Also, shorter *pohb-poaaah* and loud, vibrant, rolling *wh ohh-whaaaaohu*. Other calls include deep grumbling *grrro grrrro*... or *whrrro whrrro*... and *grrroah grrroah*... **HABITAT** Broadleaved evergreen forest, secondary forest; up to 900 m.

INDIAN ROLLER *Coracias benghalensis* 31.5–34.5 cm

(11,12) **Adult** *affinis*: Turquoise crown (duller centre), uppertail-coverts and vent, greenish-/brownish-olive mantle, scapulars and tertials, dark purplish-blue rump, vinous-brown head-sides/breast, more distinctly light purple throat with narrow pale streaks. Brilliant dark purplish-blue and light turquoise wings and outertail. (13) **Juvenile**: Browner; reduced turquoise on crown, paler, browner head-sides. **VOICE** Harsh, retching *kyak*. **HABITAT & BEHAVIOUR** Open country, cultivation, coastal scrub, urban areas; up to 1,525 m. Often on telegraph wires and other exposed perches; drops to ground in search of food.

DOLLARBIRD *Eurystomus orientalis* 27.5–31.5 cm

(14,15) **Adult** *orientalis*: Dark brown to greenish-brown above, dark bluish-purple to turquoise below with darker/browner breast and lighter blue throat-streaks; thick red bill. Pale silvery-turquoise patch on primaries. (16) **Juvenile**: Largely blackish bill, browner above, initially all-brown head, some/no turquoise on throat-centre. **Other subspecies** *E.o.deignani* (NW,NE). **VOICE** Hoarse rasping *kreck..kreck*...; *kak*; *kiak* etc., sometimes in rapid series. **HABITAT & BEHAVIOUR** Open broadleaved forest, clearings, plantations, mangroves, island forest; up to 1,000 m. Often perches on dead treetops; mostly an aerial feeder.

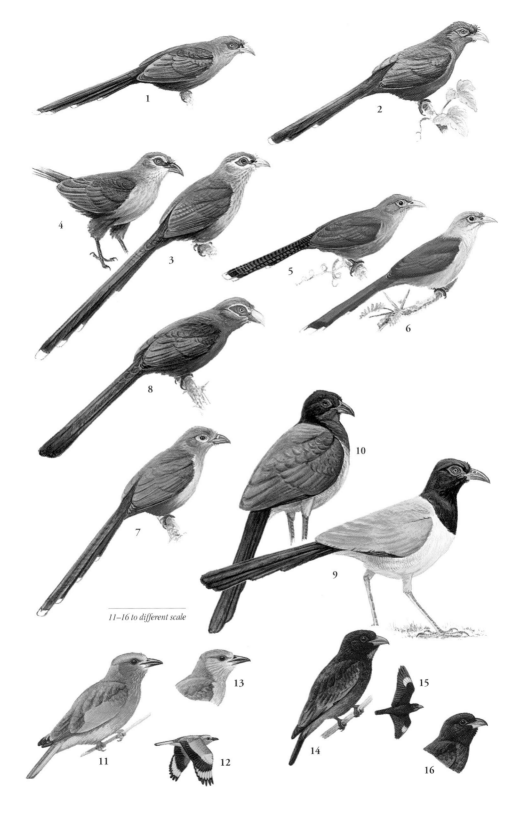

11–16 to different scale

PLATE 22 PARROTS, PARAKEETS & COMMON HOOPOE

BLUE-RUMPED PARROT *Psittinus cyanurus* 18.5–19.5 cm

(1,2) **Male** *cyanurus*: Larger/stockier than hanging parrots; mostly greyish-blue head, blackish mantle, purplish-blue back to uppertail-coverts, yellow-green covert fringing, pale greyish-/brownish-olive breast/flanks with blue tinge. Dark red wing-covert patch, red bill with dark lower mandible. Blackish underwing with mostly red coverts. (3) **Female**: Brown head with paler sides and yellower throat, mostly dark green above, mostly green breast, belly and flanks, narrow dark streaks on lower head-sides/throat, less dark red on wing-coverts, dark brown bill. (4) **Juvenile female**: Green crown/head-sides, little or no dark red on wing-coverts. **Juvenile male**: As juvenile female but may have bluer forehead/head-sides. **VOICE** Sharp, high-pitched *chi chi chi*... and *chew-ee*. Melodious trilling. **HABITAT** More open broadleaved evergreen forest, sometimes nearby plantations/cultivation; up to 300 m.

VERNAL HANGING PARROT *Loriculus vernalis* 13–15 cm

(5,6) **Male**: Very small and short-tailed. Bright green; red back to uppertail-coverts, light blue on throat/upper breast, red bill, dull orange legs/feet, whitish/pale yellow eyes; turquoise underwing with green coverts. (7) **Female**: Little or no blue on throat and breast, somewhat duller head and underparts, red of upperparts duller and mixed with some green on back and rump. **Juvenile**: Like female but back to uppertail-coverts mixed with green; eyes, legs and feet duller. **VOICE** High-pitched squeaky *tsee-sip* or *pi-zeez-eet* (mainly in flight). **HABITAT & BEHAVIOUR** Broadleaved evergreen, semi-evergreen and deciduous forest, clearings; up to 1,525 m. Has strong direct flight; often hangs upside-down; visits fruiting trees.

BLUE-CROWNED HANGING PARROT *Loriculus galgulus* 12–14.5 cm

(8) **Male**: From Vernal by dark blue crown-patch, golden mantle-patch, bright golden-yellow back-band, red patch on lower throat/upper breast, black bill, usually brown/grey eyes, greyish-brown to yellowish legs and feet. (9) **Female**: Duller, no red on lower throat/upper breast, less distinct crown and mantle-patches (particularly former), golden back-band (lacks yellow tone), duller red on lower upperparts. (10) **Juvenile**: Like female but all-green mantle, less blue on crown, smaller golden back-band, dusky-yellowish to blackish bill with yellowish tip, dull yellowish legs and feet. From Vernal by duller bill, obvious blue tinge on crown (if present), golden back-band, slightly darker underparts. **VOICE** Shrill, high-pitched *tsi* or *tsrri*, sometimes *tsi-tsi-tsi*... etc. **HABITAT** Broadleaved evergreen forest, clearings, wooded gardens and plantations, mangroves; up to 1,200 m.

ALEXANDRINE PARAKEET *Psittacula eupatria* 50–58 cm

(11) **Male** *siamensis*: Relatively large with massive red bill; green/yellowish-green head, pale blue-washed hindcrown/nape to upper ear-coverts, broad maroon-red shoulder-patch. Narrow collar (black at front, pink at rear), otherwise mostly green (duller mantle); blue-washed uppertail, yellowish undertail, green underwing-coverts. (12) **Female**: No collar or obvious blue on head, smaller/paler shoulder-patch, shorter tail-streamers. **Juvenile**: As female but duller; smaller shoulder-patch, shorter tail, duller bill. **VOICE** Loud, ringing *trrrieuw*, loud *kee-ah* and

keeak, resonant *g'raaak g'raaak*... **HABITAT** Mixed deciduous forest, temple groves; up to 915 m.

GREY-HEADED PARAKEET *Psittacula finschii* 36–40 cm

(13) **Male**: Slaty-grey head, red and yellow bill, black throat, black band behind ear-coverts and (narrowly) along hindcrown border, light blue nuchal collar, small maroon shoulder-patch, very long, purplish-blue (basally) and pale yellowish (distally) tail-streamers (undertail all yellow); turquoise-green underwing-coverts, whitish eyes. (14) **Juvenile**: Green head (darker crown, bluish-tinged head-sides), dark eyes. Upper mandible usually ruddy. (15) **First summer**: Mostly pale slaty head, no black throat or collar. **Female**: As male but no shoulder-patch or black on throat-centre, shorter tail. **VOICE** Shrill high rising *dreet dreet*...; *sweet sweet*...; *swit* etc. **HABITAT** Deciduous, pine and open broadleaved evergreen forest; cultivation. Up to 1,300 m.

BLOSSOM-HEADED PARAKEET *Psittacula roseata* 30–36 cm

(16) **Male** *juneae*: Rosy-pink forehead/head-sides, black throat/collar, orange/yellow and black bill, small maroon shoulder-patch, mostly deep turquoise tail-streamers with pale yellow tips; green underwing-coverts. (17) **Female**: Violet-grey head, blackish malar patch (no collar), shorter tail. From Grey-headed by bill (as male), maroon shoulder-patch, black on malar area, more turquoise uppertail and underwing-coverts (as male). (18) **Juvenile**: Green hindcrown, no shoulder-patch. Smaller/smaller-billed than Grey-headed, bill all yellowish, forehead/ear-coverts washed vinous-greyish, dark on malar, more turquoise uppertail, green underwing-coverts. **VOICE** Softish *pwi* and watery *drii*. **HABITAT** Deciduous and open broadleaved evergreen forest, groves, cultivation; up to 915 m.

RED-BREASTED PARAKEET *Psittacula alexandri* 33–37 cm

(19) **Male** *fasciata*: Stocky and relatively short-tailed; red and blackish bill, lilac-grey/-blue crown/head-sides, black loral line and broad malar band, yellowish-washed wing-coverts, deep pink breast, largely turquoise tail. (20) **Female**: Back bill, richer pink breast (without male's violet tinge), blue-washed head, shorter tail-streamers. (21) **Juvenile**: Dull vinous-grey forehead/head-sides, duller dark head markings, green nape, breast/upper belly. **VOICE** Shrill *ek ek*... and short sharp nasal *kaink*, repeated rapidly in alarm. Nasal honking *cheent cheent*... mixed with more grating notes. Also a raucous *kak-kak-kak-kak-kak*... **HABITAT & BEHAVIOUR** Open broadleaved evergreen, semi-evergreen and deciduous forest, temple groves; visits cultivation; up to 1,220 m. Large flocks raid crops.

COMMON HOOPOE *Upupa epops* 27–32.5 cm

(22,23) **Adult** *longirostris*: Long narrow down-curved bill, dull pale rufous crown, long black-tipped crest (often held erect, fan-like), black-and-white/-buff bars on back/rump, black wings and tail with broad white bars, dull dark pinkish throat to upper belly. Mantle pale warm brown (grey-tinged), uppertail-coverts white, flanks streaked black. **Juvenile**: Somewhat duller and paler above and browner below. **Other subspecies** *U.e.saturata* (visitor). **VOICE** Soft *hoop-boop-boop* (sometimes two notes); recalls Oriental Cuckoo. **HABITAT** Open country, semi-desert, scrub, open woodland, cultivation, gardens; up to 1,525 m.

11–23 to different scale

PLATE 23 SWIFTS

GLOSSY SWIFTLET *Collocalia esculenta* 10 cm

(1,2) **Adult** *cyanoptila*: Tiny; blackish upperside with variable dark blue to dark greenish gloss, whitish vent. Throat and upper breast dark greyish, sometimes with some paler feather fringing. **Juvenile**: Said to have stronger greenish gloss on upperside and pale grey/buff fringing on wing feathers. **VOICE** Short, grating, twittering sounds at the nest. **HABITAT & BEHAVIOUR** Over forested and open areas. Flight rapid and rather bat-like.

HIMALAYAN SWIFTLET *Collocalia brevirostris* 11.5–14 cm

(3,4) **Adult** *rogersi* (breeds NW,W; visits S): Wing 116–128 mm. Blackish-brown above with faint blue-green gloss and paler greyish rump-band, rather uniform throat and breast with darker chin (slightly paler than ear-coverts); belly and vent mid-brownish-grey. In hand, has darker shaft-streaks on breast, belly and undertail-coverts, lacks white rami, has no or only slight leg-feathering. Darker above than Germain's, with deeper tail-notch. From Black-nest by obvious tail-notch. **Juvenile**: Rump-band a little less defined, fewer leg feathers. **Other subspecies** *C.b.innominata* (visitor throughout?): Slightly larger (within range given; wing 123–132 mm, outertail 54–57.5 mm, innertail 43–49.5 mm), and has variable leg-feathering and white rami (sometimes lacking?). **VOICE** Rattling twitter. **HABITAT** Over forest, open areas; up to 2,200 m.

BLACK-NEST SWIFTLET *Collocalia maxima* 12–13.5 cm

(5,6) **Adult**: Wing 126–133 mm, outertail 47–52.5 mm, innertail 43.5–48 mm. Throat and breast rather uniform, or grading to darker chin (all a little paler than ear-coverts). In hand, shows faint darker shaft-streaks on throat and densely feathered legs. Like Germain's but somewhat bulkier, bigger-headed and longer-winged; little or no tail-notch; tends to show narrower, duller rump-band (can be almost same). From Himalayan by typically more clearly defined pale rump-band and lack of obvious tail-notch. **VOICE** Similar to Himalayan. **HABITAT** Open areas, sometimes over forest, offshore islets, urban areas; lowlands.

GERMAIN'S SWIFTLET *Collocalia germani* 11.5–12.5 cm

(7,8) **Adult** *germani*: Wing 113–123.5 mm, outertail 50–53 mm, innertail 43–46 mm. Has palest underparts (particularly lower throat and upper breast) and rump-band (whitish-grey with blackish shaft-streaks) of any swiftlet in region. Lower throat and upper breast paler than chin and obviously paler than ear-coverts. In hand, legs always unfeathered, has similar (but fainter) dark shaft-streaks on throat to Black-nest. **Other subspecies** *C.g.amechana* (extreme S) is said to have slightly duller rump-band. **HABITAT** Open areas, sometimes over forest, offshore islets; lowlands.

SILVER-RUMPED NEEDLETAIL *Rhaphidura leucopygialis* 11 cm

(9,10) **Adult**: Small but robust, blackish with prominent silvery-white lower back, rump and uppertail-coverts, short square-cut tail and very broad paddle-shaped wings, deeply pinched-in at base and pointed at tips. Has dark bluish gloss on upperparts and bare shafts (spines) extending from tail-tip (not usually

visible in field). **Juvenile**: Less glossy. **VOICE** High-pitched *tirrr-tirrr* and rapid chattering, recalling House Swift. **HABITAT & BEHAVIOUR** Broadleaved evergreen forest, clearings; up to 1,250 m. Flight fluttery and erratic.

ASIAN PALM SWIFT *Cypsiurus balasiensis* 11–12 cm

(11,12) **Adult** *infumatus*: Quite uniform greyish-brown, long slender wings, long, deep-forked tail. Tail looks long/narrow and pointed when closed; rump, head-sides, breast and belly a little paler, throat paler still. Like some swiftlets when tail closed, but tail much more slender, never glides with wings held stiffly below horizontal. **Juvenile**: Tail somewhat less sharply/deeply forked. **VOICE** Frequently uttered, high-pitched trilled *sisisi-soo-soo* or *deedle-ee-dee*. **HABITAT & BEHAVIOUR** Open country, urban areas, often near palm trees; up to 800 m. Often found in small, highly active groups.

FORK-TAILED SWIFT *Apus pacificus* 18–19.5 cm

(13,14) **Adult** *cooki*: Quite large, long sickle-shaped wings, sharply forked tail (not obvious when closed); clear-cut narrow white rump-band (often hard to see at distance). Has slightly paler throat, indistinct whitish scales on rest of underparts, and darker shaft-streaks on rump-band and throat (all hard to see in field). (15) **Adult** *pacificus* (widespread visitor): Browner above (little gloss), head slightly paler than mantle with narrow greyish-white feather margins. Rump-band broader, throat whiter, both with narrower/fainter dark streaks. **Juvenile**: Whitish secondary/inner primary tips. **VOICE** Shrill *sreee*. **HABITAT** Over forest/open areas; up to 2,565 m.

DARK-RUMPED SWIFT *Apus acuticauda* 17–18 cm

(16,17) **Adult**: Very similar to Fork-tailed Swift but lacks white rump-band, tends to have darker, more heavily marked throat, sharper tail-fork with narrower and more pointed outer feathers. **Juvenile**: Probably differs as Fork-tailed. **VOICE** Very high-pitched, rapid, sibilant, quavering *tsrr'i'i'i'i* and *tsrr'i'i'i'i'is'it* etc at nest sites. **HABITAT** Forested areas, cliffs; 1,000–2,300 m.

HOUSE SWIFT *Apus affinis* 14–15 cm

(18,19) **Adult** *subfurcatus*: Quite broad-winged; blackish with sharply contrasting broad white rump-band and distinctly whitish throat. Tail squarish, only slightly notched, has narrow dark shaft-streaks on rump-band (not visible in field). **Juvenile**: Tends to have paler-fringed wing feathers. **VOICE** Harsh rippling trilled *der-der-der-dit-derdiddidoo*, rapid shrill *sik-siksiksik-sik-sik-siksiksiksik*... etc., and staccato screaming. **HABITAT** Urban and open areas, sometimes over forest; up to 1,800 m.

PLATE 24 NEEDLETAILS, TREESWIFTS, BARN OWL & SHORT-EARED OWL

WHITE-THROATED NEEDLETAIL *Hirundapus caudacutus*
21–22 cm

(1,2) **Adult** *caudacutus*: Like Silver-backed Needletail but with clearly defined white throat and short white band from extreme forehead to upper lores; pale saddle tends to be more extensive and more whitish; has distinctive white tertial markings (not usually visible in field). (3) **Adult** *nudipes* (recorded NW): All-blackish forehead and lores, while whitish on saddle tends to be restricted to lower mantle/upper back. **Juvenile**: Greyish-brown forehead/lores, less glossy above, white of lower flanks and undertail-coverts marked with blackish. **VOICE** Rapid insect-like chattering: **trp-trp-trp-trp-trp-trp**... **HABITAT** Over forest, open areas; up to 800 m.

SILVER-BACKED NEEDLETAIL *Hirundapus cochinchinensis*
20.5–22 cm

(4,5) **Adult** *cochinchinensis*: Similar to Brown-backed but centre of saddle distinctly brownish-white, throat paler, brownish-grey (may appear whitish), lacks white spot on lores. **Juvenile**: Has some dark brown markings on white of lower flanks and undertail-coverts. **VOICE** Soft, rippling trill. **HABITAT** Forested and open areas, large rivers in or near forest; up to 800 m.

BROWN-BACKED NEEDLETAIL *Hirundapus giganteus*
21–24.5 cm

(6,7) **Adult** *indicus*: Very large and bulky swift, blackish above and dark brown below with distinctive brown saddle on lower mantle to back and pronounced white V on lower flanks and vent. Has white spot on lores (visible at close range), chin and centre of upper throat often somewhat paler. **Juvenile**: White loral spot less obvious, white of lower flanks and vent faintly marked darker. **Other subspecies** *H.g.giganteus* (resident S): Larger (24.5–26.5 cm), lacks white spot on lores. **VOICE** Rippling trill, similar to White-throated but slower. Also, squeaky **cirrwi-et**, repeated 2–3 times, and thin squeaky **chiek**. **HABITAT & BEHAVIOUR** Forested and open areas; up to 1,830 m. Has fast gliding flight; wings make loud whooshing sound when zooming overhead.

CRESTED TREESWIFT *Hemiprocne coronata* 21–23 cm

(8) **Male**: Slightly bluish-tinged grey; darker forehead crest (often erect) and wings, paler lower throat/breast, whitish belly/vent, pale rufous head-sides, upper throat and throat-sides. Flight feathers browner than blue-black wing-coverts, tertials paler. (9,10) **Female**: No rufous on head, blackish lores, dark slate ear-coverts, very thin dusky-white line along crown edge (over eye), thin dusky-white moustachial line, all-grey throat; very long, slender wings/tail, very deep tail-fork, uniform grey nape to rump, rather uniform underwing, with darker leading edge to coverts (male same). **Juvenile**: Has extensive white feather-fringing on upperparts (less obvious on mantle), paler lower back and rump, dusky-whitish underpart feathers with grey-brown subterminal bands and white tips, and broadly white-tipped tertials and flight feathers. **VOICE** Harsh, rather explosive **kee-kyew**, second note lower. When perched, **kip-KEE-kep**. **HABITAT & BEHAVIOUR** Open deciduous forest, forested and open areas; up to 1,400 m. Regularly perches upright on exposed branches.

GREY-RUMPED TREESWIFT *Hemiprocne longipennis*
18–21.5 cm

(11) **Male** *harterti*: As Crested but crown to mantle dark glossy green, lores blackish, ear-coverts dull dark chestnut, throat all grey, tertials mostly whitish-grey (contrasting sharply), tail-tip falls short of primary tips. (12,13) **Female**: Blackish ear-coverts. In flight grey back/rump contrasts with dark mantle; has contrasting blackish underwing-coverts (male same). **Juvenile**: Upperpart feathers extensively fringed rusty-brown (less so on rump), underpart feathers off-white with irregular brown subterminal bands and white tips; scapulars, flight feathers and tail broadly tipped whitish. **VOICE** Harsh, piercing **ki**, **ki-ki-ki-kew** and staccato **chi-chi-chi-chew**, sometimes a disyllabic **too-eit**, with more metallic second note. **HABITAT & BEHAVIOUR** Forested and open areas; up to 900 m. Regularly perches upright on exposed branches.

WHISKERED TREESWIFT *Hemiprocne comata* 15–16.5 cm

(14) **Male** *comata*: Small; olive-bronze body, dark glossy blue crown, nape, upper throat/throat-sides and wings, long white supercilium and malar/moustachial streak. Ear-coverts dull rufous-chestnut, slight non-erectile crest. (15,16) **Female**: Blackish ear-coverts. In flight shows dark underwing and contrasting white vent (also male). **VOICE** High-pitched shrill chattering **she-she-she-she-shoo-shee**, with higher penultimate note. Plaintive **chew** when perched. **HABITAT & BEHAVIOUR** Clearings in broadleaved evergreen forest, forest edge; up to 800 m. Spends much more time perched than other treeswifts, normally flying only short distances to feed.

BARN OWL *Tyto alba* 34–36 cm

(17,18) **Adult** *stertens*: Medium-sized to fairly large; upperside pale buffy-grey with golden-buff markings and blackish and whitish speckles (rather uniform in flight), with pale heart-shaped facial discs and white to buffy-white underparts, variably speckled blackish. Uppertail golden-buff with dark bars and greyish vermiculations. **Juvenile**: Similar to adult. **Other subspecies** *T.a.javanica* (S). **VOICE** Variety of eerie screeching, rasping and hissing sounds. **HABITAT** Cultivation, open country, saltpans, marsh and swamp borders, plantations, urban areas; up to 1,220 m.

SHORT-EARED OWL *Asio flammeus* 37–39 cm

(19) **Female** *flammeus*: Tiny ear-tufts, dark-ringed yellow eyes, broad dark streaks on buffy breast; broad dark bars on upperwing/tail, buff primary bases abut blackish primary coverts. Underwing-coverts buffish. (20) **Male**: Paler and less uniform buff than female, with less bold markings, whitish underwing (including coverts) with clear black bars on flight feathers/primary coverts. **VOICE** Male gives low, rather muffled **boo-boo-boo-boo-boo-boo**... (mainly during wing-clapping display). Hoarse rasping **cheeee-op** (mostly female). Barking **chef-chef-chef** in alarm. **HABITAT & BEHAVIOUR** Grassland, marshes, open areas; up to 1,500 m. Often easily flushed from open habitat, flying off with rather stiff rowing wingbeats. Only flies in daylight.

1–7, 8–16 and 17–20 to different scales

PLATE 25 SMALLER OWLS

ORIENTAL BAY OWL *Phodilus badius* 29 cm

(1) **Adult** *badius*: Distinctive facial shape, dark-outlined facial discs, triangular rudimentary ear-tufts, dark eyes; sparsely spotted pinkish-buff underparts, largely golden-buff nuchal band and scapulars. **VOICE** Eerie musical upward-inflected whistles, rising then fading away: *oo hlii boo hu-i-li hu-i-li hu-i-li hu-i-li* (in full or in part). **HABITAT & BEHAVIOUR** Broadleaved evergreen forest, plantations, landward edge of mangroves; up to 1,220 m, rarely to 2,200 m. Often perches quite low down on vertical plant stems.

WHITE-FRONTED SCOPS OWL *Otus sagittatus* 27–29 cm

(2) **Adult**: Relatively large and long-tailed, plumage resembling Reddish but brighter dark rufous to rufous-chestnut above (sometimes also breast), broad whitish forehead-patch (extends to ear-tufts), brown eyes, unbarred primaries. **VOICE** Territorial call is a hollow monotone whistled *hoooo*, similar to Reddish but more abrupt. **HABITAT** Broadleaved evergreen forest; up to 300 m.

REDDISH SCOPS OWL *Otus rufescens* 19 cm

(3) **Adult** *malayensis*: Dull rufescent-tinged plumage, recalling Mountain Scops but with pale buffish forehead and eyebrows, plainer upperparts, less distinct scapular markings, plain rufescent-buff underparts with distinct blackish spots (slightly highlight above with pale buff), brown eyes, broad dark-and-buff barring on primaries, pale flesh bill. **Juvenile:** Undocumented. **VOICE** Territorial call is a hollow whistled *hoooo*, fading at the end, repeated every 7–11 s. **HABITAT** Broadleaved evergreen forest; below 200 m.

MOUNTAIN SCOPS OWL *Otus spilocephalus* 20 cm

(4) **Adult** *siamensis*: Short, rounded ear-tufts, usually warm buff eyebrows, rufous-chestnut above, large white scapular markings, buffish to rufous below with white markings and dark vermiculations (no streaks), yellow eyes. (5) **Adult** *vulpes* (may occur extreme S): Deeper-toned, coarser blackish markings above, broad crown-streaks. **Juvenile:** Head/body paler and buffier with dark bars, no scapular markings. **VOICE** Territorial call is a distinctly spaced *phu-phu* or *toot-too* (every 5–7 s). **HABITAT** Broadleaved evergreen forest; 500–2,200 m.

ORIENTAL SCOPS OWL *Otus sunia* 19 cm

(6) **Adult greyish morph** *distans*: Yellow eyes, no nuchal collar, bold white scapular marks, dark streaks below. (7) **Adult rufous morph**: Black crown-streaks, obvious ear-tufts, whitish belly with blackish to rufous markings. (8) **Adult rufous morph** *stictonotus* (visitor): Paler and more rufous (less chestnut). **Juvenile:** Head/body paler with more dark bars, fewer streaks, no scapular markings. **VOICE** Loud, clear, measured *toik toik'to-toik* or shortened *toik'to-toik* (*O.s.stictonotus*). **HABITAT** Broadleaved evergreen and mixed deciduous forest and clearings; also island forest, mangroves, plantations etc. on migration; up to 2,000 m (breeds below 1,000 m).

COLLARED SCOPS OWL *Otus bakkamoena* 23 cm

(9,10) **Adult** *lettia*: Greyish variant. Broad whitish eyebrows and nuchal collar, pronounced ear-tufts, dark eyes, greyish-brown buff-marked upperparts, whitish below with fine vermiculations and sparse streaks. (11) **Adult**: Buff variant. Buffish eyebrows and nuchal collar, deep buff base colour to underparts. (12) **Juvenile:** Paler (often warmer) head and body, darker bars overall. **VOICE** Rather soft, clear, slightly falling *bouu* (every c.12 s); pitch varies (? also between sexes). Rarely a strident *kuuk-kuuk-kuuk*. **HABITAT** All types of broadleaved forest, clearings, gardens, plantations, island forest; up to 2,200 m.

COLLARED OWLET *Glaucidium brodiei* 16–16.5 cm

(13,14) **Adult** *brodiei*: Very small; buff and blackish 'imitation face' pattern on nape, speckled crown, tear-shaped streaks on belly, no prominent white markings on coverts. **Juvenile:** Crown to mantle unmarked, apart from whitish shaft-streaks on fore-crown. **VOICE** Loud, rhythmic, piping *pho pho-pho pho* (c.2 s duration), every 1–2 s (often in daytime). **HABITAT** Broadleaved evergreen forest; up to 2,565m, mostly above 600m.

ASIAN BARRED OWLET *Glaucidium cuculoides* 20.5–23 cm

(15) **Adult** *bruegeli*: Broad, rounded head, no ear-tufts, dull brown with pale buffish bars, narrow whitish eyebrows, white ventral line, whitish belly and lower flanks with broad brown streaks. (16) **Juvenile:** Diffuse pale barring above, diffuse dark barring below, streaking more diffuse, crown more speckled. (17) **Adult** *deignani* (south-eastern race): Rustier belly-streaks, grey head with whiter bars. **VOICE:** Descending, eerie quavering trill: *wu'u'u'u'u'u'u'u'u...* (c.10 s long), gradually increasing in volume. Long series of raucous double-notes, increasing in pitch/volume, preceded by mellow *hoop* notes. **HABITAT & BEHAVIOUR.** More open broadleaved forests, open areas with clumps of trees; up to 1,800 m. May perch in open during day; wags tail from side to side.

SPOTTED OWLET *Athene brama* 20–20.5 cm

(18) **Adult** *mayri*: White-spotted upperparts, white eyebrows, broken dark foreneck-collar, broken dark bars below. **Juvenile:** Apparently more washed out above, underpart bars more diffuse; belly may be lightly streaked. **VOICE** Harsh, screeching *chirurr-chirurr-chirurr...* etc., followed by or alternating with *cheevak cheevak cheevak...* Complex high screeching and chuckling. **HABITAT** Open woodland, cultivation, gardens, buildings, urban areas; up to 800 m.

BROWN HAWK OWL *Ninox scutulata* 30–31 cm

(19) **Adult** *burmanica*: Slim, small-headed, relatively long-tailed, whitish between eyes, whitish underparts with broad chestnut-brown streaks (denser on breast), pale greyish tail with broad blackish bars, golden-yellow eyes. **Juvenile:** Paler/warmer above, more diffusely marked below. **Other subspecies** *N.s.japonica* (visiting race): Slightly darker above, colder/darker markings below. **VOICE** Loud, haunting, rather deep, rising *whu-up*, repeated just over once per second. **HABITAT & BEHAVIOUR** Open forest, mangroves, also wooded parks and gardens on migration; up to 1,350 m. May be seen hawking insects at dusk (resembles some *Accipiter* species in flight).

PLATE 26 LARGER OWLS & EARED NIGHTJARS

SPOT-BELLIED EAGLE OWL *Bubo nipalensis* 61 cm

(1) **Adult** *nipalensis*: Very large, dark brown above with pale buff markings (mainly on scapulars and wing-coverts), long part-barred ear-tufts, whitish below with blackish-brown heart-shaped spots (upper breast and sides of neck appear more barred). Dark eyes, pale yellow bill. (2) **Juvenile**: Head/body whitish to buffy-white with prominent blackish-brown bars (more prominent above). **VOICE** Deep *HU HUU* or *HOO HOO* (usually c.2 s between notes), every 1–2 minutes. Loud eerie nasal moaning scream: *waayaoaah* etc. and quieter *aayao* at roost. **HABITAT** Broadleaved forests, clearings; 300–1,200 m.

BARRED EAGLE OWL *Bubo sumatranus* 45.5–46.5 cm

(3) **Adult** *sumatranus*: Like Spot-bellied but much smaller, with narrow brown-and-buffy (pale chestnut-tinged) bars on upperparts, no buff markings on scapulars or wing-coverts, narrow blackish-whitish barring on underparts and legs (denser and washed browner on breast). **Juvenile**: Like Spot-bellied but dark bars narrower and denser. **VOICE** Loud, deep *uk OOO OO* (introductory note barely audible), usually with about 2 s between notes and repeated after lengthy intervals. Also a loud quacking *gagagagogogo*. **HABITAT** Broadleaved evergreen forest, clearings, mature plantations; up to 610 m.

DUSKY EAGLE OWL *Bubo coromandus* 54–58 cm

(4) **Adult** *klossii*: Like Brown Fish Owl but quite uniform drab dark greyish-brown above, with no obvious markings, underparts much darker and greyer with less distinct streaks and denser dark vermiculations/crossbars, no whitish gorget, ear-tufts more erect, primaries unbarred, legs feathered. (5) **Juvenile**: Head/body creamy-whitish with very faint darker striations/vermiculations, wings rather plain greyish (as adult). **VOICE** Loud hollow notes at diminishing intervals: *kok kok kok-kok-kokaloo* (recalls ping-pong ball bouncing to halt). **HABITAT** Open woodland, usually near water; lowlands.

BROWN FISH OWL *Ketupa zeylonensis* 49–54 cm

(6) **Adult** *leschenault*: Rather warm buffish-brown (paler below); bold blackish-brown markings above, floppy streaked ear-tufts, strong blackish-brown and whitish/buff wing markings, whitish scapular markings and gorget, long blackish-brown streaks and narrow brown crossbars (sometimes faint) below. Eyes golden-yellow, bill greenish-grey with darker tip, no white on forehead/eyebrows. (7) **Juvenile**: Head/body pale creamy-buffish with long dark brown streaks, wings paler than adult. **VOICE** Territorial call is a deep, rapid, hollow moaning *hu who-hu* or *hup-hup-hu* with last note barely audible. Also deep mutterings, rising to maniacal laughter: *hu-hu-hu-hu-hu hu ha* or *oof uh-oof uh-oof uh-oof uh-oof uh-oof u-uh-h-HA-oo-oo-oof*, with laughter before end. **HABITAT** More open broadleaved forests near water; up to 800 m.

BUFFY FISH OWL *Ketupa ketupu* 45.5–47 cm

(8) **Adult** *aagaardi*: Like Brown but richer buff overall, broad blackish upperpart-streaks/wing markings contrasting more with underparts; has white area on forehead/eyebrows, less obvious white gorget, no crossbars below. **Juvenile**: Like Brown but body and wings richer buff. **VOICE** Long,

monotonous *bup-bup-bup-bup-bup-bup*... or *bup-bup-bup-bup-bup-bup*... like a generator, and high-pitched screeching yelps: *yiark, yark, yark, yeek* etc. Subdued, hoarse rather hissing *hyiii* or *hyiiii-ih* uttered by roosting birds. **HABITAT** Broadleaved evergreen forest near water, mangroves, plantations, wooded gardens, cultivation; up to 800 m.

SPOTTED WOOD OWL *Strix seloputo* 44.5–48 cm

(9) **Adult** *seloputo*: Like Brown but speckled/spotted white above (neck-sides barred), white/buffy-white below, mixed rich buff and with well-spaced bold blackish-brown bars (denser on breast); facial discs plain rufous-buff. **Juvenile**: Initially similar to Brown but lacks dark around eyes and contrasting even bars on wings and tail. **VOICE** Loud, abrupt booming *WHO* or *UUH* (possibly differing slightly between sexes), repeated every 8–11 s. Also a loud, deep quavering *WRRRROOH WRRRROOH WRRRROOH*... **HABITAT** Edge of broadleaved evergreen forest, logged forest, plantations, wooded parks, cultivation, sometimes mangroves; up to 305 m.

BROWN WOOD OWL *Strix leptogrammica* 47–53 cm

(10) **Adult** *laotiana*: Large, with rounded head; buffy-brown facial discs with blackish-brown border, dark eyes surrounded by dark brown/black, mostly dark brown above with whitish/buff markings on scapulars and (narrowly) across upper mantle (broken in centre); buff below (breast often dark brown), with dense dark brown bars. (11) **Juvenile**: Whitish/buffish with thin dark bars; contrasting dark brown/dull rufous bars on flight feathers/tail. **Other subspecies** *S.l.maingayi* (S). **VOICE** Deep vibrating *HU-HU-HU'HUHRRROO*, every 1–5 s. Loud eerie scream, *eeeeoooow*, or quieter, slightly vibrating *ayaarrrh*. **HABITAT** Broadleaved forests; up to 2,565 m.

MALAYSIAN EARED NIGHTJAR *Eurostopodus temminckii* 25–28 cm

(12,13) **Adult**: Darkest nightjar in region. Similar to Great Eared but much smaller, crown darker, ear-tufts less pronounced, tail darker and less contrastingly barred. Females are possibly more rufescent than males. **Juvenile**: Upperparts somewhat paler, warmer and less heavily vermiculated; pale bars on underparts duller. **VOICE** Similar to Great Eared but introductory note louder and always audible, second note shorter: *tut wee-ow*, repeated 5–7 times after shortish intervals. **HABITAT** Open areas in or near broadleaved evergreen forest; lowlands.

GREAT EARED NIGHTJAR *Eurostopodus macrotis* 40.5–41 cm

(14,15) **Adult** *cerviniceps*: Relatively large and longer-winged/-tailed; no whitish wing/tail markings. Relatively plain buffy-grey crown, dark head-sides to upper breast, thin white/buff collar, chestnut-tinged shoulders, broad tail-barring; lower breast to vent barred blackish and pale buff. Ear-tufts may be visible when perched. **Juvenile**: Paler above with fewer, more contrasting markings, paler/plainer and more chestnut wing-coverts, diffuse bars below. **VOICE** Long double whistle, after much quieter introductory note: *put PEE-OUW*. **HABITAT & BEHAVIOUR** Open areas in/near broadleaved forests; up to 1,220 m. Wingbeats leisurely; often feeds high in air.

12–15 to different scale

PLATE 27 FROGMOUTHS & NIGHTJARS

LARGE FROGMOUTH *Batrachostomus auritus* 39–42 cm

(1) **Adult:** From other frogmouths by much larger size, large white tips to upperwing-coverts and lower scapulars. Has buffy-white and blackish-barred nuchal collar and rather uniform warm brown throat and breast with a few small white markings. Eyes brown. Females are said usually to be rather duller and plainer than males. **Juvenile:** Paler/plainer, no nuchal collar or spotting on upperparts, scapulars or wing-coverts. **VOICE** Territorial call is unmistakable series of 4–8 loud bubbling trills, *prrrrrooh prrrrrooh prrrrrooh prrrrrooh...* (either rising or even-pitched), each separated by 3–6 s pauses. **HABITAT** Broadleaved evergreen forest; below 200 m.

GOULD'S FROGMOUTH *Batrachostomus stellatus* 23–26.5 cm

(2) **Adult:** Similar to females of other small frogmouths but has white spots on wing-covert tips, dark rufous-brown scales and no blackish markings below (belly/undertail-coverts whiter), more protruding bill. (3) **Adult:** Some (mainly females?) are much darker/colder and browner above; scaling below colder/browner. (4) **Juvenile:** Initially plainer; dark bars above, paler streaks on lower breast/belly. Slowly acquires adult features. **VOICE** Male territorial call is an eerie, rather weak whistled *woah-weeo*, with falling second note; occasionally only gives *weeo* notes. Female utters growling notes and rapid series of high-pitched yapping *wow* notes, 3–5 higher-pitched *wek* notes and a descending whistled *weeeoh*. **HABITAT** Broadleaved evergreen forest; below 185 m.

HODGSON'S FROGMOUTH *Batrachostomus hodgsoni* 24.5–27.5 cm

(5) **Male** *indochinae:* Similar to Javan (particularly *B.j.affinis*) but heavier black markings above and on breast, no rufous on breast, bill smaller and less protruding. (6) **Female:** Like Javan but paler, has more prominent white markings below, whiter lores, smaller bill. (7) **Juvenile:** Upperparts barred blackish and pale brown with warm tinge, no nuchal collar, underparts similar, grading to plainer and whiter from lower breast to vent. **VOICE** Up to 10 soft rising whistles: *whaaeee*, *whaaow* or *wheeow-a* etc. (intervals 1–7 s). Chuckling *whoo* notes. **HABITAT** Broadleaved evergreen and mixed evergreen/pine forest, secondary growth; 900–1,900 m, rarely down to 305 m.

JAVAN FROGMOUTH *Batrachostomus javensis* 23–24 cm

(8) **Male** *continentalis:* Warmish brown above, with buff, white and blackish speckles, vermiculations and spots, has whitish scapular spots, narrow white and black nuchal collar; underside buffy-white with more rufous throat/breast and dark vermiculations and large white markings on breast/belly. (9) **Female:** Rather dark rufous-chestnut with white and black marked nuchal collar, large white markings on scapulars, black-fringed white markings on lower throat/breast, tail faintly banded. (10) **Male** *affinis* (extreme S): Less rufescent, usually more black markings overall, more whitish markings on crown, typically a more contrastingly barred tail. **VOICE** Male gives mournful, wavering whistles, *tee-loo-eee* (*loo* descending, *eee* rising), or shorter *loo-eee*. Also, repeated *KWAH-a* or *e-ah*, longer *kwaaba*, and loud falling *whah* or *gwaa*. Female utters strange descending laughing *grra-ga-ga-ga* or *kerrr-ker-ker*.

HABITAT Broadleaved evergreen and mixed deciduous forest, forest edge, secondary growth; up to 800 m.

GREY NIGHTJAR *Caprimulgus indicus* 28–32 cm

(11–13) **Male** *hazarae:* Smaller than Large-tailed; darker crown, no rufous on nape, somewhat heavier black vermiculations above, duller/darker ear-coverts and throat, usually less whitish on lower throat (may appear as two patches), breast somewhat darker, scapulars less contrasting, with black, buff and whitish bars and vermiculations overall; less obvious whitish/buff bars across wing-coverts, smaller white wing- and tail-patches. (14) **Female:** Wing-patches smaller and buff, outertail feathers narrowly tipped brownish-white to brownish-buff. **Juvenile:** Paler than female; flight feathers narrowly tipped pale warm buff. **Other subspecies** *C.i.jotaka* (wintering form). **VOICE** Male territorial call is a rapid *tuctuctuctuctuctuctuc...* (up to 16 notes; 3–4 per second), repeated monotonously after short pauses. Fast, deep *quor-quor-quor* (possibly by females only). **HABITAT** Open broadleaved evergreen and coniferous forest, secondary growth; also open areas and gardens (non-breeders); 600–2,565 m (breeds 1,300–1,700 m).

LARGE-TAILED NIGHTJAR *Caprimulgus macrurus* 31.5–33 cm

(15–17) **Male** *bimaculatus:* Fairly large; rather pale crown with dark centre, much white on lower throat, prominent row of black scapulars with broad whitish-buff fringes, rather obvious whitish/buff bars across wing-coverts, brownish-grey tail with uneven dark bars; large white patches on wings and tail. Nape often strongly rufescent. (18) **Female:** Wing-patches smaller and buff, tail-patches much duller, buffish to buffish-white. **Juvenile:** Paler/buffier than female, duller tail-patches. **VOICE** Monotonously repeated loud, resonant *chaunk* from territorial males. **HABITAT** Open forest, secondary growth, cultivation; up to 2,000 m.

INDIAN NIGHTJAR *Caprimulgus asiaticus* 23–24 cm

(19–21) **Adult** *asiaticus* (incl. *siamensis*): Like Large-tailed but smaller, shorter-tailed and paler, distinct buff nuchal collar with darker markings, broader whitish-buff scapular fringes, typically has two large round white patches on throat; slightly smaller white/buffy-white wing-/tail-patches (tend to be slightly smaller still on females). **Juvenile:** Paler/plainer; streaking above restricted to hindcrown/nape, scapular fringes more rufous. **VOICE** Male's territorial call is a knocking *chuk-chuk-chuk-chuk-chuk-k'k'k'roo* (2–4 *chuk* notes), like ping-pong ball bouncing to rest. **HABITAT** Open dry forest, semi-desert, dry scrub and cultivation; lowlands.

SAVANNA NIGHTJAR *Caprimulgus affinis* 25–25.5 cm

(22–24) **Male** *burmanicus:* Rather uniform above, ill-defined scapular pattern (though often some contrasting warm buff fringes); white outertail feathers (often dusky-tipped). Faint buffish nuchal band, little/no pale moustachial line, normally two distinct roundish white/buffish-white throat-patches, large white wing-patches. (25) **Female:** Wing-patches slightly smaller and buff, no obvious pale or whitish tail markings. **Juvenile:** Somewhat paler. **VOICE** Male territorial call is a repeated, loud rasping *chaweez* or *chweep*. **HABITAT** Open dry dipterocarp, pine and broadleaved evergreen forest, grassland, scrub; up to 915 m.

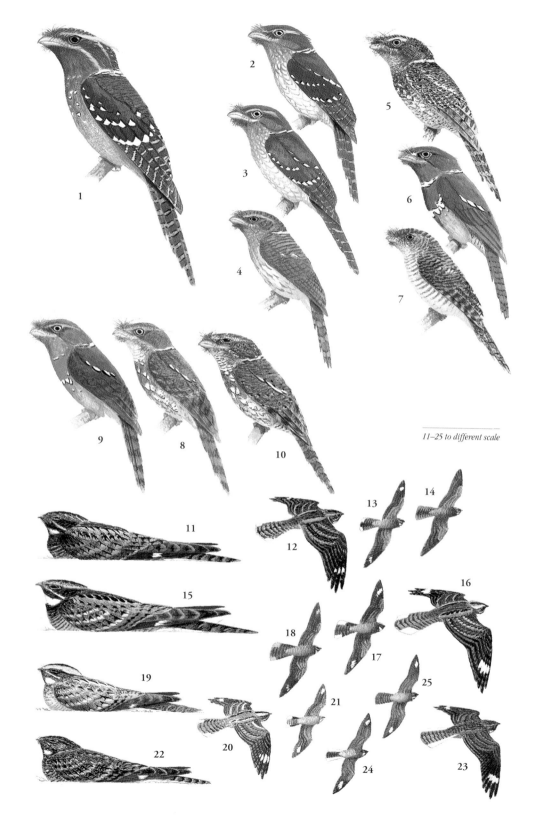

11–25 to different scale

PLATE 28 WOOD PIGEONS & IMPERIAL PIGEONS

ROCK PIGEON *Columba livia* 33 cm

(1,2) **Adult** *intermedia*: Pure stock (probably occurring wild in parts of Myanmar) predominantly grey with noticeably darker hood and breast, blackish tail-tip and paler wing-coverts with two broad blackish bars. Neck glossed green and purple. Silvery-whitish underwing-coverts conspicuous in flight. (3) **Juvenile**: Pure stock duller than adult and browner overall; head, neck and breast greyish-brown with gloss reduced or lacking, wing-coverts mostly pale greyish-brown. (4–6) **Adult variants**: Feral stock highly variable, owing to cross-breeding with domestic varieties. Can show patches of white and brown in plumage, or be all blackish. **VOICE** Song is a soft, guttural *oo-roo-coo*. **HABITAT** Cliffs, ruins, groves in open and cultivated places, urban areas; up to 1,500 m.

SPECKLED WOOD PIGEON *Columba hodgsonii* 38 cm

(7,8) **Male**: Told by combination of pale grey head, neck and upper breast, dark maroon mantle, dark maroon scapulars and lesser coverts with bold whitish speckles, dark belly and vent. Has maroon and pale grey streaks and scales on lower hindneck, upper mantle, lower breast and belly, and dark greenish to greyish legs and feet. (9) **Female**: Head and breast darker grey than male; mantle cold and rather slaty dark brown without maroon, lacks maroon on scapulars and lesser coverts, base colour of underparts dark brownish-grey without maroon. **Juvenile**: Like female but dark parts of body and wings browner with indistinct speckles on scapulars and wing-coverts. **VOICE** Deep, throaty *whock-whroooo whrrrooo*. **HABITAT** Broadleaved evergreen forest; 1,400–2,565 m.

ASHY WOOD PIGEON *Columba pulchricollis* c. 36 cm

(10,11) **Adult**: Dark slaty upperside and breast, contrasting grey head with broad buffish neck-collar and whitish throat. Upper mantle and upper breast glossed green, legs and feet red. In flight, told from Speckled Wood and Mountain Imperial Pigeons by relatively small size, dark breast, pale belly and vent, and all-dark tail. (12) **Juvenile**: Buffish neck-collar little developed and largely pale grey, no green gloss on upper mantle and upper breast, crown darker grey, wings and breast browner (breast obscurely barred dull rufous), lower breast and central abdomen tinged rufous. **VOICE** Song is a deep resonant *whoo*, given singly or repeated up to 5 times. **HABITAT** Broadleaved evergreen forest; 1,400–2,565 m.

PALE-CAPPED PIGEON *Columba punicea* 36–40.5 cm

(13,14) **Male**: Overall dark plumage with contrasting whitish-grey crown diagnostic. Upperparts purplish-maroon with faint green gloss on sides and back of neck, more strongly iridescent mantle and back, and dark slate-coloured rump and uppertail-coverts, with ear-coverts, throat and underparts vinous-brown, undertail-coverts slaty-grey, tail and flight feathers blackish, and orbital skin and base to pale bill red. (15) **Female**: Like male but crown generally greyish.

(16) **Juvenile**: Wing-coverts and scapulars duller than adult with rufous fringes, crown initially concolorous with mantle, gloss on upperparts much reduced, underparts greyer. **VOICE** Undocumented. **HABITAT** Broadleaved evergreen forest, secondary growth, sometimes mangroves, island forest and more open areas (mainly during migratory movements); up to 800 m.

GREEN IMPERIAL PIGEON *Ducula aenea* 42–47 cm

(17,18) **Adult** *sylvatica*: Similar to Mountain Imperial but upperparts mostly dark metallic green (may be hard to discern) with variable rufous-chestnut gloss; head, neck and underparts rather uniform vinous-tinged pale grey, undertail-coverts dark chestnut, tail all dark. **Juvenile**: Duller above than adult; head, neck and underparts paler, virtually without vinous tones. **Other subspecies** *D.a.polia* (southern S). **VOICE** Song is a very deep, repeated *wah-whhoo*; *wah-whhrrooo* or *wah-wahrroo* etc. Also gives a deep *boooo* or *huuooo* and rhythmic purring *crrhhoo*. **HABITAT** Broadleaved evergreen, semi-evergreen, mixed deciduous and island forest, mangroves, sometimes secondary habitats; lowlands.

MOUNTAIN IMPERIAL PIGEON *Ducula badia* 43–51 cm

(19,20) **Adult** *griseicapilla*: The largest pigeon in the region. Distinguished by mostly purplish-maroon mantle and wing-coverts, bluish-grey crown and face, white throat, vinous-tinged pale grey neck (more vinous at rear) and underparts, whitish-buff undertail-coverts and dark tail with contrasting broad greyish terminal band. Red eyering and red bill with pale tip. (21) **Juvenile**: Similar to adult but has less pink on hindneck, rusty-brown fringes to mantle feathers, wing-coverts and flight feathers. (22) **Adult** *badia*: (S): Upperparts more extensively and intensely purplish-maroon (including rump), crown and face duller and more vinous-grey (contrasts less with hindneck) and darker, stronger vinous-pink tinge to underparts, contrasting more with (buffish) undertail-coverts. **VOICE** Song is a loud, very deep *uh, WROO-WROO* or *uhOOH-WROO-WROO* (introductory note only audible at close range) or just *uOOH-WROO*. Repeated after rather long intervals. **HABITAT & BEHAVIOUR** Broadleaved evergreen forest; up to 2,565 m (mostly in mountains). Usually in pairs or small flocks; regularly visits fruiting trees.

PIED IMPERIAL PIGEON *Ducula bicolor* 38–41 cm

(23,24) **Adult** *bicolor*: Unmistakable. White with contrasting black primaries and secondaries and black tail with much white on outer feathers. **Juvenile**: White feathers have buffish tips, particularly on upperside. **VOICE** A deep but rather quiet *cru-croo* or *croo croo-oo*. Deep, resonant purring *rruuu* or *wrrooom*, repeated after 1–3 s intervals. Also *whoo whoo whoo hoo hoo*, with notes descending in pitch and becoming progressively shorter. **HABITAT & BEHAVIOUR** Island forest, sometimes mangroves and coastal mainland forest; lowlands. Gregarious, generally seen in small flocks; larger aggregations on offshore islands for roosting and breeding.

PLATE 29 DOVES & CUCKOO DOVES

ORIENTAL TURTLE DOVE *Streptopelia orientalis* 31–33 cm

(1,2) **Adult** *agricola*: Resembles Spotted Dove but larger, bulkier, shorter-tailed and darker overall, with rufous fringes to lower mantle and wing-coverts, broader rufous fringes to scapulars, barred rather than spotted sides of neck, and bluish-slate rump and uppertail-coverts. Crown bluish-grey (forehead paler and more buffish), sides of head, neck, upper mantle and throat to belly rather uniform pale vinous-brownish, undertail-coverts grey. In flight, shows greyish tail-tips and lacks prominent pale bar across upperwing-coverts. (3) **Juvenile**: Somewhat paler with narrower, paler rufous fringes to lower mantle, scapulars and wing-coverts, paler fringes to breast, much smaller or absent neck-patch. (4) **Adult** *orientalis* (wintering race): Larger and greyer, less vinous on head to upper mantle and underparts, and has rather more distinct breast-band/collar, contrasting with the paler creamy throat and paler buffish belly. **VOICE** Song is a husky *wu,whrroo-whru ru* (sometimes without last note) or faster *er-her-herher*. **HABITAT** Open forest, secondary growth, scrub, cultivation; up to 1,800 m.

SPOTTED DOVE *Streptopelia chinensis* 30–31 cm

(5,6) **Adult** *tigrina*: Told by broad black collar from sides to back of neck with conspicuous white spots, long graduated tail with extensive white tips to outer feathers, and broad pale greyish bar across outer greater coverts to carpal (prominent in flight). Rest of upperside greyish-brown with indistinct dark streaks and narrow light edging, crown and ear-coverts pale grey, neck and underparts pale vinous-brownish, throat and vent whitish, primaries and secondaries blackish. (7) **Juvenile**: Much browner; warmer, less vinous-pink below, distinct buff fringes to upperparts, wing-coverts and breast, almost no grey on crown and wing-coverts, much less distinct dark neck-collar with buffish-brown bars. **VOICE** Song is a soft repeated *wu hu'crrroo*; *wu-crrroo* or *wu huuu-croo*, or more hurried *wu-hwrrroo.. wu-hwrrroo..wu-hwrrroo* etc. **HABITAT** Open areas, open woodland, scrub, cultivation, parks and gardens; up to 1,800 m.

RED COLLARED DOVE *Streptopelia tranquebarica* 23–24.5 cm

(8) **Male** *humilis*: Relatively small and compact with distinctive brownish vinous-red plumage, pale bluish-grey head (except throat), black hindneck-bar, grey rump and uppertail-coverts, rather short square-cut dark tail with broad white tips on outer feathers, and blackish flight feathers. Undertail-coverts whitish. Vent whitish; in flight, square-cut tail has whitish corners. (9,10) **Female**: Similar pattern to male but body and wing-coverts mostly brownish, less grey on head. (11) **Juvenile**: Like female but hindneck-bar absent, upperparts, wing-coverts and breast fringed buffish, primaries, primary coverts and alula tipped dull rufous, and crown rufescent-tinged. **VOICE** Song is soft, throaty, rhythmically repeated *croodle-oo-croo*. **HABITAT** Drier open country, scrub, cultivation; lowlands.

BARRED CUCKOO DOVE *Macropygia unchall* 38–41 cm

(12,13) **Male** *tusalia*: Slender proportions, long graduated tail with no white or grey markings and dark rufescent upperside (including tail) with broad blackish bars distinctive. Head paler brown and unbarred, underparts buffish-brown, breast vinous-tinged and finely barred blackish; has violet and green gloss on nape, upper mantle and (less intensely) breast; primaries and secondaries all dark. General plumage tones quite variable. (14) **Female**: Like male but underparts paler buffish with dense blackish bars (throat and vent plainer). (15) **Juvenile**: Similar to female but all-barred head and neck. **VOICE** Song is a deep *who-OO* or *wu-OO*, repeated every 1–2 s up to 12 times or more; sometimes a quicker *wuOO* or longer *wuOOO*. **HABITAT** Broadleaved evergreen and semi-evergreen forest, forest edge, clearings; 500–1,800 m.

LITTLE CUCKOO DOVE *Macropygia ruficeps* 28–33 cm

(16,17) **Male** *assimilis*: Resembles Barred in shape but smaller, crown distinctly rufous-chestnut, upperparts and tail without bars, underparts more uniform, breast rufous-buff with heavy whitish scales, underwing-coverts rufous-buff, upperwing-coverts dark brown with chestnut fringes. (18) **Female**: Resembles male but breast heavily mottled blackish, wing-coverts more distinctly fringed chestnut. (19) **Male** *malayana* (presumably this race extreme S): Blackish mottling on breast, somewhat darker overall, with broader chestnut fringes to wing-coverts. (20) **Female**: Heavier black mottling on lower throat and upper breast; otherwise differs as male. **Juvenile**: Similar to female but mantle and belly a little more barred, with bolder markings on lower throat and breast. **VOICE** Song is a soft monotonous *wup-wup-wup-wup-wup*..., with c. 2 notes per second. Each bout consists of up to 40 notes. **HABITAT** Broadleaved evergreen forest, sometimes adjacent deciduous forest, forest edge; 500–1,800 m.

PEACEFUL DOVE *Geopelia striata* 21–21.5 cm

(21,22) **Male**: Resembles a miniature Spotted Dove but upperparts greyer with dark bars rather than streaks, hindneck, sides of neck and flanks barred black and white, centre of breast unbarred vinous-pink, forehead and face distinctly pale bluish-grey, orbital skin pale grey-blue. (23) **Juvenile**: Duller, less contrasting bars on hindneck, rather uniform dark brownish and buffish-brown bars on crown, upperparts and wing-coverts, less distinct bars on underparts but extending further across breast (which almost lacks vinous-pink), and warm buffish fringes to tail and flight feathers. **Female**: Like male but bars extend further onto breast, possibly with less distinctly blue-grey forecrown. **VOICE** Song is a high-pitched soft trilling, leading to a series of rapidly delivered short *coo* notes. **HABITAT** Scrub in open country and along coasts, parks, gardens, cultivation; lowlands.

PLATE 30 GREEN PIGEONS

CINNAMON-HEADED GREEN PIGEON *Treron fulvicollis* 25.5–26 cm

(1) **Male** *fulvicollis*: Rufous-chestnut head and neck. (2) **Female**: Similar to Thick-billed but red-based bill distinctly narrower, eyering much narrower, crown greener, has yellowish thighs and streaked (not barred) undertail-coverts. **Juvenile**: Both sexes initially similar to female; male soon shows patches of adult plumage. **VOICE** Song is similar to Little Green but less whining, more syllabic. **HABITAT** Freshwater swamp forest, mangroves, coastal forest and secondary growth; lowlands.

LITTLE GREEN PIGEON *Treron olax* 20–20.5 cm

(3) **Male**: Told by bluish-grey hood (throat whiter), maroon mantle, scapulars and lesser coverts, and orange patch on upper breast. Tail blackish-slate with paler grey terminal band, bill slaty with yellowish-green tip. (4) **Female**: From other green pigeons by combination of dark grey crown, dark green upperparts, pale greyish throat, dull green underparts, pale buffish undertail-coverts with dark green streaks, and bill. **Juvenile**: Both sexes initially like female but a little darker above, crown less distinctly grey, scapulars, tertials and lesser coverts tipped chestnut (obscurely on mantle); male soon shows patches of adult plumage. **VOICE** Song is high-pitched, rather nasal and well structured: roughly *wiiiiii-iiu-iiu iiu-iiui iiui-iiuwu*. Repeated after shortish intervals. **HABITAT** Broadleaved evergreen forest, freshwater swamp forest, secondary growth; below 200 m.

PINK-NECKED GREEN PIGEON *Treron vernans* 26.5–32 cm

(5) **Male** *griseicapilla*: Like Orange-breasted but grey head grades to vinous-pink nape, neck and breast-sides (breast-centre orange), greyer-green above, grey uppertail with blackish subterminal band and much narrower pale grey tips to outer feathers. Undertail blackish with narrow pale grey tips, undertail-coverts dark chestnut. (6) **Female**: From Orange-breasted by more uniform, greyer upperparts (including nape) and tail (as male). **Juvenile**: Both sexes initially like female but tertials browner, scapulars and tertials fringed whitish to buffish, and primaries tipped browner; male soon shows patches of adult plumage. **VOICE** A series of bubbling and gargling notes, leading to a series of harsh grating sounds. Foraging flocks utter a hoarse rasping *krrak, krrak*... **HABITAT** Scrub, cultivated areas, mangroves, peat and freshwater swamp forest, island forest; lowlands.

ORANGE-BREASTED GREEN PIGEON *Treron bicincta* 29 cm

(7) **Male** *bicincta*: Green head with grey nape, green (tinged brownish) above, vinous-pink and orange patches on breast, grey central tail feathers. Rufescent undertail-coverts, broad grey terminal band on blackish undertail. (8) **Female**: Lacks vinous-pink and orange breast-patches. From other green pigeons by contrasting grey nape, brownish cast to green of upperparts, lack of obvious eyering, dark-based bill (no red) and tail (as male). **Juvenile**: Initially as female but nape less grey, scapulars/tertials fringed dull buffish (vaguely on mantle), some rufescent fringes on lesser coverts, pale-tipped primaries; male soon shows patches of adult plumage. **VOICE** Song is a mellow wandering whistle and subdued gurgling. Calls include a repeated *ko-WRRROOOK* and *kreeeeew-kreeeeew-kreeeew*.

HABITAT More open deciduous and semi-evergreen forest, secondary growth, sometimes broadleaved evergreen forest; up to 800 m.

POMPADOUR GREEN PIGEON *Treron pompadora* 25.5–26 cm

(9) **Male** *phayrei*: Like Thick-billed but lacks broad eyering, bill more slender and greyish, has orange wash on breast and yellower-tinged throat. Undertail-coverts brick-red. (10) **Female**: From Thick-billed as male (except breast wash) plus short-streaked (not scaled) undertail-coverts. **Juvenile**: Initially like female but darker above, less grey on crown, pale tips to primaries, indistinct paler tips to mantle, scapulars and tertials; male rapidly shows patches of adult plumage. **VOICE** Song is a series of wandering pleasant whistles, up and down scale. **HABITAT** Broadleaved evergreen and semi-evergreen forest; up to 800 m.

THICK-BILLED GREEN PIGEON *Treron curvirostra* 25.5–27.5 cm

(11) **Male** *nipalensis*: Thick pale greenish bill with red base, broad greenish-blue eyering, grey crown, maroon mantle, scapulars and lesser coverts, and all-green throat and underparts. Undertail-coverts dull chestnut. (12,13) **Female**: Green above, dark green-scaled creamy-buff undertail-coverts, whitish-scaled dark green thighs. **Juvenile**: Initially like female but has some rusty fringes on tips of scapulars, tertials and primaries; male soon shows patches of adult plumage. **Other subspecies** *T.c.curvirostra* (S). **VOICE** Song is similar to Little but fuller, lower-pitched and broken more into separate phrases. Calls with guttural hissing or growling when foraging. **HABITAT** Broadleaved evergreen, semi-evergreen and mixed deciduous forest, secondary growth, sometimes mangroves; up to 1,200 m.

WEDGE-TAILED GREEN PIGEON *Treron sphenura* 33 cm

(14) **Male** *sphenura*: Broad wedge-shaped tail (all grey below), large maroon upper mantle/shoulder-patch, green below, apricot wash on crown/breast; pale cinnamon undertail-coverts, blue bill-base and thin eyering. (15,16) **Female**: Crown, upperparts and breast all green (forehead slightly yellower), undertail-coverts creamy-buff with dark green centres. *T.s.robinsoni* is smaller and darker with darker, less contrasting forehead. (17) **Male** *robinsoni* (presumably this race extreme S): Smaller (26.5–30.5 cm), darker, little/no apricot on crown/breast, maroon of upperparts restricted to shoulder-patch; undertail-coverts as female. **Juvenile**: Initially like female. **VOICE** Song is a rather high-pitched *phruuuuah-po phuu phuuuuu phuu-phu phuo-oh po-oh-oh-po-po-ohpopopo puuuuuuuah puuooaha wo-pi-ohaauah* etc. **HABITAT** Broadleaved evergreen forest; 600–2,565 m.

WHITE-BELLIED GREEN PIGEON *Treron sieboldii* 33 cm

(18) **Male** *murielae*: Very similar to Wedge-tailed Green Pigeon but belly mostly greyish-white, undertail-coverts creamy-whitish with dark green centres, undertail blackish with very narrow grey terminal band, maroon of upperparts confined to upper scapulars and shoulder-patch, bill brighter blue. (19) **Female**: From Wedge-tailed by underpart colour and undertail pattern (as male). **VOICE** A mournful, protracted *o-aooh* or *oo-whooo*, the first note higher-pitched; repeated several times. Also a short *pyu* in alarm. **HABITAT** Broadleaved evergreen forest, forest edge, clearings; 950–2,000 m.

PLATE 31 EMERALD DOVE, NICOBAR PIGEON, GREEN PIGEONS & JAMBU FRUIT DOVE

EMERALD DOVE *Chalcophaps indica* 23–27 cm

(1,2) **Male** *indica*: Unmistakable: metallic green mantle and wings, blue-grey crown and nape, white forehead and eyebrow and dark vinous-pinkish lower head-sides and underparts; whitish to pale grey double band on back (conspicuous in flight), white patch on lesser coverts, red bill. (3) **Female:** Like male but head, mantle and breast much browner, belly paler and more buffish, grey restricted to forehead and eyebrow, no white on wing. (4) **Juvenile:** Resembles female but crown, mantle and breast darker brown, most of plumage barred rufous-buff (less on centre of crown and mantle, boldest on breast), almost lacks green on upperside. **VOICE** Song is a deep soft ***tit-whoooo*** or ***tik-whooOO*** (short clicking introductory note barely audible), repeated at c.1 s intervals up to 25 times. **HABITAT & BEHAVIOUR** Broadleaved evergreen, semi-evergreen and mixed deciduous forest; up to 1,500 m. Often flushed from forest tracks, trails and stream-beds.

NICOBAR PIGEON *Caloenas nicobarica* 40.5–41 cm

(5,6) **Adult** *nicobarica*: All-dark plumage with white uppertail-coverts and short white tail. Head, neck (including long hackles) and breast blackish-slate with golden-green and blue gloss, rest of plumage mostly blue and green with copper highlights on upperparts, bill blackish with short 'horn' near base of upper mandible. (7) **Juvenile:** Duller and browner with rather uniform dark greenish-brown head, mantle and underparts, no neck hackles and very dark brownish-green tail with blue tinge (retained for several years). **VOICE** Harsh guttural croaking or barking ***ku-RRAU*** and deep low reverberating ***rrr-rrr-rrr-rrr***... Usually silent. **HABITAT & BEHAVIOUR** Small wooded islands, dispersing to but rarely seen in mainland coastal forest. Mostly terrestrial, running from danger or flying up to hide in trees.

LARGE GREEN PIGEON *Treron capellei* 35.5–36 cm

(8) **Male:** Large size, very stout bill, yellowish eye-ring, legs and feet, green upperparts, all-green head (greyish around face) and yellow-orange breast-patch distinctive. Undertail-coverts dark chestnut-brown. (9) **Female:** Like male but breast-patch yellowish, undertail-coverts creamy-buff with dark green mottling. **Juvenile male:** Like female but breast-patch more orange-tinged, undertail-coverts pale rufous. **Juvenile female:** Like female. **VOICE** Song is a series of variable deep nasal creaking notes: ***oo-oo-aah oo-oo-aah aa-aa-aah*** and ***oooOOah oo-aah*** etc. Calls include deep conversational grumblings and growlings. **HABITAT** Broadleaved evergreen forest, freshwater swamp forest, forest edge and clearings, specialising on figs; below 200 m.

YELLOW-FOOTED GREEN PIGEON *Treron phoenicoptera* 33 cm

(10) **Male** *annamensis*: Grey crown and nape, pale green throat, yellowish-green neck and upper breast, pale grey-green upperparts, grey lower breast and belly and yellow legs and feet. Has small pinkish-maroon shoulder-patch, bright yellowish-olive tail with grey terminal half and dark maroon undertail-coverts with creamy-buff bars. **Female:** Tends to show less distinct shoulder-patch. **Juvenile:** Both sexes are paler and duller than female, with little or no shoulder-patch. **VOICE** Series of c.10 beautiful modulated mellow musical whistles, recalling Orange-breasted but louder and lower-pitched. **HABITAT** Mixed deciduous forest, secondary growth; lowlands, sometimes up to 800 m.

PIN-TAILED GREEN PIGEON *Treron apicauda* 30.5 cm (tail-prongs up to 10 cm more)

(11) **Male** *apicauda*: Wedge-shaped grey tail (outer feathers blackish near base) with greatly elongated and pointed central feathers (prongs). Has bright blue naked lores and base of rather slender bill, mostly rather bright green body, apricot flush on breast, green belly (any white markings restricted to vent) and chestnut undertail-coverts with outer webs fringed buffish-white. (12,13) **Female:** Like male but breast all green, may show less chestnut (and more whitish) on undertail-coverts, central tail feathers shorter (still distinctly elongated and pointed). **Juvenile male:** Tail-prongs shorter and blunter, wing-coverts rounder, creating different pattern of yellow fringes on wing; primary tips faintly tinged pale grey-green. **VOICE** Song is a series of musical, wandering whistles: ***ko-kla-oi-oi-oi-oilli-illio-kla***, possibly produced by duetting pair. Said to be more tuneful and less meandering than that of Wedge-tailed. **HABITAT** Broadleaved evergreen forest; 500–1,830 m.

YELLOW-VENTED GREEN PIGEON *Treron seimundi* 26–28 cm (tail-prongs up to 5 cm more)

(14,15) **Male** *seimundi*: Like Pin-tailed but tail-prongs much shorter, generally darker green, has maroon shoulder-patch, whitish belly-centre, mostly yellow undertail-coverts with narrow green centres. Bill blue with horn-grey tip, naked lores and eyering blue, forecrown golden-tinged, upper breast with pinkish-orange wash. (16) **Female:** Undertail-coverts have broader green centres, no maroon shoulder-patch, breast greener. **VOICE** Song is a high-pitched ***pooaah po-yo-yo-pooaah***. **HABITAT** Broadleaved evergreen forest, forest edge; 300–950 m.

JAMBU FRUIT DOVE *Ptilinopus jambu* 26.5–27 cm

(17) **Male:** Greenish upperparts, crimson face, white eyering and white underparts with pink flush on foreneck and upper breast diagnostic. Bill orange-yellow, undertail-coverts chestnut. (18) **Female:** Mostly green with greyish-purple face, white eyering, maroon central stripe on throat, paler vent and buffish undertail-coverts. (19) **Juvenile:** Like female but face brownish and central throat whitish (washed dull rufous). Initially has warm brown fringing on upperparts, wing-coverts and tertials. **VOICE** Soft ***hooo***, repeated after short intervals. **HABITAT** Broadleaved evergreen forest, rarely mangroves; up to 1,200 m.

8–19 to different scale

PLATE 32 MASKED FINFOOT, CRAKES, WATERCOCK & GALLINULES

MASKED FINFOOT *Heliopais personata* 52–54.5 cm

(1) **Male**: Black throat/upper foreneck with white border, black forecrown/line along crown-side, yellow bill with small horn at base (spring only?). Brown above, greyer nape to mantle, dark brown eyes, bright green legs/feet. (2) **Female**: Throat, upper foreneck and much of lores whitish, less black on forecrown, no horn, yellow eyes. **Juvenile**: As female but browner above, no black on forecrown, more mottled black on neck, paler bill. **VOICE** Rather high-pitched bubbling (like air blown through tube into water), possibly followed by clucks that increase in tempo. **HABITAT & BEHAVIOUR** Rivers in broadleaved evergreen forest, mangroves, swamp forest, sometimes pools/lakes away from forest; up to 800 m. Secretive. Quite grebe-like; head jerks back/forth when swimming. Awkward on land.

WHITE-BREASTED WATERHEN *Amaurornis phoenicurus* 28.5–36 cm

(3) **Adult** *phoenicurus*: Dark brownish-slate above, white face and foreneck to upper belly, deep rufous-chestnut vent. Mostly yellowish-green bill with red at base, red eyes, yellowish legs/feet. (4) **Juvenile**: Browner above, darker lores/forehead/ear-coverts, broken bars below, brown eyes, dull bill. **VOICE** Weird bubbling, roaring, grunting and croaking: ***kru-ak kru-ak kru-ak-a-wak-wak***; ***krr-kwaak-kwaak krr-kwaak-kwaak*** etc. Long series of ***kwaak*** or ***kook*** notes. Quick ***pwik*** contact notes. **HABITAT** Smaller vegetated wetlands, wet places in open forest (including islands), mangroves, roadsides; up to 800 m.

WHITE-BROWED CRAKE *Porzana cinerea* 19–21.5 cm

(5) **Adult**: Grey neck-sides to upper flanks, blackish mask bordered by white streaks. Blackish-mottled slaty-grey crown, blackish and buffish streaks above, pinkish-cinnamon vent, greenish-yellow bill (red at base), greenish legs. **Juvenile**: Crown to mantle paler/browner, head-sides to flanks paler grey, face pattern less distinct, no red at bill-base, greyer legs. **VOICE** Loud nasal chattering ***chika*** (rapidly repeated 10–12 times) from both sexes. Also a loud ***kek-kro*** when foraging, repeated nasal ***bee*** notes and quiet, repeated ***charr-r*** when alarmed. **HABITAT** Well-vegetated freshwater lakes, floating mats of vegetation, marshes, sometimes overgrown ditches/rice paddies; lowlands.

WATERCOCK *Gallicrex cinerea* Male 41–43 cm; female 31–36 cm

(6) **Male breeding**: Relatively large, mostly blackish; red-based yellow bill, long red frontal shield, longish red legs, grey to buff fringing above, warm brown fringing on rump/uppertail-coverts, pale-barred vent. (7) **Male non-breeding**: Like female non-breeding, but possibly shows broader, more defined bars below. (8,9) **Female breeding**: Dark brown above with buff feather fringes, greyer fringing on hindneck, upper mantle and wing-coverts; head-sides pale buff, cheeks brownish, buffy-white below, with narrow wavy greyish-brown bars, deeper buff lower foreneck/upper breast and undertail-coverts, whiter throat-/abdomen-centre. Greenish bill and legs/feet; white

leading edge to wing in flight (also male). Non-breeders have somewhat heavier bars below. (10) **Juvenile**: As female non-breeding but broader, warmer buff streaks above, crown narrowly streaked buff, head-sides/underparts rich buff with narrow dark bars (may be almost lacking), white of throat in centre only; respective sexes smaller than adults. **VOICE** Territorial call is 10–12 ***ogh*** or ***kok*** notes, then 10–12 quicker, deeper, metallic booming ***ootoomb*** notes, and finally, 5–6 ***kluck*** notes. Nasal ***krey*** in alarm. **HABITAT & BEHAVIOUR** Freshwater marshes/grassland, rice paddies; lowlands. Usually skulking.

PURPLE SWAMPHEN *Porphyrio porphyrio* 28.5–42 cm

(11) **Adult** *poliocephalus*: Large/robust, big red bill/frontal shield, red legs. Extensively purple-blue, silver wash on head, dark turquoise throat/foreneck/wings (tertials greener), blackish belly-centre, white undertail-coverts. (12) **Juvenile**: Duller than adult, hindneck to rump mixed with brown, foreneck and breast duller, lower belly whiter, bill and 'frontal shield' smaller and duller (latter almost lacking), legs and feet much duller. (13) **Adult** *viridis* (W[south],C[south],SE,S): Smaller; mostly blackish-brown upperparts, turquoise shoulders. **VOICE** Extended series of powerful, rattling nasal notes: ***quin-quinkrrkrrquinquinquinkrrkrr...*** Sonorous chuckling and cackling. Contact call is a soft ***puk-puk...***, alarm call a rising nasal blast, ***cooah*** or ***gooweh***. **HABITAT & BEHAVIOUR** Freshwater marshes, swamps, reedbeds, well-vegetated lakes; up to 400 m. Usually quite conspicuous.

COMMON MOORHEN *Gallinula chloropus* 30–35 cm

(14) **Adult** *chloropus*: Dark; white flank-line/lateral undertail-coverts, red bill (yellow tip)/frontal shield. Yellow-green legs/feet (orange-red above joint). Bill, frontal shield, legs and feet duller when worn; may lose flank-line. (15) **Juvenile**: Browner above, much paler/browner head-sides/underside, whitish throat/belly-centre (undertail-coverts as adult), buffier flank-line (may be lost when moulting), greenish-brown bill/frontal shield, duller legs. **Other subspecies** *G.c.orientalis* (south S): Smaller/darker, relatively large shield. **VOICE** Loud ***krrruk***, ***kurr-ik*** or ***kark***. Also, soft ***kook***, loud ***kekuk*** or ***kittick***, and hard ***keh-keh*** alarm. **HABITAT & BEHAVIOUR** Freshwater lakes, pools, marshes, ditches etc., flooded rice fields; up to 800 m. Cocks tail, flashing undertail-coverts. Mostly swims but also walks on land.

COMMON COOT *Fulica atra* 40.5–42.5 cm

(16) **Adult** *atra*: Blackish; white bill/frontal shield. White trailing edge to secondaries in flight, greenish legs/feet. (17) **Juvenile**: Plumage browner-tinged, throat and centre of foreneck whitish, belly paler, frontal shield smaller. **VOICE** Male combat call is explosive ***pssi*** or ***pyee*** (sharper in alarm); female equivalent is croaking ***ai*** or ***u***, becoming rapid ***ai-oeu-ai-ai-oeu...*** etc. in alarm. Contact calls are short ***kow***, ***kowk***, ***kut*** or sharper ***kick*** notes. Male also utters a series of hard, smacking ***ta*** or ***p*** notes. **HABITAT & BEHAVIOUR** Freshwater lakes, marshes; lowlands. Usually seen swimming; patters along surface when disturbed. Sometimes walks on land.

3–10 to different scale

PLATE 33 CRAKES & RAILS

RED-LEGGED CRAKE *Rallina fasciata* 22–25 cm

(1) **Adult**: Chestnut-tinged brown upperside, dull chestnut head and breast, black-and-whitish bars on wing-coverts and flight feathers, bold blackish and whitish ventral bars, red legs. (2) **Juvenile**: Like adult but duller, buffier, less bold wing markings and ventral barring, brownish-yellow legs. **VOICE** Male territorial call is a loud rapid hard (6–9 note) *UH-UH-UH-UH-UH-UH*..., repeated every 1.5–3 s. Females sometimes join in with sudden quacking nasal *brrr*, *brr'ay* or *grr'erh* notes. Often calls during night. **HABITAT** Streams and wet areas in broadleaved evergreen forest, forest edge, clearings and secondary growth, sometimes wet areas in cultivation; below 200 m.

SLATY-LEGGED CRAKE *Rallina eurizonoides* 26–28 cm

(3) **Adult** *telmatophila*: Larger than Red-legged, duller/colder above, unmarked wings, greyish to black legs. (4) **Juvenile/first winter**: Like Red-legged but larger, bigger-billed, no bars/spots on wing-coverts, paler-faced. **VOICE** Territorial call is said to be a persistent *kek-kek kek-kek kek-kek kek-kek*... Subdued *krrrr* when alarmed and long drumming *krrrrrrrr-ar-kraa-kraa-kraa-kraa*. Often calls at night. **HABITAT** Streams and wet areas in broadleaved evergreen forest and secondary growth, grassy vegetation in plantations, also marshes and gardens on passage; up to 1,500 m.

SLATY-BREASTED RAIL *Gallirallus striatus* 26–31 cm

(5) **Adult** *albiventer*: Chestnut crown, dull olive-brown above with black-and-white mottling and barring, grey head-sides and breast, with blackish-and-whitish barring ventrally; longish reddish bill, dark legs. (6) **Juvenile**: Duller and paler, streaked blackish above, paler and browner below with duller bars, shorter bill. **VOICE** Territorial call is a series of sharp, stony *kerrek* or *trrrik* notes; may run together to form kind of song, lasting up to 30 s. Also low *kuk* and *ka-ka-kaa-kaa* from courting males. **HABITAT** Marshes, reedbeds, mangroves, wet rice paddies, waterside vegetation, sometimes more open/drier areas; up to 1,300 m (mostly lowlands).

WATER RAIL *Rallus aquaticus* 27–30 cm

(7) **Adult** *indicus*: Like Slaty-breasted Rail but no chestnut on crown, grey supercilium, broad dark brownish eyestripe, buffy olive-brown upperparts with broad blackish streaks, broader underpart bars, paler legs. **First winter**: Browner with some pale scales on breast. **VOICE** Series of well-spaced, drawn-out, squealing, grunting *grui* or *krueeh*, rising in crescendo to series of longer high-pitched whistles (like squealing piglets). Also sharp *tic* notes, followed by wheezy screaming *wheee-ooo* and sharp *krrihk*. **HABITAT** Freshwater marshes, reedbeds; up to 400 m.

BLACK-TAILED CRAKE *Porzana bicolor* 21–24 cm

(8) **Adult**: Rufescent upperside, blackish tail, slaty-grey head, neck and underparts, brick-red legs. (9) **Juvenile**: Upperparts mixed with blackish-brown, brownish tinge below. **VOICE** Male territorial call is a long trill, up to 13 s, like Ruddy-breasted Crake but more obviously descending and usually preceded

by subdued harsh rasping *waak-waak* (not audible at distance); also recalls Little Grebe. Contact call is a high-pitched *kek* or *kik*. **HABITAT** Small swampy areas and overgrown streams in or near broadleaved evergreen forest and secondary growth, adjacent to wet cultivation; 1,000–1,460 m.

BAILLON'S CRAKE *Porzana pusilla* 19–20.5 cm

(10) **Adult** *pusilla*: Small; short greenish bill, olive-brown above with blackish and white streaks/speckles, blue-grey supercilium and underparts, black-and-white bars on rear flanks and vent, greenish legs. (11) **Juvenile**: Lacks blue-grey; whitish throat to belly-centre, rufous-buff on upper breast and upper flanks. **VOICE** Usually silent but may give a short *tac* or *tyiuk* when alarmed. Territorial call is a creaky rasping *trrrr-trrrrr* (like sound of nail along teeth of comb), repeated every 1–2 s and sometimes preceded by dry *t* sounds. **HABITAT** Freshwater marshes, reedbeds, vegetated wetlands; up to 1,400 m.

SPOTTED CRAKE *Porzana porzana* 21–24 cm

(12) **Male non-breeding**: Largely brownish below, with many white speckles/bars, plain buff undertail-coverts. (13) **Male breeding**: More bluish-grey underlying head, neck and breast markings, brighter red bill-base. (14) **First winter**: Whitish throat, denser white speckling on head and sides of neck, duller bill. **Female**: As male non-breeding but tends to show less grey on head, more white speckles. **VOICE** May utter sharp *tck* notes when alarmed. Territorial call is a short, loud, rather high-pitched ascending *kwit* or *whitt*, c.1 per s, often for several minutes. **HABITAT** Marshes, reedbeds; lowlands.

RUDDY-BREASTED CRAKE *Porzana fusca* 21–26.5 cm

(15) **Adult** *fusca*: Uniform, rather cold dark olive-brown above, reddish-chestnut head with indistinct narrow whitish bars on greyish-black rear flanks and vent, blackish bill with greenish base, reddish legs. (16) **Juvenile**: Whitish underside with dense dull brownish-grey vermiculations/mottling, dull brown legs/feet. **Other subspecies** *P.f.erythrothorax* (visitor): Larger, a shade paler overall, less reddish below. **VOICE** Territorial call is hard *tewk* or *kyot*, every 2–3 s, the sequence often speeding up and usually followed by a long, high, slightly descending trill (3–4 s long). Trill recalls Black-tailed Crake. Low *chuck* contact call. **HABITAT** Freshwater marshes, reedbeds, sometimes more open wetlands, wet rice paddies, drier cultivation, mangroves (mainly on passage); up to 700 m.

BAND-BELLIED CRAKE *Porzana paykullii* 27 cm

(17) **Adult**: Like Slaty-legged but has darker, colder brown crown and upperside, paler, more extensive chestnut below, some whitish and dark bars on wing-coverts, salmon-red legs, greenish-slate bill with pea-green base. (18) **First winter**: Washed-out head-sides and breast (vaguely barred), purplish-brown legs. **VOICE** Usually silent. Territorial call is a loud metallic clangour running into brief trills (likened to sound made by wooden rattle). **HABITAT & BEHAVIOUR** Freshwater swamps, vegetated wetlands, wet areas in or near broadleaved evergreen forest; lowlands. Very skulking.

PLATE 34 GREATER PAINTED-SNIPE, EURASIAN WOODCOCK & SNIPES

GREATER PAINTED-SNIPE *Rostratula benghalensis* 23–26 cm

(1–3) **Female** *benghalensis*: Darker/more uniform than snipes; white spectacles, belly and band around shoulder, slightly drooping bill, blackish crown with buffish median stripe, buffish mantle-lines, dark maroon-chestnut remainder of head, neck and upper breast. Barred tail/flight feathers, largely clear white underwing-coverts. (4,5) **Male**: Plumage somewhat paler and much more variegated, spectacles buffish, head-sides, neck and upper breast mostly greyish-brown, with large rich buffish markings on wing-coverts. **Juvenile**: Resembles male but wing-coverts greyer with smaller buff markings. **VOICE** Female territorial call is a series of 20–80 or so short *kook*, *oook* or *koh* notes (like sound made by blowing into empty bottle), usually given at dusk and night. A single *kook* during roding display. May give a loud explosive *kek* when flushed. **HABITAT & BEHAVIOUR** Marshy and swampy areas, wet rice paddies (particularly when overgrown); lowlands. Quite secretive; mainly crepuscular. Feeds by probing in soft mud and sweeping bill from side to side in shallow water. Stands motionless for long periods. When flushed, flies short distance, with rather slow erratic wingbeats, legs trailing. Female has low 'roding' display flight; both sexes perform spread-wing displays.

EURASIAN WOODCOCK *Scolopax rusticola* 33–35 cm

(6,7) **Adult**: Resembles some snipes but larger, hindcrown broadly barred black, upperparts more softly patterned with rufescent-brown and buff (no lengthwise pale stripes), underparts entirely barred brown and buff. In flight appears heavy and robust with broad, rounded wings. **VOICE** Usually silent when flushed but occasionally gives harsh snipe-like *scaap* notes. During roding display, utters weak, high-pitched *chissick* or *pissipp*, interspersed with low, guttural *aurk-aurk-aurk*. **HABITAT & BEHAVIOUR** Forest, secondary growth, dense cover along streams; up to 2,565 m. Prefers damp areas; usually solitary. May be flushed from concealed position in daytime; flies with heavier wingbeats than snipes. Territorial males perform roding display at dawn and dusk, flying in regular circuits low over treetops, with slow deliberate wingbeats.

WOOD SNIPE *Gallinago nemoricola* 28–32 cm

(8–10) **Adult**: Relatively large, bulky and short-billed; pronounced buff stripes and scaling on distinctly dark upperparts, lower breast to vent entirely barred, no gingery breast-patch. In flight, wings appear relatively broad and rounded, with densely dark-barred underwing-coverts. (11) **Juvenile**: Mainly differs by finer, whiter fringes to mantle and scapulars, paler buff fringes to median coverts. **VOICE** Often silent when flushed but may give a deep, guttural croak or *che-dep che-dep*... **HABITAT & BEHAVIOUR** Streams, rivers and other wet areas in or near broadleaved evergreen forest and secondary growth, marshes and swamps with thick cover; recorded at 1,310–2,075 m. Usually solitary; rarely flies far when flushed.

PINTAIL SNIPE *Gallinago stenura* 25–27 cm

(12–14) **Adult**: Like Common but bill shorter, pale supercilium broader than dark eyestripe at bill-base, narrower pale brown to whitish scapular edges, tail only projects slightly beyond wing-tips, primaries only project slightly beyond tertials. Legs greyish/brownish-green. In flight, tail looks somewhat shorter, almost all of toes extend beyond tail-tip, more contrasting sandy-buff lesser/median coverts, almost no trailing edge to secondaries, more heavily barred underwing-coverts, almost no white on tail corners. Usually 24–28 tail feathers, 6–9 outer pairs pin-like. (15) **Juvenile**: Narrower whitish edges to mantle/scapulars, narrower/more even whitish-buff wing-covert fringes. **VOICE** When flushed, may utter short, rasping *squok*, *squack* or *squick*, rather weaker/lower-pitched than call of Common. **HABITAT & BEHAVIOUR** Open marshy areas, rice paddies; up to 1,800 m. Often in drier areas than Common; flight typically shorter/more direct.

SWINHOE'S SNIPE *Gallinago megala* 27–29 cm

(16–18) **Adult**: Very like Pintail. Bill longer (relatively as Common), tail projects more beyond wings, primaries may project clearly beyond tertials; wings slightly longer/more pointed, toes project less, more white on tail (less than Common). Slightly larger and larger/squarer-headed than Pintail/Common, crown-peak more behind eye (eye also further back), heavier-chested. Legs thicker than Common, usually thicker than Pintail, often rather yellow (greenish/greenish-yellow). In spring, face and neck-sides/flanks (sometimes breast) may look quite dusky/heavily barred (distinctly darker than Pintail/Common). Usually 20 (18–26) tail feathers, outer ones broader than Pintail. (19) **Juvenile**: Narrower whitish edges to mantle and scapulars, clear whitish-buff fringes to wing-coverts and tertials. **VOICE** Usually silent when flushed. May call like Pintail (same pitch) but possibly slightly less hoarse, rather thinner and quite nasal with slight rattling quality. **HABITAT & BEHAVIOUR** Marshy areas, rice paddies and their margins. In drier, possibly less open places than Pintail/Common. Take-off rather slow/laboured compared to Pintail/Common. Flight rather direct, usually for short distance.

COMMON SNIPE *Gallinago gallinago* 25–27 cm

(20–22) **Adult** *gallinago*: Relatively long bill, dark eyestripe broader than pale supercilium at bill-base, bold pale buff/buffish-white lengthwise stripes above, largely white belly/vent, no obvious white wing-covert tips, tail clearly projects beyond closed wings. In flight, prominent white trailing edge to secondaries, panel of unbarred white on underwing-coverts, toes project only slightly beyond tail, little white on outer-tail (more than Pintail/Swinhoe's). (23) **Juvenile**: Mantle and scapulars with fine whitish lines, wing-coverts more narrowly fringed buffish-white. **VOICE** When flushed, regularly gives rasping, often slightly rising *scaaap*; more drawn out than Pintail and Swinhoe's. **HABITAT & BEHAVIOUR** Open marshy areas, rice paddies; lowlands. Flight fast and erratic, often zig-zagging.

JACK SNIPE *Lymnocryptes minimus* 17–19 cm

(24–26) **Adult**: Smaller/shorter-billed than other snipes; dark crown-centre, 'split supercilium', dark mantle and scapulars with purple/green gloss and prominent buff lengthwise lines, no bars below, dark-streaked foreneck, upper breast and flanks; all-brown, slightly wedge-shaped tail, unbarred white panel on underwing-coverts. **VOICE** Usually silent when flushed but sometimes utters low, weak, barely audible *gah*. **HABITAT & BEHAVIOUR** Marshy areas, ditches; up to 1,500 m. Often solitary. Feeds with nervous rocking action. Freezes when approached and difficult to flush. Flight often appears rather weak and fluttery, typically only covering short distance.

PLATE 35 GODWITS & DOWITCHERS

BLACK-TAILED GODWIT *Limosa limosa* 36–40 cm

(1,2) **Adult non-breeding** *melanuroides*: Told by combination of fairly large size, long blackish legs, rather long neck, long straight bicoloured bill with pinkish basal half, and rather plain brownish-grey plumage with somewhat paler head-sides, neck and breast, short whitish supercilium and whitish belly and vent. In flight shows pronounced white upperwing-bar, broad white band across rump and uppertail-coverts contrasting with mostly black tail, and white underwing with dark border. Legs and feet dark grey. (3) **Male breeding**: Sides of head, neck and upper breast mostly reddish-rufous, mantle and scapulars boldly marked blackish with some chestnut, rest of underparts whitish with variable blackish bars. (4) **Female breeding**: Larger, longer-billed and duller than male breeding, retaining greater proportion of greyish non-breeding plumage. (5) **Juvenile**: Like female breeding but crown streaked brown and cinnamon, mantle and scapulars rather boldly marked with dark grey-brown and chestnut, wing-coverts dark grey-brown with cinnamon-buff fringing, neck and breast initially washed with rufous-buff. **VOICE** Single or repeated yelping *kip* notes in flight. Feeding flocks utter chattering *kett* and *chuk* notes. **HABITAT & BEHAVIOUR** Mud- and sandflats, coastal pools, marshes, sometimes wet rice paddies; lowlands. Usually found in flocks. Feeds by picking and forward-probing, often in deeper water than Bar-tailed.

BAR-TAILED GODWIT *Limosa lapponica* 37–41 cm

(6,7) **Adult non-breeding** *lapponica*: Similar to Black-tailed Godwit but upperparts buffier and distinctly streaked, bill slightly upturned, legs somewhat shorter. In flight lacks white wing-bar, back to uppertail-coverts white, tail white with blackish bars, underwing duller and less distinctly dark-bordered. (8) **Male breeding**: Head, neck and underparts almost entirely reddish-chestnut; has bold chestnut markings on upperparts. (9) **Female breeding**: Larger and longer-billed than male, but modest change from non-breeding plumage, with darker-marked upperparts and deep apricot wash on head-sides, neck and breast. (10) **Juvenile**: Like adult non-breeding but crown and upperparts have brown centres and broad bright buff edges, with buffish-brown wash and fine dark streaks on neck and breast. (11) **Adult non-breeding** *baueri* (recorded C southwards): Dark back and rump, dark-barred uppertail-coverts and dark-barred underwing-coverts. **VOICE** Flight calls include abrupt high *kik* or *kiv-ik* (often repeated), barking *kak-kak* and nasal *ke-wuh* or *kirruc*. **HABITAT & BEHAVIOUR** Mudflats, sandflats, beaches, coastal pools. Often feeds on open mud/sand and in shallower water than Black-tailed.

LONG-BILLED DOWITCHER *Limnodromus scolopaceus* 27–30 cm

(12,13) **Adult non-breeding**: Similar to Asian but smaller, basal half of bill greenish, upperside somewhat plainer, neck and upper breast rather plain brownish-grey, legs shorter, paler, greyish- to brownish-green. In flight shows unmarked white back, heavily dark-barred rump to uppertail, somewhat darker inner primaries and secondaries with narrow, defined white trailing edge and finely dark-barred underwing-coverts. (14) **Adult breeding**: Similar to Asian but upperparts boldly mottled rather than streaked, supercilium and sides of head noticeably paler, underparts paler with dark speckles and bars on neck, breast, flanks and vent. Bill and leg colour similar to adult non-breeding. (15) **Juvenile**: Resembles adult non-breeding but mantle and scapulars dark brown with fine chestnut fringes, sides of head and breast washed buff. **VOICE** Typical flight and contact call is a single or repeated sharp *kik* or *keek*. When alarmed, may give a longer, shriller *keeek* (singly or in short series). **HABITAT & BEHAVIOUR** Coastal marshes, freshwater and brackish pools, sometimes mudflats. Feeds by continuous vertical probing, usually in knee-deep water.

ASIAN DOWITCHER *Limnodromus semipalmatus* 34–36 cm

(16,17) **Adult non-breeding**: Most likely to be confused with godwits. Similar to Bar-tailed Godwit (*L.l.baueri*) but somewhat smaller, shorter-necked and shorter-legged, with rather flattish forehead and straight all-black bill with slightly swollen tip (sometimes paler at extreme base). In flight, uppersides of inner primaries, secondaries and greater coverts appear somewhat paler than rest of wing (may appear rather translucent), underwing pale with unmarked white coverts (similar to Bar-tailed *L.l.lapponica*), back to uppertail-coverts white with dark markings, uppertail largely unbarred (somewhat paler than Bar-tailed *L.l.baueri* and quite unlike *L.l.lapponica*). (18) **Male breeding**: From similar Bar-tailed Godwit by largely white vent, size, shape and distinctive bill. (19) **Female breeding**: Head, neck and underparts slightly duller than male. (20) **Juvenile**: Similar to adult non-breeding but mantle, scapulars and tertials blacker with narrow, neat pale buff fringes, neck and breast strongly washed buff and indistinctly dark-streaked. **VOICE** In flight utters occasional airy *chaow* or *chowp*, yelping *chep-chep* and soft *kiaow*. **HABITAT & BEHAVIOUR** Mudflats, coastal marshes and pools. Feeds by continuous vertical probing, usually in knee-deep water. Gregarious; often associates with godwit flocks.

PLATE 36 CURLEWS & JACANAS

LITTLE CURLEW *Numenius minutus* 29–32 cm

(1,2) **Adult**: Similar to Whimbrel but much smaller (not much larger than Pacific Golden Plover) and finer-billed, pale supercilium contrasts more sharply with blackish eyestripe, underparts more buffish. In flight, back to uppertail-coverts concolorous with mantle, underwing-coverts mostly buffish-brown. Legs and feet yellowish to bluish-grey. **Juvenile**: Similar to adult. VOICE In flight, excited whistled 3–4 note *weep-weep-weep*... or *qwee-qwee-qwee*..., recalling Whimbrel but sharper and higher-pitched. Also rougher *tchew-tchew-tchew* and harsh *kweek-ek* when alarmed. HABITAT & BEHAVIOUR Short grassland, barren cultivation, margins of fresh water and sometimes coastal wetlands; lowlands. May be tame. Feeds mostly by picking.

WHIMBREL *Numenius phaeopus* 40–46 cm (female slightly larger and longer-billed than male)

(3,4) **Adult** *phaeopus*: Distinctive. Fairly large; bill longish and markedly kinked downward towards tip, upperside rather cold greyish-brown with whitish to pale buffish mottling, prominent blackish lateral crown-stripes and eyestripe, broad whitish supercilium and buffish-white neck and breast with heavy dark streaks. In flight, upperside appears all dark with contrasting clean white back and rump, underwing-coverts mostly plain whitish. Legs/feet dull bluish-grey. (5) **Juvenile**: Clear buff markings on scapulars and tertials, breast buffier with slightly finer streaks. (6) **Adult** *variegatus* (widespread but scarcer): Lower back and rump concolorous with mantle and shows heavy dark bars on underwing-coverts. Intergrades occur. See other curlews. VOICE In flight utters diagnostic clear whinny or titter: *dididididididi*... or *puhuhuhuhuhuhu*..., varying in intensity. Also single plaintive *curlee* notes. HABITAT & BEHAVIOUR Coastal wetlands, mangroves, marshes, large rivers; lowlands. Gregarious. Feeds mostly by picking rather than probing.

EURASIAN CURLEW *Numenius arquata* 50–60 cm (female larger and longer-billed than male)

(7,8) **Adult non-breeding** *orientalis*: Like Whimbrel but larger, bill longer and more strongly and gently downcurved, head more uniform with slightly darker crown and indistinct supercilium, upperparts rather more coarsely marked with whitish to pale buff, has more pronounced blackish streaks on neck, breast and upper belly. In flight shows stronger contrast between outer and inner upperwing, contrasting white back and rump (latter with some dark mottling) and largely white underwing-coverts. Legs and feet bluish-grey. (9) **Juvenile**: Like adult breeding but even more buffish, breast and flanks more narrowly dark-streaked, more contrasting tertial pattern, and somewhat shorter and less downcurved bill. **Adult breeding**: Has more buffish fringing on upperparts and somewhat more buffish base colour to sides of head, neck and breast. VOICE Loud, rising, ringing *cour-lee* or *cour-loo*, uttered with varying emphasis, and low *whaup* or *were-up*. Loud, rapid stammering *tyuyuyuyu*... or *tututu*... when agitated. HABITAT & BEHAVIOUR Mud- and sandflats, coastal wetlands, large rivers; lowlands. Gregarious. Feeds mostly by deep probing into soft mud.

EASTERN CURLEW *Numenius madagascariensis* 60–66 cm (female larger and longer-billed than male)

(10,11) **Adult non-breeding**: Like Eurasian but larger and longer-billed, appears more uniform, with browner/buffier underparts. In flight shows rather uniform rufescent-tinged greyish-brown back and rump, and dense dark bars on underwing-coverts. Legs and feet dull blue-grey. (12) **Adult breeding**: Upperpart fringes and back to uppertail distinctly washed rufous, sides of head and neck washed rufous, rest of underparts warmer-tinged. **Juvenile**: Similar to adult non-breeding but has extensive neat buffish-white markings on upperparts and wing-coverts, finer dark streaks on underparts, and shorter bill. VOICE Call is *coor-ee*, similar to Eurasian but flatter-sounding and less fluty. Also gives strident *ker-ee ker-ee*... or *carr-eeir carr-eeir*... when alarmed, and occasional bubbling trills. HABITAT & BEHAVIOUR Mud- and sandflats. Feeds mostly by deep probing.

PHEASANT-TAILED JACANA *Hydrophasianus chirurgus* 29–31.5 cm (breeding tail to 25 cm more)

(13) **Adult breeding**: Mostly glossy blackish-brown with white head and foreneck, shiny yellow-buff hindneck (bordered black), very long, pointed blackish tail and mostly white wings. Outer primaries and primary tips largely blackish, the latter with strange pendant-like extensions, upperparts often slightly paler with faint purple gloss. (14,15) **Adult non-breeding**: Crown, centre of hindneck and upperparts drab brown with whitish bars on crown and hindneck, white to pale buff supercilium extending in broad buff band down neck-side, underparts all white with black eyestripe extending down neck-side and broadly across breast, median and lesser coverts largely greyish-brown with some blackish bars, tail shorter. In flight mostly white wings distinctive. See Grey-headed Lapwing (in flight). (16) **Juvenile**: Resembles adult non-breeding but crown mostly rather pale rufous-chestnut with blackish-brown feather-centres, no obvious supercilium, rufous to rufous-buff fringes to upperparts, neck washed pale rufous-chestnut (less distinctly buff on sides), median and lesser coverts more rufescent, black on breast ill-defined. VOICE During breeding season gives a series of deep rhythmic *t'you*, *me-e-ou* or *me-onp* notes, and nasal mewing *jaew* or *tewn* notes. Other calls include a sharp, high-pitched *tic-tic-tic*..., nasal *brrr-brrp* and high-pitched, whining *eeeaaar* when alarmed. HABITAT & BEHAVIOUR Well-vegetated freshwater marshes, swamps, lakes and pools, sometimes apparently less suitable habitats on passage, including mangroves and large rivers; up to 400 m. Gregarious outside breeding season.

BRONZE-WINGED JACANA *Metopidius indicus* 26.5–30.5 cm

(17) **Adult**: Black head, neck and underparts (glossed green), white supercilium, bronze-olive lower mantle, scapulars and wing-coverts, chestnut-maroon back to uppertail and vent; purple/green-glossed lower hindneck. (18) **Juvenile**: Crown, nape and loral eyestripe dull chestnut, neck-sides, lower foreneck and upper breast deep rufous-buff, rest of underparts white with dark-barred thighs, uppertail-coverts barred blackish and pale chestnut, tail black and white with buff and/or bronze-green tinge. VOICE Short low harsh guttural grunts and a wheezy piping *seek-seek-seek*... HABITAT Well-vegetated freshwater marshes, swamps, lakes, pools; up to 400 m.

13–18 to different scale

PLATE 37 SANDPIPERS

SPOTTED REDSHANK *Tringa erythropus* 29–32 cm

(1,2) Adult non-breeding: Resembles Common but distinctly paler overall, bill longer, more slender and finer-tipped; more distinct white supercilium, no streaks on underparts, longer legs. In flight, upperside appears rather uniform apart from unbarred white back. **(3) Adult breeding**: Upperside blacker, head, neck and underparts almost uniform blackish. Some (mainly females) have faint pale scales on head, neck and underparts. **(4) Juvenile**: Recalls adult non-breeding but brownish-grey overall with finely white-speckled upperparts and wing-coverts, dark-streaked neck and closely dark-barred breast to undertail-coverts. **VOICE** Loud, rising *chu-it*, given in flight. Also a conversational *uck* when feeding, and short *chip* when alarmed. **HABITAT & BEHAVIOUR** Freshwater marshes, flooded rice paddies, coastal pools, large rivers; up to 400 m. Gregarious. Often feeds in quite deep water.

COMMON REDSHANK *Tringa totanus* 27–29 cm

(5,6) Adult non-breeding *eurhinus*: Told by combination of size, plain-looking brownish-grey upperside, whitish underside with fine dark breast-streaks, stoutish straight red bill with dark distal half, and bright red legs and feet. Sides of head greyish with neat whitish eyering, but lacks pronounced supercilium. In flight shows diagnostic white secondaries and white-tipped inner primaries. **(7) Adult breeding**: Upperparts browner with small blackish markings, head, neck and underparts more heavily dark-streaked. **(8) Juvenile**: Similar to adult breeding but has neat pale buffish spotting and spangling on upperparts and wing-coverts, more narrowly streaked breast and often more yellowish-orange legs and feet. **Other subspecies** *T.t.craggi, terrignotae, ussuriensis* (ranges unclear; only separable by minor detail in breeding plumage). **VOICE** Typical call is a plaintive *teu-hu-hu*, particularly in flight. When alarmed, gives a long mournful *tyuuuu* and rapid repetition of call. **HABITAT** Coastal wetlands, lowland marshes, large rivers.

MARSH SANDPIPER *Tringa stagnatilis* 22–25 cm

(9,10) Adult non-breeding: Resembles Common Greenshank but smaller and slimmer with distinctly thin straight blackish bill and proportionately longer legs, no bold streaks on head, neck or mantle, no obvious dark loral stripe, but shows broad white supercilium. Upperside fairly uniform greyish, blacker on lesser and median coverts, underside white, legs and feet greenish. In flight, upperside appears fairly uniform with contrasting white back to uppertail-coverts. **(11) Adult breeding**: Upperside boldly patterned with black, with distinct dark speckles and streaks on crown, neck and breast, and dark arrow-shapes extending along flanks; legs and feet often yellowish-

tinged. **Juvenile**: Like adult non-breeding but mantle to wing-coverts browner-tinged with narrow dark subterminal bars and pale buff fringes on feathers. **VOICE** Repeated plaintive mellow *keeuw* or *plew*, higher-pitched, thinner and less ringing than Common Greenshank. Loud *yip*, *yup* or *chip* (often repeated rapidly) when alarmed. **HABITAT** Various wetlands, mudflats, marshes, large rivers; lowlands.

COMMON GREENSHANK *Tringa nebularia* 30–34 cm

(12,13) Adult non-breeding: Medium-sized to largish with rather long neck, stout-based and slightly upturned greenish-grey bill with darker tip, and long greenish legs. Crown, ear-coverts, hind-neck, mantle and sides of breast prominently streaked, rest of upperside greyish with somewhat darker lesser coverts, underparts white, has distinctly dark loral stripe and lacks white supercilium behind eye. In flight appears rather uniform above, back to uppertail contrastingly white with dark bars on longer uppertail-coverts and tail, toes extending beyond tail-tip. Legs and feet greyish-green, sometimes greenish-yellow or dull yellowish, basal half of bill often tinged bluish-grey. **(14) Adult breeding**: Some scapulars have prominent blackish centres, crown, neck and breast heavily streaked and spotted blackish. **Juvenile**: Like adult non-breeding but upperside slightly browner-tinged with clear pale buff fringes, median and lesser coverts darker, neck and breast-streaks somewhat bolder. **VOICE** Distinctive flight call is a loud clear ringing *teu-teu-teu* or *chew-chew-chew*. When alarmed, utters a throaty *kiu kiu kiu* or *kyoup-kyoup-kyoup*, recalling Common Redshank, and a sharp *tchuk* or *chip*. **HABITAT** Various wetlands, mudflats, large rivers; up to 400 m.

NORDMANN'S GREENSHANK *Tringa guttifer* 29–32 cm

(15,16) Adult non-breeding: Very similar to Common but legs shorter (particularly above joint) and yellower, neck shorter, bill distinctly bi-coloured, crown, nape and sides of breast more uniform and only faintly streaked, upperside much plainer, without obvious dark markings, has more white above eye and paler lores. In flight shows all-white uppertail-coverts and rather uniform greyish tail; toes do not extend beyond tail-tip. Legs and feet yellow to greenish-yellow or brownish-yellow. **(17) Adult breeding**: Much more boldly marked, feathers of upperside largely blackish with whitish spots and spangling, head and upper neck heavily dark-streaked, with distinctive broad blackish crescentic spots on lower neck and breast and darker lores. **(18) Juvenile**: Like adult non-breeding but crown and upperparts tinged pale brown, fringes of scapulars and tertials have whitish notching, wing-covert fringes pale buff, breast has slight brown wash and faint dark streaks at sides. **VOICE** Flight call is a distinctive *kwork* or *gwaak*. **HABITAT** Mud- and sandflats, sometimes other coastal wetlands.

PLATE 38 SANDPIPERS

GREEN SANDPIPER *Tringa ochropus* 21–24 cm

(1,2) **Adult non-breeding**: Smallish and quite short-legged; crown, hindneck, sides of breast and upperparts blackish-brown with olive tinge, dull buff speckling on mantle, scapulars and wing-coverts, prominent white lores and eyering. Similar to Wood and Common. Differs from former by lack of prominent supercilium behind eye, plainer crown and hind-neck, darker upperparts, more demarcated breast-band and greener legs and feet. From latter by more blackish upperparts and lack of white spur between breast-band and shoulder. In flight, white rump and uppertail-coverts contrast very sharply with almost uniformly dark upperside, tail white with two or three broad blackish bands. Legs and feet dull greyish-green. (3) **Adult breeding**: Bold streaks on crown, neck and breast and quite distinct white speckles on upperparts and wing-coverts. **Juvenile**: Like adult non-breeding but upperparts and breast browner-tinged, with less distinct small deep buff spots on scapulars and tertials. **VOICE** Loud, sharp *klU-Uweet-wit-wit* and *tluee-tueet*, usually given in flight. Sharp *wit-wit-wit* when alarmed. **HABITAT & BEHAVIOUR** Various lowland wetlands, rarely mudflats; up to 400 m. Occasionally bobs rear end of body.

WOOD SANDPIPER *Tringa glareola* 18.5–21 cm

(4,5) **Adult non-breeding**: Told by combination of smallish size, longish straight bill, long broad whitish supercilium, dark brown upperparts with faint buffish speckles, lightly streaked foreneck and upper breast, and pale greenish-yellowish legs and feet. In flight appears quite uniform above, with contrasting darker flight feathers and white rump. (6) **Adult breeding**: Upperparts more blackish with much bolder whitish speckles and fringes; crown, neck and upper breast clearly streaked. **Juvenile**: Similar to adult non-breeding but upper-parts and wing-coverts browner with finer and denser buff speckles, has more defined streaking on foreneck and upper breast. **VOICE** Nervous *chiff-if* or *chiff-iff-iff*, particularly in flight. Sharp *chip* (often rapidly repeated) when alarmed. **HABITAT & BEHAVIOUR** Marshes, flooded rice paddies, lake margins, large rivers, rarely mudflats; up to 400 m. Gregarious.

TEREK SANDPIPER *Xenus cinereus* 22–25 cm

(7,8) **Adult non-breeding**: Smallish size, long upturned blackish bill with yellowish base, shortish orange-yellow legs. Upperside rather plain brown-ish-grey with darker median and lesser coverts, with suggestion of dark lines on scapulars; underparts white with some faint streaks on neck and breast. In flight, upperside appears rather uniform, with distinctive broad white trailing edge to secondaries (recalls Common Redshank). Legs and feet bright orange to orange-yellow, sometimes green-ish-yellow. (9) **Adult breeding**: Upperparts much clearer grey with prominent black lines on scapulars, bill all dark.

(10) **Juvenile**: Similar to adult non-breeding but upperside dark-er and browner, scapulars narrowly fringed buffish, wing-coverts finely fringed light buffish, has indistinct short blackish lines on scapulars and yellower base of bill. **VOICE** In flight utters low rip-pling trilled *du-du-du-du-du*... and shorter mellow *chu-du-du*. Sharp *tu-li* when alarmed. **HABITAT & BEHAVIOUR** Mud- and sandflats, saltpans and other coastal wetlands. Runs rather fast.

COMMON SANDPIPER *Actitis hypoleucos* 19–21 cm

(11,12) **Adult non-breeding**: Told by smallish size, medium-short straight bill, shortish legs, plain brownish upperside and white underparts with greyish-brown lateral breast-patches, separated from shoulder by prominent white 'spur'. Tail longish, extending well beyond closed wing-tips, legs and feet greyish-olive to dull yellowish-brown. In flight appears rather uniformly dark above with contrasting long white wing-bar across greater covert tips and middle of inner primar-ies. See much smaller Temminck's Stint. (13) **Adult breeding**: Upperparts slightly glossy greenish-brown with faint dark streaks and dark bars on larger feathers, lateral breast-patches browner with dark streaks, almost meeting across upper breast. (14) **Juvenile**: Like adult non-breeding but upperparts narrowly fringed buff with some darker subterminal markings, wing-coverts with prominent buff tips and subdued dark barring. **VOICE** Call is a high-pitched plaintive ringing *tsee-wee-wee*... or *swee-swee-swee*..., mainly given in flight. Sometimes gives sin-gle *sweet* or longer *sweeee-eet* when alarmed. Song is an excited, rising, repeated *kittie-needie* (often given on winter-ing grounds). **HABITAT & BEHAVIOUR** Various wetlands, mudflats, tidal creeks, coastal rocks, lakes, rivers; up to 800 m. Often 'bobs' rear end of body. Flies with short flicking wingbeats.

GREY-TAILED TATTLER *Heteroscelus brevipes* 24–27 cm

(15,16) **Adult non-breeding**: Resembles some larger *Tringa* sandpipers but upperside uniform grey, sides of head and upper breast rather plain pale grey, with prominent white supercilium (extending behind eye), rather stout straight bill with yellowish basal half, shortish yellow legs. Throat and rest of underparts unmarked white. In flight, com-pletely grey upperside with somewhat darker outer wing distinc-tive. (17) **Adult breeding**: Ear-coverts, sides of throat and neck finely streaked grey, breast and upper flanks scaled grey, chang-ing to more V-shaped markings on lower flanks, base of bill duller. **Juvenile**: Like adult non-breeding but upperparts and wing-coverts have neat whitish spots and fringes; outer fringes of tail feathers notched white. **VOICE** Plaintive *tu-weet* or *tu-whip* (sometimes repeated), usually given in flight. Alarm calls are more hurried *tu-wiwi*, *twi-wi* and *twiwiwi*. **HABITAT & BEHAVIOUR** Reefs, rocky shores, mud- and sandflats, sometimes saltpans and prawn ponds, rarely inland rivers. Gait recalls Com-mon Sandpiper. Occasionally gregarious.

PLATE 39 SANDPIPERS & RUFF

RUDDY TURNSTONE *Arenaria interpres* 21–24 cm

(1,2) **Adult non-breeding** *interpres*: Smallish and robust with short stout blackish bill, short orange-red legs and feet and complex blackish pattern on sides of head and breast. Head mostly dark brown with paler lores/cheeks and supercilium, upperside mixed dark brown, blackish and dull rufous-chestnut, remainder of underparts white. (3) **Male breeding**: Head crisply patterned black and white, upperparts boldly marked blackish and orange-chestnut. (4) **Female breeding**: Head pattern duller than male, crown more streaked and washed brown, upperpart pattern less clear-cut. (5) **Juvenile**: Resembles adult non-breeding but has reduced dark pattern on sides of head and breast, whitish submoustachial stripe, broad buffish to buffish-white fringing on upperparts and wing-coverts, and somewhat duller legs and feet. **VOICE** Usual call is a rapid rattling *tuk tuk-i-tuk-tuk*, *trik-tuk-tuk-tuk* or *tuk-e-tuk*. Utters low *tuk* notes when foraging and sharp *chik-ik* and *kuu* or *teu* when flushed or alarmed. **HABITAT & BEHAVIOUR** Mud- and sandflats, beaches, saltpans and other coastal wetlands. Turns over seaweed and small stones and digs holes in search of food; also scavenges. Walks with distinctive rolling gait.

GREAT KNOT *Calidris tenuirostris* 26–28 cm

(6,7) **Adult non-breeding**: Told by combination of medium size, rather attenuated shape with longish, broad-based, slightly downward-tapering blackish bill and shortish dark legs, grey upperside with dark shaft-streaks, rather nondescript pale greyish head, neck and upper breast, with darker streaks and grey to black spots on sides of breast and upper flanks. Has indistinct white supercilium and white throat, belly and vent. In flight, upperside appears rather uniform but with blacker primary coverts, white uppertail-coverts contrasting with dark tail, underwing-coverts mostly white. (8) **Adult breeding**: Upperside boldly marked with black, scapulars bright chestnut with black markings, head and neck have bold black streaks, and breast and flanks show dense black spots (centre of breast may be solidly black). (9) **Juvenile**: Similar to adult non-breeding but crown to mantle more prominently streaked blackish, scapulars blackish-brown with whitish to buffish-white fringes, wing-coverts with blackish arrow-shaped markings and broad whitish to whitish-buff fringes, breast washed buffish and more distinctly dark-spotted. **VOICE** In flight may give muffled *knut* or *nyut* notes and a harsher *chak-chuka-chak* and *chaka-ruk-chak* when flushed or alarmed. **HABITAT & BEHAVIOUR** Mud- and sandflats, sometimes coastal pools and saltpans. Feeds mainly by probing. Gregarious.

RED KNOT *Calidris canutus* 23–25 cm

(10,11) **Adult non-breeding** *canutus*: Similar to Great but smaller and more compact with relatively larger head and shorter neck, shorter, straighter bill, usually more distinct dark loral stripe, better defined whitish supercilium, more uniformly grey upperside, no black spots on underparts and usually smaller, more V-shaped flank markings. In flight shows uniform dark scales/bars on rump and uppertail-coverts, greyer tail, and less white on underwing-coverts. Legs and feet dull olive-green. (12) **Adult breeding**: crown, nape and mantle boldly streaked blackish, scapulars boldly patterned blackish and chestnut, face and underparts deep reddish-chestnut, vent whiter with dark markings. Note size and shortish bill and legs. (13) **Adult post-breeding**: Largely blackish scapulars; moults to non-breeding plumage head first. (14) **Juvenile**: Similar to adult non-breeding but mantle, scapulars and wing-coverts browner with prominent buffish-white fringes and dark subterminal markings, breast and flanks washed buff and finely dark-streaked. **VOICE** When foraging and in flight, may give occasional soft nasal *knut* or *wutt* notes. Sudden *kikkik* when flushed or alarmed. **HABITAT & BEHAVIOUR** Mostly mud- and sandflats. Feeds by probing but also picks from surface. Gregarious.

RUFF *Philomachus pugnax* Male 29–32 cm, female 22–26 cm

(15) **Male non-breeding**: Told by combination of size, rather hunch-backed and pot-bellied appearance, longish neck, relatively small head, shortish, slightly drooping bill, and longish, usually orange to yellowish legs. Plumage rather variable. Crown and upperside greyish-brown with pale buff to whitish fringes, underside mainly whitish with greyish wash and mottling on foreneck and upper breast, no obvious supercilium but whiter face. In flight shows broad-based wings and shortish tail, toes project beyond tail-tip, upperside rather nondescript with broad white sides to lower rump and uppertail-coverts and narrowish white wing-bar. Legs and feet pinkish-red or orange-red to dull yellowish or dull greenish). (16) **Male breeding**: In full plumage, attains remarkable long head-, neck- and breast-plumes (forming broad loose 'ruff'), varying in colour from black or white to rufous-chestnut, with or without bars and streaks. Has greenish or yellowish to reddish naked, warty facial skin, usually mostly pinkish bill and typically orange to reddish-orange legs and feet. (17) **Male breeding/non-breeding (transitional)**: Face feathered, bill bicoloured, patchy plumage. (18) **Female non-breeding**: Notably smaller than male. In flight both sexes show broad-based wings, broad white sides to rump, narrowish white wing-bar, toes projecting beyond short tail. (19) **Female breeding**: Lacks plumes and ruff. Rather nondescript greyish-brown with whiter face, blackish markings on centres of upperparts and wing-coverts, and variable bold blackish markings on neck and breast; belly and vent whitish. (20) **Juvenile male**: Upperside like breeding female but with simpler warm buff to whitish fringing; head-sides to breast rather uniform buff, legs and feet dull yellowish-brown to dull greenish. (21) **Juvenile female**: Usually darker buff on neck and breast than juvenile male, and smaller. **VOICE** Often silent but may give occasional low *kuk* or *wek* notes in flight. **HABITAT & BEHAVIOUR** Marshes, grassy areas, rice paddies, coastal pools, rarely mudflats; lowlands. Feeds mostly by surface pecking but often wades in fairly deep water.

PLATE 40 SMALL SANDPIPERS

SANDERLING *Calidris alba* 18–21 cm

(1,2) **Adult non-breeding**: Told by combination of smallish size, shortish straight black bill, pale grey ear-coverts and upperside and snowy-white underside. Often shows contrasting dark area at bend of wings; legs and feet blackish, lacks hind toe. In flight shows very prominent broad white bar across upperwing. (3) **Adult breeding**: Brighter individuals are very similar to Red-necked Stint but larger, with dark streaks on somewhat duller, more chestnut sides of head, throat and breast (including lower breast-sides), mostly chestnut centres of scapulars and no hind toe. In flight shows much broader white wing-bar. (4) **Adult breeding variant**: Duller (fresh) bird, with faint rufous/chestnut on head/breast, more contrasting breast markings. (5) **Juvenile**: Similar to adult non-breeding but has darker streaks on crown and hindneck, blackish mantle and scapulars, boldly patterned with buffish-white and buff-washed breast with dark streaks at sides. **VOICE** Typical flight call is a quiet liquid *klit* or *twik* (often repeated), sometimes extending to short trill. **HABITAT & BEHAVIOUR** Sand- and mudflats, beaches, sometimes saltpans, large rivers. Feeds by rapid probing and pecking, runs very fast.

SPOON-BILLED SANDPIPER *Calidris pygmeus* 14–16 cm

(6,7) **Adult non-breeding**: Resembles Red-necked and Little Stints but has diagnostic spatulate-shaped bill (less obvious in profile). Also has somewhat bigger head, whiter forehead and breast and broader white supercilium. (8) **Adult breeding**: Apart from bill, like Red-necked Stint but scapulars more uniformly fringed rufous-buff. (9) **Juvenile**: Very similar to Red-necked and Little Stints (apart from bill) but has whiter forehead/face, somewhat darker, more contrasting lores/ear-coverts, more uniform buff/buffish-white fringes to mantle and scapulars. **VOICE** Quiet rolling *preep* and shrill *wheet*, usually in flight. **HABITAT & BEHAVIOUR** Mud- and sandflats, sometimes sandy beaches, saltpans, prawn ponds. Often stands more upright than Red-necked Stint. Feeds in shallow water and on wet mud, either sweeping bill from side to side or patting surface with bill.

LITTLE STINT *Calidris minuta* 14–15.5 cm

(10,11) **Adult non-breeding**: Very similar to Red-necked. At close range, looks slightly slimmer and longer-legged with somewhat finer, often slightly drooping bill, with broader dark centres to feathers of upperparts, grey areas of head and breast usually more streaked, sometimes a more diffuse, greyish breast-band. Legs and feet blackish. (12) **Adult breeding**: Very similar to Red-necked. At close range, appears slightly slimmer and longer-legged with somewhat finer, often slightly drooping bill, with broader dark centres to feathers of upperparts, grey areas of head and breast usually more streaked, sometimes a more diffuse, greyish breast-band. Legs and feet blackish. (13) **Juvenile**: From Red-necked, on average, by more contrastingly patterned head, darker-centred and more rufous-edged upperpart feathers (especially lower scapulars, tertials and wing-coverts) and more coarsely streaked breast-sides. Recalls Long-toed but has less contrasting head pattern, much less heavily streaked neck and breast, shorter neck, and dark legs and feet. **VOICE** In flight may give sharp staccato *kip* or *tit* notes, sometimes extending to short trill. **HABITAT & BEHAVIOUR** Saltpans, prawn ponds, mudflats, large rivers. Feeding action similar to Red-necked.

RED-NECKED STINT *Calidris ruficollis* 14–16 cm

(14,15) **Adult non-breeding**: Small; shortish straight black bill, uniform greyish above with dark shaft-streaks, white below, fairly distinct greyish lateral breast-patches with slight dark streaks. Supercilium white, legs/feet blackish. (16) **Adult breeding**: Cheeks/ear-coverts, lower throat and centre of upper breast plain rufous/brick-red, supercilium whitish to brick-red, face whiter around bill-base, mantle/scapulars with blackish central markings and rufous to brick-red fringes, tertials/wing-coverts mostly fringed greyish-white, breast-sides usually whitish with dark streaks. (17) **Adult pre-breeding**: In fresh plumage, little rufous/chestnut on head/breast, greyer mantle/scapular fringes. (18) **Juvenile**: Darker above than adult non-breeding, mantle and upper scapulars blackish with pale warm fringes, lower scapulars grey with dark subterminal markings and whitish fringes, tertials grey with whitish to buffish fringes, wing-coverts edged whitish, breast-sides washed pinkish-grey and faintly streaked; sometimes shows faint whitish mantle-lines, rarely shows obvious 'split supercilium'. **VOICE** Flight call is thin *kreep* or *creek*. Sometimes shorter *krep*, *kiep* or *klyt* or short trill in alarm. **HABITAT & BEHAVIOUR** Coastal pools, mud- and sandflats, also large rivers, other inland wetlands; up to 400 m. Feeds with rapid pecking action, sometimes probes.

TEMMINCK'S STINT *Calidris temminckii* 13.5–15 cm

(19,20) **Adult non-breeding**: From other stints by attenuated shape with rather long tail (often projects slightly beyond closed wings), relatively uniform cold greyish-brown upperside, plain-looking, drab brownish-grey ear-coverts and breast (can be slightly paler in centre), greenish-yellow to yellow or yellowish-brown legs and feet. Resembles miniature Common Sandpiper. In flight shows distinctive white tail-sides. Legs and feet greenish- to brownish-yellow. (21) **Adult breeding**: More dull olive-brown above, with irregular blackish feather-centres and rufous fringes on mantle and scapulars, head-sides/breast washed brown, indistinct darker streaks on head-sides and neck/breast. (22) **Juvenile**: Similar to adult non-breeding but mantle, scapulars and wing-coverts browner with narrow buff fringes and blackish subterminal markings, sides of head and breast washed buffish. **VOICE** In flight utters distinctive rapid stuttering *tirrr* (often repeated) or longer *tirrr'r'r* or *trrrrrit*. **HABITAT** Muddy freshwater wetlands and rice paddies, large rivers, saltpans, prawn ponds, rarely mudflats; up to 400 m.

LONG-TOED STINT *Calidris subminuta* 14–16 cm

(23,24) **Adult non-breeding**: Resembles Red-necked and Little but longer-necked, bill finer with pale-based lower mandible, browner above with larger dark feather-centres, neck-sides/breast washed brown and distinctly streaked darker, legs/feet yellowish-brown to greenish (may be pale orange-yellow) with distinctly longer toes. (25) **Adult breeding**: Crown rufous with dark streaks, upperparts and tertials broadly fringed rufous, neck-sides and breast washed creamy-buff and very distinctly dark-streaked (breast may be slightly paler in centre). (26) **Juvenile**: Like adult breeding but has prominent white mantle-lines, greyer lower scapulars. **VOICE** In flight gives soft liquid *kurrrip* or *chirrup* and shorter *prit*. **HABITAT & BEHAVIOUR** Marshes, wet rice paddies, coastal pools, rarely mudflats; lowlands. When alarmed may stand erect with neck stretched up.

PLATE 41 SMALLER SANDPIPERS & RED-NECKED PHALAROPE

SHARP-TAILED SANDPIPER *Calidris acuminata* 19–21 cm

(1,2) **Adult non-breeding**: Distinguished by size, medium-length, slightly down-tapering dark bill, rich dark brown crown, prominent whitish supercilium, dull foreneck and breast with diffuse dark streaks, and dull greenish to yellowish legs and feet. Has fairly prominent pale eyering, upperparts rather nondescript, mostly dull greyish-brown with pale buffish to whitish fringes. Recalls much smaller Long-toed Stint. (3) **Adult breeding**: Crown distinctly rufous with dark streaks, mantle and scapulars blackish-brown with mostly bright rufous fringes, streaks on neck and upper breast more distinct, bold dark brown arrowhead markings on lower breast, upper belly and flanks. (4) **Juvenile**: Resembles breeding adult but supercilium and throat plainer and whiter, neck-sides and breast rich buff with little dark streaking, rest of underparts unmarked white. **VOICE** Flight call is a soft *ueep* or *wheep* (often repeated). Also gives a twittering *teet-teet-trrt-trrt* or *prtt-wheet-wheet*. **HABITAT & BEHAVIOUR** Marshes, fish ponds, mudflats. Often feeds on drier margins of wet habitats.

DUNLIN *Calidris alpina* 17–21 cm

(5,6) **Adult non-breeding** *sakhalina*: Like Curlew Sandpiper but somewhat shorter-necked and shorter-legged, bill slightly shorter and less strongly downcurved, supercilium less distinct, foreneck and upper breast duller with fine streaks. In flight shows dark centre to rump and uppertail-coverts. Also resembles Broad-billed Sandpiper but slightly larger and less elongated, legs relatively longer and always blackish, bill slightly narrower and more gently downcurved (not distinctly kinked at tip), never shows obvious 'split supercilium', wing-coverts more uniform. (7) **Male breeding**: Large black belly-patch, neck and breast whitish with distinct dark streaks, supercilium whitish, mantle and scapulars mostly bright rufous-chestnut with some black subterminal markings and whitish fringes. (8) **Juvenile**: Mantle and scapulars blackish with rufous, buff and whitish fringing, wing-coverts neatly fringed buff, head-sides, neck and upper breast washed buffish-brown, has extensive blackish streaks on hindneck, breast and belly. **VOICE** Flight call is a characteristic harsh *treeep* or *kreee*. Utters soft twittering notes when foraging. **HABITAT & BEHAVIOUR** Mudflats, saltpans, prawn ponds, large rivers; up to 400 m. Feeding action similar to Curlew Sandpiper.

CURLEW SANDPIPER *Calidris ferruginea* 19–21.5 cm

(9,10) **Adult non-breeding**: Distinguished by size, relatively long downcurved blackish bill, fairly long blackish legs, rather plain greyish upperside, prominent white supercilium and white underparts with indistinct streaky greyish wash on breast. In flight, upperside appears rather uniform with narrow white bar along tips of primary and greater coverts and distinctive white band on lower rump and uppertail-coverts. (11) **Female breeding**: Head/underparts deep reddish-chestnut, with dark crown-streaks, whitish facial markings, scaling on breast/belly and largely white vent; mantle/scapulars boldly patterned chestnut, black and whitish. (12) **Juvenile**: Like non-breeding adult but upperparts browner with buff-and-dark scaly pattern, head and breast washed peachy-buff and faintly dark-streaked. **Male breeding**: Slightly deeper reddish-chestnut

below than female with fewer whitish scales. **Juvenile**: Like adult non-breeding but browner above with neat pale buff fringes and dark subterminal markings, head-sides and breast washed pale peachy-buff and faintly dark-streaked. **VOICE** Flight call is a distinctive rippling *kirrip* or *prrriit*. **HABITAT & BEHAVIOUR** Mud- and sandflats, coastal pools, large rivers; lowlands. Feeds by pecking and vigorous probing, often in deeper water than Dunlin.

BROAD-BILLED SANDPIPER *Limicola falcinellus* 16–18 cm

(13,14) **Adult non-breeding** *sibirica*: Resembles some stints but larger, bill longer and noticeably kinked downwards at tip. Upperside rather uniform grey with dark streaks and somewhat darker lesser coverts, has prominent white supercilium, typically shows narrow white lateral crown-streak ('split supercilium'), underside crisp white with narrow dark streaks on breast (mostly at sides). In flight shows dark leading edge to upperwing-coverts. Smaller and much shorter-legged than Dunlin and Curlew Sandpiper. (15) **Adult breeding**: Fresh plumage (May). Crown blackish, offsetting white 'split supercilium', ear-coverts tinged pinkish-brown, upperparts and wing-coverts blackish with rufous to pale chestnut and whitish fringes, prominent lengthwise white lines along edge of mantle and scapulars, and boldly dark-streaked neck and breast. When worn, upperparts may appear largely blackish, neck and breast washed pinkish-brown and even more densely streaked. (16) **Juvenile**: Similar to adult breeding (fresh) but white mantle-lines more prominent, wing-coverts broadly fringed buff. **VOICE** In flight gives a dry trilled *trrreet* or *chrrreeit* and shorter *trett*. **HABITAT & BEHAVIOUR** Mud- and sandflats, saltpans, coastal pools. Feeding action similar to Dunlin and Curlew Sandpiper; slower than that of stints.

RED-NECKED PHALAROPE *Phalaropus lobatus* 17–19 cm

(17,18) **Adult non-breeding**: Small size, needle-like blackish bill, isolated blackish mask, mostly grey upperparts and mostly white underparts diagnostic. Has indistinct long whitish mantle-lines, whitish fringes to scapulars and wing-coverts, grey-washed breast-sides and grey streaks on flanks. In flight, upperwing appears rather blackish with contrasting narrow white band along tips of greater coverts and primary coverts. (19) **Female breeding**: Striking. Head, neck and upper breast slate-grey with broad rufous-chestnut band running from behind ear-coverts to upper foreneck. Face blackish, small mark over eye and throat white, upperparts blackish-slate with broad warm buff lines bordering mantle and scapulars. (20) **Male breeding**: Similarly patterned to female breeding but duller and more washed out. (21) **Juvenile**: Similar to adult non-breeding but crown and upperparts blackish, with broad rufous-buff mantle-lines and rufous to buff fringes to scapulars; neck-sides and upper breast washed vinous-pinkish, dark streaks on neck and breast-sides. **First winter**: Like adult non-breeding but has blacker crown, upperparts and wing-coverts, with only a few grey feathers. **VOICE** In flight may give a short sharp *kip* or *twick*, harsher *cherp* or squeaky *kirrik* or *kerrek*. **HABITAT & BEHAVIOUR** Open sea, coastal pools, sometimes mudflats, rarely inland rivers and pools; up to 400 m. Habitually swims, often spinning around; also wades when feeding. Normally gregarious.

PLATE 42 THICK-KNEES, BLACK-WINGED STILT, PIED AVOCET & CRAB-PLOVER

EURASIAN THICK-KNEE *Burhinus oedicnemus* 40–44 cm

(1,2) **Adult** *indicus*: From other thick-knees by smaller size, much smaller bill, streaked upperparts, neck and breast, and lack of prominent black head markings. Upperparts and scapulars pale sandy-brown, with blackish and white bands along smaller wing-coverts and mostly grey greater coverts. In flight shows blackish secondaries and primaries, latter with relatively small white patches. (3) **Juvenile**: Scapulars, inner wing-coverts and tertials fringed rufous-buff, with less obvious dark bars along wing-coverts and whiter tips to greater coverts. **VOICE** Territorial call consists of slurred whistles: *kiki-week* and *kiweek* etc., which build in pitch and volume to loud series of clear *kur-lee* phrases before dying away again. Otherwise gives loud, haunting, rising *kur-lee* and more churring *churrrrreee*. Normally calls at dusk and during night. **HABITAT & BEHAVIOUR** Dry barren areas, semi-desert, sand-dunes, scrub, riverine sandbanks; lowlands. Mostly crepuscular and nocturnal. Rests in shade during daytime.

GREAT THICK-KNEE *Esacus recurvirostris* 49–54 cm

(4,5) **Adult**: Quite large with long legs and longish, thick, slightly upturned black bill with yellow base. Forehead white, crown and upperparts pale sandy-greyish, head-sides and throat white with sharply contrasting black lateral crown-stripe, ear-coverts and submoustachial patch, rest of underparts whitish with brownish wash on foreneck and upper breast, and buff-washed undertail-coverts. Has narrow blackish and whitish bands along lesser coverts. In flight, upperwing shows contrasting, mostly grey greater coverts, mostly black secondaries, black primaries with large white patches, underwing mostly white with black-tipped flight feathers and primary coverts. **Juvenile**: Initially has buffish fringes and spots on upperparts. **VOICE** Territorial call is a series of wailing whistles with rising inflection: *kree-kree-kree kre-kre-kre-kre-kre*... etc. Gives a loud harsh *see-eek* when alarmed. **HABITAT & BEHAVIOUR** Shingle and sandbanks along large rivers, sand-dunes, dry lake shores, sometimes coastal mud- and sandflats, saltpans; lowlands. Mainly crepuscular and nocturnal.

BEACH THICK-KNEE *Esacus neglectus* 53–57 cm

(6,7) **Adult**: Similar to Great but slightly larger, bill bulkier with less upcurved upper mandible, crown and nape blackish, forehead and lores black, upper lesser coverts blacker. In flight, upperwing shows mostly grey secondaries and mostly white inner primaries, underwing all white, apart from black-tipped secondaries and outer primaries. **Juvenile**: Upperparts slightly paler with buffy fringes, duller bands along upper lesser coverts, median and greater coverts grey-brown with narrow buffish-white fringes and faint dark subterminal markings. **VOICE** Territorial call is a repeated harsh wailing *wee-loo*. Other

calls include an occasional rising *quip-ip-ip* and weak *quip* or *peep* when alarmed. **HABITAT & BEHAVIOUR** Undisturbed sandy beaches and sandflats, often near mangroves. Mostly crepuscular and nocturnal.

BLACK-WINGED STILT *Himantopus himantopus* 35–40 cm

(8,9) **Adult non-breeding** *himantopus*: Black and white plumage, slim build, medium-long needle-like blackish bill and very long pinkish-red legs diagnostic. Mostly white with grey cap and hindneck, black ear-coverts and black upper mantle, scapulars and wings. (10) **Male breeding**: Head and neck typically all white. Can have variable amounts of grey and black on head and hindneck. (11) **Female breeding**: Like male but mantle and scapulars browner. (12) **Juvenile**: Crown and hindneck brownish-grey, upperparts and wing-coverts greyish-brown with buffish fringes. **VOICE** Typically utters sharp nasal *kek* and yelping *ke-yak*. Monotonous high-pitched *kik-kik-kik-kik*... when alarmed. **HABITAT & BEHAVIOUR** Borders of open wetlands, saltpans, coastal pools, large rivers; up to 800 m. Gregarious.

PIED AVOCET *Recurvirostra avosetta* 42–45 cm

(13,14) **Male**: Black and white plumage, long, narrow, strongly upturned blackish bill and long bluish-grey legs diagnostic. Predominantly white with black face, crown and upper hindneck and mostly black scapulars, median and lesser coverts and primaries. (15) **Juvenile**: Dark parts of plumage obscured with dull brown, white of mantle and scapulars mottled pale greyish-brown. **Female**: Bill shorter and more strongly upturned than in male. **VOICE** Clear melodious liquid *kluit*, often repeated. Harsher, more emphatic *kloo-eet* and shrill *krrree-yu* when alarmed. **HABITAT & BEHAVIOUR** Coastal pools, mud- and sandflats, lakes, large rivers; lowlands. Usually feeds in shallow water.

CRAB-PLOVER *Dromas ardeola* 38–41 cm

(16,17) **Adult**: Very distinctive. Medium-sized to largish; bill very thick, pointed and blackish, legs long and bluish-grey, plumage predominantly white with contrasting black mantle and scapulars and mostly black upperside of primaries, primary coverts, secondaries and outer greater coverts. Sometimes has blackish speckles on hindcrown and nape. (18) **Juvenile**: Hindcrown and nape more heavily speckled blackish, upperparts mostly greyish with paler brownish-grey scapulars and wing-coverts, dark of upperwing greyer. **VOICE** Flight call is a nasal yappy *kirruc*. Also gives a repeated barking *ka* or *ka-how* and *kwerk-kwerk-kwerk-kwerk*... A sharp whistled *kew-ki-ki* and *ki-tewk* also recorded from breeding grounds. **HABITAT & BEHAVIOUR** Undisturbed sandy beaches, dunes, mud- and sandflats. Mainly a crepuscular and nocturnal feeder. Likely to be found in family parties or small flocks.

PLATE 43 SMALLER PLOVERS & PRATINCOLES

COMMON RINGED PLOVER *Charadrius hiaticula* 18–20 cm

(1,2) **Adult non-breeding** *tundrae*: Like Little Ringed but slightly larger/more robust, breast-band broader and less even, base of lower mandible dull orange, legs/feet orange. In flight shows prominent white upperwing-bar. (3) **Male breeding**: From Little Ringed by orange bill with black tip, orange legs and feet and broader, less even black breast-band, with no obvious eyering or white band across midcrown. (4) **Juvenile**: Like adult non-breeding but breast-band narrower, has buffish fringes and narrow dark subterminal markings above, bill all dark, legs/feet duller, more yellowish. From Little Ringed by size and proportions, colder-toned upperside, whiter forehead and supercilium, lack of obvious eyering, often more orange-tinged legs/feet, and white wing-bar. **Female breeding**: Like male but ear-coverts and breast-band brownish-black. **VOICE** Mellow rising ***too-lee***, usually given in flight. Also a short ***wip*** and, when alarmed, soft low ***too-weep***. **HABITAT & BEHAVIOUR** Mud- and sandflats, saltpans, coastal pools, large rivers; up to 400 m. Feeding action and wingbeats slightly slower than Little Ringed.

LONG-BILLED PLOVER *Charadrius placidus* 19–21 cm

(5,6) **Adult non-breeding**: Recalls Little Ringed but larger and even more slender and attenuated in shape; has longer bill, broader dark band across forecrown, broader buff supercilium and narrower, more even breast-band. Bill blackish with some dull yellow at base of lower mandible, legs and feet pinkish-yellow. In flight, upperwing shows narrow white central bar, narrow white trailing edge to secondaries, greyish area on outer secondaries and inner primaries (forming faint panel) and more contrasting blackish primary coverts. (7) **Adult breeding**: Has white forehead and supercilium, broad black band across forecrown and narrow even black breast-band. Lacks black lores and ear-coverts of Little Ringed and has less prominent eyering. (8) **Juvenile**: Initially differs from adult by neat warm buff fringes above, no dark band across midcrown, more buffish supercilium and greyish-brown breast-band. Likely to resemble adult non-breeding once it reaches the region. **VOICE** Clear rising ***piwee*** or ***piwii-piwii-piwii***... and musical ***tudulu***. **HABITAT** Larger rivers, dry fields, rarely mud- and sandflats, beaches; up to 400 m.

LITTLE RINGED PLOVER *Charadrius dubius* 14–17 cm

(9,10) **Adult non-breeding** *jerdoni*: From other small plovers by rather dainty proportions, small-headed appearance, rather attenuated rear end, slender dark bill, pinkish to yellowish legs/feet, white collar, complete breast-band (may be slightly broken in centre) and uniform upperwing (in flight). Rest of head and upperside greyish-brown, apart from buffish-white forehead and indistinct supercilium; has narrow pale yellowish eyering. (11) **Male breeding**: Lores, ear-coverts and breast-band black, forehead and supercilium white; prominent black band across forecrown, backed by distinctive narrow white band and pronounced broad yellow eyering. (12) **Juvenile**: Like adult non-breeding but upperside somewhat sandier-brown with warm buff fringes and indistinct darker subterminal markings, breast-band browner and restricted more to lateral patches, supercilium more buffish. **Female breeding**: Eyering narrower, ear-coverts/breast-band browner. **Other subspecies** *C.d.curonicus* (wintering race). **VOICE** Territorial call is a repeated harsh ***cree-ah*** (often dur-

ing display flight). Typical call is a plaintive ***pee-oo*** (***pee*** stressed). Also, shorter ***peeu*** and rapid ***pip-pip-pip-pip***... in alarm. **HABITAT & BEHAVIOUR** Large rivers, lakes, marshes, rice fields, coastal pools; up to 800 m. Display involves gliding with wings raised in V and (on ground) puffing-out of breast, tail-fanning and prancing.

ORIENTAL PLOVER *Charadrius veredus* 22–25 cm

(13–15) **Adult non-breeding**: Recalls sand plovers but larger and slimmer-looking with longer neck, legs and wings and slenderer bill, typically also longer and more pronounced supercilium and buffish-brown upper breast. When fresh, upperparts and wing-coverts have narrow rufous to warm buff fringes. Legs and feet yellow to orange (tinged pinkish to greenish). In flight shows distinctive, very long, all-dark wings with paler upperwing-coverts. (16) **Male breeding**: Mostly whitish head/neck, rufous-chestnut breast-band with broad black lower border. (17) **Female breeding**: Like adult non-breeding but upper breast with rufescent wash. (18) **Juvenile**: Like fresh adult non-breeding but has more pronounced and paler buff fringing on upperparts and wing-coverts. **VOICE** Occasional sharp whistled ***chip-chip-chip***, short piping ***klink*** and various trilled notes. **HABITAT & BEHAVIOUR** Dry mud near water, short grassy areas, sometimes saltpans, mud-/sandflats; lowlands. Runs very fast, flight fast, high and rather erratic.

ORIENTAL PRATINCOLE *Glareola maldivarum* 23–24 cm

(19–21) **Adult breeding**: Graceful, rather tern-like, short bill, long pointed wings, short forked tail. Crown and upperparts uniform warmish grey-brown, neck/breast paler and more buffish, lores blackish, throat and upper foreneck buff with narrow black border, prominent red base to lower mandible. In flight, looks uniform above with sharply contrasting white rump/uppertail-coverts, underwing blackish-brown with mostly chestnut coverts. (22) **Adult non-breeding**: Duller neck, breast and throat, paler lores, broken throat-border, less red on bill. (23) **Juvenile**: Similar to non-breeding adult but crown and upperside greyish-brown with prominent whitish to buff fringes and blackish subterminal markings, throat paler, neck-sides and breast streaked/mottled greyish-brown, bill all dark. **VOICE** A sharp tern-like ***kyik*** or ***kyeck***, ***chik-chik*** and ***chet*** etc., usually in flight. Also a loud ***cherr*** and rising ***trooeet***. **HABITAT** Marshes, large rivers, lakes, dry rice paddies and open country, coastal pools; up to 800 m.

SMALL PRATINCOLE *Glareola lactea* 16–19 cm

(24–26) **Adult breeding**: Easily told from Oriental by smaller size, much paler/greyer upperside, paler throat without dark border, pale buffish-grey breast. Lores black. In flight, shows broad white band across secondaries and inner primaries, black trailing edge to secondaries, tail almost square-cut with broad black terminal band. (27) **Adult non-breeding**: Lores paler, throat faintly streaked. (28) **Juvenile**: Similar to adult non-breeding but chin white, lower throat bordered by brownish spots/streaks, upperparts/wing-coverts with indistinct buffish fringes and brownish subterminal bars, tail tipped buffish-brown. **VOICE** In flight gives a high-pitched ***prrip*** or ***tiririt***. Also a short ***tuck-tuck-tuck***... **HABITAT & BEHAVIOUR** Large rivers, dry margins of lakes and marshes, rarely coastal pools and sandy areas; up to 400 m. Highly gregarious.

PLATE 44 SMALLER PLOVERS

KENTISH PLOVER *Charadrius alexandrinus* 15–17.5 cm

(1,2) **Adult non-breeding** *dealbatus*: From other small plovers by combination of plain upperside, white nuchal collar, and well-defined and rather narrow dark lateral breast-patches. Bill blackish, legs rather long, bluish-grey to greyish, sometimes distinctly olive or pinkish. In flight shows obvious white bar across upperwing and white outertail feathers. (3,4) **Adult non-breeding**: Worn, faded individuals can be very pale and greyish above ('bleached'). (5) **Male breeding**: White forehead and short supercilium, black patch on midcrown, strongly rufous-washed remainder of crown and nape, broad blackish eyestripe, well-defined narrow black lateral breast-patches. (6) **Male breeding variant**: Less well marked. (7) **Female breeding**: Usually has little or no rufous on crown and nape, may lack black on head and breast markings shown by male (more like adult non-breeding). (8) **Juvenile**: Like adult non-breeding but somewhat paler-headed, forehead and supercilium washed buff, upperparts and wing-coverts neatly fringed buff, lateral breast-patches somewhat paler and more diffuse. **Other subspecies** *C.a.alexandrinus* (visitor NW): Always shows dark greyish legs and feet. **VOICE** In flight may utter soft *pit* or *pi* notes and hard trilled *prrr* or *prrrtut*, harsher than similar call of Lesser Sand. Plaintive *too-eet* or *pweep* when alarmed. During display flight, utters repeated sharp rattling *tjekke-tjekke-tjekke*... **HABITAT & BEHAVIOUR** Beaches, sand- and mudflats, coastal pools, large rivers, dry lake margins; up to 400 m. In breeding season male performs stiff-winged display flights with body tilting from side to side. Pair displays include wing- and tail-spreading.

MALAYSIAN PLOVER *Charadrius peronii* 14–16 cm

(9) **Male**: Similar to breeding male Kentish Plover but slightly smaller and shorter-billed, upperparts and wing-coverts with prominent pale fringes (appear scaly or mottled), narrower black lateral breast-patches which extend in complete band below white nuchal collar; legs and feet often tinged yellowish or pinkish. (10,11) **Female**: Lacks black markings. From Kentish by rufous-washed ear-coverts and lateral breast-patches and scaly upperparts; crown always washed rufous. (12) **Juvenile**: Slightly duller than female. **VOICE** Soft *whit* or *twik*, recalling Kentish. **HABITAT & BEHAVIOUR** Undisturbed sandy, coralline and shelly beaches, sometimes nearby mudflats. Usually encountered in pairs.

LESSER SAND PLOVER *Charadrius mongolus* 19–21 cm

(13,14) **Adult non-breeding** *schaeferi*: From other small plovers (except Greater Sand) by broad lateral breast-patches and lack of white nuchal collar. Upperside sandy greyish-brown with whitish forehead and supercilium. Best separated from Greater by combination of following subtle features: smaller size, neater proportions, rounder head, shorter and blunter-tipped bill (length roughly equal to distance from base of bill to rear of eye), tibia obviously shorter than tarsus, dark grey to greenish-grey legs and feet, toes only projecting slightly beyond tail-tip in flight. Bill length varies from longest in this subspecies to shortest in *C.m.mongolus*. (15) **Male breeding**: Distinctive, with black forehead, lores and ear-coverts and deep orange-rufous sides of neck and broad breast-band. May show very small whitish markings on sides of forehead. (16) **Female breeding**: Much duller, with less orange-rufous on neck and breast and browner forehead and mask. (17) **Juvenile**: Like adult non-breeding but upperparts and wing-coverts fringed buffish, supercilium washed buff and often less pronounced, lateral breast-patches mixed with buffish. (18) **Adult non-breeding** *mongolus* (?recorded): Bill smaller. (19) **Male breeding**: White forehead, bisected by vertical black line, narrow blackish upper border to breast-band. **VOICE** In flight, rather short sharp hard *kruit* or *drrit* notes; also a hard *chitik* and *chi-chi-chi*. **HABITAT** Mud- and sandflats, coastal pools, rarely large rivers and other inland wetlands; lowlands.

GREATER SAND PLOVER *Charadrius leschenaultii* 22–25 cm

(20,21) **Adult non-breeding** *leschenaultii*: Very similar to Lesser but differs by combination of following subtle features: larger size, longer appearance, squarer head, longer bill with more tapered tip (length greater than distance from base of bill to rear of eye), longer tibia (may appear almost as long as tarsus), typically somewhat paler legs and feet (usually tinged greenish or yellowish), toes projecting distinctly beyond tail-tip in flight. (22) **Male breeding**: Plumage like Lesser (*C.m.mongolus*) but has narrower orange-rufous breast-band, with no black upper border. (23) **Female breeding**: Like adult non-breeding but with narrow orange-brown breast-band. (24) **Juvenile**: Differs in same way as Lesser. **VOICE** A trilled *prrrirt*, *kyrrrr trr* and *trrri* etc., softer and longer than similar calls of Lesser, recalling Ruddy Turnstone. **HABITAT & BEHAVIOUR** Mud- and sandflats, beaches, saltpans, coastal pools, rarely large rivers on passage. Often associates with Lesser, but generally less common.

PLATE 45 LARGER PLOVERS & LAPWINGS

PACIFIC GOLDEN PLOVER *Pluvialis fulva* 23–26 cm

(1,2) **Adult non-breeding**: Medium-sized, short-billed and rather nondescript with distinctive golden spangling on upperside, pale buffish-grey head-sides, neck and breast with dusky-grey streaks and mottling. Has prominent dark patch on rear ear-coverts. In flight shows rather uniform upperside with indistinct narrow whitish wing-bar and dull underwing with dusky-grey coverts. (3) **Male breeding**: Face, ear-coverts, foreneck, centre of breast and belly black, with broad white band extending from lores over and behind ear-coverts and down breast-sides and white flanks, and vent with black markings. (4) **Juvenile**: Similar to adult non-breeding but crown, nape and upperparts much more boldly patterned with gold or yellowish-buff, head-sides, neck and breast strongly washed golden, the latter finely spotted/streaked darker. **Female breeding**: Tends to have less black on underparts. **VOICE** In flight utters clear rapid *chu-it*, recalling Spotted Redshank. Also a more drawn-out *klu-ee* and more extended *chu-EE*. **HABITAT** Cultivated and dry areas, coastal habitats; up to 800 m.

GREY PLOVER *Pluvialis squatarola* 27–30 cm

(5,6) **Adult non-breeding**: Only likely to be confused with Pacific Golden but larger, stockier and bigger-headed with stouter bill and relatively shorter legs, upperside more uniform and distinctly greyish with whitish speckling and spangling, has whitish (rather than buffish) supercilium, mostly greyish sides of head and whiter base colour to neck and breast. In flight shows prominent white bar across upperwing, white uppertail-coverts, boldly barred tail and largely whitish underwing with diagnostic black axillaries. (7) **Male breeding**: Face, ear-coverts, foreneck, centre of breast and belly black, with very broad white band extending from lores over and behind ear-coverts and down breast-sides; has black mid-flanks and white vent. Upperside boldly spangled with silvery-white. (8) **Juvenile**: Similar to adult non-breeding but upperside blacker with more defined yellowish-white to yellowish-buff speckles and spangling, neck and breast washed yellowish-buff and more distinctly dark-streaked. **Female breeding**: Typically somewhat browner above, with less black on sides of head, and variable amounts of white admixed with black of underparts. **VOICE** Flight call is a loud plaintive melancholy *tlee-oo-ee*. Sometimes gives a shorter *tloo-ee*. **HABITAT & BEHAVIOUR** Mud- and sandflats, beaches, coastal pools. Gregarious.

NORTHERN LAPWING *Vanellus vanellus* 28–31 cm

(9,10) **Adult non-breeding**: Looks black and white at a distance with distinctive long, thin, swept-back crest. Crown and crest black, sides of head mixed buffish and whitish with black facial patch and line through ear-coverts, upperparts and wing-coverts mostly dark glossy green with some buffish fringes, underparts white with broad blackish breast-band and orange-rufous undertail-coverts. In flight shows distinctive, very broad wings with black flight feathers, pale band across tips of outer primaries and sharply contrasting white underwing-coverts. (11) **Male breeding**: Buff of head-sides replaced by white, lores and throat black (joining breast-band). (12) **Female breeding**: Like breeding male but lores and throat

marked with white. (13) **Juvenile**: Similar to adult non-breeding but upperparts and wing-coverts more prominently fringed warm buff, crest shorter. **VOICE** Calls with loud shrill *cheew* and clear *cheew-ip* or *wee-ip*. **HABITAT** Open country, cultivation, marshes; up to 400 m.

RIVER LAPWING *Vanellus duvaucelii* 29–32 cm

(14,15) **Adult**: Told by black crown and long crest (not always visible), black face, black stripe down centre of throat to uppermost breast and whitish remainder of head and neck. Bill, legs and feet black, underparts white with sandy greyish-brown breast-band and small black belly-patch; has curious black spur on bend of wing (often hidden). In flight, upperwing shows broad white band and narrow black band over median and lesser coverts, tail-tip black. (16) **Juvenile**: Black of head partly obscured by brownish feather-tips, upperparts and wing-coverts sandy-brown with buff fringes and slightly darker subterminal markings. **VOICE** Typical call is a sharp high-pitched *tip-tip* or *did did did*..., sometimes ending with *to-weet* or *do-weet*. **HABITAT & BEHAVIOUR** Large rivers and surrounds; up to 400 m. Breeding display (on ground) includes stooping, spinning and upstretching.

GREY-HEADED LAPWING *Vanellus cinereus* 34–37 cm

(17,18) **Adult non-breeding**: Relatively large size, mostly plain brownish-grey head, neck and upper breast, rather long yellowish bill with black tip, and yellowish legs and feet diagnostic. Chin and centre of throat whitish, with broad, partly obscured, blackish breast-band. In flight shows diagnostic white greater coverts and secondaries (above and below). See Pheasant-tailed Jacana (in flight). (19) **Juvenile**: Head, neck and breast brownish, breast-band vague or absent, upperparts and wing-coverts neatly fringed with buffish. **Adult breeding**: Head, neck and upper breast grey, with neat broad blackish breast-band. **VOICE** Plaintive *chee-it*, often repeated and, when alarmed, a rasping *cha-ha-eet* and sharp *pink*. **HABITAT & BEHAVIOUR** Marshes, wet rice paddies, cultivation; up to 400 m. Gregarious in main wintering areas.

RED-WATTLED LAPWING *Vanellus indicus* 31.5–35 cm

(20,21) **Adult** *atronuchalis*: Black hood and upper breast, white patch on ear-coverts, red facial skin, black-tipped red bill. Cold sandy greyish-brown above with narrow white band across upper mantle, remainder of underparts whitish, legs long and yellow. In flight shows prominent white band along greater upperwing-coverts, blackish flight feathers, white band across rump and uppertail-coverts and mostly black tail with white corners. (22) **Juvenile**: Dark of hood and breast duller, throat whitish, facial skin duller/reduced, bill and legs/feet duller. **VOICE** Typical call is a loud rapid *did-ee-doo-it* (first note often repeated). During display flight utters frenzied series of typical calls, interspersed with *did-did-did*... or *kab-kab-kab*... Sharp incessant *trint* and high-pitched *pit* notes when alarmed. **HABITAT & BEHAVIOUR** Margins of lakes and large rivers, marshes, agriculture, wasteland; up to 400 m. Usually found in pairs or family parties. Display flight involves short, dipping wingbeats, downward swoops and acrobatic tumbling dives.

PLATE 46 JAEGERS & INDIAN SKIMMER

POMARINE JAEGER *Stercorarius pomarinus* 47–61.5 cm
(including tail-streamers to 11.5 cm)

(1) **Adult pale morph non-breeding**: Variable. Less contrast between cap and collar than breeding, neck-sides/throat mottled dark brown, tail-coverts barred whitish, tail-streamers shorter, usually not twisted. (2) **Adult pale morph breeding**: Relatively large/heavy; blackish-brown with broad whitish collar, large whitish area on breast/belly, broad twisted tail-streamers (often broken/absent). Bill bicoloured, neck-sides washed yellowish, flanks may be barred whitish; male's breast-band often reduced to lateral patches. Dark wings with whitish shaft-streaks at base of primaries, narrow white crescent at base of primaries on underwing. (3) **Juvenile pale morph**: Usually cold medium brown with rather plain head and contrasting dark face; mantle/back narrowly barred buff, scapulars/coverts darker with buff tips, vent broadly barred whitish. Contrasting pale bars on uppertail-coverts, underwing-coverts and axillaries, distinctive double pale patch on underwing (pale-based primary coverts and primaries), only slightly protruding, thumb-shaped tail-streamers. Combination of dark head, prominently pale-barred uppertail-coverts and underwing pattern diagnostic. Some have mostly pale head, paler lower breast to belly and pale-barred flanks, and are best told by contrasting dark face and double pale patch on underwing. (4) **Second-winter pale morph**: Similar to non-breeding adult but underwing-coverts like juvenile. (5) **Juvenile dark morph**: Head/body blackish-brown with pale-barred tail-coverts. Scapulars/coverts darker than pale morph, with less distinct pale tips, narrower pale markings on underwing-coverts (same double pale patch on primaries). **Adult dark morph**: Rare. Blackish-brown with similar primary pattern to pale morph. Intermediates very rare. **First-winter pale morph**: Like juvenile but with pale hindcollar, no pale tips above. **Third-winter pale morph**: Lower breast/belly whiter than adult, may lack bars on greater underwing-coverts. HABITAT & BEHAVIOUR Open seas, sometimes inshore. Normal flight quite slow, gull-like; piratical flight relatively laboured.

PARASITIC JAEGER *Stercorarius parasiticus* 42–54.5 cm
(including tail-streamers to 10.5 cm).

(6) **Adult pale morph non-breeding**: Cap less distinct, has more dark markings on underparts (including breast-band of dark mottling), pale-edged mantle and pale-barred tail-coverts; tail-streamers may be lacking. (7) **Adult pale morph breeding**: Similar to Pomarine but smaller/slimmer with narrower, darker bill, small white patch on extreme forehead, somewhat paler greyish-brown scapulars/wing-coverts, paler yellowish wash on neck-sides, mostly white underparts with variable clean grey breast-band (sometimes only lateral patches), dusky vent and pointed tail-streamers. In flight, wings somewhat slimmer and narrower-based than Pomarine. (8) **Juvenile pale morph**: Highly variable. Head/underbody quite plain rufescent-/cinnamon-tinged brown to mostly pale. Some show obvious paler head. On plumage, generally best told from Pomarine by presence of small pale forehead-patch, pale rusty to bright rufous nuchal band, streaks on head and neck and/or rufescent to warm-tinged head/underbody. Lacks contrasting dark face, rarely has double pale patch on underside of primary coverts/primaries. Dark-headed birds lack obvious whitish bars on tail-coverts shown by Pomarine. Some have diagnostic broad whitish crescent (not shaft-streaks) on upperside of primary bases. (9) **Second-winter pale morph**: From non-

breeding adult as Pomarine but lacks double pale underwing-patch. (10) **Juvenile dark morph**: On plumage, best told from Pomarine by all-dark underwing-coverts, including primary coverts. **Adult dark morph**: Best separated from Pomarine by size, shape, tail and behaviour. A range of intermediates with pale morph occur. **First-winter pale morph**: As juvenile but develops pale areas on head and body; warmer-tinged individuals lose such tones. **Third-winter pale morph** Gradually becomes more like adult non-breeding. HABITAT & BEHAVIOUR Open seas, sometimes close inshore. Compared to Pomarine, normal flight typically faster and more falcon-like with occasional shearwater-like glides; piratical flight faster and more acrobatic, often chasing terns and gulls for up to several minutes but rarely attacking birds themselves.

LONG-TAILED JAEGER *Stercorarius longicaudus* 47–67.5 cm
(including tail-streamers to 26.5 cm)

(11) **Adult non-breeding** *pallescens*: Tail-streamers shorter or lacking. Best told from Parasitic and Pomarine by size, shape and virtual lack of any whitish flash on primaries (particularly below). (12) **Adult breeding**: Similar to Parasitic but somewhat slighter in build, with shorter but relatively thicker bill, noticeably paler, greyer upperparts/coverts and longer central tail feathers. Looks smaller with more elongated rear end, upperwing-coverts contrast with blackish primaries, only outermost two of which have white shafts (forming narrow line on forewing), underwing all dark (apart from white shaft on leading primary), tail-streamers usually longer than width of inner wing, breast/upper belly whitish, darkening to grey on lower belly/vent. (13) **Juvenile pale morph**: Typically greyer, more boldly patterned than Parasitic (never rufescent); upperpart feathers/coverts tipped/barred whitish to buffish. Looks slightly longer-bodied (behind wings) and longer-tailed (noticeably attenuated rear end), usually only two white shaft-streaks on upperside of primaries, strongly pale-barred underwing-coverts/axillaries. Strikingly greyish plumage, with whitish head and/or belly or greyish head/breast and whitish belly diagnostic. (14) **Juvenile dark morph**: On plumage, best told from Parasitic by two (normally) white shaft-streaks on upperside of primaries and bolder barring on tail-coverts and often axillaries. (15) **Second winter**: Similar to adult non-breeding but underwing-coverts barred. **First winter**: Like juvenile but upperparts/wing-coverts plain greyish-brown, belly cleaner/whiter, central tail feathers more pointed, usually longer. **Third winter**: As adult non-breeding but may show a few pale bars on underwing-coverts. HABITAT & BEHAVIOUR As Parasitic but normal flight lighter/less purposeful, often recalls smallish gull or tern; piratical attacks less confident and briefer.

INDIAN SKIMMER *Rynchops albicollis* 40–43 cm

(16,17) **Adult breeding**: Black above, white forehead, collar and underparts, long deep orange bill (paler tip) with longer lower mandible; white trailing edge to upperwing, forked tail with mostly blackish central feathers. (18) **Juvenile**: Bill dusky-orange with blackish tip, crown and nape paler, brownish-grey with darker mottling, mantle, scapulars and wing-coverts paler and more greyish-brown with whitish to pale buffish fringes. **Adult non-breeding**: Somewhat duller/browner above. VOICE High, nasal *kap* or *kip* notes (mainly in flight). HABITAT & BEHAVIOUR Large lowland rivers, lakes, rarely coastal wetlands. Feeds in flight, skimming lower mandible through water; wingbeats slow, graceful. Usually found singly, in pairs or small parties.

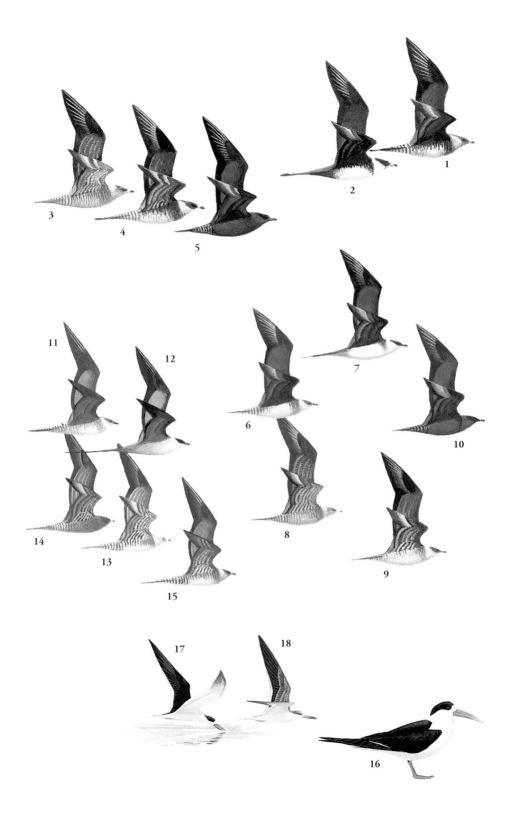

PLATE 47 LARGER GULLS

BLACK-TAILED GULL *Larus crassirostris* 45–48 cm

(1,2) **Adult non-breeding**: Dark grey above, white tail with broad black band. Head/neck and underparts white, greyish streaked hindcrown/nape, longish yellow bill with red tip and black band, legs/feet greenish-yellow, eyes pale yellowish, eyering red; mostly blackish outer primaries (above), broad white trailing edge to secondaries. (3) **Adult breeding**: All-white head and neck. (4,5) **First winter**: Told by dark-tipped pinkish bill, rather uniform greyish-brown body with contrasting whitish forehead, throat, rump, uppertail-coverts and vent, diagnostic blackish tail with narrow white terminal band. (6) **Second winter**: Similar to adult non-breeding but mantle/scapulars mixed with brown, upperwing somewhat paler/browner. HABITAT & BEHAVIOUR Mud- and sandflats, coasts, coastal pools. Often associates with other gulls.

THE HERRING GULL COMPLEX: *Larus argentatus*, *L. heuglini* & *L. vegae*

Forms of Herring Gull *L. argentatus* and Lesser Black-backed Gull *L. fuscus* have received much attention in recent years. There is increasing evidence that some forms, previously regarded as subspecies, may be full species. Recent studies on breeding grounds, combined with examination of specimens, is providing a more scientifically reliable foundation for identification in winter. Much more work is required to determine reliable identification criteria for each form. Basic points to bear in mind while trying to identify these large gulls are: **1**. A gathering of at least several similar birds will provide a more important sample than a single individual. It is often possible to assign groups of similar-looking birds to a form more confidently. When two or more forms are thought to be present side by side, it may help to look for common features among them, rather than devote too much time to a bird that looks 'different' from the others; this may be an extreme/atypical variant, more difficult to identify than the majority type. **2**. An assessment of moult (mainly primary moult), with respect to time of year, will often provide more reliable identification pointers than subjective assessments of size, mantle shade etc. The accounts below outline what are currently thought to be the basic features of the forms known/likely to occur.

HERRING GULL *Larus argentatus* 60–67 cm

L.a.mongolicus: **Adult**: Least known of complex. Slightly larger than Vega; should look larger than Heuglin's (side by side). Legs/feet pinkish, roughly same shade of grey above as Vega (perhaps fractionally paler with slight bluish tinge), may tend to show more black on primaries. Moult appears to commence even earlier than Vega, although it is unclear whether it is continuous or suspended during migration. In February/March, like Vega, already shows white head, while Heuglin's still shows head-streaking. On current knowledge, probably not safely separable in field from Vega in any plumage. HABITAT Coasts. Not yet definitely recorded.

HEUGLIN'S GULL *Larus heuglini* 58–65 cm

(7,8) **Adult non-breeding** *tamyrensis*: From Vega by yellow legs/feet, slightly darker grey above, more black on primaries. Eyes usually pale. Moult starts later than Vega; any large gull with white head and retained, faded/worn primaries in September/October is likely to be this species. By February/March, still has obvious head-streaks of non-breeding plumage and may still have outermost primaries growing, while most or all Vega will have white heads of breeding plumage. *L.h.heuglini* (could occur):

Slightly darker grey above (similar to European Lesser Black-backed *L.fuscus graellsii*), slightly more black and smaller white markings on primaries. (9) **Adult breeding**: Head and neck all white. (10,11) **First winter**: Moults in new scapulars and tertials, which are greyer with more diffuse darker central markings and less defined pale borders; head and underside somewhat whiter, particularly face, head and neck. (12) **Second winter**: Like first winter, but mantle, back and scapulars largely grey. **Juvenile**: White of head, underside, rump and uppertail-coverts heavily streaked/mottled dull brownish, upperparts/wing-coverts dark brownish with whitish to brownish-white fringing/notching, tail mostly blackish with dark-speckled white base and narrow white terminal band, bill blackish, legs/feet dull pinkish. In flight, upperwing quite blackish, with contrasting paler median coverts and slightly paler, dark-tipped inner primaries (paler when worn). HABITAT Coasts, sand-/mudflats, coastal pools, lowland lakes.

VEGA GULL *Larus vegae* 57–64 cm

(13,14) **Adult non-breeding** *birulai*: Slightly bulkier than Heuglin's, pinkish legs/feet, paler grey above (similar to European Herring *L.a.argentatus*), more white on primaries. Fairly heavy head/neck-streaks, usually dark eyes (c.75%). An important difference is primary moult timing (starts summer, complete about November), up to four months ahead of Heuglin's. Thus, in September/October, has fresh/still growing outer primaries (creates rather stumpy-ended look) and has acquired dark head-streaks of non-breeding plumage; at this time, Heuglin's still has old/worn outer primaries and white head of breeding plumage. (15) **Adult breeding**: Head and neck all white. (16,17) **First winter**: Best separated from Heuglin's by paler greater upperwing-coverts, somewhat paler inner primaries. (18) **Second winter**: From Heuglin's by same features as first winter; additionally has paler grey on upperparts. **Juvenile**: Head/neck/underside/rump/uppertail-coverts more heavily dark-marked than Heuglin's (often looks mostly brown, with whiter face/neck), bold pale notches on tertial fringes; paler greater upperwing-coverts and inner primaries (in flight). **First/second winter** From Heuglin's by paler greater upperwing-coverts and inner primaries. HABITAT Coasts. Not yet definitely recorded.

PALLAS'S GULL *Larus ichthyaetus* 58–67 cm

(19,20) **Adult non-breeding**: Large; blackish band on yellowish bill, dark mask, comparatively pale grey above, small amount of black on outer primaries. Legs and feet dull yellowish, hindcrown faintly dark-streaked. In flight, upperwing shows white outer primaries with black subterminal markings and white outer primary coverts. (21) **Adult breeding**: Black head, broken eyering, bill has yellower base, more red near tip, legs/feet brighter. (22,23) **First winter**: From second-winter Heuglin's/Vega by dark mask and hindcrown-streaks, densely dark-marked lower hindneck/breast-sides, paler grey on mantle, back and scapulars, mostly grey, unbarred greater coverts, and white rump, uppertail-coverts and tail-base, contrasting sharply with broad blackish subterminal tail-band. (24) **Second winter**: More similar to adult non-breeding but shows remnants of dark markings on median, lesser and primary coverts, mostly black outer primaries and narrow blackish subterminal tail-band. VOICE Occasionally gives a deep low *kyow-kyow* and nasal crow-like *kraagh* or *kra-ah*. HABITAT & BEHAVIOUR Coasts, sand- and mudflats, coastal pools, large rivers; up to 400 m. Regularly scavenges and parasitises other birds.

PLATE 48 SMALLER GULLS, BRIDLED & SOOTY TERNS

BROWN-HEADED GULL *Larus brunnicephalus* 42–46 cm

(1,2) **Adult non-breeding**: Like Black-headed but a little larger, bulkier, thicker-billed and thicker-necked, with pale eyes. In flight shows broader and more rounded wings with distinctive, broadly black-tipped outer primaries, enclosing up to three white 'mirrors', and more extensively blackish underside of primaries with white 'mirrors' near wing-tip. (3) **Adult breeding**: Has dark brown hood with broken white eye-ring and paler face, bill uniform dark red. (4,5) **First winter**: From Black-headed, on plumage, by black outer primaries, broader black tips to inner primaries (above and below) and whitish patch extending over primary coverts and inner primaries on upperwing. **VOICE** Like Black-headed but deeper and gruffer. **HABITAT** Large rivers and lakes, coasts, coastal pools; up to 400 m.

BLACK-HEADED GULL *Larus ridibundus* 35–39 cm

(6,7) **Adult non-breeding**: Relatively small and slim with rather narrow black-tipped red bill, dark red legs and feet and pale grey upperside. Head mainly white, with prominent dark ear-spot and dark smudges on side of crown. Eyes dark. In flight, upperwing appears very pale with prominent white leading edge to outer wing and smallish black tips to outer primaries; underwing pattern mirrors this but coverts all greyish, outer primaries having more black and less white. (8) **Adult breeding**: Has dark brown hood with broken white eye-ring and uniform darker red bill. (9,10) **First winter**: At rest resembles non-breeding adult but bill paler and duller with more contrasting dark tip, legs and feet duller and more pinkish, with greyish-brown centres to median and lesser coverts, inner greater coverts and tertials. In flight, upperwing shows broad greyish-brown band across coverts and broad blackish band along secondaries and tips of primaries, with blackish subterminal tail-band. **VOICE** Typical calls are a high-pitched screaming *kyaaar* and *karrr*. Contact calls include short *kek* and deeper *kuk* notes. **HABITAT** Large rivers, lakes, coasts, coastal pools; up to 400 m.

SLENDER-BILLED GULL *Larus genei* 37–42 cm

(11,12) **Adult non-breeding**: Like Black-headed but longer-necked and longer-billed, has longer, more sloping forehead, all-white head (sometimes with faint ear-spot) and pale eyes. (13) **Adult breeding**: Head white, bill dark, sometimes appearing almost blackish (particularly at distance), underparts may be washed pink. (14,15) **First winter**: Apart from shape, differs from Black-headed by paler, more orange bill with less obvious dark tip, much fainter head markings, pale eyes and longer, paler legs. In flight shows less contrasting band across upperwing-coverts (feather-centres paler) and a little more white on outer primaries. **VOICE** Like that of Black-headed but slightly deeper, lower-pitched and more nasal. **HABITAT** Coastal pools.

BLACK-LEGGED KITTIWAKE *Rissa tridactyla* 37–42 cm

(16,17) **Adult non-breeding** *pollicaris*: Relatively dark grey upperparts and upperwing, grey nape, vertical blackish bar behind eye, yellowish bill, shortish dark brown to blackish legs (rarely tinged pinkish to reddish). Tail is slightly notched. Rather narrow outer wing turns whitish before neat black tip. (18) **Adult breeding**: Head all white. (19,20) **First winter**: Differs from non-breeding adult by distinctive upperwing pattern, with broadly black outer primaries and black diagonal band across coverts, contrasting sharply with largely whitish secondaries and inner primaries. Has black-tipped tail, black bill (may be slightly paler at base); head as non-breeding adult but may show black band across hindneck. **VOICE** Likely to be silent, but may give a short nasal *kya* in flight, or short knocking *kt kt kt*... when alarmed. **HABITAT & BEHAVIOUR** Open seas, rarely inshore. Flight more tern-like than other gulls, with quick stiff wingbeats.

BRIDLED TERN *Sterna anaethetus* 37–42 cm

(21) **Adult non-breeding** *anaethetus*: Distinguished by combination of size, dark brownish-grey upperside, thin whitish nuchal band, whitish forehead-patch (speckled darker) and blackish crown, nape and mask. Has uneven paler tips to upperparts and wing-coverts, deeply forked tail and blackish bill, legs and feet. In flight shows dark upperwing and mostly whitish underwing with darker secondaries, inner primaries and outer primary tips. (22–24) **Adult breeding**: Clean white forehead and short eyebrow contrast with black eye-stripe, crown and nape, lacks paler tips on brownish-grey of upperparts and upperwing. In flight, leading edge of upper lesser coverts may appear slightly darker. (25) **Juvenile**: Has whitish tips and dark subterminal bars on upperparts and wing-coverts, breast-sides sullied brownish-grey, head pattern similar to adult non-breeding. **VOICE** Usual calls include a staccato yapping *wep-wep*... **HABITAT & BEHAVIOUR** Open seas, islets. Flight is very buoyant with rather elastic wingbeats.

SOOTY TERN *Sterna fuscata* 42–45 cm

(26) **Adult non-breeding** *nubilosa*: Similar to Bridled but larger, upperparts and upperwing blacker and more uniform, no whitish eyebrow or nuchal band. On underwing in flight, whitish coverts contrast more sharply with the uniformly blackish flight feathers. (27–29) **Adult breeding**: From Bridled by concolorous blackish crown, hindneck and upperside, broader square-cut white forehead-patch (without white eyebrow), wing pattern (as adult non-breeding) and blackish tail with more contrasting white edge. (30) **Juvenile/first winter**: Mostly sooty-blackish, with contrasting whitish vent, whitish tips on mantle to uppertail-coverts, scapulars, tertials and wing-coverts, and mostly whitish underwing-coverts. **First summer**: Intermediate between juvenile and adult non-breeding, underside variably dark-marked (particularly breast and flanks). **VOICE** Typical calls include a high-pitched *ker-wacki-wah* and shorter *kraark*. **HABITAT** Open seas, islets.

PLATE 49 LARGER TERNS

CASPIAN TERN *Sterna caspia* 48–55 cm

(1–3) **Adult non-breeding**: Unmistakable. Larger than other terns with diagnostic thick red bill. Crown, nape and mask mostly black, with whiter, dark-mottled forecrown, black subterminal marking on bill-tip. In flight, upperwing has grey-edged blackish outer primaries, underwing with contrasting, mostly blackish outer primaries. (4) **Adult breeding**: Forehead to nape and mask all black. (5) **First winter**: Similar to adult non-breeding but secondaries, primary upperwing-coverts and tail somewhat darker; may show slightly darker centres to upperwing-coverts. **VOICE** A loud deep croaking *kraah* and *kra-krah* and hoarse *kretch*. **HABITAT** Coastal pools, mud- and sandflats, sometimes lakes, large rivers; lowlands.

RIVER TERN *Sterna aurantia* 38–46 cm (including outertail feathers up to 23 cm)

(6) **Adult non-breeding**: Medium-sized with rather thick dark-tipped yellow bill, reddish legs and feet and only very little dark coloration at tips of outer primaries (more when worn). Has mostly black mask and nape and greyish crown with dark streaks; underparts greyish-white. Note habitat. (7) **Adult breeding**: Bill uniform orange-yellow, forehead to nape and mask black, upperwing all grey with paler primaries and primary coverts (forms striking flash), with noticeably long streamer-like outertail feathers. Some individuals retain this plumage outside the breeding season. (8) **Juvenile**: Has dark-tipped yellow bill, blackish mask, blackish streaks on crown, nape, ear-coverts and throat-sides, whitish supercilium, blackish-brown fringes to mantle feathers, scapulars, tertials and wing-coverts, and blackish-tipped primaries. **First winter**: Similar to non-breeding adult but retains juvenile tertials, primaries and tail feathers. In flight gives a rather high nasal *kiaah* or *hiaah*. When displaying gives more extended, rapidly repeated disyllabic calls: *kierr-wick kierrwick-kierr-wick*..., often accelerating to crescendo. **HABITAT & BEHAVIOUR** Large rivers, sometimes lakes; up to 400 m. Flight strong and purposeful.

LESSER CRESTED TERN *Sterna bengalensis* 35–40 cm

(9–11) **Adult non-breeding** *bengalensis*: Like Great Crested but smaller, bill narrower and yellowish-orange, more solid black hindcrown and 'mane' on nape, paler grey on upperside; when worn, shows darker outer primaries and bar on secondaries. (12) **Adult breeding**: Crown and nape black, including extreme forehead (white on Great Crested), bill more orange. (13) **Juvenile**: From Great Crested, apart from size and bill, by darker upperside of inner primaries. (14) **First winter**: Greater and median upperwing-coverts plainer grey than Great Crested (not illustrated), head pattern as adult non-breeding. **VOICE** Typical flight call is a harsh *krrrik-krrrik*. **HABITAT** Open seas, coasts, mud- and sandflats.

GREAT CRESTED TERN *Sterna bergii* 45–49 cm

(15–17) **Adult non-breeding** *velox*: Combination of largish size, rather stocky build, long, thickish, cold yellow to greenish-yellow bill and darkish grey upperside distinctive. Has white face and forecrown, blackish mask, blackish hindcrown and nape with white streaks and well-defined whitish tertial fringes. In flight shows mostly uniform wings with darker-tipped outer primaries. Worn feathers on upperwing are darker and their presence creates a patchy appearance. (18) **Adult breeding**: Has brighter yellow bill, extreme forehead white, crown and nape black, the latter with a shaggy crest. (19) **Juvenile**: Bill slightly duller than non-breeding adult, feathers of mantle, back, scapulars and tertials brownish-grey with whitish fringes, dark brownish-grey to blackish centres to wing-coverts, secondaries and outer primaries, and darker tail. In flight shows four dark bands across upperwing-coverts and secondaries and rather uniformly dark outer primaries and primary coverts. (20) **Second winter**: As non-breeding adult but retains juvenile outer primaries, primary coverts and secondaries, tail typically darker with variable dark subterminal band. **First winter**: Similar to juvenile but with uniform grey mantle and scapulars. Juvenile wing-coverts are gradually lost, often resulting in patchy appearance. **Other subspecies** *S.b.cristata* (? recorded Gulf of Thailand): Smaller and noticeably paler grey above, closer to Lesser. **VOICE** Usual calls include a harsh grating *krrrik*, *kerrer* and *kerrak*, particularly in flight. **HABITAT** Open seas, coasts, mud- and sandflats, islets.

CHINESE CRESTED TERN *Sterna bernsteini* 43 cm

(21–23) **Adult non-breeding**: Similar to Great Crested Tern but smaller with prominently blackish-tipped yellow bill and much paler grey on upperside. Size intermediate between Lesser and Great Crested Terns. In flight differs from both by sharp contrast between pale grey upperwing and blackish outer primaries. (24) **Adult breeding**: Forehead to nape black, with similar shaggy nuchal crest to Great. Black-tipped yellow bill diagnostic. **Juvenile/immature**: Not yet documented. **HABITAT** Open seas, coasts.

PLATE 50 SMALLER TERNS & BROWN NODDY

ROSEATE TERN *Sterna dougallii* 33–39 cm (including tail-streamers to 11 cm)

(1,2) **Adult non-breeding** *bangsi*: Very similar to Common but more slimly built, grey of upperside paler, has longer tail (unless broken) with all-white outer feathers which project well beyond closed wing-tips, bill somewhat longer and slenderer. May show pinkish-flushed underparts. When fresh, inner edges of primaries white, forming defined white line along inner edge of closed wing (lacking on Common). In flight shows paler, more uniform upperparts and upperwing-coverts (back contrasts less with rump and uppertail-coverts), with whiter secondaries and less dark on primaries; underwing only has faint dark markings on outer primary tips. (3,4) **Adult breeding**: Bill black with red on base to basal half only, underparts often flushed pink, tail-streamers very long. In flight differs from Common by paler and plainer upperwing, whiter secondaries and inner primaries, darker greyish outermost primaries, no dark wedge on mid-primaries. (5) **Juvenile**: From Common by all-blackish bill, legs and feet, darker forecrown (initially all dark), usually bolder blackish subterminal markings on mantle feathers, scapulars and tertials (latter may be almost completely blackish) and broad white upper edge to closed primary tips. (6) **First winter/summer**: Similar to non-breeding adult, but in flight upperwing shows dark bands across lesser coverts and secondaries and somewhat darker leading edge of outer wing. (7) **Adult breeding** *korustes* (? west S): Tends to be larger and paler grey above with less black on bill. **VOICE** A distinctive, incisive, clicky *dju-dik*, particularly in flight, and low rasping *kraak*, *zraaach* or *aaahrk* when agitated. **HABITAT & BEHAVIOUR** Open seas, coasts, mud- and sandflats, beaches, islets. Typically flies with shallower, stiffer and faster wingbeats than Common.

BLACK-NAPED TERN *Sterna sumatrana* 30–35 cm

(8) **Adult breeding** *sumatrana*: Crown all white, sharply defined nape-band; blackish bill and legs/feet. Can show pinkish flush on underparts. (9) **Adult non-breeding**: Told by combination of white head with narrow black band from eyes to hindnape, blackish bill, legs and feet and very pale grey on upperside. Has some dark streaks on hindcrown. In flight shows uniform very pale grey upperwing with blackish outer edge of outermost primary. Wings appear very whitish at a distance. (10) **Juvenile**: Bill initially dusky-yellow but soon turns blackish; has white forehead and lores, variable dark streaks on crown, well-defined black band from eye to nape, blackish subterminal markings on mantle feathers, scapulars, tertials and wing-coverts, dark-centred tail feathers, darker grey secondaries and darker grey primaries with white inner edges, which form defined line along inner edge of closed wing. Generally similar to Roseate but with different head pattern; dark markings on upperside narrower, more crescent-shaped and typically paler. **First winter**: Similar to adult non-breeding but with darker band across lesser upperwing-coverts, retained juvenile primaries and darker greyish markings on tertials and tail. **VOICE** May give a sharp *kick*, *tsii-chee-ch-chip* and hurried *chit-chit-chit-er*, particularly in flight. **HABITAT** Open seas, coasts, beaches, islets.

COMMON TERN *Sterna hirundo* 33–37 cm (including tail-streamers to 8 cm)

(11,12) **Adult non-breeding** *tibetana*: Medium-sized with fairly slender, pointed blackish bill, dark red legs and feet, white forehead and lores, blackish mask and nape and medium-grey mantle, back, scapulars and wing-coverts. Mostly likely to be confused with Roseate but somewhat thicker-set, lacks white upper edge to closed primary tips, has shorter tail with noticeably grey outer fringes to feathers and somewhat shorter bill. In flight, darker grey of upperparts and upperwing contrasts with white rump and uppertail-coverts (more so in breeding plumage), upperwing has mostly grey secondaries with only narrow white trailing edge and more dark on primaries, lesser and primary coverts; underwing shows more extensive dark tips to outer primaries. See Whiskered Tern. (13,14) **Adult breeding**: Bill orange-red with black tip, legs and feet dark red, forehead to nape black; develops long tail-streamers (outer feathers). Best distinguishing features from Roseate are slight grey wash to underparts (lower ear-coverts and cheeks slightly whiter), more uniform closed primary tips and shorter tail-streamers (not projecting beyond closed wing-tips). In flight, upperwing differs by darker secondaries, somewhat paler outermost primaries (apart from tips) and distinctive dark wedge on mid-primaries; underwing shows dark trailing edge to outer primaries. (15) **Juvenile (late)**: Base of bill extensively orange (blackens with age), legs and feet orange, head pattern similar to adult non-breeding; mantle, scapulars, tertials and wing-coverts have dark brown subterminal markings and, initially, buffish fringes. In flight, upperwing shows pronounced blackish band at leading edge of lesser coverts; dark secondaries, outer primaries and primary coverts contrast with rest of upperwing. *S.h.longipennis* has mostly blackish bill and dark legs and feet. (16) **First winter/summer**: Similar to adult non-breeding but upperwing has somewhat bolder dark bands across lesser coverts and secondaries. (17) **Adult breeding** *longipennis* (autumn sight records from Gulf of Thailand): Mostly black bill, greyer upperparts and underparts, more contrasting white cheek-stripe and dark reddish-brown legs and feet. **VOICE** Typical calls include a harsh *kreeeah* or *kreeeerh*, short *kik* notes, a rapid *kye-kye-kye-kye*… and *kirri-kirri-kirri*. **HABITAT & BEHAVIOUR** Coastal habitats, open ocean, occasionally large rivers and inland lakes.

BROWN NODDY *Anous stolidus* 40–45 cm

(18,19) **Adult** *pileatus*: Rather uniform dark chocolate-brown plumage with whitish forehead, grey crown, broken white eyering, and long wedge-shaped tail (slightly cleft when spread) distinctive. In flight shows paler brownish band across upper-wing-coverts and paler brownish underwing-coverts. (20) **Juvenile**: Feathers of crown, mantle, scapulars and wing-coverts have indistinct pale buffish fringes, forecrown somewhat browner, rarely whitish. See juvenile Sooty Tern. **VOICE** Occasionally utters a harsh *kaark* and *kwok kuok*… **HABITAT** Open seas, islets.

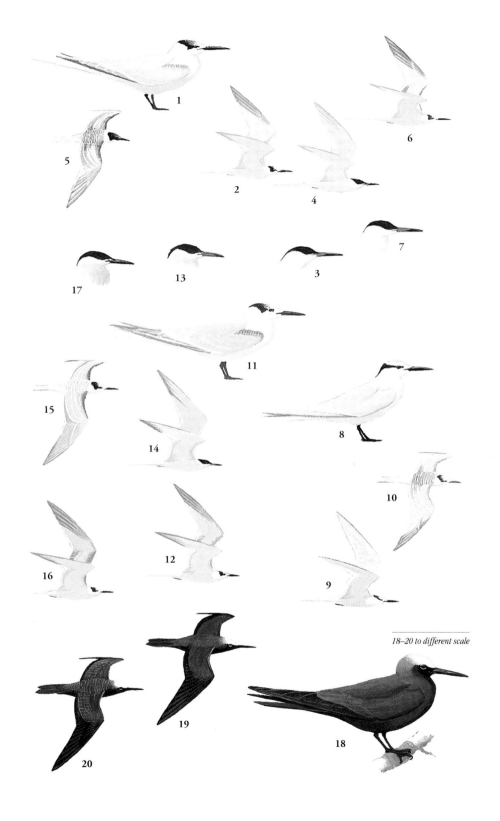

18–20 to different scale

PLATE 51 GULL-BILLED TERN & SMALLER TERNS

GULL-BILLED TERN *Sterna nilotica* 35–38 cm

(1–3) **Adult non-breeding** *affinis*: Combination of size, white head with blackish ear-coverts, pale silvery-grey rump and uppertail and shallow tail-fork distinctive. Recalls Whiskered but much larger and larger-billed, with longer and more slender wings. (4) **Adult breeding**: Forehead to nape black. (5,6) **First winter**: Similar to adult non-breeding but secondaries and upper primary coverts somewhat darker, tail dark-tipped; may show odd darker centres and whiter tips to upper-wing-coverts. **Other subspecies** *G.n.nilotica* (? recorded). **VOICE** Flight calls include a low nasal *ger-erk* and *kay-vek* and loud metallic *kak-kak*. Nasal *kvay-kvay-kvay*... when alarmed. **HABITAT** Coasts, mudflats, sandflats, coastal pools, lakes, large rivers; lowlands.

LITTLE TERN *Sterna albifrons* 22–25 cm

(7,8) **Adult non-breeding** *sinensis*: Small size, long-billed and short-tailed appearance distinctive. Bill, legs and feet dark, lores and forecrown white, hindcrown blackish with white streaks, band through eye and nape black, rump to tail-centre white (sometimes grey). In flight shows rather uniform grey upperside and upperwing with narrow dark band on leading edge of lesser coverts and blackish outermost primaries with white shafts. (9,10) **Adult breeding**: Bill yellow with black tip, legs and feet orange to yellow; has black crown, central nape and eyestripe and contrasting defined white forehead-patch. (11) **Juvenile**: Similar to non-breeding adult but with dark subterminal markings on mantle, scapulars, tertials and wing-coverts. In flight shows dark leading edge to upperwing and often has largely whitish secondaries and inner primaries; outer primaries less sharply contrasting. **First winter/first summer**: Like adult non-breeding. **Other subspecies** *S.a.albifrons* (recorded in winter west S): Slightly darker grey on upperside, longer tail-streamers and dark shafts on outer primaries. **VOICE** Sharp high-pitched *kik* or *ket* notes, particularly in flight, and a harsh rasping *kyik* when alarmed. Also a rapidly repeated *kirrikikki kirrikikki*... **HABITAT & BEHAVIOUR** Coasts, beaches, saltpans, mud- and sandflats, large rivers; lowlands. Flies with rapid wingbeats; often hovers.

BLACK-BELLIED TERN *Sterna acuticauda* 30–33 cm

(12) **Adult non-breeding**: Owing to habitat, most likely to be confused with River Tern. Differs by much smaller size, bill slenderer and orange with darker tip, often shows some blackish mottling on belly and vent; forehead and crown sometimes all black. (13) **Adult breeding**: Forehead to nape and mask black, bill uniform orange, with grey breast and blackish

belly and vent, contrasting with whitish head-sides and throat. Distinguished by combination of bill, upperwing (similar to that of River), deeply forked tail and dark underparts. (14) **Juvenile**: Best separated from River by size, bill (as adult non-breeding), lack of whitish supercilium and whiter sides of neck and lower sides of head. **VOICE** Flight call is a clear piping *peuo*. **HABITAT** Large rivers, sometimes large lakes, marshes; up to 400 m.

WHISKERED TERN *Chlidonias hybridus* 24–28 cm

(15,16) **Adult non-breeding** *javanicus*: Smallish and rather compact with relatively short, blackish bill, blackish mask and hindcrown/nape, white crown with dark streaks at rear, dark reddish legs and feet, and shortish tail. In flight shows relatively short, broad wings, rather uniform grey upperside, and upperwing with darker secondaries and outer primaries and somewhat darker inner primaries and shallow tail-fork. Superficially resembles smaller *Sterna* terns but note size, shape, bill and habitat. (17) **Adult breeding**: Distinctive, with dark red bill, legs and feet, black forehead to nape, white throat and lower sides of head and dark grey remainder of underparts, contrasting with white vent and underwing-coverts. Grey of underside often appears blackish at distance. (18) **Juvenile**: Mantle, scapulars, tertials and innermost wing-coverts fawn-brown with blackish subterminal markings and narrow buff fringes, forming a distinctive 'saddle' effect; otherwise similar to non-breeding adult but forecrown and face washed brownish-buff. **First winter**: Similar to adult non-breeding. **VOICE** Short hoarse rasping *kersch* and repeated short *kek* notes, mainly given in flight. **HABITAT** Coastal pools, mud- and sandflats, marshes, lakes, large rivers, wet rice paddies; up to 400 m.

WHITE-WINGED TERN *Chlidonias leucopterus* 20–24 cm

(19,20) **Adult non-breeding**: Similar to Whiskered but has finer bill and distinctive head pattern, with blackish area restricted to hindcrown, thin line on centre of nape and isolated roundish ear-patch ('headphones'). In flight shows white rump and uppertail-coverts, upperwing with darker outer primaries and dark bands across lesser coverts and secondaries. (21) **Adult breeding**: Easily told by combination of black head, body and underwing-coverts and whitish upperwing-coverts, rump and tail-coverts. (22) **Adult non-breeding/ breeding (transitional)**: Patchy plumage. (23) **Juvenile**: Differs from Whiskered in same way as adult non-breeding; additionally has distinctly darker and more uniform 'saddle'. **First winter**: Similar to adult non-breeding. **VOICE** May give a harsh high-pitched *kreek* and harsh creaking *kesch*, particularly in flight. **HABITAT** Coasts, coastal pools, marshes, wet rice paddies, lakes, large rivers; up to 800 m.

PLATE 52 BAZAS, ORIENTAL HONEY-BUZZARD, BAT HAWK & BLACK EAGLE

JERDON'S BAZA *Aviceda jerdoni* 46 cm

(1–3) **Adult** *jerdoni*: Relatively small, with long, erectile, white-tipped blackish crest, warm brown sides of head and nape, paler and warmer area on upperwing-coverts, dark mesial streak, indistinct rufous breast-streaks and broad rufous bars on belly and vent. Resembles some hawk eagles (particularly juveniles) but smaller, tips of primaries fall closer to tail-tip (at rest). In flight, broad wings have strongly 'pinched-in' bases; shows slightly contrasting paler and warmer band across upperwing-coverts, cinnamon-rufous and white bars on underwing-coverts, fewer dark bars on flight feathers and three unevenly spaced blackish tail-bands. See Crested Goshawk. (4,5) **Juvenile**: Head mostly buffish-white with blackish streaks, breast plainer, bars on belly and vent often broken; has four evenly spaced dark tail-bands (subterminal one broadest). **VOICE** A rather high-pitched, airy *pee-weeeow* or *fiweeoo* and shorter *ti-wuet*, repeated 3–4 times. When agitated, a very high-pitched *chi chichitchit chit-chit* and *chu chit-chit chu-chit chu-chit* etc., interspersed with *he-he-hew* or descending *he-he-wi-wiwi*. **HABITAT & BEHAVIOUR** Broadleaved evergreen forest, freshwater swamp forest; up to 1,700 m. Rarely soars high over forest; often travels and hunts below canopy.

BLACK BAZA *Aviceda leuphotes* 31.5–33 cm

(6–8) **Adult** *syama*: Relatively small, head black with long erectile crest, upperside mostly black, prominent white markings on scapulars, variable white and chestnut markings on greater coverts, tertials and secondaries; whitish remainder of underparts with black band on breast, many chestnut bars on belly, and black vent. In flight, underwing shows black coverts and primary tips and grey secondaries, contrasting with whitish remainder of primaries; has rather broad wings and shortish tail. (9) **Juvenile**: Duller overall, upperside more brownish-black with more white markings; narrow whitish streaks on throat and brown streaks on white of upper breast. **Other subspecies** *A.l.leuphotes* (breeds W,NW): Apparently tends to have more chestnut and white on upperparts, mostly chestnut breast-band and less barring on more rufous-buff lower breast and belly. **VOICE** A plaintive, high-pitched, rather shrill *chi-aah*, *tchi'euuah* or *tcheeoua*, with stressed first syllable; often repeated. **HABITAT & BEHAVIOUR** Broadleaved evergreen and deciduous forest, freshwater swamp forest, other habitats on migration; up to 1,500 m. Often in small flocks, particularly during migration. Flight rather crow-like; glides and soars on level wings.

ORIENTAL HONEY-BUZZARD *Pernis ptilorhyncus* 55–65 cm

(10–12) **Male pale morph** *ruficollis*: Relatively large with rather small head, longish neck and short crest or tuft on hindcrown. Highly variable. Typically has greyish sides of head and pale underparts with dark throat-border and mesial streak, gorget of dark streaks on lower throat/upper breast and warm brown to rufous bars on lower breast to vent. Eyes brown, cere grey. May have mostly cinnamon-rufous or whitish head and underparts, the latter with streaks and/or bars or unmarked. In flight shows relatively long, rather broad wings and rather long narrow tail with two complete, well-spaced blackish

bands (often appears blackish with pale central band); underwing typically whitish with complete blackish trailing edge, narrow dark bars on coverts and (usually) three blackish bands across primaries and outer secondaries. Dark markings on flight feathers are also visible from above. (13) **Female pale morph**: Eyes yellow. In flight, from below, shows narrower tail-bands, four narrower blackish bands across primaries and outer secondaries, and narrower dark trailing edge to wing. Neither of latter two features is visible from above. Typically has browner sides of head and upperparts than male. See hawk eagles and *Buteo* buzzards. (14,15) **Adult dark morph**: Mostly dark chocolate-brown head, body and wing-coverts. (16) **Adult dark morph variant**: White bars/scales on underbody and underwing-coverts (*P.p.torquatus* only?). (17,18) **Juvenile pale morph**: Equally variable. Typically shows paler head, neck, underparts and underwing-coverts than adult. Has less distinct dark bands across underside of flight feathers and three or more dark tail-bands. May have dark mask and/or streaked underparts. Eyes yellow. **Other subspecies** *P.p.torquatus* (south W,S), *orientalis* (only visiting subspecies). **VOICE** A high-pitched screaming whistled *wheeew*. **HABITAT & BEHAVIOUR** Broadleaved evergreen and deciduous forest, open wooded country; up to 1,800 m (breeds mostly below 1,220 m). Holds wings level when soaring, often slightly arched when gliding. Flight display involves shallow upward swoop and almost vertical upstretching of wings, which are briefly winnowed.

BAT HAWK *Macheiramphus alcinus* 46 cm

(19,20) **Adult** *alcinus*: Falcon-like appearance, blackish-brown plumage, dark mesial streak on contrasting whitish throat and centre of upper breast. Has broken white eyering and variable amount of white on breast. In flight, most likely to be confused with Peregrine Falcon but, apart from distinctive plumage, wings appear longer and broader-based. (21) **Juvenile**: Browner with paler base to upper tail and more extensive whitish areas on underparts. **VOICE** A high, yelping *kwik kwik kwik kwik...* **HABITAT & BEHAVIOUR** Open areas in or near broadleaved evergreen forest, vicinity of bat-caves; lowlands. Mostly hunts at night, with rapid flight on shallow stiff wingbeats.

BLACK EAGLE *Ictinaetus malayensis* 69–81 cm

(22,23) **Adult** *malayensis*: Blackish overall, yellow cere and feet. Has rather long tail with indistinct narrow pale bands; closed wing-tips fall close to/beyond tail-tip. In flight shows unmistakable long broad wings with pinched-in bases and well-spread 'fingers', and longish tail. See *Aquila* eagles and dark morph Changeable Hawk Eagle. (24,25) **Juvenile**: Head, neck and underparts pale buffish with heavy blackish streaks; some pale tips on upperparts and wing-coverts. In flight also shows pale buffish underwing-coverts with blackish streaks and more obviously pale-barred underside of flight feathers and tail. **VOICE** A shrill yelping *wee-a-kwek* etc., particularly during display flight. **HABITAT & BEHAVIOUR** Broadleaved evergreen forest and nearby open areas; 800–2,565 m. Soars with wings in V, often spiralling gently downwards into forest clearings. Display flight involves steep dives through U-loop, up to near-vertical stall.

PLATE 53 KITES, WHITE-BELLIED SEA EAGLE & SHORT-TOED SNAKE EAGLE

BLACK KITE *Milvus migrans* 55–60 cm

(1–3) **Adult** *govinda*: Rather nondescript dull brownish plumage and longish tail with shallow fork distinctive. Head, mantle and underparts indistinctly streaked darker, tail with indistinct narrow dark barring, cere, legs and feet yellow. In flight, outer wing is broadly fingered and angled backwards, paler diagonal band across coverts contrasts with mostly blackish remainder of upperwing, inner primaries somewhat paler; underwing similar but with uniform coverts and variably sized (usually small) whitish patch at base of primaries. (4,5) **Juvenile**: Crown, upper mantle, breast and belly streaked whitish to pale buff; rest of upperside and wings (including underwing-coverts) have whitish to pale buff tips; shows rather contrasting dark mask. (6,7) **Adult** *lineatus* (visitor throughout): Larger (61–66 cm), with more rufescent-tinged body and tail, and typically paler forehead, face and throat. In flight, underwing usually shows extensive whitish area on inner primaries with dark barring and whitish bases to blackish outer primaries. See harriers. (8,9) **Juvenile**: Like juvenile *govinda* but with broader, whiter streaks and feather-tips, and more prominent blackish mask. **VOICE** A high-pitched whinnying ***pee-errrr*** or ***ewe-wirrrrr***. **HABITAT & BEHAVIOUR** Open areas, coastal habitats, large rivers, cities; up to 800 m. Spends much time soaring and gliding, with wings slightly arched; twists tail.

BRAHMINY KITE *Haliastur indus* 44–52 cm

(10,11) **Adult** *indus*: Bright cinnamon-rufous plumage and contrasting whitish head, neck and breast with dark shaft-streaks diagnostic. Outer primaries largely blackish. (12,13) **Juvenile**: Recalls Black Kite but smaller, with shorter, rounded tail, overall warmer-tinged plumage and less obviously streaked crown and nape. In flight shows shorter, broader wings, some rufous markings on upperwing-coverts, rounded tail-tip and distinctive, unbarred buffish-white area across underside of primaries, contrasting with darker secondaries and black tips of outer primaries. *H.i.intermedius* (S) tends to have narrower dark shaft-streaks on whitish parts of plumage. **VOICE** A thin, high, stressed note followed by a hoarse gasping: ***tsss, herhehhe-hhehhehheh***... A drawn-out, mewing ***kyeeeer*** or ***kyerrh***. **HABITAT & BEHAVIOUR** Coastal areas, large lakes and rivers; mostly lowlands. Often scavenges around harbours.

WHITE-BELLIED SEA EAGLE *Haliaeetus leucogaster* 70–85 cm

(14,15) **Adult**: Very large, with grey upperparts and wings, white head, neck and underparts, and short, diamond-shaped white tail with blackish base. In flight shows bulging secondaries and relatively narrow outer wing, white coverts contrasting sharply with blackish remainder of underwing.

(16,17) **Juvenile**: Upperparts and wings mostly dark brownish, head, neck and underparts dull cream to buffish with dingy brownish wash across breast, tail off-white with broad dark brownish subterminal band. In flight, upperwing shows paler band across median coverts and paler area on inner primaries; underwing has warm buffish coverts and large whitish patch on primaries, contrasting with blackish secondaries and tips of primaries. See Pallas's Fish, Tawny and Imperial Eagles. (18) **Third year**: Resembles adult but has duller breast and underwing-coverts, paler underside of secondaries and black-tipped whitish underside of primaries. **VOICE** A loud, honking ***kank kank kank***... or ***blank blank blank blank***... shorter, quicker ***ken-ken-ken-ken***... and ***ka ka kaa***... **HABITAT & BEHAVIOUR** Rocky coasts, islets, sometimes larger inland waterbodies; up to 800 m (breeds in lowlands). Glides and soars with wings in V. Aerial courtship display includes acrobatic somersaults, side-slipping and stoops.

SHORT-TOED SNAKE EAGLE *Circaetus gallicus* 62–67 cm

(19,20) **Adult pale individual**: Medium-sized with rather big-headed, top-heavy appearance, yellow to orange-yellow eyes, longish unfeathered legs and relatively long wings, which reach tail-tip at rest. Pale wing-coverts, underparts whitish with indistinct markings. In flight, shows long broad wings (distinctly pinched-in at base), narrow dark barring and trailing edge on otherwise pale and rather featureless underwing, and three bands across undertail (terminal one broadest). (21) **Adult dark individual**: Distinctive dark hood, extensive dark barring below and darker bands across underwing. Plumage very variable. Head may be mostly pale and underparts and underwing can be very pale and rather featureless, but always shows tail-banding and some dark markings on underwing. Upperside normally shows contrastingly pale lesser and median coverts. See juvenile Crested Serpent Eagle and Rufous-bellied Hawk Eagle. **Juvenile**: Shows uniform narrow pale tips to wing feathers, paler and more contrasting median and lesser upperwing-coverts, pale-tipped greater coverts and poorly marked underwing, without dark trailing edge. **VOICE** May give plaintive musical whistled ***weeo*** or longer ***weeooo***, sometimes followed by gull-like ***woh-woh-woh*** or ***quo-quo-quo***. **HABITAT & BEHAVIOUR** Open and coastal areas; lowlands. Flies with rather slow, heavy wingbeats; soars with wings held flat or slightly raised, with gently drooping primaries; frequently hovers.

PLATE 54 OSPREY, FISH EAGLES & WHITE-TAILED EAGLE

OSPREY *Pandion haliaetus* 55–63 cm

(1) **Adult male** *haliaetus*: Fairly large size, uniform dark brown upperside and contrasting white head and underparts with dark line through eye and dark streaks on breast (often forming complete band) distinctive. (2) **Adult female**: Breast-band broader. In flight, adults show long, rather slender wings (typically angled back from carpal joints and bowed), relatively shortish tail, white underwing-coverts with contrasting blackish primary coverts and tips to greater coverts, and evenly barred tail. (3) **Juvenile**: Upperparts and wing-coverts broadly fringed white to buffish, breast markings less defined. **VOICE** May give series of hoarse, falling whistles: *piu-piu-piu-piu*... **HABITAT & BEHAVIOUR** Lakes, large rivers, sea coasts; up to 800 m. Catches fish in feet in plunge-dive onto surface of water; often hovers over water.

PALLAS'S FISH EAGLE *Haliaeetus leucoryphus* 76–84 cm

(4,5) **Adult**: Recalls Grey-headed but larger, head, neck and upper mantle warm buffish to whitish, has darker brown upperside, dark brown thighs and vent, and blackish base of tail. In flight shows longer, straighter wings and longer blackish tail with broad white central band. (6,7) **Juvenile**: Similar to White-bellied Sea Eagle but underparts more uniformly dark, narrow pale supercilium contrasts with blackish mask, tail blackish-brown. In flight shows similar underwing pattern but coverts mostly dark brown with whitish band across median coverts to axillaries, outer primaries all dark. Whitish primary flashes rule out White-tailed Eagle. (8) **Second/third year**: Similar to juvenile but underside paler and more uniform. In flight, underwing shows broader whitish band across median coverts, and almost all-dark flight feathers. **VOICE** A series of loud, guttural notes, repeated up to 14 times or more: *kha-kha-kha-kha*...; *gho-gho-gho-gho*...; *gao-gao-gao-gao*... etc. Calling may speed up and run to a higher-pitched excited yelping. **HABITAT** Large lakes and rivers, marshes; lowlands.

WHITE-TAILED EAGLE *Haliaeetus albicilla* 70–90 cm

(9,10) **Adult** *albicilla*: Very large size, nondescript brownish plumage, big yellow bill and short, diamond-shaped white tail diagnostic. Has paler brown to creamy-whitish hood and upper breast, mostly blackish secondaries and primaries, indistinct darker streaks on head and body, and mottled wing-coverts. (11–13) **Juvenile**: Upperparts and wing-coverts mostly darker, warmish brown with blackish tips, head and underparts blackish-brown with pale streaks on neck and breast, bill dusky-greyish, tail feathers broadly bordered blackish. In flight shows distinctive combination of very broad, parallel-edged wings, dark underwing with whitish axillaries and narrow whitish bands across coverts, and whitish spikes on tail feathers. See White-rumped and Cinereous Vultures, Himalayan Griffon and

Aquila eagles. (14) **Second/third year**: Broad buffish-white line on underwing-coverts, brown-buff belly to vent. **Third/fourth year**: Similar to juvenile but body darker. In flight shows less prominent whitish bands across underwing-coverts and white tail with narrow blackish terminal band. **VOICE** A loud rapid yelping *klee-klee-klee-klee-klee-klee*... **HABITAT & BEHAVIOUR** Large lakes and rivers, open country; recorded in lowlands. Soars with wings held level or only slightly raised; glides on level wings or with outer wing slightly depressed.

LESSER FISH EAGLE *Ichthyophaga humilis* 51–68 cm

(15–17) **Adult** *humilis*: Like Grey-headed Fish Eagle but smaller, with somewhat paler upperparts, wing-coverts and breast, and dull greyish tail with darker terminal band (often appears rather uniform). In flight, underwing similar but may show whitish bases to outer primaries, undertail dark brownish with only slightly contrasting dark terminal band. (18,19) **Juvenile**: From Grey-headed by paler upperparts, plainer head and breast, with only vague paler streaks, no whitish supercilium, more contrasting white vent, darker tail. **Other subspecies** *I.h.plumbea* (W,NW): Averages 20% larger (within size range given above). **VOICE** Various deep, yelping and whining gull-like sounds: *yow*; *yow-ow*; *ow-ow-ow-ow*; *yow-yow-yow-yow*; *yaa'aaah*; *eeyaauuah*; *yow-eee-aaa...yow-aaa* etc. **HABITAT & BEHAVIOUR** Larger rivers in forest; lowlands. Spends long periods perched in waterside trees. Glides and soars on level wings.

GREY-HEADED FISH EAGLE *Ichthyophaga ichthyaetus* 69–74 cm

(20–22) **Adult**: Rather large and long-necked, with plain greyish hood, sharply contrasting white thighs and vent, and rounded white tail with broad black terminal band. Upperparts and wing-coverts greyish-brown, breast mostly warm brown to brownish-grey. In flight, wings appear rather broad and rounded, white tail-base and vent contrasting sharply with all-dark wings. (23,24) **Juvenile**: Head, neck, breast and upper belly mostly warm brownish, with narrow white supercilium and whitish streaks on crown, sides of head, foreneck and breast; upperside browner-tinged than adult, tail dark with whitish mottling showing as faint pale bands. In flight, underwing-coverts mostly whitish, flight feathers mostly whitish with darker tips and some faint narrow darker bars towards their tips. Immature plumages poorly documented. Gradually develops darker underwing and adult tail pattern. (25) **Second/third year**: Whitish patches on primaries, white thighs and vent, dark end to tail. **VOICE** During courtship display utters a powerful barking *kroi-ork* and repeated loud eerie *tiu-weeeu*. **HABITAT & BEHAVIOUR** Lakes, swamps, large rivers; lowlands. Soars with wings held level or in shallow V.

PLATE 55 VULTURES

WHITE-RUMPED VULTURE *Gyps bengalensis* 75–85 cm

(1–3) **Adult**: Blackish plumage with contrasting white neck-ruff, lower back and rump. Has mostly greyish-brown naked head and longish neck, and rather short thick dark bill with pale bluish-grey upper mandible. In flight shows very broad wings with well-spaced fingers, short tail, distinctive white patch on back and rump, mostly greyish secondaries and inner primaries (above and below) and diagnostic white underwing-coverts with black leading edge. See White-bellied Sea Eagle. (4,5) **Juvenile**: Browner overall, neck-ruff dark brownish, back and rump dark brownish, head and neck mostly covered with whitish down, bill blackish, lesser and median wing-coverts vaguely streaked paler, underparts narrowly streaked whitish. In flight shows rather uniform dark plumage with short narrow whitish bands across underwing-coverts; leading edge of under-wing-coverts is darker than greater underwing-coverts. See White-tailed Eagle. Gradually attains adult features with age. **Second/third year**: Like juvenile but primary and greater under-wing-coverts mostly whitish (shows some whitish feathers on lower back and beginnings of short buffy neck-ruff). **VOICE** Often silent but gives occasional grunts, croaks, hisses and squeals at nest sites, roosts and when feeding. **HABITAT** Open country, vicinity of abattoirs, cliffs; up to 1,350 m.

SLENDER-BILLED VULTURE *Gyps tenuirostris* 80–95 cm

(6–8) **Adult**: Told by mostly rather pale sandy-brown body and wing-coverts and contrasting naked blackish head and longish neck. Has narrow head profile and relatively long slender dark bill, relatively small pale neck-ruff, whitish lower back and rump, dark-centred greater coverts (above and below) and dark greyish legs and feet. In flight, relatively uniform pale upper- and underwing-coverts and underbody contrast with dark head and neck and blackish secondaries and primaries. (9,10) **Juvenile**: Neck-ruff browner, upperwing-coverts duller and browner and vaguely streaked, underparts faintly streaked. **VOICE** Occasional hissing and cackling sounds. **HABITAT** Open country; lowlands. **NOTE** Formerly united with Indian Vulture *G. indicus*, as Long-billed Vulture *G. indicus* (see Rasmussen and Parry 2001).

HIMALAYAN GRIFFON *Gyps himalayensis* 115–125 cm

(11–13) **Adult**: Huge and bulky with shortish, thick pale bill, pale head, thickish neck and mostly sandy-buffy body and wing-coverts. Neck-ruff brownish-buff, legs and feet pinkish. In flight, plumage resembles Slender-billed Vulture but head pale, upper body and wing-coverts much paler and more contrasting, underwing-coverts (including greater coverts) uniformly whitish with narrow dark leading edge. (14,15) **Juvenile**: Similar to White-rumped Vulture but considerably larger and more heavily built, with whitish streaks on mantle to uppertail-coverts and scapulars, broader, more prominent whitish streaks on upper- and underwing-coverts and underparts, and paler legs and feet. In flight, plumage very similar to White-rumped but underwing-coverts typically have longer, more clearly separated buffish bands, leading edge of underwing-coverts same colour as greater underwing-coverts (not darker). (16) **Subadult**: Develops paler underbody and upperwing-coverts, aiding separation from White-rumped. **VOICE** Occasional grunts and hissing sounds. **HABITAT** Open country; recorded in lowlands.

CINEREOUS VULTURE *Aegypius monachus* 100–110 cm

(17,18) **Adult**: Huge size, uniform blackish-brown plumage. Bill larger than other vultures, pale crown and nape contrast with black face and foreneck, legs and feet greyish-white. In flight shows very broad, relatively straight-edged wings; appears all dark except for narrow pale line at base of flight feathers. (19) **Juvenile**: Plumage even blacker, head and neck mostly blackish. **HABITAT** Open country; lowlands.

RED-HEADED VULTURE *Sarcogyps calvus* 81–85 cm

(20,21) **Male**: Blackish plumage, red head, neck, legs and feet. Has yellowish eyes, pale dark-tipped tertials and secondaries, white frontal part of neck-ruff and white lateral body-patches. In flight, these white areas and pale band across bases of flight feathers (less pronounced on upperwing) contrast sharply with black remainder of wings and body. (22,23) **Juvenile**: Dark brown above with narrow pale fringing, paler brown below, with buff shaft-streaks, head and neck pinkish with some whitish down, eyes brown, legs and feet pinkish, vent whitish, flight feathers uniform (above and below). In flight shows similar underside pattern to adult, apart from all-dark flight feathers and whitish vent. **Female**: Eyes dark brown to dark red. **VOICE** Occasional squeaks, hisses and grunts. **HABITAT** Open country and wooded areas, dry deciduous forest with rivers; lowlands.

PLATE 56 HARRIERS

WESTERN MARSH HARRIER *Circus aeruginosus* 48–56 cm

(1–3) **Male** *aeruginosus*: Recalls Eastern Marsh but markings on head, neck and breast browner, ear-coverts paler, dark of upperparts and wing-coverts brown and more uniform, lower underparts and thighs rufous-chestnut. In flight also shows buff leading edge to lesser upperwing-coverts. (4–6) **Female**: Similar to juvenile Eastern Marsh but shows dark eye-line that extends down side of neck; lacks neck-streaks. In flight shows smaller pale flash on underside of primaries; normally shows broad creamy-buff leading edge to inner wing and creamy-buff breast-band. (7,8) **Juvenile**: Resembles female but initially lacks creamy-buff on wing-coverts and breast. Male gradually acquires grey parts of plumage with age. VOICE May give weak *kyik* or cackling *chek-ek-ek-ek-ek*... HABITAT Marshes, rice paddies, open areas; lowlands.

EASTERN MARSH HARRIER *Circus spilonotus* 48–56 cm

(9–11) **Male** *spilonotus*: Similar to Pied but shows black streaks on neck and breast and lacks large white patches on upperwing-coverts. Has pale scaling on upperparts and wing-coverts. In flight, darker lesser upperwing-coverts are apparent. (12–14) **Female**: Resembles Pied but belly and thighs dull rufous. In flight further differs by lack of pale leading edge to lesser upperwing-coverts, thinner bars on uppertail with plain central feathers, extensively dull chestnut-brown underwing-coverts and less boldly marked underside of secondaries. Other harriers ruled out by combination of grey on wings and tail, streaked head and breast and rufescent belly and thighs. (15,16) **Juvenile** (dark individual illustrated): Rather uniform dark brown (faint paler area across breast) with pale hood, with or without dark crown and band across lower throat; head-sides rather uniform, variable darker streaking on neck, pronounced creamy-buff streaks sometimes on mantle. In flight, blackish-tipped creamy-greyish underside of primaries, contrasting with dark remainder of underwing, distinctive. Male gradually acquires grey plumage parts with age. VOICE May utter a kite-like mewing *keeau*, particularly at roost sites. HABITAT & BEHAVIOUR Marshes, rice paddies, open areas; up to 800 m. Large number may gather at roost sites. Glides with wings in shallow V.

HEN HARRIER *Circus cyaneus* 44–52 cm

(17–19) **Male** *cyaneus*: Grey plumage with contrasting white lower breast to undertail-coverts. When perched, wing-tips fall well short of tail-tip. In flight shows distinctive combination of all-black, 'five-fingered' outer primaries (above and below), darker trailing edge to rest of wing (more prominent below) and obvious unmarked white band across uppertail-coverts. See Black-shouldered Kite. (20–22) **Female**: Rather nondescript brownish, with dark-barred wings and tail and dark-streaked pale neck and underparts. Heavy arrowhead or drop-shaped markings on thighs and undertail-coverts (wide arrowhead shapes on undertail-coverts); wing-tips fall well short of tail-tip at rest. In flight shows clearly defined broad white uppertail-covert band; has two well-marked dark bands on upperside of secondaries (terminal one broadest and most obvious); underwing has broadest dark band along trailing edge, the other two differing in width and variably spaced, but with pale bands between them reaching wing; dark tips to inner primaries and dark, unpatterned axillaries. (23,24) **Juvenile**: Similar to female (underparts streaked) but generally rustier, with darker underside of secondaries. Boldly streaked underparts, narrow whitish collar. VOICE May give a rapid, quacking chatter, *quek-ek-ek-ek*, *quik-ik-ak-ik-uk-ik* etc. HABITAT & BEHAVIOUR Open areas; up to 1,500 m. Glides with wings in shallow V.

PIED HARRIER *Circus melanoleucos* 43–46 cm

(25–27) **Male**: Unmarked black head, mantle, back, upper breast and median coverts, large whitish patch on lesser coverts. In flight, black outer primaries (above and below) and black band across upperwing-coverts contrast sharply with mostly pale remainder of wings. See Black-shouldered Kite. (28–30) **Female**: Separated from other female harriers by whitish area along upper edge of lesser coverts, grey outer edge to wing-coverts and secondaries, and almost unmarked whitish thighs and vent. In flight, from above, shows distinctive combination of whitish leading edge to lesser coverts, whitish uppertail-covert band, uniformly barred tail and grey primary coverts and flight feathers with dark bars; also has broadly dark-tipped primaries and darker trailing edge to wing. Relatively pale underwing, narrower dark bands across secondaries than Hen. (31,32) **Juvenile**: Relatively uniform dark rufous-brown wing-coverts, dark rufous-brown underparts. Resembles Eastern Marsh but more rufous-brown. In flight shows narrow whitish uppertail-covert band and, from below, distinctive combination of darkish rufous-brown body and wing-coverts, indistinct paler bands across blackish secondaries (tapering towards body) and pale greyish primaries with dark bars restricted to tips and inner feathers (leading edge also darker). VOICE Displaying male gives *keee-veeee* calls and female utters a rapid *kee-kee-kee* or rapid, chattering *chak-chak-chak-chak*... Otherwise usually silent but occasionally utters a rapid *wek-wek-wek*. HABITAT & BEHAVIOUR Marshes, grassland, open areas, cultivation; up to 800 m. Glides with wings in shallow V.

PLATE 57 ACCIPITERS

SHIKRA *Accipiter badius* 30–36 cm

(1–3) **Male** *poliopsis*: Pale grey sides of head and upperparts, white throat with faint grey mesial streak and dense narrow orange-rufous bars on breast and belly diagnostic. Tail has central and outer pairs of feathers plain grey, the rest with 3–4 dark cross-bars, outer primary tips blackish, eyes orange-red to scarlet. Barring below sometimes more pinkish and less marked. In flight, underwing appears rather whitish with some dark bars across dark-tipped outer primaries and indistinct warm buffish markings on coverts. See Eurasian Sparrowhawk. (4,5) **Female**: Larger; eyes yellow, upperside washed brownish (particularly nape and mantle), underparts more coarsely barred rufous. In flight undertail shows 7–8 narrow dark bands on outer feathers. (6,7) **Juvenile**: Crown, upperparts and wing-coverts brown with paler fringes. Has warm-tinged dark brown mesial streak, tear-drop breast-streaks turning to barring on flanks and spots on thighs, five complete narrow dark bands across upper-tail (subterminal one broadest) and greenish-yellow to yellow eyes. In flight shows even dark bars across whole of whitish underside of flight feathers. Best separated from similar Besra by larger size, spots on thighs, paler upperside and narrower dark tail-bands. See Crested Goshawk. **VOICE** A loud harsh thin *titu-titu* and long, drawn-out screaming *iheeya iheeya*... **HABITAT & BEHAVIOUR** Deciduous, open broadleaved evergreen, mixed broadleaved and coniferous forest, open areas, cultivation; up to 1,600 m. Often seen hunting in open.

CHINESE SPARROWHAWK *Accipiter soloensis* 29–35 cm

(8) **Male**: Similar to Shikra but grey of plumage considerably darker, breast pale pinkish to pinkish-rufous (either unbarred or indistinctly barred), belly whitish; closed wing-tips fall more than halfway along visible part of uppertail. Eyes dark brownish-red (cere prominent and orange). In flight shows diagnostic, mostly whitish underwing with contrasting broadly black-tipped primaries, dark grey trailing edge to secondaries and pinkish-buff tinge to unmarked coverts. (9) **Female**: Usually has somewhat darker, more rufous breast and upper belly, often with some faint greyish barring on latter, and underwing-coverts typically more rufous-tinged; eyes yellow to orange-yellow. (10,11) **Juvenile**: Eyes like female. Difficult to separate from Shikra, Japanese Sparrowhawk and Besra. Important features at rest include: slate-greyish crown and sides of head contrasting with dark brown upperparts, short pale supercilium (not extending obviously behind eye), barred thighs, relatively long primary projection, distinct chestnut tinge to neck-streaks, upperpart fringing and underpart markings, and four visible complete dark bands on uppertail. In flight, pointed wing-tips and unmarked underwing-coverts are distinctive; shows only two dark bands across inner secondaries (apart from dark trailing edge); undertail has three visible complete dark bands but five narrower ones on outer feathers. **VOICE** Usually silent. A rapid, shrill, nasal, accelerating *kee pe-pe-pe-petu-petu* (descending in pitch) on breeding grounds. **HABITAT & BEHAVIOUR** Open country, wooded areas. Often seen in migrating flocks over forest; up to 1,500 m. Often in flocks during migration.

JAPANESE SPARROWHAWK *Accipiter gularis* 25–31 cm

(12–14) **Male**: Similar to Besra but upperside tends to be paler, mesial streak faint or lacking, has rather diffuse pale pinkish-rufous barring on breast, belly and flanks, uppertail has narrow dark bands (usually four complete ones visible), closed wing-tips fall about halfway along tail. Eyes deep red. In flight, wings appear more pointed. See Eurasian Sparrowhawk. (15,16) **Female**: Larger than male, with orange-yellow to yellow eyes, distinctly browner upperparts, more prominent mesial streak and more obviously barred underparts. From Besra by noticeably darker upperside with less contrasting crown, much narrower mesial streak, lack of breast-streaks, dense but even greyish-brown bars on breast, belly and flanks, and uppertail-bands (see male). See much larger Eurasian. (17) **Juvenile female**: Difficult to separate from Besra but mesial streak normally much thinner, breast-streaks less pronounced (never black), often less heavily marked belly and flanks and narrower dark bands on uppertail (as adult); may show slaty-grey hindcrown contrasting somewhat with mantle. In flight, from above, shows narrower, less distinct dark bands across flight feathers and tail than Besra; underside very similar. Eyes yellow. **HABITAT & BEHAVIOUR** Open country, forest edge, lightly wooded areas; up to 1,500 m. Often seen in flocks during migration.

BESRA *Accipiter virgatus* 26–32 cm

(18,19) **Male** *affinis*: Distinguished by combination of very dark slate-greyish upperside (sometimes slightly purplish-tinged), prominent dark mesial streak, broad blackish and rufous-chestnut streaks on centre of upper breast, and broad rufous-chestnut bars on lower breast, upper belly and thighs. Eyes orange to deep red; closed wing-tips fall less than one third along tail, uppertail usually with four visible dark bands broader or equal to intervening pale bands. Resembles miniature Crested Goshawk but lacks crest, darker above. In flight, wings appear relatively short, rounded and blunter than in other small accipiters; undertail shows three complete dark bands but 5–6 narrower ones on outermost feathers (distal one broader). (20,21) **Female**: Larger, with yellow eyes, and browner-tinged upperside with contrasting blackish crown and nape. (22) **Juvenile female**: Difficult to separate from Shikra and Japanese Sparrowhawk but has more prominent dark mesial streak, blacker breast-streaks and even-width dark and pale tail-bands. In flight also shows blunter wings. Also differs from Japanese by lack of any contrast between hindcrown and mantle and, in flight, by broader, more pronounced dark bands across upperside of flight feathers and tail. **VOICE** A loud squealing *ki-weeer* and rapid *tchew-tchew-tchew*... **HABITAT & BEHAVIOUR** Broadleaved evergreen and mixed broadleaved forest; up to 2,000 m, commoner at higher levels. Generally hunts birds inside wooded habitats and less likely to be seen soaring overhead than other accipiters.

PLATE 58 ACCIPITERS & BUZZARDS

CRESTED GOSHAWK *Accipiter trivirgatus* 40–46 cm (birds in S are somewhat smaller)

(1,2) **Male** *indicus*: Combination of relatively large size, short crest, slaty crown and sides of head, brownish-grey upperparts, dark mesial streak, streaked breast and barred belly distinctive. Mesial streak blackish, sides of breast rufous-chestnut, streaks on central breast and broad bars on belly rufous-chestnut; uppertail greyish with three complete broad blackish bands (pale bands of equal width), eyes yellow to orange-yellow, legs relatively short and stout, closed wing-tips fall close to base of tail. In flight wings appear broad, blunt-tipped and rounded with bulging secondaries (pinched-in at base); underside shows four dark bands across flight feathers, three broad dark bands across central tail feathers and four narrow bands across outermost tail feathers. See juvenile Shikra, female and juvenile Besra and Jerdon's Baza. (3) **Juvenile**: Generally similar to adult but eyes yellow, sides of head and upperparts browner, has rufous to buffish feather fringes on crown and nape, pale buffish fringing on mantle and wing-coverts, streaked ear-coverts, underparts washed buffish and mostly streaked brown, bars restricted to lower flanks and thighs. **Female**: Larger, with browner-tinged crown and sides of head and browner breast-streaks and bars on belly. **VOICE** A shrill, screaming *he he hehehehe* and high-pitched squeaking *chiup* when alarmed. **HABITAT & BEHAVIOUR** Broadleaved evergreen, deciduous and mixed broadleaved and coniferous forest; up to 1,800 m. Performs display flights with shallow, winnowing, bowed wings and fluffed-out undertail-coverts.

EURASIAN SPARROWHAWK *Accipiter nisus* 28–38 cm

(4–6) **Male** *nisosimilis*: Distinguished by combination of size, slaty-grey upperside, orange-rufous wash on cheeks, narrow orange-rufous streaks on throat, faint orange-rufous bars on breast, belly and flanks, and faint darker bands on uppertail (subterminal one noticeably broader). Often shows faint narrow pale supercilium, eyes orange-red to orange-yellow, has no isolated mesial streak. In flight appears relatively long-winged and long-tailed. (7,8) **Female**: Larger, with more prominent whitish supercilium, somewhat browner-tinged upperside, more obvious dark uppertail-bands and darker, more pronounced markings below. Combination of size, prominent supercilium, unstreaked breast and tail pattern rule out Japanese and Besra. (9) **Juvenile**: Best separated from other smaller accipiters by combination of size, heavy rufous-chestnut to blackish barring on underparts, and tail pattern (like female). Some can show more streak-like markings or arrowhead shapes on breast. **VOICE** May give a loud, shrill *kyi-kyi-kyi*... when alarmed. **HABITAT** Forested and open areas; up to 1,830 m (mainly in mountains).

NORTHERN GOSHAWK *Accipiter gentilis* 48–62 cm

(10) **Male** *schvedowi*: Most likely to be confused with female Eurasian Sparrowhawk. Usually considerably larger, white supercilium more pronounced, crown and sides of head darker than mantle, lower sides of head and throat rather uniform whitish, rest of underparts barred brownish-grey. In flight appears proportionately longer-winged, shorter-

tailed and heavier-chested, underwing has much finer, less pronounced dark barring on coverts and much less contrasting darker bands across flight feathers. (11,12) **Female**: Considerably larger than male, grey of upperside browner-tinged, eyes orange-yellow (*vs* orange-red), banding on underwing more obvious. (13,14) **Juvenile female**: Darker and browner above than adult, with buffish to whitish fringes, supercilium less distinct and buffish, neck and underparts buff with bold dark brown streaks; uppertail has distinct irregular broad dark bands. In flight also shows more bulging secondaries and heavier markings on underwing, with dark streaks/spots on pale buffish coverts. Eyes yellow. **VOICE** May give loud, guttural *kyee-kyee-kyee*... in alarm. **HABITAT** Wooded country, sometimes more open areas; up to 2,500 m.

RUFOUS-WINGED BUZZARD *Butastur liventer* 38–43 cm

(15–17) **Adult**: Size and shape recalls Grey-faced Buzzard but has mostly greyish head and underparts, contrasting with mostly rufous-brown to rufous-chestnut upperside. Has indistinct dark streaks on crown, neck and breast, lacks dark mesial stripe, uppertail strongly rufescent. In flight, mostly uniform rufous-chestnut upperside of flight feathers and rump to tail, coupled with relatively plain whitish underwing-coverts and indistinctly patterned undertail, diagnostic. (18) **Juvenile**: Head browner with narrow white supercilium; upperparts, lesser wing-coverts, breast and belly duller and more brownish. **VOICE** A shrill *pit-piu* with higher first note. **HABITAT** Dry deciduous forest, secondary growth; up to 800 m.

GREY-FACED BUZZARD *Butastur indicus* 41–49 cm

(19–21) **Male**: Size, rather slim build and relatively large-headed appearance recalls both accipiters and *Buteo* buzzards. Crown, upperside and breast mostly rather plain greyish-brown with greyer sides of head, yellow eyes, white throat, blackish submoustachial and mesial stripes, greyish-brown and white bars on belly and three dark bands across tail. At rest, closed wing-tips fall not far short of tail-tip. In flight, wings straighter and longer than in accipiters and much narrower than *Buteo* buzzards; upperwing shows rufescent bases to primaries, underwing rather pale with darker trailing edge (primary tips blackish), some dark markings on coverts, and indistinct narrow dark bands across flight feathers; pale undertail with three dark bands and plainer outer feathers. See Jerdon's Baza. (22) **Juvenile**: Crown and neck brown, narrowly streaked white, broad white supercilium contrasts with greyish-brown sides of head, underparts dull whitish with pronounced dark streaks, mesial streak narrower, upperparts and wing-coverts browner with pale tips (particularly latter). Underwing and tail similar to adults. **Female**: Tends to have more prominent supercilium, browner-tinged ear-coverts and more whitish barring on breast. **Adult dark morph**: Rare. Head, body and wing-coverts (above and below) dark brown, rest of wings and tail typical. **Juvenile dark morph**: Differs primarily by dark brown eyes. **VOICE** A plaintive high-pitched *tik HWEEER* or *tik H'WEEER* (introductory note audible at fairly close range). **HABITAT & BEHAVIOUR** Open coniferous, broadleaved and mixed forest, secondary growth, open areas; up to 1,800 m. Flight rather direct with fast wingbeats and interspersed glides. Soars with wings held level.

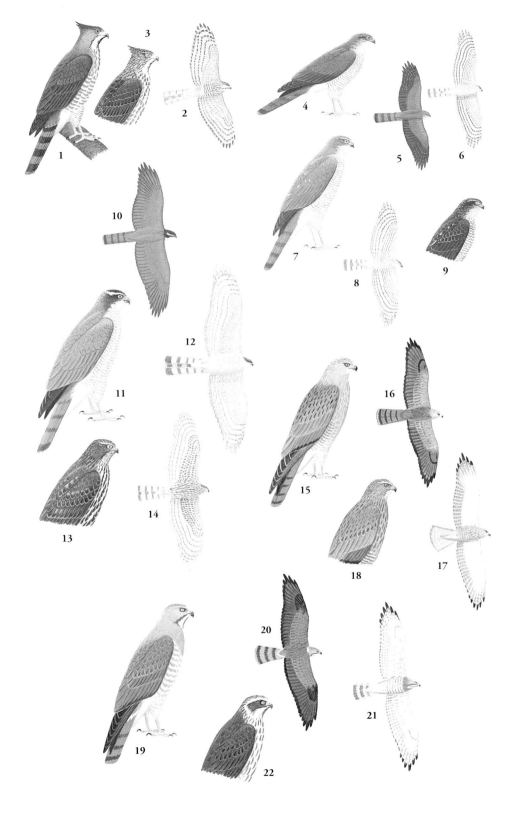

PLATE 59 *AQUILA* EAGLES

GREATER SPOTTED EAGLE *Aquila clanga* 65–72 cm

(1–3) **Adult**: Differs from similar large dark eagles by relatively shorter wings, smallish bill and shortish tail. In flight, wings appear relatively short and broad, upperside rather uniformly dark with paler area on bases of primaries and narrow pale band across uppertail-coverts; underwing rather uniformly dark with distinctive whitish patch or crescent at base of outer primaries. (4–6) **Juvenile**: Blackish, with pronounced whitish spots on upperwing-coverts, and whitish tips to scapulars, tertials, most other wing feathers and tail; has broad pale buffish streaks on belly and thighs (sometimes also or only on breast or lacking altogether). In flight, whitish bands across upperwing-coverts and whitish band across uppertail-coverts contrast sharply with dark upperparts, rest of wing-coverts and secondaries; underwing shows darker coverts than flight feathers, paler bases of primaries than adult and faint dark bars across secondaries and inner primaries. (7) **Subadult**: Exhibits a mixture of adult and juvenile features. (8,9) **Juvenile pale morph**: Mostly buffy or creamy head, body and wing-coverts (as adult pale morph), whitish tips to upperwing-coverts, secondaries, inner primaries and tail. (10) **Juvenile pale morph**: Younger individual with rufescent-brown body and wing-coverts. **Adult pale (*'fulvescens'*) morph**: Rare. Has mostly buffish to rufous body, median and lesser upper- and underwing-coverts. **VOICE** Series of short quick high-pitched notes: ***hi-hi-hi-hi-hi***...; ***hihi hihi-hi***... etc. **HABITAT & BEHAVIOUR** Marshes, lakes, rivers, open country; up to 400 m. Soars on flattish wings, glides with primaries distinctly angled downwards.

TAWNY EAGLE *Aquila rapax* 64–71 cm

(11–13) **Adult pale morph** *vindhiana*: Difficult to separate from pale morph Greater Spotted but has somewhat larger bill, longer neck, fuller and longer 'trousers' and yellowish eyes. In flight, underwing shows paler inner primaries and bases of outer primaries, without well-defined whitish patch or crescent. (14,15) **Adult dark morph**: Rare. Difficult to separate from Steppe at rest but somewhat more powerfully built, lacks rufescent nape-patch and has dark throat. Often adopts a more upright posture; at very close range, gape typically ends below centre of eye (extends behind eye in Steppe). In flight, shows distinctive underwing pattern, with greyish inner primaries and bases of outer primaries contrasting with uniformly dark secondaries. Best separated from spotted eagles by combination of size, structure, underwing pattern and yellowish eyes. (16,17) **Juvenile pale morph**: Whitish tips to upperwing-coverts, secondaries, inner primaries and tail. When fresh, has strongly rufescent head, body and wing-coverts. **Juvenile dark morph**: Similar to adult but with creamy tips to upperwing-coverts, secondaries, inner primaries and tail. **VOICE** May give a repeated barking *kowk*. **HABITAT & BEHAVIOUR** Open country; recorded in lowlands. Glides with inner wing slightly raised and primaries slightly angled downwards.

STEPPE EAGLE *Aquila nipalensis* 76–80 cm

(18–20) **Adult** *nipalensis*: Larger, and larger-billed, than other large, uniformly dark eagles. Best separated from Greater Spotted and dark morph Tawny by combination of size, structure, full 'trousers', rufous-buff nape-patch, somewhat paler throat and distinct dark barring on secondaries. At very close range, gape typically ends behind eye. In flight, wings and tail distinctly longer than spotted eagles. Underwing pattern distinctive, with mostly blackish primary coverts, and contrasting darker trailing edge to and dark barring across flight feathers. See Black Eagle. (21–23) **Juvenile**: Head, body and wing-coverts paler and more grey-brown, with whitish tips to greater and primary upperwing-coverts, secondaries and tail feathers, and broader, whiter band across uppertail-coverts. In flight, easily separated from other large dark eagles by broad whitish trailing edge to underwing-coverts (wide band across underwing). (24) **Subadult**: Lacks obvious whitish band on underwing but is already developing distinctive adult-like underwing. **VOICE** May give a repeated, deep barking *ow* or slightly hoarse *akh akh akh akh*... **HABITAT & BEHAVIOUR** Open country; lowlands. Soars on flatter wings than Greater Spotted.

IMPERIAL EAGLE *Aquila heliaca* 72–83 cm

(25–27) **Adult**: Unmistakable large blackish-brown eagle with large head and bill, golden-buff supercilium, ear-coverts, nape and hindneck, prominent white markings on upper scapulars, pale undertail-coverts and broadly black-tipped greyish tail. In flight shows almost uniformly blackish underwing and pale undertail-coverts. See Black Eagle. (28–30) **Juvenile**: Recalls pale morph Greater Spotted and Tawny but larger, with diagnostic distinct dark streaks on nape, neck, breast and wing-coverts (above and below). In flight also shows a pale greyish wedge on inner primaries. **VOICE** Repeated deep, barking *owk*. **HABITAT & BEHAVIOUR** Open country, cultivation; up to 400 m. In flight, wings held more level than other eagles.

PLATE 60 CRESTED SERPENT EAGLE, COMMON BUZZARD & EAGLES

CRESTED SERPENT EAGLE *Spilornis cheela* 56–74 cm

(1,2) **Adult** *burmanicus*: Large head, mostly dark brownish plumage. Prominent yellow cere, facial skin and eyes, short full, white-marked blackish crest on nape/hindneck; small white spots on median and lesser coverts, paler, warm-tinged head-sides, neck and underparts, with black-bordered whitish speckles turning to short bars on lower breast to undertail-coverts. Very broad-winged in flight; from below, shows distinctive darkish body/underwing-coverts, broad white band across underwing contrasting with broad black trailing edge, and black tail with broad white central band. See Oriental Honey-buzzard and hawk eagles. (3,4) **Juvenile**: Head scaled black and whitish with blackish ear-coverts; whitish tips/fringes above, whitish below, usually with faint buffish wash and dark streaks on throat-centre, breast and belly; has whitish tail with three complete blackish bands. In flight shows mostly whitish underwing, with buff-washed and dark-streaked wing-coverts, many fine dark bars across underside of flight feathers and indistinct broad darker trailing edge. See hawk eagles and Short-toed Snake Eagle. (5) **Adult** *malayensis* (S): Distinctly smaller, darker head-sides and underparts, more pronounced markings below. **VOICE** Rather vocal, particularly when soaring. Utters a loud plaintive high-pitched 2–4 note *hwiii-hwi*; *h'wi-hwi*; *hwi-hwi-hwi*; *h'wee hew-hew*; *hii-hwi-hwi* etc., sometimes introduced by spaced *hu-hu-hu-hu*... 'Song' is a sustained crescendo: *ha-ha-ha-ha hu-hu-hu-hu-h'weeooleeoo*. **HABITAT & BEHAVIOUR** Broadleaved evergreen, deciduous and peatswamp forest, secondary forest; up to 1,600 m. Soars with wings in shallow V. Displaying pairs soar with head and tail raised, dive at one another and undertake short flights with wings winnowed shallowly below horizontal.

COMMON BUZZARD *Buteo buteo* 51–57 cm

(6–8) **Adult pale morph** *japonicus*: Very variable. Combination of size, robust build, rather large head, mostly dark brown upperside and mostly whitish underparts with variable, large dark brown patch across belly distinctive. Typically shows dark brown and whitish streaks on crown and neck, more whitish sides of head with dark eye-stripe, heavy brown throat-streaks (particularly at sides), sparse brown breast-streaks and greyish-brown uppertail with numerous faint narrow darker bars. In flight shows broad rounded wings and shortish rounded tail; upperwing usually has paler area across primaries, underwing with contrasting blackish outer primary tips and blackish carpal patches, rest of underwing rather pale with whiter primaries and rather narrow dark trailing edge; has numerous indistinct narrow dark bars across underside of flight feathers and tail. See Osprey. (9–11) **Adult dark morph**: Body and wing-coverts blackish-brown, broader terminal tail-band; rest of underwing as pale morph. **Juvenile pale morph**: Like adult but has less heavily streaked underparts, narrower, paler and more diffuse trailing edge to underwing and evenly barred tail, without broader subterminal band. **VOICE** A plaintive, far-carrying mewing *peeeooo* or *peee-oo*, stressed at start. **HABITAT & BEHAVIOUR** Open country, open forest and forest edge, cultivation; up to 2,565 m. Soars with wings in shallow V and tail spread; glides on level wings; often hovers.

BONELLI'S EAGLE *Hieraaetus fasciatus* 65–72 cm

(12,13) **Adult** *fasciatus*: Dark brown above, whitish below with dark streaks on foreneck to breast and dark-barred thighs. Whitish patch on mantle, relatively uniform greyish tail with broad blackish subterminal band, no crest. In flight shows distinctive, faintly barred greyish underwing with whitish leading edge to mostly black coverts, and grey tail with prominent black subterminal band. (14–16) **Juvenile**: Head, upperparts and coverts paler/browner, uppertail browner with even, narrow darker bars; underparts warm buffish with dark streaks on lower throat and breast. In fresh plumage, head, underparts and underwing-coverts are rufous; this fades to dull rufous in time, later to buffy and, in some cases, to creamy. In flight, from below, shows warm buffish wing-coverts usually with distinctive dark tips to greater and primary coverts forming a narrow dark line across underwing; undertail evenly and finely dark-barred. See hawk eagles. **VOICE** A repeated shrill melodious *iub* and longer whistled *eeeoo* (lower-pitched at end) during display flight. **HABITAT & BEHAVIOUR** Forested areas, often near cliffs; 800–1,900 m. Glides on flat wings.

BOOTED EAGLE *Hieraaetus pennatus* 50–57 cm

(17–19) **Adult pale morph**: Relatively small with pale crown, dark sides of head and mostly whitish underparts. Pale scapulars, uppertail-coverts, and band across wing-coverts contrast with mostly dark remainder of upperside. In flight, whitish under-wing-coverts and pale wedge on inner primaries contrast sharply with otherwise blackish underwing, undertail greyish with indistinct dark terminal band and central feathers. (20,21) **Adult dark morph**: Head/body quite uniform dark brown. Tail shape/pattern (as pale morph), contrasting paler scapulars and uppertail-coverts and pale band across upperwing-coverts (in flight) rule out Black Kite. (22) **Adult rufous morph**: Shows strongly rufescent head, body and underwing-coverts. **Juvenile**: As adult but has prominent white trailing edge to wings and tail in fresh plumage. **VOICE** May give a clear shrill chattering *ki-ki-ki*... or longer *kee-kee-kee*... **HABITAT & BEHAVIOUR** Open and wooded areas, cultivation; up to 800 m. When gliding and soaring, holds wings slightly forwards and level, or with primaries angled slightly downwards; sometimes twists tail like Black Kite.

RUFOUS-BELLIED EAGLE *Hieraaetus kienerii* 53–61 cm

(23,24) **Adult** *formosae*: Blackish sides of head and upperside, white throat and upper breast and otherwise rufous-chestnut underparts diagnostic. Has slight crest and narrow dark streaks on breast to undertail-coverts. In flight, from below, shows mostly rufous-chestnut wing-coverts, pale leading edge to wings, and narrow dark bars across rather pale greyish flight feathers and tail (latter with blackish subterminal band). (25,26) **Juvenile**: Brown above, head-sides whitish with blackish eyeline, whitish below with black flank-patch. In flight, shows whitish underwing-coverts with broken dark trailing edge and narrower trailing edge to flight feathers and tail. From similar hawk eagles by dark upperside with brown primaries, blackish eyeline and flank-patch, indistinctly barred tail, underwing-covert pattern and lack of obvious crest. See Short-toed Snake Eagle. **VOICE** Fairly clear but low-pitched series of notes ending with very thin breathless note: *WHI-WHI-WHI-WHI yii*. See Changeable Hawk Eagle. **HABITAT & BEHAVIOUR** Broadleaved evergreen forest; up to 2,000 m. Usually glides and soars with wings held level.

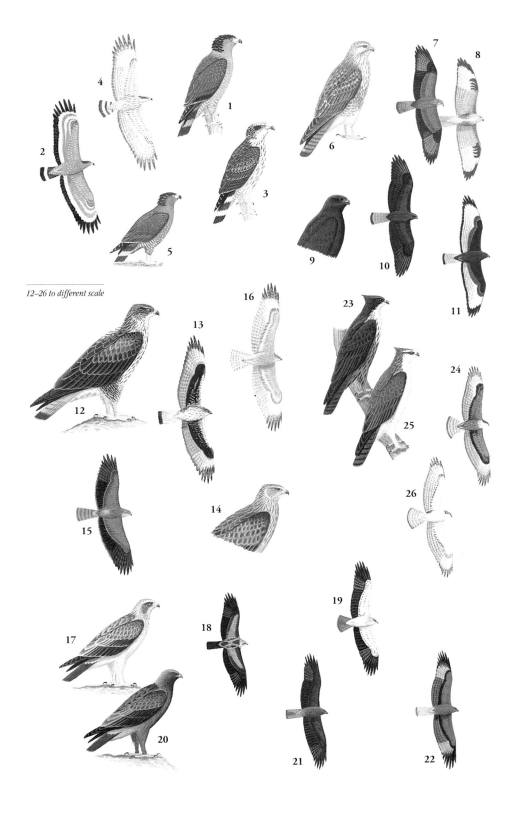

12–26 to different scale

PLATE 61 HAWK EAGLES

CHANGEABLE HAWK EAGLE *Spizaetus cirrhatus* 61–75 cm

(1–3) **Adult pale morph** *limnaetus*: Rather non-descript brown above, whitish below with dark mesial streak, dark streaks on breast and belly, and faint narrow rufous barring on thighs and undertail-coverts; has four dark bands on tail (terminal one is broader), crest distinctly short. In flight shows broad, rather parallel-edged wings. From other hawk eagles by combination of lack of belly-barring, relatively plain underwing-coverts, and undertail pattern with three rather narrow dark bands and a broader dark terminal band. See Bonelli's Eagle and Oriental Honey-buzzard. (4,5) **Adult dark morph**: Blackish overall with greyer, broadly dark-tipped tail. In flight, underwing shows greyer bases to flight feathers. Recalls Black Eagle but wings much more parallel-edged, lacks barring on underwing and undertail (apart from terminal band). See Common Buzzard. (6–8) **Juvenile pale morph**: Head, neck and underparts almost unmarked whitish; has prominent whitish fringes to upperpart feathers (particularly wing-coverts) and narrower, more numerous dark tail-bands (lacks wide dark terminal band). In flight, underside similar to adult apart from paler body and wing-coverts and tail pattern. **Juvenile dark morph**: Like adult but may show some dark barring on underside of flight feathers and tail. See Black Eagle. **VOICE** A somewhat ascending series of loud, shrill, high-pitched whistles, terminated by a thin, stressed, high-pitched note: *wi-wiwiwiwi-hii*; *wi-wi-wi-wi-wi-wi-wi-hiii*; *kwi-kwi-kwi-kwiii* etc. Also *k'wi-wi* or *kerWI-WI* recalling Crested Serpent Eagle. Juveniles give shrill *klit-klit* and *klit-kli* with stressed second note. **HABITAT & BEHAVIOUR** Broadleaved evergreen and deciduous forest; up to 2,000 m. Soars and glides with wings held level. During display flight, stretches neck forwards, lifts tail and holds wings in shallow V.

MOUNTAIN HAWK EAGLE *Spizaetus nipalensis* 66–75 cm

(9–11) **Adult** *nipalensis*: Similar to pale morph Changeable but has long erectile white-tipped blackish crest, whitish bars on rump, broader dark mesial streak, broad dark bars on belly, and equal-width dark and pale tail-bands. In flight from below, wings somewhat broader and more rounded (more pinched-in at base of secondaries), tail relatively shorter, wing-coverts with heavy dark markings, dark tail-bands broader. (12,13) **Juvenile**: From Changeable by distinctive crest, pale to warm buff head and underparts, darker-streaked crown, hindneck and sides of head, and buff-barred rump. In flight from below also differs by shape, and equal-width pale and

dark tail-bands. Underwing-coverts plain creamy-white. **VOICE** A shrill *tlueet-weet-weet*. **HABITAT & BEHAVIOUR** Broadleaved evergreen, deciduous and mixed forests; 600–2,565 m. Glides with wings held level; soars with wings in shallow V.

BLYTH'S HAWK EAGLE *Spizaetus alboniger* 51–58 cm

(14–16) **Adult**: Sides of head and crown to mantle distinctly blacker than other hawk eagles, underparts whitish with prominent black mesial streak, bold blackish breast-streaks and bold blackish bars on belly, thighs and vent, tail blackish with pale greyish broad central band and narrow tip. Crest long and erectile, blackish or with fine white tip. In flight shows whitish underwing with heavy blackish bars on coverts, blackish bands across flight feathers and distinctive tail pattern. See Crested Serpent Eagle. (17,18) **Juvenile**: Crown, hindneck and ear-coverts sandy-rufous, upperside browner than adult with whitish fringes, underparts plain pale buff to whitish with buffish breast and flanks, tail whitish with two or three medium-width dark bands and slightly broader dark terminal band, underwing-coverts plain creamy-whitish; crest similar to adult. From Mountain by smaller size, more rufescent unstreaked head and hindneck, and different tail pattern, with four dark bands on upperside. In flight, also differs by shorter, more parallel-edged wings. Moults directly into adult plumage. **VOICE** A very high-pitched, fast, slightly metallic *wiiii-hi*, *eeee'ha*, *wiii'a* or *wee'ah*, and shrill *pik-wuee* with slightly rising second note. **HABITAT & BEHAVIOUR** Broadleaved evergreen forest; up to 1,700 m. Soars on level wings.

WALLACE'S HAWK EAGLE *Spizaetus nanus* 46 cm

(19–21) **Adult** *nanus*: Similarly patterned to Blyth's but smaller, browner overall, sides of head and hindneck rufescent-brown with blackish streaks, crest broadly white-tipped, tail greyish with three dark bands (terminal one slightly broader). In flight, underside differs by buffish-white base colour to flight feathers, warm buffish coverts with narrow dark barring and tail pattern. See Jerdon's Baza. Best separated from Mountain by much smaller size and tail pattern. Note habitat and range. (22,23) **Juvenile**: Very similar to Blyth's but has broad white tip to crest. **VOICE** A shrill high-pitched *yik-yee* or *kliit-kleeik*, with upward-inflected second note. Fledged juveniles give up to eight high-pitched breathless whistles: *yii-yii-yii-yii*... and *ee-ee-ee-ee-eeee*. **HABITAT** Broadleaved evergreen forest; below 200 m.

PLATE 62 BLACK-SHOULDERED KITE, FALCONETS & PEREGRINE FALCON

BLACK-SHOULDERED KITE *Elanus caeruleus* 31–35 cm

(1,2) **Adult** *vociferus*: Relatively small size, rather pale grey upperside with contrasting black lesser and median coverts. Whitish head-sides and underparts, black eyebrow, shortish white tail with grey central feathers. In flight, wings appear rather pale with contrasting black median and lesser upperwing-coverts and underside of primaries. See male Hen Harrier. (3) **Juvenile**: Crown streaked darker, grey of upperparts tinged browner with whitish-buff tips to feathers, tail darker-tipped, ear-coverts and breast initially washed with warm buff, breast and flanks sparsely and narrowly streaked with brown. **VOICE** Soft piping *pii-uu* or *pieu* (particularly when displaying). Sharp *gree-ah* or harsh, screaming *ku-eekk* when alarmed. **HABITAT & BEHAVIOUR** Open country, semi-desert, cultivation; up to 1,500 m. Glides and soars with wings raised; often hovers. Male courtship display includes mock dive-attacks at female.

WHITE-RUMPED FALCON *Polihierax insignis* 25–26.5 cm

(4,5) **Male** *cinereiceps*: Told by smallish size, long tail, pale greyish ear-coverts and forehead to upper mantle with blackish streaks, white rump and uppertail-coverts, and unmarked whitish underparts. Rest of upperparts dark slate-grey. Nuchal collar often whiter than crown. (6) **Female**: Resembles male but crown to upper mantle deep rufous. (7) **Juvenile**: Both sexes similar to male but lower nape/upper mantle broadly rufous, rest of upperparts washed with brown. **VOICE** A long falling whistle. **HABITAT & BEHAVIOUR** Open deciduous woodland, clearings in deciduous forest; up to 700 m. Often perches (in concealed or exposed position) for long periods. Flight direct, with rapid wingbeats.

COLLARED FALCONET *Microhierax caerulescens* 15.5–18 cm

(8,9) **Adult** *burmanicus*: Told by very small size, black ear-covert patch and upperside, broad white forehead and supercilium (latter meeting white nuchal collar), and chestnut throat. Thighs and vent chestnut, breast-centre and belly variable, white to chestnut. (10) **Juvenile**: Pale areas of forehead, sides of head and supercilium washed pale chestnut, throat whitish, chestnut of underparts paler and restricted mainly to undertail-coverts. **VOICE** A high-pitched *kli-kli-kli* or *killi-killi-killi*. **HABITAT & BEHAVIOUR** Deciduous forest, clearings in broadleaved evergreen and mixed forests; up to 1,830 m. Perches in exposed places for long periods. Flight direct and rapid, shrike-like.

BLACK-THIGHED FALCONET *Microhierax fringillarius* 15–17 cm

(11) **Adult**: Similar to Collared but lacks white nuchal collar, has much less white on forehead and supercilium, more black on ear-coverts, whiter throat and black lower flanks (extending to thighs). **Juvenile**: Similar to adult but pale areas of forehead, sides of head and supercilium washed very pale chestnut, throat white, chestnut of underparts much paler. **VOICE** A shrill, squealing *kweer WEEK*. **HABITAT** Clearings in broadleaved evergreen forest, forest edge, partly wooded cultivation and parkland; up to 1,500 m.

PEREGRINE FALCON *Falco peregrinus* 38–48 cm

(12–14) **Adult** *japonensis* (*calidus*?): Told by large size, slate-grey upperside, broad blackish moustachial streak and whitish lower sides of head and underparts with dark bars on flanks and belly to undertail-coverts. Has somewhat paler back and rump and indistinct bands on uppertail (terminal one broader). In flight, wings appear broad-based and pointed, tail shortish, underwing uniformly darkish (due to dense dark barring), with darker-tipped primaries and darker trailing edge. (15,16) **Juvenile**: Upperparts and wing-coverts duller with narrow warm brown to buffish fringes, forehead and supercilium whitish with indistinct dark streaks, lower head-sides and underparts buffy with dark streaks (turning to chevrons on vent), has some broken buffish bars on uppertail. In flight, underwing similar to adult but coverts more boldly marked. See smaller Eurasian Hobby and Amur Falcon. (17,18) **Adult** *peregrinator* (recorded C): Strongly rufous-washed underparts (usually barred) with whiter throat and sides of neck, buffish tail-tip and rufous-washed underwing-coverts. (19) **Juvenile**: Darker, browner upperside than *japonensis*, no obvious whitish forehead-patch or supercilium, strongly rufous-washed underparts and underwing-coverts. (20,21) **Adult** *ernesti* (resident S): Smaller than *japonensis*, with darker upperside (can appear blackish), solid blackish sides of head and duller breast to vent with denser dark barring. **VOICE** May give shrill *kek-kek-kek*... when alarmed. **HABITAT & BEHAVIOUR** Various open habitats including wetlands, coastal habitats, offshore islets, cliffs; up to 2,000 m. Large, powerful falcon that captures birds in mid-air, usually after a spectacular stoop.

1–3, 4–11 and 12–21 to different scales

PLATE 63 SMALLER FALCONS

COMMON KESTREL *Falco tinnunculus* 30–34 cm

(1–3) **Male** *interstinctus* (throughout): Medium-sized; slaty-grey crown, nape and rump to upper-tail, broad black subterminal tail-band, rufous remainder of upperparts and wing-coverts with blackish markings. Has contrasting dark mous-tachial/cheek-stripe and pale buffish underparts with dark streaks/spots on breast, belly and flanks. Wing-tips fall short of dark subterminal tail-band on perched birds. In flight, underwing appears largely whitish with dark markings (mainly on coverts), tail quite strongly graduated. (4–6) **Female:** Typically lacks grey in plumage (may show grey on uppertail-coverts and uppertail); crown and nape warm brown with dark streaks, has dark line behind eye and long, dark moustachial stripe, uppertail rufous with narrow blackish bars and broad black sub-terminal band, rufous of upperparts duller and paler than male with more numerous and distinct dark bars (less spotted), underparts more heavily dark-streaked. **Juvenile:** Like female (both sexes) but upperparts, wing-coverts, flight and tail feath-ers tend to be more strongly and heavily marked, uppertail-coverts rufescent grey-brown. **Other subspecies** *F.t.tinnuncu-lus* (recorded NW,C): Somewhat paler-toned and less heavily marked with paler grey parts of plumage. **VOICE** A sharp, pierc-ing *keee-keee-keee*..., in a rapid series or singly. Also *kik* notes given singly or repeated, and trilling *kreeeee* or *wrreeee* when agitated. **HABITAT & BEHAVIOUR** Various open habitats, culti-vation, urban areas, cliffs; up to 2,000 m. Often hovers. Flies with shallow, winnowy wingbeats.

AMUR FALCON *Falco amurensis* 28–31 cm

(7,8) **Male:** Slaty-grey overall with paler grey underparts, rufous-chestnut thighs and vent and red eyering, cere, legs and feet. In flight, diagnostic white underwing-coverts contrast sharply with blackish remainder of underwing. (9,10) **Female:** Similar to adult Eurasian Hobby but with dark-barred upperparts and uppertail, buffy-white thighs and vent, and different bare-part colours (similar to male). In flight, differs by whiter base colour of underwing (particularly coverts) and more pronounced dark and pale bars on undertail. Thighs and under-tail-coverts are buffy. See much larger Peregrine Falcon. (11,12) **Juvenile:** Similar to Eurasian Hobby but upperparts and wing-coverts more broadly and prominently tipped/fringed buff, has dark-barred upperparts and uppertail, pale parts of head, underparts and underwing somewhat whiter, legs and feet red-dish, eyering and cere pale yellow. (13) **First-summer male:** Variable, showing mixed characters of adult and juvenile. **VOICE** A shrill screaming *kew-kew-kew*... at roost sites. **HABITAT & BEHAVIOUR** Various open habitats, wooded areas; up to at least 400 m. Likely to be encountered in flocks. Often hovers.

MERLIN *Falco columbarius* 25–30 cm

(14–16).**Male** *insignis*: Told by fairly small size and compact shape, rather uniform, bluish-grey upperside, blackish flight feathers, broad black-ish subterminal tail-band and warm buffish to rufescent-buff underparts with rather narrow dark streaks on breast, belly and flanks. Has only indistinct darker moustachial/cheek-stripe, fairly pronounced buffish-white supercilium, rufous nuchal collar and a few bro-ken narrower dark bars on uppertail. Legs and feet orange to yellowish. In flight shows rather short, broad but pointed wings, shortish tail, heavy pale-and-dark markings on underwing, and broad whitish and blackish bands on undertail. (17–19) **Female:** Resembles Common Kestrel, juvenile Amur Falcon and Eurasian Hobby. Differs from all by combination of small size, compact shape, faint moustachial/cheek-stripe, fairly prominent pale supercilium, rather drab brown crown and upperside with paler buffish-brown markings (including uppertail) but no blackish bars and heavier brown underpart-streaking. Lacks bicoloured upperwing of kestrels. See much larger, darker Peregrine Falcon. **Juvenile:** Like female but upperparts tend to be darker brown. **VOICE** A shrill chattering *quik-ik-ik-ik* or *kek-kek-kek* when alarmed; a coarse lower-pitched *zek-zek-zek* given by females. **HABITAT** Open areas, cultivation; up to 400 m. Flight is rapid and direct; does not hover.

EURASIAN HOBBY *Falco subbuteo* 30–36 cm

(20–22) **Adult** *streichi*: Similar to Peregrine Fal-con but smaller, moustachial stripe narrower, upperparts more uniform, uppertail unbarred, breast and belly heavily streaked blackish, thighs and vent reddish-rufous. In flight shows more slender wings. (23,24) **Juvenile:** Crown, upper-parts and wing-coverts duller with narrow pale buffish feather fringes, has dark streaking on underparts and buffish vent. From Peregrine Falcon by size, shape, lack of obvious pale supercili-um, and plainer, deeper buff or rufous vent. **VOICE** May give a rapid sharp scolding *kew-kew-kew-kew*... **HABITAT & BEHAV-IOUR** Wooded and open areas; up to 2,000 m. Flight swift and dashing. Does not hover.

ORIENTAL HOBBY *Falco severus* 27–30 cm

(25,26) **Adult** *severus*: All-blackish head-sides, buffish-white throat and forecollar and reddish-rufous remainder of underparts. Upperside slate-grey with darker flight feathers. In flight also shows distinctive reddish-rufous underwing-coverts. Size and shape recalls Eurasian. (27,28) **Juvenile:** Resembles adult but upperparts and wing-coverts darker and browner with narrow pale feather-fringes, breast to vent rufous with blackish drop-like streaks on breast and belly, outertail feathers barred. In flight shows rufous underwing-coverts with indistinct darker markings. See larger Peregrine Falcon (partic-ularly subspecies *peregrinator*). **VOICE** A high-pitched rapid *ki-ki-ki-ki-ki*... or *hiu-hiu-hiu-hiu-hiu-hiu*..., repeated at intervals. **HABITAT & BEHAVIOUR** Open areas in broadleaved evergreen and deciduous forest, secondary growth, cultivation, mangroves, vicinity of limestone cliffs; up to 1,525 m. Flight swift and dashing; does not hover.

PLATE 64 DARTER, CORMORANTS & SPOONBILLS

DARTER *Anhinga melanogaster* 85–97 cm

(1,2) **Adult non-breeding** *melanogaster*: Similar to cormorants but easily distinguished by longish slender pointed bill, long thin neck and relatively long tail. Head, neck and mantle mostly dark brown with pale throat and long whitish stripe extending from eye down sides of neck, prominent white streaks on upper mantle, scapulars and upperwing-coverts. **Adult breeding**: Crown, hindneck and base colour of upper mantle blackish, foreneck more chestnut. **Juvenile**: Somewhat paler and browner, underside buffish-white with contrasting dark flanks and vent, buff-fringed upperwing-coverts and narrow pale tail-tip. **VOICE** On breeding grounds utters strange gruff, rather nasal *uk ukukukuk-errr uk-uk* or *ok ok ok ok ukukukukuk-err rerr-rerr-rer-ruh*. **HABITAT & BEHAVIOUR** Lakes, marshes, large rivers; up to 800 m. Swims on open water; sometimes submerges, with only snake-like neck visible. In flight, often spends time soaring.

LITTLE CORMORANT *Phalacrocorax niger* 51–54.5 cm

(3,4) **Adult non-breeding**: Relatively small and short-necked with distinctive shortish, stubby bill. Mostly blackish-brown, scapulars and wings greyer with black feather edges, chin whitish, bill mostly dull greyish flesh-colour. In flight, appears relatively short-necked, small-winged and long-tailed. (5) **Adult breeding**: Head, neck and underparts black with bluish to greenish gloss and dense silvery-white streaks on crown, ear-coverts and nape, bill blackish. (6) **Juvenile**: Similar to adult non-breeding but browner overall, head and neck paler and browner, throat whitish, underparts streaked/scaled pale brownish. Has paler crown and hindneck and darker belly than other cormorants. **HABITAT & BEHAVIOUR** Various wetlands, mainly fresh water but also estuaries and mangroves; up to 800 m. Flies with regular, rather fast wingbeats.

INDIAN CORMORANT *Phalacrocorax fuscicollis* 61–68 cm

(7,8) **Adult non-breeding**: Similar to Little but larger, bill relatively long and slender, head, neck and underparts blacker with whitish lower head-sides and throat, and uneven whitish to pale brown streak-like markings on foreneck and breast, base colour of scapulars and wings browner. In flight appears longer-necked, larger-winged and shorter-tailed; more closely resembles Great but smaller, slimmer and thinner-necked with smaller, more oval-shaped head and proportionately longer tail. (9) **Adult breeding**: Apart from size and shape, similar to Little but has silvery peppering over eye, distinctive white tuft on rear side of head, and browner base colour of scapulars and wings. (10) **Juvenile**: Upperside browner than adult non-breeding, underparts mostly whitish with dark brown smudging and streaks on foreneck and breast and dark brown flanks. Best separated from Great by size, shape, much thinner

bill, dark ear-coverts, less extensive and duller gular skin and darker breast. **HABITAT** Various wetlands in both fresh and salt water; lowlands.

GREAT CORMORANT *Phalacrocorax carbo* 80–100 cm

(11,12) **Adult non-breeding** *sinensis*: Much bigger and larger-billed than other cormorants. Head, neck and underparts black with prominent white area on lower head-sides and upper throat; has browner scapulars and wings with black feather-edges and extensive yellow facial and gular skin. In flight, apart from large size, appears relatively thick-necked, large-winged and short-tailed, with squarish head and slightly kinked neck. (13) **Adult breeding**: Has dense white streaks forming sheen across sides of crown and neck, more orange facial skin and darker gular skin, larger and more defined white area on ear-coverts and throat, greenish-glossed scapulars and wings, and large white thigh-patch. (14) **Juvenile**: Upperside much browner than adult non-breeding, sides of head and underparts mostly whitish, with dark brown streaks on foreneck and upper breast, and dark brown flanks and thighs. Apart from size and bill, differs from similar Indian by more extensive, yellower facial and gular skin, whitish ear-coverts and sparser, more contrasting breast markings. Gradually attains adult plumage. **VOICE** Usually silent but utters a variety of deep, guttural calls at breeding colonies. **HABITAT & BEHAVIOUR** Various wetlands in both fresh and salt water; up to 400 m. Flies with slower wingbeats than other cormorants.

EURASIAN SPOONBILL *Platalea leucorodia* 82.5–89 cm

(15) **Adult non-breeding** *major*: Very similar to Black-faced but larger, has all-white forehead and cheeks and pale fleshy-yellow patch on upperside of bill-tip ('spoon'). (16) **Adult breeding**: Separated from Black-faced by same features as adult non-breeding. Additionally, shows yellow-orange throat skin; patch on upperside of bill-tip is yellower than on adult non-breeding. (17,18) **Juvenile**: Easily separated from Black-faced by dull pinkish bill and loral skin. **HABITAT** Lowland marshes, lakes; could also occur on tidal mudflats.

BLACK-FACED SPOONBILL *Platalea minor* 76 cm

(19) **Adult non-breeding**: All-white plumage, long spatulate all-black bill, black facial skin encircling base of bill. Eyes dark. (20) **Adult breeding**: Yellowish to buffish nuchal crest and breast-patch, reddish eyes. At close range, shows narrow yellow crescent over eye. (21) **Juvenile**: Similar to adult non-breeding but has blackish edges to outer primaries and small blackish tips to primaries, primary coverts and secondaries (particularly former). **HABITAT & BEHAVIOUR** Tidal mudflats, coastal pools. Likely to be encountered in groups.

15–21 to different scale

PLATE 65 EGRETS

LITTLE EGRET *Egretta garzetta* 55–65 cm

(1,2) **Adult non-breeding** *garzetta*: From other white egrets by combination of size, mostly dark bill and blackish legs with yellow to greenish-yellow feet (can be hard to see when muddy). Bill may have small (variable) amount of pale yellowish to flesh colour at base of lower mandible (often difficult to see), facial skin dull greenish to yellowish-grey. In flight, legs and feet extend well beyond tail-tip. (3) **Adult breeding**: Has pronounced nape-, back- and breast-plumes, facial skin and feet often more reddish during courtship, bill blackish. **Juvenile**: Similar to adult non-breeding. **VOICE** Hoarse, grating *kgarrk* or longer *aaahk* when flushed. Also various guttural calls at breeding colonies. **HABITAT & BEHAVIOUR** Various open freshwater and coastal wetlands, cultivation; up to 800 m. Gregarious.

CHINESE EGRET *Egretta eulophotes* 68 cm

(4,5) **Adult non-breeding**: Very similar to white morph Pacific Reef but legs longer (tarsus longer than bill), bill somewhat more slender and pointed, upper mandible black to brownish-black, lower mandible yellowish-flesh to yellowish with contrasting blackish terminal third. Facial skin pale greenish to greenish-yellow. In flight, very similar to Little, with legs and feet extending well beyond tail-tip. At rest, differs from Little by mostly dull greenish legs and feet and more extensive pale area on lower mandible. (6) **Adult breeding**: Recalls Little but has yellow to orange-yellow bill and distinctive shaggy nape-plumes (crest). Facial skin light blue to grey-blue, legs blackish with greenish-yellow to yellow feet. **Juvenile**: Similar to adult non-breeding. **HABITAT & BEHAVIOUR** Tidal mudflats, mangroves. Usually gregarious.

PACIFIC REEF EGRET *Egretta sacra* 58 cm

(7) **Adult dark morph non-breeding** *sacra*: Overall dark greyish plumage. Often has whitish chin and throat-line, bill as in white morph but facial skin may be greyer. (8) **Adult dark morph breeding**: Shortish plumes on nape, back and breast; bill, legs and feet often yellower. **Adult white morph non-breeding**: Shorter-legged and somewhat less elegant than other white egrets (except Cattle). Told by size, bill length and colour, and leg colour. Facial skin greenish; upper mandible greenish-horn with variable amount of blackish to dark brownish, lower mandible horn- to greenish-yellow with slightly darker tip; legs and feet mostly olive-green to yellowish. Very similar to Chinese but legs shorter (tarsus always shorter than bill), bill somewhat thicker and less pointed, typically with paler upper mandible (darker on culmen) and less contrasting dark tip to lower mandible. In flight, only feet and small amount of legs project behind tail-tip. **Adult white morph breeding**: Differs as dark morph. **Juvenile**: Similar to adult non-breeding. Dark morph is a somewhat paler smoky-grey. **VOICE** An occasional grunting *ork* when foraging and harsh *squak* when flushed. **HABITAT & BEHAVIOUR** Rocky shores, islets, beaches, sometimes mudflats. Usually found singly or in pairs.

GREAT EGRET *Casmerodius albus* 85–102 cm

(11,12) **Adult non-breeding** *modestus*: Considerably larger than other egrets; very long neck, dagger-like yellow bill (extreme tip may be black), blackish legs and feet (upper tibia often yellowish). Facial skin olive-yellow. Only likely to be confused with smaller Intermediate but more elegant, neck longer and more strongly kinked (though long and thin when held outstretched), head thinner and bill much longer. At close range, shows diagnostic pointed extension of facial skin below/behind eye. In flight, retracted neck is more deeply bulging. (13) **Adult breeding**: Has very long back-plumes and very short coarse breast-plumes. During courtship, bill turns black, facial skin cobalt-blue, legs reddish. **Juvenile**: Similar to adult non-breeding. **VOICE** May utter a harsh but high-pitched rolling *krr'rr'rr'rra* when flushed. Various guttural calls at breeding colonies. **HABITAT & BEHAVIOUR** Various inland and coastal wetlands, rice paddies, mangroves; up to 400 m. Gregarious. Flies with slower wingbeats than Intermediate.

INTERMEDIATE EGRET *Mesophoyx intermedia* 65–72 cm

(14,15) **Adult non-breeding**: Easily confused with Great. Differs primarily by smaller size, considerably shorter bill, more rounded head, shorter and less distinctly kinked neck and more hunched appearance. At close range, facial skin does not extend in point below/behind eye. In flight, retracted neck has less pronounced downward bulge. Recalls Cattle but much larger and more graceful, with longer neck and bill, less rounded head and longer, darker legs. Facial skin pale yellow to greenish-yellow, legs all blackish. (16) **Adult breeding**: Long back-plumes, longish breast-plumes, yellow bill, sometimes with black/dark brown on tip and ridge of upper mandible (blacker with yellow base during courtship); facial skin, legs and feet as adult non-breeding. **Juvenile**: Similar to adult non-breeding. **VOICE** May give a harsh croaking *kwark* or *kuwark* when flushed. Distinctive buzzing sounds during display at breeding colonies. **HABITAT & BEHAVIOUR** Various wetlands; up to 400 m. Gregarious. Wingbeats more rapid than Great, slower and more graceful than Cattle. Often raises crown feathers.

CATTLE EGRET *Bubulcus ibis* 48–53 cm

(17,18) **Adult non-breeding** *coromandus*: Smaller and stockier than other egrets, often appearing rather hunched. Has shortish neck, rather rounded head with pronounced 'jowl', relatively short thick yellow bill and blackish legs and feet (often tinged brownish to greenish). Facial skin yellowish to greenish-yellow. Only likely to be confused with Intermediate but considerably smaller, with notably shorter bill and legs (legs and feet somewhat paler) and much shorter neck without obvious kink. In flight shows shorter, rounder wings and much less downward-bulging neck; legs and feet extend less beyond tail-tip. (19) **Adult breeding**: Head and neck extensively rufous-buff, with short rufous-buff nape and breast-plumes, long rufous-buff back-plumes and more yellowish legs and feet. During courtship, bill, legs and feet turn pinkish-red. **Juvenile**: Like adult non-breeding but may show blackish legs and feet and grey tinge to plumage. **VOICE** Sometimes gives quiet croaking *ruk* or *RIK-rak* in flight. Low conversational rattling at roost sites. **HABITAT & BEHAVIOUR** Various wetlands, cultivation (usually avoids saline wetlands); up to 800 m. Gregarious. Often feeds near cattle, on disturbed insects.

PLATE 66 HERONS, POND HERONS, NIGHT HERONS & GREAT BITTERN

GREY HERON *Ardea cinerea* 90–98 cm

(1,2) **Adult non-breeding** *jouyi*: Greyish upperparts and wing-coverts, mostly whitish head, foreneck and underparts, broad black head-stripes, extending as long plumes, blackish streaks on foreneck/upper breast. Thick dull yellowish bill, black shoulder-patch. Mostly greyish wing-coverts contrast with blackish flight feathers, underwing similar but with darker leading edge to coverts; black band down body-side, white leading edge to wing. (3) **Adult breeding**: Bill bright orange-yellow, has elongated white scapular plumes; during courtship, bill, legs and feet become deeper orange to vermilion. (4) **Juvenile**: Plumage shows less contrast; crown dark greyish, nape-plumes short, neck-side grey, duller band on side, dull bill. **VOICE** Loud, harsh, abrupt *krahnk*, particularly in flight. Also a deep, grating *raark* when flushed. **HABITAT** Various inland and coastal wetlands, rice paddies, mangroves; up to 800 m.

GREAT-BILLED HERON *Ardea sumatrana* 114–115 cm

(5,6) **Adult breeding** *sumatrana*: Larger than juvenile Grey, no black in plumage, neck and upperside darker brownish-grey, has pale streaks on scapulars, foreneck and breast, dull greyish belly/vent; uniformly dark wings. **Adult non-breeding**: Duller plumes on scapulars/breast. **Juvenile**: Warmer-tinged than adult non-breeding, upperparts tipped buff to rufous-buff, neck and underparts tinged rufous, lower foreneck and breast more broadly streaked whitish. **VOICE** Occasional loud harsh croaks. Also, unnerving loud guttural roars during breeding season (mainly at night). **HABITAT & BEHAVIOUR** Mangroves, islets, undisturbed beaches. Solitary or in pairs.

PURPLE HERON *Ardea purpurea* 78–90 cm

(7,8) **Adult** *manilensis*: Black crown/nape-plumes, rufous-chestnut neck with black lines down sides/front, dark chestnut-maroon belly, flanks and vent. Bill, legs and feet mostly yellowish. Smaller/slimmer than Grey, upperparts darker with chestnut-maroon shoulder-patch and wash on scapulars. In flight, recalls Grey but upperwing shows darker coverts and buff (not white) markings near wing-bend and mostly chestnut-maroon underwing-coverts; at distance, feet look bigger and extend slightly further beyond tail-tip, retracted neck is more deeply bulging. (9,10) **Juvenile**: Head-sides/hindneck duller, more buffish, with less defined dark markings, lacks nape-plumes, dark brown above with warm buffish-brown fringing, buffier-brown belly/vent, browner underwing-coverts. See Great Bittern. **VOICE** Flight call similar to Grey but thinner and higher-pitched. Loud, hoarse *raanka* and *raank* calls noted at roosting sites. **HABITAT & BEHAVIOUR** Well-vegetated freshwater wetlands, marshes, lakes, reedbeds, large rivers, occasionally coastal wetlands; up to 400 m. More secretive than Grey.

INDIAN POND HERON *Ardeola grayii* 45 cm

(11) **Adult breeding**: Head, neck and breast brownish-buff with long white head-plumes, throat whitish, mantle and scapulars dark brownish-maroon, greater upperwing-coverts washed buff. **Adult non-breeding**: Possibly indistinguishable from other pond herons. **Juvenile**: Possibly indistinguishable from other pond herons. **VOICE** May give a gruff

rolling *urrh urrh urrh*... and abrupt hollow *okh* in flight. Repeated conversational *wa-koo* at breeding sites. **HABITAT** Various freshwater wetlands, sometimes coastal pools; lowlands.

CHINESE POND HERON *Ardeola bacchus* 45–52 cm

(12,13) **Adult non-breeding**: Rather nondescript at rest, but in flight shows white wings and tail. Head to breast mostly buffish with bold dark brown streaks, mantle/scapulars darkish olive-brown, rest of plumage white. Bill yellowish with dark tip (may also have darker upper mandible), legs/feet greenish-yellow to yellow. Possibly indistinguishable from other pond herons, but perhaps shows more obvious dusky tips to outermost primaries than Javan. (14) **Adult breeding**: Chestnut-maroon head, neck and breast, white throat, blackish-slate mantle and scapulars. **Juvenile**: More spotted below than adult non-breeding, brownish tail markings and inner primaries, grey-washed upperwing-coverts. **VOICE** Harsh squawk in alarm. **HABITAT** Freshwater wetlands, also mangroves, tidal pools; up to 800 m.

JAVAN POND HERON *Ardeola speciosa* 45 cm

(15) **Adult non-breeding**: Possibly indistinguishable from other pond herons but may show less obvious dusky tips to outermost primaries than Chinese. (16) **Adult breeding**: Pale brownish-buff to creamy-whitish head and neck, white head-plumes, deep cinnamon-rufous breast and blackish-slate mantle and scapulars diagnostic. **Juvenile**: Possibly indistinguishable from other pond herons. **VOICE** Similar to other pond herons. **HABITAT** Various wetlands, particularly along coast; lowlands.

BLACK-CROWNED NIGHT HERON *Nycticorax nycticorax* 58–65 cm

(17,18) **Adult non-breeding** *nycticorax*: Robust; mostly grey with black crown and mantle/scapulars. Blackish bill and lores, yellow legs/feet, long whitish nape-plumes. Bulky/big-headed in flight, with broad, rounded wings. (19) **Juvenile**: Larger, stockier and thicker-billed than pond herons; dark brown wings/tail, buffish to whitish drop-like spots on mantle, scapulars and upperwing-coverts. See much smaller Little Heron and small bitterns. **Adult breeding**: Black of plumage glossed bluish-green, lores and legs go red during courtship. **VOICE** Deep hollow croaking *kwok*, *quark* or more sudden *guk*, particularly in flight. **HABITAT & BEHAVIOUR** Lowland marshes, swamps, rice paddies, mangroves. Gregarious. Mainly feeds at night, roosting in thick cover by day. Mostly seen at dusk and dawn.

GREAT BITTERN *Botaurus stellaris* 70–80 cm

(20,21) **Adult** *stellaris*: Large size, overall buffish plumage, cryptically patterned with black streaks and vermiculations. Thick yellowish bill, blackish crown and submoustachial stripe, plain rufous-buff head-sides, more golden-buff neck-sides, greenish legs/feet; base colour below whiter than above. Heavy and broad-winged in flight, upperside of flight feathers blackish-brown with broad rufous-brown bars, contrasting somewhat with coverts. **VOICE** May give harsh, nasal *kau* or *krau* in flight. Territorial call (unlikely to be heard) is a slow deep resonant far-carrying boom, *up-RUMBH*. **HABITAT** Well-vegetated freshwater marshes, reedy ditches; up to 400 m.

PLATE 67 LITTLE HERON, MALAYAN NIGHT HERON & BITTERNS

LITTLE HERON *Butorides striatus* 40–48 cm

(1,2) **Adult** *javanicus*: Mostly slaty-greyish; black crown/nape-plumes (often raised untidily), whiter head-sides, throat and breast-centre, black streak below ear-coverts, narrow whitish/buffish-white scapular and wing-covert fringing. Dark bill with yellower-based lower mandible, olive-yellow facial skin, dull yellowish-orange legs/feet. (3,4) **Juvenile**: Browner above, with less uniform dark crown/nape, indistinct buffish markings on crown, mantle and lesser coverts, underparts streaked dark brown and whitish, legs and feet dull greenish to yellowish-green. **Other subspecies** *B.s.actophilus* (northern Thailand), *amurensis* (visitor, recorded S). **VOICE** May give a distinctive short harsh *skeow*, *k-yow* or *k-yek* when flushed, and a high-pitched, raspy *kitch-itch itch* when alarmed. **HABITAT** Mangroves, tidal mudflats, offshore islands, rivers and streams in or near forest, lakes; up to 900 m.

MALAYAN NIGHT HERON *Gorsachius melanolophus* 48–51 cm

(5) **Adult** *melanolophus*: Stocky and thick-necked with shortish bill and legs. Shows distinctive combination of deep rufous sides of head and neck, black crown and long crest, black streaks down foreneck and breast, and chestnut-tinged brown upperparts and wing-coverts with fine blackish vermiculations. Belly and vent densely marked blackish and whitish, tail blackish, facial skin bluish to greenish-blue, legs and feet greenish. In flight, from above, shows rufous secondaries with broad blackish subterminal band, white-tipped rufous primary coverts and buff-tipped blackish primaries. Facial skin may turn reddish when breeding. (6) **Juvenile**: Duller than adult with dense irregular whitish to buffish and greyish bars and vermiculations overall. Crown and nape blacker with more pronounced white markings, throat whitish with broken dark mesial streak. In flight, shows more contrast between upperwing-coverts and flight feathers. **VOICE** Territorial call is a series of 10–11 deep *oo* notes, given at c.1.5 s intervals; heard between dusk and dawn. **HABITAT & BEHAVIOUR** Swampy areas and streams in broadleaved evergreen and mixed deciduous forests, freshwater swamp forest, secondary forest, bamboo; up to 1,220 m. Very secretive, feeding mostly at night.

YELLOW BITTERN *Ixobrychus sinensis* 36–38 cm

(7,8) **Male**: Small, skinny and long-necked, long dagger-like bill. Told by light brown/buffy coloration, contrasting blackish crown, rather cold olive-brown mantle/scapulars to uppertail-coverts, white underside with vague darker lines down foreneck/upper breast. Often has strongly vinous-washed head-/neck-sides and upperparts (particularly when breeding). In flight, buff greater upperwing-coverts and plain whitish underwing-coverts contrast with blackish flight feathers/tail. Rest of upperwing-coverts gradually become darker towards leading edge. Bill yellow-horn with dark ridge of upper mandible and often tip, legs and feet yellowish-green (yellower when breeding). (9,10) **Juvenile**: Like female but has bold dark streaks above, bolder dark streaks below. From other small bitterns by buffish upperside with dark streaks; contrasting buffish base colour to upperwing-coverts, plain whitish underwing-coverts. **Female**: More uniform and mostly warm brown above; may be vaguely streaked, almost lacks dark on crown, shows obvious warm brown lines down foreneck to upper breast. Lacks vinous wash. **VOICE** Territorial call is a series of low *ou* notes.

In flight may give staccato *kak-kak-kak*. **HABITAT & BEHAVIOUR** Densely vegetated freshwater wetlands, reedbeds, sometimes rice paddies; up to 800 m. May freeze, with neck upstretched when approached.

VON SCHRENCK'S BITTERN *Ixobrychus eurhythmus* 39–42 cm

(11,12) **Male**: Resembles Cinnamon but crown (apart from blackish median stripe), ear-coverts, mantle to back and scapulars rich dark chestnut, contrasting strongly with mostly buffish underparts/wing-coverts. Single dark chestnut line from chin to upper breast-centre. In flight, differs from Yellow by chestnut upperparts and leading edge of upperwing-coverts (particularly patch at wing-bend) and greyer, less contrasting upperside of flight feathers and more silvery-grey underwing with dark markings on coverts. Has similar plain whitish underwing-coverts. (13,14) **Female**: Similar to Cinnamon but has much bolder white to buff speckling/spotting above. In flight, easily separated by mostly blackish-grey flight feathers, tail and underwing colour (similar to adult male). **Juvenile**: Like female. **HABITAT & BEHAVIOUR** Swampy areas or pools in or near forest or secondary growth, sometimes in more open, well-vegetated wetlands; lowlands. Secretive, usually seen in flight.

CINNAMON BITTERN *Ixobrychus cinnamomeus* 38–41 cm

(15,16) **Male non-breeding**: Almost uniform rich cinnamon-rufous upperside. Mostly warm buffish below with indistinct dark chestnut line from centre of throat to centre of upper breast. In flight, almost uniform rich cinnamon-rufous wings (paler below) are diagnostic. Yellowish eyes and facial skin (as other small bitterns). (17) **Female**: Upperside slightly duller and darker with vague buffish speckling on scapulars and upperwing-coverts; underparts have dark brown lines down sides of neck and upper breast, and darker central line. (18,19) **Juvenile**: Duller/darker above than female, narrow buffish streaks on head-sides, dense buffish speckling and feather fringing on upperparts and upperwing-coverts, darker streaking below, wings a shade duller and darker. **Male breeding**: Eyes and facial skin turn red, yellow of bill becomes more orange. **VOICE** Territorial call is a throaty, 9–18 note *ukh-ukh-ukh-ukh-ukh-ukh-ukh...* (tailing off towards end), repeated after lengthy intervals. Flight call is a low, clicky *ikh* or *ikh-ikh*. **HABITAT & BEHAVIOUR** Rice paddies, marshes, various freshwater wetland habitats; up to 1,830 m. Usually seen in flight.

BLACK BITTERN *Dupetor flavicollis* 54–61 cm

(20,21) **Male** *flavicollis*: Told by combination of size, all-blackish ear-coverts/upperside, long dagger-like bill and blackish legs/feet. Lacks head-plumes/crest. Throat and breast whitish with broad dark chestnut to blackish streaks and plain yellowish-buff patch on sides of neck and upper breast, lower underparts sooty-greyish, bill horn to yellowish-horn with dark tip and ridge of upper mandible. In flight shows rather broad, all-dark wings. (22) **Female**: Like male but dark parts of plumage browner, breast-streaking more rufescent. (23) **Juvenile**: Like female but crown/upperside with narrow rufous fringing, breast washed buffish-brown. **VOICE** Territorial call is described as a loud booming. **HABITAT & BEHAVIOUR** Marshy freshwater wetlands, rice paddy margins, freshwater swamp forest, mangroves; lowlands. Usually seen in flight.

PLATE 68 IBISES & STORKS

GLOSSY IBIS *Plegadis falcinellus* 55–65 cm

(1,2) **Adult non-breeding** *falcinellus*: Mostly dark brownish, white-streaked head/neck, green-glossed scapulars/wing-coverts. Bill pale brownish, legs/feet dark brownish, narrow white border to lores; all-dark wings. (3) **Adult breeding**: Head, neck and body mostly deep chestnut, forecrown glossed green, much of plumage purplish-tinged, no streaks on head and neck but clear white border to lores; bill mostly flesh-coloured. **Juvenile**: Dull, little green gloss above, head/neck densely mottled whitish, throat whitish, no white around lores. **VOICE** May give a low harsh *graa* and subdued grunting sounds in flight. **HABITAT** Lowland marshy wetlands.

BLACK-HEADED IBIS *Threskiornis melanocephalus* 75–76 cm

(4,5) **Adult non-breeding**: White plumage, blackish downcurved bill, naked blackish head and upper neck, blackish legs and feet. In flight, bare reddish skin shows through underwing-coverts. **Adult breeding**: Variable yellowish wash on mantle and breast, greyish wash on scapulars and tertials, white plumes extending from lower neck and elongated tertials. **Juvenile**: Brownish to greyish-white feathering on head and neck, black-edged/tipped outer primaries, blackish bare skin showing through underwing-coverts. **VOICE** Peculiar vibrant grunting sounds at nesting colonies. **HABITAT** Lowland marshy wetlands, mudflats, mangroves.

WHITE-SHOULDERED IBIS *Pseudibis davisoni* 75–85 cm

(6,7) **Adult**: Larger than Glossy, white collar (faintly bluish), longer greyish bill, dull red legs/feet. Naked blackish head, dark greenish-blue gloss on upperwing. In flight, shows white patch on inner lesser upperwing-coverts. **Juvenile**: Dull collar and legs, less glossy wings, shorter bill. Similar white wing-patch. **VOICE** Territorial calls are repeated loud, unearthly hoarse screams: ***ERRRRRRH*** or ***ERRRRRRRROH***, accompanied by rhythmic, moaning ***errh errh errh…*** (by female?). Also screams mixed with honking ***OWK OWK OWK OWK…*** and more subdued ***ohhaaa ohhaaa…*** and ***errrr-ah***. **HABITAT** Pools/streams and marshy areas in open lowland forest.

GIANT IBIS *Pseudibis gigantea* 102–106.5 cm

(8,9) **Adult**: Huge size; long downcurved, pale horn-coloured bill, naked greyish head and neck with black bars at rear, mostly blackish-slate body, contrasting grey wings with black feather-tips. Has a faint greenish gloss on body and deep red eyes, legs and feet. In flight shows strongly contrasting upperwing pattern and completely dark underwing. **Juvenile**: Has short black feathers on back of head and neck, shorter bill, brown eyes. **HABITAT** Pools, streams and marshy areas in open lowland forest.

BLACK STORK *Ciconia nigra* 95–100 cm

(10,11) **Adult**: Overall glossy greenish- to purplish-black, with white lower breast, belly, undertail-coverts and inner underwing-coverts. Bill, orbital skin, legs and feet red. **Juvenile**: Patterned like adult but dark parts of plumage mostly dark brown, white parts somewhat duller. Has pale brown flecks on neck and breast, pale brown tips to scapulars and upperwing-coverts, and mostly dull greyish-olive bill, orbital skin, legs and feet. **HABITAT** Freshwater marshes, pools and ditches, rivers, cultivation, open areas; up to 700 m.

WOOLLY-NECKED STORK *Ciconia episcopus* 75–91 cm

(12,13) **Adult** *episcopus*: Glossy purplish-/greenish-black; black cap, contrasting white neck and vent. Bill blackish with some dark red at tip and along ridge of upper mandible; facial skin dark grey, legs and feet dull red, bronzy area along inner upperwing-coverts and short, forked black tail (appears white due to extended undertail-coverts). **Juvenile**: Patterned like adult but dark parts of plumage mostly dull brown, with feathered forehead and duller bill, legs and feet. **HABITAT & BEHAVIOUR** Marshes, freshwater swamp forest, pools and streams in open forest; below 300 m. Not very gregarious. Bill-clatters at nest, with head resting back on mantle.

STORM'S STORK *Ciconia stormi* 75–91 cm

(14,15) **Adult**: Similar to Woolly-necked but bill bright red, facial skin dull orange with a broad golden-yellow area around eye, lower foreneck glossy black, lacks bronzy area along inner wing-coverts. **Juvenile**: Blackish parts of plumage browner, bill dark-tipped, facial skin, legs and feet duller. **HABITAT & BEHAVIOUR** Freshwater swamp forest, rivers, streams and pools in broadleaved evergreen forest; lowlands. Solitary or in pairs; rarely in small loose groups. Performs bill-clattering displays at nest sites.

LESSER ADJUTANT *Leptoptilos javanicus* 122.5–129 cm

(16) **Male non-breeding**: Bill thick (culmen straight), mostly horn-coloured, mostly yellowish head/neck, more vinous head-sides, pale forehead, dark legs/feet; all-blackish wings, with white patch on inner underwing-coverts. (17) **Male breeding**: Oval coppery spots near tips of median upperwing-coverts and narrow whitish edges to lower scapulars, tertials and inner greater coverts; sides of head redder. **Female**: As male non-breeding but bill shorter, less massive. **Juvenile**: Duller above, downier head/neck. **VOICE** Deep guttural sounds at nest. **HABITAT & BEHAVIOUR** Freshwater marshes, pools in or near open forest, swamp forest, mangroves, sometimes rice paddies and open areas including mudflats; lowlands. Flies with neck retracted (like Grey Heron).

GREATER ADJUTANT *Leptoptilos dubius* 145–150 cm

(18) **Adult non-breeding**: Larger than Lesser, deeper bill (culmen convex), more uniform pinkish head and neck, pronounced drooping neck-pouch, white neck-ruff, greyer upperside with still paler, greyer greater coverts and tertials; greyer underwing with more whitish markings on coverts, sooty-grey undertail-coverts. (19) **Adult breeding**: Blacker face, redder head/neck, paler, bluer-grey above, bright saffron-yellow neck-pouch. **Juvenile**: Bill narrower (more like adult Lesser), denser pale brownish to grey down on head/neck, wings initially all dark but soon with paler underwing-coverts and brown band across greater coverts and tertials. **HABITAT** Freshwater marshes, pools in/near open drier forests, freshwater swamp forest, sometimes rice fields, open areas; up to 800 m.

PLATE 69 STORKS & CRANES

MILKY STORK *Mycteria cinerea* 92–97 cm

(1,2) **Adult non-breeding**: Resembles Painted but plumage all white, apart from blackish primaries, secondaries and tail, has limited dark red head-skin. Bill pale pinkish-yellow, legs and feet dull pinkish-red. (3) **Adult breeding**: White parts of plumage suffused very pale creamy-buffish, bill bright yellow to orange-yellow, bare head brighter red, legs and feet deep magenta. (4,5) **Juvenile**: Similar to Painted but has browner, more uniform head and neck, paler lesser and median upperwing-coverts (hardly contrasting with mantle), no defined darker breast-band and slightly less extensive naked head-skin. In flight shows off-whitish tips to underwing-coverts, creating overall paler appearance. **HABITAT & BEHAVIOUR** Tidal mudflats, mangroves. Normally gregarious; likely to be encountered with other storks.

PAINTED STORK *Mycteria leucocephala* 93–102 cm

(6,7) **Adult non-breeding**: Mostly white with black and white median and lesser coverts and breast-band, pink-washed inner greater coverts and tertials, and blackish flight feathers and tail. Has long thick pinkish-yellow bill which droops slightly at tip, naked orange-red head and pinkish-red to brownish-red legs and feet. In flight shows white barring on black underwing-coverts. (8) **Adult breeding**: Head-skin redder, bill pinkish-peach, legs and feet brighter reddish-magenta, has brighter pink on tertials etc. (9,10) **Juvenile**: Head and neck pale greyish-brown with whitish streaks, naked head-skin dull yellowish and reduced to a patch around eye to throat, mantle feathers and greater coverts pale greyish-brown with whitish fringes, lesser and median coverts obviously darker, with whitish fringes, back to uppertail-coverts creamy-whitish; underparts dull whitish with indistinct but defined dusky breast-band. Often has slight pinkish suffusion on tertials. In flight shows uniformly dark underwing-coverts. **HABITAT & BEHAVIOUR** Lowland marshes, lakes, freshwater swamp forest, sometimes wet rice paddies; up to 1,000 m on passage. Often in flocks; associates with other large waterbirds.

ASIAN OPENBILL *Anastomus oscitans* 68–81 cm

(11,12) **Adult non-breeding**: Broad dull horn-coloured to greyish bill with open space between mandibles. Relatively small, with mostly dull greyish-white plumage (including head) and contrasting glossy black lower scapulars, tertials, primaries, secondaries and tail. Legs and feet pinkish to greyish-pink. **Adult breeding**: Whiter with redder legs at onset of breeding season. **Juvenile**: Like adult non-breeding but head, neck, mantle, scapulars and breast brownish-grey, bill brownish and initially shorter with no space between mandibles, legs and feet duller. **HABITAT & BEHAVIOUR** Freshwater marshes, rice paddies, ditches through cultivation; up to 700 m. Very gregarious. Birds clatter bills at nest.

WHITE STORK *Ciconia ciconia* 100–115 cm

(13,14) **Adult *asiatica*?**: Similar to Asian Openbill and Milky but shows straight pointed red bill and red legs and feet. Plumage all white (including head and tail), apart from contrasting black lower scapulars, tertials, greater coverts, primaries and secondaries. **Juvenile** Has browner greater upper-wing-coverts and brownish-red bill, legs and feet. **HABITAT** Marshes, rice paddies, open areas; recorded in lowlands.

BLACK-NECKED STORK *Ephippiorhynchus asiaticus* 121–135 cm

(15) **Female *asiaticus***: Huge and mostly white, with glossy black head, neck, back to tail, greater and median coverts, tertials and lower scapulars. Has distinctly long black bill, very long red legs, strong blue to greenish and purplish gloss on black of plumage (particularly head and neck) and bright yellow eyes. In flight shows white wings with broad black central band (above and below). (16) **Male**: Brown eyes. (17,18) **Juvenile**: Head, neck and upperparts dull brown with whitish lower back to base of tail, flight feathers blackish-brown, rest of underparts whitish, bill dark olive-brown, legs and feet dull olive. In flight shows all-dark wings. Gradually attains adult plumage and soon shows suggestion of distinctive adult wing pattern. **HABITAT & BEHAVIOUR** Lowland freshwater marshes, marshy areas and pools in open forest, rarely also mud- and sandflats. Occurs singly or in pairs; very conspicuous.

SARUS CRANE *Grus antigone* 152–156 cm

(19,20) **Adult *sharpii***: Huge and rather uniform grey; mostly naked red head/upper neck (brighter when breeding). Blackish primaries/primary coverts, mostly grey secondaries, pale reddish legs and feet. (21) **Juvenile**: Head and upper neck buffish and feathered, overall plumage duller with brownish-grey feather-fringes, those of upperparts more cinnamon-brown. **VOICE** Loud trumpeting (usually duetting pairs). **HABITAT & BEHAVIOUR** Marshy grassland, open country, rice paddies; lowlands. Pairs perform dancing display, including wing-spreading, bowing, head-lowering and leaps into air.

COMMON CRANE *Grus grus* 110–120 cm

(22,23) **Adult *lilfordi***: Huge size, greyish plumage, mostly blackish head and upper neck, with red patch on crown, broad white band from ear-coverts down side of upper neck. Long drooping tertials mixed with black. In flight, blackish primaries and secondaries contrast with grey wing-coverts. (24) **First winter**: Head/upper neck warm buffish to grey, rest of plumage (particularly above) often mixed with brown; may show whitish/buffy-whitish patch behind eye. Smaller than Sarus, much shorter bill, dark markings on inner coverts, tertials and secondaries, dark legs. More like adult by first spring, fully adult by third winter/spring. **VOICE** Flight calls include loud, flute-like bugling ***kroob***, ***krrooab*** and ***kurr*** etc., higher-pitched ***klay***, croaking ***rrrrrrrer*** and various honking sounds. Similar calls also given on ground, including duets by bonded pairs: ***kroo-krii-kroo-krii***… **HABITAT** Marshes, open areas, less disturbed cultivation; recorded at c. 400 m.

19–24 to different scale

PLATE 70 SPOT-BILLED PELICAN, TROPICBIRDS & FRIGATEBIRDS

SPOT-BILLED PELICAN *Pelecanus philippensis* 127–140 cm

(1,2) **Adult breeding**: Huge; mostly whitish, yellowish-pink bill with dark spots along upper mandible, pinkish pouch with heavy purplish-grey mottling, dark bluish to purplish lores, tufted dusky nape and hindneck, blackish legs and feet. Rump, tail-coverts and underwing-coverts variably washed cinnamon-pinkish, underparts variably flushed pink, with faint yellowish-buff patch on lower foreneck and upper breast. In flight shows dark greyish flight feathers (above and below) and dull underwing-coverts with obvious whitish band along greater coverts. (3) **Juvenile**: Similar to adult non-breeding but sides of head, nape, hindneck, mantle and upperwing-coverts browner, with paler fringes to mantle feathers and upperwing-coverts, unmarked yellower bill, plain dull pinkish pouch, duller lores and pinkish-grey legs and feet. In flight shows browner flight feathers but similar underwing-pattern. **Adult non-breeding** Lacks pink/cinnamon plumage-washes, no yellowish-buff patch on lower foreneck/upper breast. HABITAT Lakes, lagoons, large rivers, estuaries, mudflats; up to 800 m.

RED-TAILED TROPICBIRD *Phaethon rubricauda* 46–48 cm (tail-streamers up to 35 cm more)

(4,5) **Adult** *westralis?*: Told by combination of red bill and tail-streamers and almost completely white plumage. Has narrow black mask and blackish shaft-streaks on primaries, primary coverts, innermost wing-coverts, inner secondaries and outertail feathers, and black chevrons on tertials. Body and wings often flushed pink. (6) **Juvenile**: Easily distinguished from other tropicbirds by greyish to blackish bill and lack of obvious black markings on upperside of primaries and primary coverts. HABITAT Open seas, islets.

WHITE-TAILED TROPICBIRD *Phaethon lepturus* 38–41 cm (tail-streamers up to 40 cm)

(7,8) **Adult** *lepturus*: White with narrow black mask, diagonal black band across upperwing-coverts, mostly black upperside of outer primaries and very long white tail-streamers with black shafts. Bill yellowish to orange. (9) **Juvenile**: Lacks black band across upperwing, has black bars on crown, coarse, well-spaced black bars/scales on mantle to uppertail- and upperwing-coverts, and black-tipped tail feathers with no streamers. Bill yellowish-cream with indistinct dark tip (greyish pre-fledging). HABITAT Open seas, islets.

GREAT FRIGATEBIRD *Fregata minor* 86–100 cm

(10) **Male** *minor*: Overall blackish plumage diagnostic, but Lesser Frigatebirds with dull whitish axillaries can cause confusion. (11) **Female**: From other frigatebirds by combination of pale greyish throat, black belly and black inner underwing-coverts. (12) **Juvenile**: From other frigatebirds by all-black inner underwing-coverts. (13) **Immature**: Gradually loses breast-band and attains blackish parts of plumage of respective adults. HABITAT Open seas, islets.

LESSER FRIGATEBIRD *Fregata ariel* 71–81 cm

(14,15) **Male** *ariel*: Overall blackish plumage with prominent whitish patches extending from sides of body to inner underwing-coverts diagnostic. Some individuals have much duller patches and may be mistaken for Great at long distance. Has red gular pouch. (16) **Female**: Combination of black hood, belly and lower flanks and white remainder of underparts, extending in stripe onto inner underwing-coverts, diagnostic. (17) **Juvenile**: Similar to female but has rufous to brownish-white head, and black breast-band enclosing white collar. Apart from size, and unless black mottling on belly present, perhaps indistinguishable from Christmas Island. (18) **Immature second stage**: Gradually loses breast-band and acquires black plumage parts of respective adults. HABITAT Open seas, islets.

CHRISTMAS ISLAND FRIGATEBIRD *Fregata andrewsi* 92–102 cm

(19) **Male**: Overall blackish plumage with contrasting white belly-patch diagnostic. (20) **Female**: Similar to Lesser Frigatebird but larger, with white belly and black bar extending from base of forewing to side of breast. (21) **Juvenile**: Apart from size, possibly not safely separable from Lesser but always shows white belly and possibly has broader black breast-band and broader white spur on inner underwing-coverts. (22) **Immature second stage**: Gradually loses breast-band and acquires black plumage parts of respective adults. HABITAT Open seas, islets.

each genus to different scale

PLATE 71 BOOBIES, SHEARWATERS & STORM-PETRELS

MASKED BOOBY *Sula dactylatra* 74–86 cm

(1) **Adult** *personata*: White plumage, with contrasting black primaries, secondaries, tertials and tail. Blackish facial skin ('mask'), pale yellowish bill, dark greyish legs and feet, white underwing-coverts with only a small dark area on primary coverts. (2) **Juvenile**: Head, neck, upperparts and upperwing-coverts rather warm brown, has dark brown band across underwing-coverts and browner primaries and secondaries than adult. Similar to Brown but upperparts and upperwing-coverts somewhat paler and warmer brown, has narrow whitish band across upper mantle, white underwing-coverts with a clearly defined dark central band, whiter underparts and dark legs and feet. Gradually attains parts of adult plumage. HABITAT Open seas, islets.

RED-FOOTED BOOBY *Sula sula* 68–72.5 cm

(3) **Adult white morph** *rubripes*: Like Masked but smaller and slimmer, tail and tertials white, bill and facial skin light blue-grey and pinkish, legs and feet rose-red, shows large blackish patch on primary underwing-coverts. Plumage may have apricot flush, particularly on crown and hindneck. (4) **Adult intermediate morph**: Similar to white morph but has brown mantle, back and wing-coverts (above and below). (5) **Juvenile**: Rather uniform dark greyish-brown with darker primaries, secondaries and tail, dark grey bill, dark grey facial skin and yellowish-grey to flesh-coloured legs and feet. (6) **Immature white morph**: Gradually attains adult features. Often shows diffuse darker breast-band; soon has untidy whitish areas on wing-coverts. **Adult brown morph**: Similar to juvenile but bill, facial skin, legs and feet as adult white morph. May show apricot flush on crown and hindneck. HABITAT Open seas, oceanic islets; sometimes coastal waters.

BROWN BOOBY *Sula leucogaster* 73–83 cm

(7,8) **Adult** *plotus*: Dark chocolate-brown plumage with contrasting white lower breast to vent. In flight, underwing-coverts also white apart from dark leading edge, incomplete dark diagonal bar and dark primary coverts. Bill pale yellowish, facial skin blue to blue-grey, legs and feet pale yellow to greenish-yellow. (9) **Juvenile**: Brown of plumage somewhat paler, white of plumage washed dusky-brownish, bill and facial skin mostly pale bluish-grey, legs and feet dull pink to pale yellowish. Gradually attains adult plumage. HABITAT Open seas, islets.

STREAKED SHEARWATER *Calonectris leucomelas* 48–49 cm

(10,11) **Adult**: Mostly greyish-brown upperside and upperwing, white underparts, white underwing-coverts with dark patches on primary coverts, distinctive white head with variable dark streaking on crown, nape and ear-coverts. Crown and ear-coverts may be mostly dark, offsetting white eye-ring, bill pale grey to pinkish-grey with darker tip. HABITAT & BEHAVIOUR Open seas; very rarely inland. During calm conditions, flight direct but rather languid, with outer wing slightly angled backward; often glides on bowed wings.

WEDGE-TAILED SHEARWATER *Puffinus pacificus* 41–46 cm

(12,13) **Adult pale morph**: Similar to Streaked but upperside darker and browner (including crown and sides of head), primary underwing-coverts mostly white, tail longer and pointed (wedge-shaped when fanned). (14) **Adult dark morph**: Most likely to be confused with Short-tailed but larger and broader-winged, with much longer, pointed tail (toes do not extend beyond tail-tip), with more uniformly dark underwing, pinkish feet, head not contrastingly dark. HABITAT & BEHAVIOUR Open seas. In calm weather, flight rather lazy, with much gliding and banking, wings held forward and bowed.

SHORT-TAILED SHEARWATER *Puffinus tenuirostris* 41–43 cm

(15,16) **Adult**: Smaller and slimmer than other shearwaters in region. Overall dark sooty-brown with pale chin, slightly paler breast and belly, and prominent whitish area along centre of underwing, contrasting with dark base and border; toes extend beyond tip of short tail. Bill, legs and feet dark. HABITAT & BEHAVIOUR Open seas. Flight direct, consisting of a flapping rise followed by a long downward glide.

SWINHOE'S STORM-PETREL *Oceanodroma monorhis* 20 cm

(17,18) **Adult**: Identified by combination of small size, forked tail and all-dark body. Upperwing has contrasting paler diagonal bar across coverts and indistinct whitish shaft-streaks on base of primaries, underwing uniformly dark. HABITAT & BEHAVIOUR Open seas, sometimes inshore. Has erratic swooping, bounding flight pattern.

10–18 to different scale

PLATE 72 PITTAS

EARED PITTA *Pitta phayrei* 20–24 cm
(1) **Male**: Rather long, slender bill; blackish crown-centre, head-sides and nape, long buffy-whitish supercilium (feathers often protrude beyond nape like ears); buffish below with dark-scaled flanks. (2) **Female**: Crown-centre, nape and sides of head browner than male, underparts more heavily dark-marked. **Juvenile**: Duller brown than female with no dark submoustachial stripe, all-buffish crown-sides and supercilium, shorter 'ears' and dark brown breast, with some lighter, rufous shaft-streaks. **VOICE** Song is an airy whistled *wheeow-whit*, repeated after rather lengthy intervals. Short dog-like whine when alarmed. **HABITAT** Broadleaved evergreen and mixed deciduous forest, bamboo; up to 900 m, sometimes 1,500 m.

BLUE-RUMPED PITTA *Pitta soror* 20–22 cm
(3) **Male** *flynnstonei*: Like Rusty-naped but crown and nape pale blue (slightly green-tinged), lower back and rump (mainly latter) distinctly blue, breast and belly paler and more buffish. (4) **Female**: Duller; mostly greenish crown and nape, upperparts browner-tinged with less blue on rump, underparts even paler. (5) **Juvenile**: Head-sides/throat buffier than Rusty-naped, richer buff markings above, less heavy breast markings. **VOICE** Song is a repeated short, full *weaoe* or *weeya* (slightly inflected). Call is a short *ppew*, *eau* or *cho*. **HABITAT** Broadleaved evergreen and semi-evergreen forest, sometimes mixed deciduous forest; 400–1,460 m.

RUSTY-NAPED PITTA *Pitta oatesi* 21–25 cm
(6) **Male** *oatesi*: Mostly deep rufous head/underparts, dull green above (rump sometimes blue-tinged), well-defined narrow blackish post-ocular stripe. Throat paler, underparts may have pinkish tinge. (7) **Juvenile**: Dark brown upperside/breast, whitish crown-streaks, whitish-buff spots on upperparts, wing-coverts and breast; whitish-buff supercilium, whitish head-sides with indistinct dark streaks, whitish throat. **Female**: Duller than the male; brown tinge above, vaguely dark-scaled lower throat/upper breast. **Other subspecies** *P.o.deborah* (presumably this in extreme S): Blue rump, strongly pinkish throat and underparts. **VOICE** Song is a sharp *chow-whit*, recalling Blue Pitta. **HABITAT** Broadleaved evergreen forest, bamboo; 800–2,565 m, locally down to 390 m.

GIANT PITTA *Pitta caerulea* 28–29 cm
(8) **Male** *caerulea*: Pale greyish head, black crown-/nape-centre, black eyestripe, blue above, broken necklace. (9) **Female**: Base colour of head warm buffish-brown, crown-centre darker-scaled than male, has narrow black nuchal collar, rufescent-brown upperside, with blue lower rump to tail and deeper buff underparts. (10) **Juvenile**: Dull dark brown above, dull dark blue tail, dirty whitish/pale buff below, broad smudgy dark breast-band, indistinctly scaled head and upper breast, bill reddish at base and tip. **VOICE** Loud airy *hwoo-er* or *whee-er*, every 5–10 s. **HABITAT** Broadleaved evergreen forest, bamboo; below 200 m.

BLUE PITTA *Pitta cyanea* 19.5–24 cm
(11) **Male** *cyanea*: Blue above, orange-scarlet rear crown-sides/nape, pale bluish-whitish below with black spots/bars. In flight, shows small white patch at base of primaries. (12) **Female**: Duller; browner above, orange-scarlet restricted more to nape and often duller, more buffish/whitish below with heavier dark markings. (13) **Juvenile**: Dark brown above with warm buff streaks, dark-scaled buffish-brown crown-sides, dark eye-stripe, duller blue uppertail-coverts/tail, mostly dark brown breast/belly with warm buff streaks; bill reddish at first. **Other subspecies** *P.c.aurantiaca* (SE): More yellowish-orange on head. **VOICE** Song is loud *peroo-whit* (*peroo* drawn-out, *whit* sharper/shriller). Rasping *skyeew* in alarm. **HABITAT** Broadleaved evergreen and moister mixed deciduous forest; up to 1,500 m.

BANDED PITTA *Pitta guajana* 21–24 cm
(14) **Male** *irena*: Crown-sides bright yellow, nape vivid orange-red; blue-black below, orange-rufous bars on breast-sides, white band on inner wing-coverts/secondaries, white throat with yellower sides. (15) **Female**: Breast to undertail-coverts whitish to buffish with narrow dark barring; less orange-red on nape. (16) **Juvenile**: Duller than female; all-buffish crown-sides, supercilium and lower nape (scaled darker), browner head-sides, dark brown breast with buff spots/streaks, duller wing-band, initially orange-red base and tip of bill. **VOICE** Song is a repeated short *pouw* or *poww*. Whirring, slightly explosive *kirr* or *pprrr* in alarm. **HABITAT** Broadleaved evergreen forest, secondary forest; up to 610 m.

BAR-BELLIED PITTA *Pitta elliotii* 19.5–21 cm
(17) **Male**: Vivid green above, blackish mask, pale green lower throat, greenish-yellow breast, yellow remainder of underparts with narrow dark bars, dark bluish centre of abdomen. Blue tail/undertail-coverts. (18) **Female**: Warm buffy-brown crown/breast, blackish-brown head-sides, buffish cheek-streaks, no blue below. (19) **Juvenile**: Initially rather uniform dark brown with darker sides of head, paler throat, pale buff spots on crown, mantle, wing-coverts and breast, and orangey-red bill with darker base. **VOICE** Song is a loud whistled *chawee-wu* (only *wee-wu* audible at distance) repeated every 9–12 s. Harsh, shrill *jeeow* or *jow* when alarmed. **HABITAT** Various broadleaved forests, bamboo; up to 400 m.

GURNEY'S PITTA *Pitta gurneyi* 18.5–20.5 cm
(20) **Male**: Blue crown/nape, black forecrown and head-sides, yellow below with black centre of breast and belly to undertail-coverts, and black-barred flanks. Upperside warm dark brown, tail turquoise-tinged deep blue. (21) **Female**: Crown and nape buffy-rufous, sides of head blackish-brown with paler streaks on lores and cheeks, throat whitish, rest of underparts pale buffy-whitish with dark bars, tail blue. (22) **Juvenile**: Forehead to nape, breast and upper belly dark brown with buff streaks (broader/more spot-like on nape), rest of upperside, head-sides and tail similar to female; initially has fleshy-orange base and tip of bill. **VOICE** Song is a short, explosive *lilip*, repeated every 2–6 s. Female may give more subdued *llup*. Harsh falling *skyeew* when alarmed. **HABITAT** Broadleaved evergreen forest, secondary forest, old rubber plantations near forest; below 200 m.

PLATE 73 PITTAS & TYPICAL BROADBILLS

HOODED PITTA *Pitta sordida* 16.5–19 cm

(1,2) **Adult** *cucullata*: Black head, dark brown crown to nape-centre, green body and greater coverts, turquoise-blue lower rump, uppertail-coverts and median/lesser covert patch, red vent; large white area on primaries. (3) **Juvenile**: Duller above/on head-sides, brownish below, white throat, pinkish-red vent; reddish bill-base/tip. **Other subspecies** *P.s.muelleri* (extreme S): Black crown, more white on primaries. **VOICE** Song is repeated loud, perky *whep-whep* or *whew-whew*. Short *skyew* in alarm. **HABITAT & BEHAVIOUR** Broadleaved evergreen forest, secondary forest, moist mixed deciduous forest, bamboo; up to 750 m (mostly lowlands). Often sings from trees.

GARNET PITTA *Pitta granatina* 14–16.5 cm

(4) **Adult** *coccinea*: Black head with scarlet-red crown/nape, crimson-red belly/vent. Narrow pale blue line along rear crown/nape-side, deep purplish above, purplish-black breast, iridescent azure/light blue wing-covert patch. (5) **Juvenile**: Mostly dark brown with paler throat and some red on nape and vent, wing-coverts and tail duller than adult, bill initially reddish at base and tip. **VOICE** Song is a long whistle (c.1.5 s), swelling in volume. Like Rail-babbler but has slight upward inflection and ends abruptly. May give purring *prrr prrr prrr...* in alarm. **HABITAT** Broadleaved evergreen forest; below 200 m.

BLUE-WINGED PITTA *Pitta moluccensis* 18–20.5 cm

(6,7) **Adult**: Told by blackish head with buff crown-sides/supercilium and white throat, green mantle and scapulars and plain buff underparts with red vent. Upper chin blackish, rump, uppertail-coverts and tail-tip deep violet-blue, tail blackish, upperwing-coverts mostly deep violet-blue. In flight shows very large white patch on primaries. (8) **Juvenile**: Head and upperparts duller, crown-sides/supercilium dark-scaled, blue of plumage duller, chin whiter, vent washed-out pinkish, tail-tip green; orangey-red base/tip of bill. Smaller white wing-patch in flight. **VOICE** Song is a loud, clear *taew-laew taew-laew* (with stressed *laew* notes), repeated every 3–5 s. Harsh *skyew* when alarmed. **HABITAT & BEHAVIOUR** Relatively open broadleaved evergreen and mixed deciduous forest, secondary growth, bamboo; also parks, gardens and mangroves on migration; up to 800 m. Regularly sings from quite high in trees.

MANGROVE PITTA *Pitta megarhyncha* 18–21 cm

(9) **Adult**: Like Blue-winged but bill much longer, crown drabber and more uniform brown (almost lacks black in centre), underparts slightly duller, chin whitish. (10) **Juvenile**: Duller. Separated from similar Blue-winged by same characters as adult. **VOICE** Song is similar to Blue-winged but more slurred and hurried: *wieuw-wieuw*. **HABITAT** Mangroves.

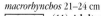

BLACK-AND-RED BROADBILL *Cymbirhynchus macrorhynchos* 21–24 cm

(11) **Adult** *malaccensis*: Black upperparts and chin/cheeks, dark maroon-red rump, uppertail-coverts and underparts with narrow black breast-band, long white streak along scapulars to tertials, turquoise-blue upper mandible and yellowish lower mandible. In flight, also shows whitish band

at base of flight feathers. (12) **Juvenile**: Browner overall; some dark red on rump to uppertail-coverts, lower throat and vent, white streak restricted to scapulars, whitish-tipped upperwing-coverts. **VOICE** Accelerating series of short grating cicada-like notes. Rasping *wiark* and rapid series of *pip* notes when alarmed. **HABITAT & BEHAVIOUR** Broadleaved evergreen and semi-evergreen forest and forest edge near water, freshwater swamp forest, mangroves; up to 300 m. Unobtrusive, often sitting still for long periods.

SILVER-BREASTED BROADBILL *Serilophus lunatus* 16–17 cm

(13) **Male** *lunatus*: Pale brownish upperparts, greyish-white forehead and underparts, prominent broad black supercilium. Rump and uppertail-coverts dark rufous, wings black with mostly warm, light brown tertials and broad greyish-blue bases to flight feathers, tail black with white tips and fringes to outer feathers. In flight, from below, shows whitish band along base of flight feathers. (14) **Female**: Like male but shows thin whitish necklace across upper breast. **Juvenile**: Duller-billed than adult. **Other subspecies** *S.l.rothschildi* (extreme S): Greyer crown, head-sides, throat and breast, more rufous-chestnut back to uppertail-coverts and tertials. *S.l.elisabethae* (NE,SE), *stolidus* (northern S). **VOICE** Melancholy *ki-uu* (*uu* lower). Also, high staccato trilled *kitikitikit...* (mainly in flight). **HABITAT & BEHAVIOUR** Lower/middle storey of broadleaved evergreen forest, sometimes mixed deciduous forest, bamboo; 300–1,800 m. Usually in small, slow-moving parties.

BANDED BROADBILL *Eurylaimus javanicus* 21.5–23.5 cm

(15) **Male** *harterti*: Dull vinous-reddish head/underparts, dark above with large yellow markings. Head/breast greyer-dark, narrow blackish breast-band, turquoise-blue bill. (16) **Female**: Lacks breast-band. (17) **Juvenile**: Mostly pale buffish/yellowish below, with vague streaks, browner crown/head-sides, yellow eyebrow, pale yellow spots/streaks on mantle, yellow-tipped wing-coverts, mostly horn-coloured bill. **VOICE** Sharp whistled *wheeoo*, then a loud, rising, frantic series of notes. Also a brief, rather nasal *whee-u* (*ee* stressed), falling *kyeeow*, rolling *keowrr* and yelping *keek-eek-eek*. **HABITAT & BEHAVIOUR** Middle storey of broadleaved evergreen and semi-evergreen forest, wetter mixed deciduous forest; up to 1,100 m. Usually in small, slow-moving parties.

BLACK-AND-YELLOW BROADBILL *Eurylaimus ochromalus* 13.5–15 cm

(18) **Male** *ochromalus*: Small; black head/breast-band, white collar; pinkish-white to yellow below, yellow eyes. (19) **Female**: Breast-band broken in centre. (20) **Juvenile**: Duller; whitish throat, dark chin, pale yellowish eyebrow, indistinct dark breast-streaks (no band). **VOICE** Frantic, rapid notes, starting slowly and downslurred, before gaining speed and momentum. Lacks introductory note of Banded, ends abruptly. Has similar *kyeeow* and *keowrr* call notes. **HABITAT & BEHAVIOUR** Middle and upper storey of broadleaved evergreen forest; up to 700 m. Male display involves wing-stretching and tail-wagging.

11–20 to different scale

PLATE 74 BROADBILLS & LEAFBIRDS

GREEN BROADBILL *Calyptomena viridis* 15–17 cm

(1) **Male** *continentis*: Chunky, rounded, short-tailed; bright deep green with black patch on rear ear-coverts and broad black bars on wing-coverts. Has broad tuft of feathers on top of bill and small black spot in front of eye. (2) **Female**: Duller, with no black markings, tuft of feathers on top of bill much smaller. **Juvenile**: Like female but breast paler, vent greenish-white. **VOICE** Soft bubbling trill, starting quietly and increasing in tempo: *toi toi-oi-oi-oi-oick*. Other calls include *goik-goik* and *goik-goik-doyik* (*doyik* faster and higher), a loud *oik*, a frog-like bubbling rattled *oo-turrr*, and mournful whistles. **HABITAT & BEHAVIOUR** Broadleaved evergreen forest; up to 800 m. Unobtrusive, in middle storey; visits fruiting figs. Male's display includes wing-flashing, head-bobbing, gaping and rico-cheting from perch to perch.

LONG-TAILED BROADBILL *Psarisomus dalhousiae* 24–27 cm

(3) **Adult** *dalhousiae*: Mostly green; long blue tail (black below), bold black and yellow head pattern, blue crown-patch and markings on rear of collar. Variable blue tinge below. White patch at base of primaries in flight. (4) **Juvenile**: Crown, nape and ear-coverts dark green, more uniformly green below, darker upper mandible. **Other subspecies** *P.d.psittacinus* (extreme S), *cyanicauda* (SE). **VOICE** Loud, high-pitched, piercing whistles, *tseeay* or *pseew*, repeated 5–8 times. Sometimes gives single sharp *tseeay* and short rasping *psweep*. **HABITAT & BEHAVIOUR** Broadleaved evergreen forest; 500–2,000 m. Usually in flocks, rather shy.

DUSKY BROADBILL *Corydon sumatranus* 25–28.5 cm

(5) **Adult** *laoensis*: Blackish-brown; buffish bib, big dark reddish bill (tip greyish). Dull purplish orbital skin, concealed orange streaks on back, white markings on outertail feathers; white patch at base of primaries in flight. (6) **Juvenile**: Browner; darker, less contrasting throat and upper breast, less white on wings and tail, more pinkish bill and orbital skin, no orange streaks on back. **Other subspecies** *C.s.sumatranus* (extreme S). **VOICE** 6–8 shrill, screaming, upward-inflected thin whistles: *hi-ky-ui ky-ui ky-ui...* or *ky-ee ky-ee ky-ee ky-ee...* Also, shrill falling *pseeoo* and piercing *tsiu*; occasional quavering *ch wit* in flight. **HABITAT & BEHAVIOUR** Middle/upper storey of broadleaved evergreen and semi-evergreen forest, wetter areas in mixed deciduous forest; up to 1,000 m. Usually in small flocks; sits rather still on branches for long periods.

GREATER GREEN LEAFBIRD *Chloropsis sonnerati* 20.5–22.5 cm

(7) **Male** *zosterops*: Stout bill, all-green plumage apart from black face and bib and purple-blue malar band. Blue shoulder-patch (usually concealed in field). (8) **Female**: Stout bill, all-green plumage, sharply demarcated yellow throat and eyering. Blue malar band faint. (9) **Juvenile**: Similar to female but blue malar band fainter or absent; has yellowish submoustachial band. **VOICE** Sings with liquid musical whistles and brief chattering notes, *wi-i chaka-wiu chi-wiu...* etc. **HABITAT** Middle to upper storey of broadleaved evergreen forest, rarely mangroves; up to 915 m.

LESSER GREEN LEAFBIRD *Chloropsis cyanopogon* 16–19 cm

(10) **Male** *septentrionalis*: Like Greater Green but smaller, much smaller-billed; has yellowish forehead and border to bib, no blue shoulder-patch. (11) **Female**: All green with golden-green forehead and blue/purplish-blue malar band. Somewhat deeper green than Blue-winged, no blue on shoulder, wings or tail. From Golden-fronted by greener forehead, shorter, less curved bill. (12) **Juvenile**: Very like Greater Green but smaller, smaller-billed, less defined yellow throat, no obvious eyering. (13) **Male** *cyanopogon* (extreme S): Much less yellow on forehead/bordering bib (more like Greater Green). **HABITAT** Broadleaved evergreen forest, open forest, forest edge; up to 700 m.

BLUE-WINGED LEAFBIRD *Chloropsis cochinchinensis* 16.5–18.5 cm

(14) **Male** *chlorocephala*: Extensive turquoise-blue on wings/tail, extensive yellowish-bronze on head/upper breast. (15) **Female**: Blue on wings/tail diagnostic (less than on male); crown/nape more golden-tinged than Lesser Green, malar band less defined. *C.c.moluccensis* tends to show more defined golden nape. (16) **Juvenile**: Like female but almost lacks any blue on face and malar area, crown and nape greener. (17) **Male** *moluccensis* (extreme S): Even yellower forecrown and border to bib, more defined golden nape. **Other subspecies** *C.c.serithai* (S): Intermediate with *moluccensis*. *C.c.cochinchinensis* (SE, south NE), *kinneari* (north NE). **VOICE** Sings with musical *pli-pli-chu-chu* and *chi-chi-pli-i* etc. Also, high *chi-chi-chi* and *chi'ii* and rattling *pridit*. **HABITAT & BEHAVIOUR** Broadleaved evergreen and mixed deciduous forest; up to 1,500 m. Often seen in small parties, joins bird-waves.

GOLDEN-FRONTED LEAFBIRD *Chloropsis aurifrons* 18–19 cm

(18) **Adult** *pridii*: Shining golden-orange forecrown, purple-blue throat/malar, rather slender, slightly downcurved bill. Broad yellowish lower border to bib. (19) **Juvenile**: Green; purple-blue and black malar, blue on shoulder, golden forehead (duller than adult). **Other subspecies** *C.a. incompta* (south W) and *inornata* (W,C,NE,SE): No obvious yellow bib-border. **VOICE** Song is complex, squeaky and scratchy but quite melodious, incorporating mimicry. **HABITAT** Dry dipterocarp and mixed deciduous forest, sometimes broadleaved evergreen and semi-evergreen forest, secondary growth; up to 1,220 m.

ORANGE-BELLIED LEAFBIRD *Chloropsis hardwickii* 18.5–20.5 cm

(20) **Male** *hardwickii*: From other leafbirds by dull yellowish-orange lower breast to vent. (21) **Female**: Dull yellowish-orange centre to abdomen and undertail-coverts, broad purplish-blue malar band. (22) **Juvenile**: Underparts uniform light green, little blue on malar, no blue shoulder-patch. Like Blue-winged but darker above, little blue on wings and tail, bill longer and slightly downcurved. **VOICE** Highly variable song: jumpy phrases of *chip*, *tsi*, *chit* and *chi* notes; monotonous *shrittitit* and *shrit* notes or *chit-wiu chit-wiu chit-wiu...*; melodious *chip-chip-chip-chip-irr chirriwu-i pichu-pi* etc. Also a loud *chissick* in flight. **HABITAT** Broadleaved evergreen forest, forest edge; 600–2,000 m, locally down to 390 m.

PLATE 75 ASIAN FAIRY BLUEBIRD, SHRIKES & RAIL-BABBLER

ASIAN FAIRY BLUEBIRD *Irena puella* 24.5–26.5 cm

(1) **Male** *puella*: Shining deep blue upperparts and undertail-coverts, blackish head-sides, remainder of underparts, tail and wings (apart from median and lesser coverts). Eyes red. (2) **Female**: Dull turquoise-blue, blackish tail and flight feathers, reddish eyes. See Maroon-breasted Philentoma. **Juvenile**: As female but duller, wings browner. **Other subspecies** *I.p.malayensis* (extreme S). **VOICE** Loud, liquid *tu-lip wae-waet-oo*. Loud liquid *wi-it*, *wait*, *pip* etc. and quavering *u-iu*. **HABITAT & BEHAVIOUR** Broadleaved evergreen forest, sometimes mixed deciduous forest; up to 1,525 m. Often near fruiting trees in small flocks.

TIGER SHRIKE *Lanius tigrinus* 17–18.5 cm

(3) **Male breeding**: Grey crown and nape, black forehead and mask, all-whitish underparts. Resembles Burmese but has blackish bars/scales on deep rufous-brown upperparts, warm brown uppertail, no white wing-patch. (4) **Female breeding**: Somewhat duller with more prominently barred/scaled upperparts and buff-tinged flanks with blackish scales; has whitish patch on lores and narrow white supercilium. (5) **Juvenile**: Duller than female, crown/head-sides uniform warmish brown with blackish bars/scales, pinkish base to lower mandible. Bolder dark scales on head/body than Brown, no obvious dark mask. **Adult non-breeding**: Forehead to upper mantle rather uniform brownish, mask duller. **VOICE** Scolding chatter in alarm. Also a subdued sharp *tchick*. **HABITAT & BEHAVIOUR** Forest edge, secondary growth; up to 300 m. Skulking.

BROWN SHRIKE *Lanius cristatus* 19–20 cm

(6) **Male** *confusus*: Uniform brown above, black mask, whitish supercilium, whitish below with rich buffish wash on sides. No white wing-patch, greyish-white forehead, brighter rufous-chestnut tinge to rump/uppertail-coverts. (7) **Female**: Often slightly duller; cream-tinged supercilium, fine dusky vermiculations on breast and flanks. (8) **Juvenile**: Duller; narrow blackish and some buffish scales above, whiter below, dark scales/bars on sides, shorter supercilium, pink-based lower mandible. Told by brown base colour above, pale supercilium, dark mask. (9) **Male** *superciliosus* (recorded S): Rich chestnut above (crown brightest), defined white forehead/supercilium. (10) **Male** *lucionensis* (widespread): Pale grey crown, less distinct supercilium, grey-washed mantle/scapulars. **Other subspecies** *L.c.cristatus* (throughout). **VOICE** Harsh *chak-ak-ak-ak-ak* in alarm. High-pitched squawks. Song consists of rich varied chattering. **HABITAT** Open country, cultivation, gardens, secondary growth; up to 2,000 m (mainly lowlands).

BURMESE SHRIKE *Lanius collurioides* 19–21 cm

(11) **Male** *collurioides*: Black forehead and mask, rufous-chestnut above, whitish below. Crown and nape slaty-grey, upperparts unbarred, has white patch at base of primaries and blackish, strongly white-edged uppertail. (12) **Female**: Duller above, whitish lores and sometimes a very narrow whitish supercilium (broken over eye). (13) **Juvenile**: Like female but crown/nape warm brownish to greyish-brown with blackish-and-buff bars, mask duller and streaked buffish, upperparts,

lesser and median coverts paler with blackish scales/bars, rest of wing fringed paler, white wing-patch smaller/almost absent; wavy blackish-brown bars on breast, flanks and thighs. **VOICE** Song is subdued, quiet, rapid and scratchy, including much repetition and varied mimicry. Alarm call is a loud, rapid harsh chattering: *chikachikachitchit*, *chekoochekoochitititititit* and *chetetetetet* etc. and a harsh single *jao*. **HABITAT** Clearings and open areas in various kinds of forest (particularly pine), cultivation; up to 1,800 m (breeds above 900 m).

LONG-TAILED SHRIKE *Lanius schach* 25–28 cm

(14) **Adult** *longicaudatus*: Black head with white throat. Relatively large; long blackish tail, rufous-chestnut above, rufous-chestnut flanks and vent, and prominent white patch at base of primaries. (15) **Juvenile**: Crown and nape whitish-buff to pale greyish, extreme forehead and supercilium whiter, lores and ear-coverts browner than adult, mantle mostly buffish, black bars/scales on crown, mantle and scapulars (vaguely on back to uppertail-coverts); wavy blackish-brown bars on breast, flanks and vent. Browner tail and browner wings with mostly buffish, black-scaled lesser and median coverts, rufous-buff-fringed greater coverts, and smaller white patch. **Other subspecies** *L.s.tricolor* (NW). **VOICE** Song is a subdued, scratchy warbling (with mimicry). Loud, scolding drawn-out *chaak-chaak* in alarm. **HABITAT** Open areas, cultivation, gardens, secondary growth, sometimes forest edge; up to 1,800 m.

GREY-BACKED SHRIKE *Lanius tephronotus* 22.5–25.5 cm

(16) **Adult**: Uniform grey crown, mantle and scapulars, black mask, no white wing-patch, rufous-chestnut rump and uppertail-coverts, rufescent flanks; almost no supercilium. (17) **Juvenile**: Crown to back cold brownish-grey, scaled/barred blackish and dull pale buff to dull rufous, mask duller, back to uppertail-coverts more rufescent with black bars, underparts more buffish with blackish scales (plainer on upper throat and vent), tertials and wing-coverts fringed rufescent. Best separated from Long-tailed by greyish mantle and scapulars and lack of white wing-patch. **First winter**: More similar to adult but mask duller, wings and underparts similar to juvenile, may have slightly paler mantle with brown tinge. **VOICE** Call is harsh and grating. Song is subdued and scratchy, incorporating much mimicry. **HABITAT** Open country, cultivation, secondary growth; up to 2,000 m.

RAIL-BABBLER *Eupetes macrocerus* 29 cm

(18) **Adult** *macrocerus*: Rather slim, with long neck, bill and tail. Overall warm brown, buffy-rufous forehead, chestnut-red crown, hindneck, throat and foreneck, long black band from bill-base through ear-coverts to neck, long white supercilium/neck-stripe, reddish-rufous breast. Strip of blue skin on neck-side inflates when calling. (19) **Juvenile**: Resembles adult but shows dull chestnut crown and hindneck, warmer upperparts, somewhat duller head/neck-stripes, orange-rufous foreneck and breast (without red), whitish throat and greyer belly. **VOICE** Long, thin, drawn-out monotone whistle, 1.5–2 s in duration. Very similar to Garnet Pitta but purer, higher-pitched and not rising at end. Also, popping frog-like notes when agitated. **HABITAT & BEHAVIOUR** Broadleaved evergreen forest; up to 900 m. Walks on forest floor, jerking head like chicken; very shy.

PLATE 76 DRONGOS & CROWS

BLACK DRONGO *Dicrurus macrocercus* 27–28.5 cm

(1) **Adult** *thai*: All blackish (slight bluish-glossed); long, deeply forked tail; often shows a small white loral spot. (2) **First winter**: Throat duller than adult (may be streaked greyish/whitish), upper breast and wings duller; has prominent whitish scales on tail-coverts and breast/belly, whitish markings on under-wing-coverts and wing-bend. **Juvenile**: Duller, tinged sooty-brown; vague paler scales on breast/belly. **Other subspecies** *D.m.cathoecus* (northern Thailand; also only visiting form): Larger. **VOICE** Harsh *ti-tiu*, rasping *jeez* or *cheece* and *cheece-cheece-chichuk* etc. **HABITAT** Open country, cultivation, roadsides, scrub; up to 1,220 m (breeds mostly in lowlands).

ASHY DRONGO *Dicrurus leucophaeus* 25.5–29 cm

(3) **Adult** *mouhoti* (breeds NW, north NE; visitor elsewhere): Dark steely-grey (somewhat paler below); darker lores, shallower tail-fork than Black. (4) **Adult** *nigrescens* (resident S): Blacker above, darker below, mainly throat/breast; intergrades occur in north. (5) **Adult** *leucogenis* (visitor throughout): Pale ashy-grey; black forehead, whitish lores, ear-coverts and vent. (6) **Adult** *salangensis* (visitor C,SE,S): Like *leucogenis* but a shade darker with mostly grey ear-coverts. **Juvenile**: Dull; paler throat/vent. **Other subspecies** *D.l.bondi* (resident W,NE[south],SE), *hopwoodi* (recorded in winter NW,NE). **VOICE** Wheezy whistled *phuuuu* and *hieeeeeer*, loud *tchik wu-wit tchik wu-wit*. Mixed chattering, shrill whistles and harsh notes; can mimic. **HABITAT** Open forest, secondary growth (also mangroves, coastal scrub in S); up to 2,565 m.

CROW-BILLED DRONGO *Dicrurus annectans* 27–32 cm

(7) **Adult**: Bulkier than Black Drongo, tail relatively shorter/broader with shallower fork and more strongly upcurled outer tips, bill thicker-based and longer, lacks loral spot. (8) **First winter**: White spots/scales on breast to vent. Breast-spots help rule out Black. **Juvenile**: Browner than adult. **VOICE** Musical whistles, churrs and chattering, including thin rising *hee'weeiit* and *heeer-wu-wit-it*, mixed with harsh chatters. **HABITAT** Broadleaved evergreen and sometimes mixed deciduous forest. Mangroves, plantations and secondary growth in winter/on passage. Up to 1,445 m (breeds below 800 m).

BRONZED DRONGO *Dicrurus aeneus* 22–23.5 cm

(9) **Adult** *aeneus*: Relatively small and small-billed; black plumage with very strong dark blue to greenish-blue gloss on upperparts, throat and breast distinctive. **Juvenile**: Sooty-brown with some gloss on crown, mantle, wings and upper breast. **First winter** Less brilliantly glossed above than adult, gloss below mostly on upper breast. **HABITAT** Broadleaved evergreen, semi-evergreen and deciduous forest, forest edge, secondary growth; up to 2,000 m.

LESSER RACKET-TAILED DRONGO *Dicrurus remifer* 25–27.5 cm (tail-shafts/rackets to 40 cm more)

(10) **Adult** *tectirostris*: Square tail-tip, very long, extended bare shafts of outer feathers, terminating in longish pendants (often broken or absent). Short tufted feathers on forehead overlap bill and create distinctive flat-headed appearance; plumage strongly glossed dark blue to greenish-blue on upperside, throat and breast. **Juvenile**: Duller, with no tail extensions. **Other subspecies** *D.r.peracensis* (south of c.16°N): Narrower, much longer ribbon-like tail-pendants (intergrades in north of range). **VOICE** Loud, musical and very varied, including much mimicry. **HABITAT** Broadleaved evergreen forest, sometimes semi-evergreen forest; 700–2,565 m.

SPANGLED DRONGO *Dicrurus hottentottus* 29–33 cm

(11) **Adult** *hottentottus*: Longish, slightly down-curved bill, squarish-ended tail with strongly up-/inward-curled outer tips. Greenish-glossed wings, tail and uppertail-coverts, hair-like forehead plumes (usually hidden). **Juvenile**: Body blackish-brown, wings/tail less shiny, outertail-tips less curled, forehead plumes much shorter. **Other subspecies** *D.h.brevirostris* (visiting race). **VOICE** Loud *chit-wiii* (*chit* stressed, *wiii* rising), and single *wiii* notes. **HABITAT & BEHAVIOUR** Various broadleaved forests, secondary growth; sometimes parks and gardens on migration; up to 2,000 m (mostly lowlands). Often in flocks, feeding in flowering trees.

GREATER RACKET-TAILED DRONGO *Dicrurus paradiseus* 33–35.5 cm (tail-rackets to 30 cm more)

(12) **Adult** *rangoonensis*: Relatively large; tall crest, forked tail with (usually) twisted pendants (often absent). (13) **Adult** *hypoballus* (S): Slightly smaller; crest shorter. **Juvenile**: Browner; short crest, no tail extensions. **First winter**: From adult by white bars on undertail-coverts and vaguely on belly, white specks on lower breast. **Other subspecies** *D.p.paradiseus* (W[south],C,SE). **VOICE** Very varied. Loud musical whistles, harsh screeching/churring and much mimicry. **HABITAT** Various broadleaved forests, secondary growth, plantations; up to 1,700 m (mainly lowlands).

HOUSE CROW *Corvus splendens* 40–43 cm

(14) **Adult** *insolens*: Broad dull greyish collar encompassing nape, upper mantle, rear ear-coverts, neck and breast diagnostic. Smaller, slimmer and thinner-necked than Large-billed, with much shorter, slenderer bill. (15) **Adult** *protegatus* (recorded S): Paler, more contrasting brownish-grey collar. **Juvenile**: Somewhat duller and browner, particularly head and body. **VOICE** Flat toneless dry *kaaa-kaaa* (weaker than Large-billed), rasping *ka* or down-turned *kow* and low-pitched *kowk*. **HABITAT & BEHAVIOUR** Open and urban areas, cultivation; up to 1,525 m. Roosts communally.

LARGE-BILLED CROW *Corvus macrorhynchos* 48–59 cm

(16) **Adult** *macrorhynchos*: Longish bill with strongly arched culmen, peaked crown, rather wedge-shaped tail. (17) **Juvenile**: Duller and less glossy. (18) **Adult** *levaillantii* (W,NW,NE,C): Smaller (45–48 cm); squarer tail-tip, usually less arched culmen. **VOICE** Throaty dry *khaa*, *kwaa*, *kaa kaa* or *kaaa-kaaa*, low *kaak*, higher *awa awa awa...* Nasal *quank quank quank* has been attributed to *C.m.levaillantii* only. **HABITAT & BEHAVIOUR** Open forest and woodland, open areas and cultivation, urban areas, mangroves; up to 2,565 m. Usually seen in pairs but tends to roost communally.

PLATE 77 JAYS, MAGPIES & TREEPIES

CRESTED JAY *Platylophus galericulatus* 31–33 cm

(1) **Adult** *ardesiacus*: Blackish plumage, white patch on neck-side, slightly forward-pointing long, erect crest. (2) **Juvenile**: Tinged warm brown above, whitish bars below; buffy wing-covert spots, short crest with buffish tips. (3) **Immature**: Like adult but paler bars on underparts and whitish shaft-streaks on throat and breast. **VOICE** Song is a strange fluty phrase, preceded by an abrupt shrill high-pitched whistle: *psssssiu HI-WU* (repeated every few seconds). Usual call is a very rapid grating metallic rattle: *tit'it'it'it'it'it'it'it'it...* **HABITAT & BEHAVIOUR** Middle/lower storey of broadleaved evergreen forest; up to 750 m. Shy; in pairs or small parties.

BLACK MAGPIE *Platysmurus leucopterus* 39–41 cm

(4) **Adult** *leucopterus*: All black with prominent white band along greater coverts and tertials; fairly long, broad tail. Short, tufted crest on forehead, reddish eyes. **Juvenile**: Body somewhat browner, crest shorter. **VOICE** Loud discordant metallic *keh-eh-eh-eh-eh*, resonant bell-like *tel-ope* and *konting-ka-longk* and xylophone-like *tok-tok teklingk-klingk-klingk* etc. **HABITAT & BEHAVIOUR** Broadleaved evergreen forest, forest edge, sometimes mangroves; below 200 m. Quite shy.

EURASIAN JAY *Garrulus glandarius* 31–34 cm

(5) **Adult** *leucotis*: Black cap and broad submoustachial band, white head-sides and throat, buffish-grey upperparts. Forehead white with black streaks, lower rump and uppertail-coverts white (prominent in flight), underparts light buffish with greyer upper breast; has blue, black and whitish barring on wing-coverts and secondaries. **Juvenile**: Darker; more rufescent body. **VOICE** Sings with various subdued musical notes (including mimicry) and clearer mewing. Call is a harsh screeching *skaaaak skaaaak...* **HABITAT & BEHAVIOUR** Open broadleaved evergreen, pine, mixed evergreen/pine and deciduous forest; up to 1,800 m. Usually in small, rather slow-moving parties.

RED-BILLED BLUE MAGPIE *Urocissa erythrorhyncha* 65–68 cm (including tail up to 47 cm)

(6) **Adult** *magnirostris*: Red bill, black hood, blue upperparts, very long white-tipped blue tail. Broad white band from hindcrown to hindneck, whitish remainder of underparts, red legs and feet. (7) **Juvenile**: Dark areas of head and upper breast much duller and browner, upperparts and wing-coverts browner (latter pale-tipped); has more white on crown, greyer bill, duller legs and feet. **VOICE** Sharp raucous *chweh-chweh-chweh-chweh...* or *chwit-wit-wit...* and shrill *shrii* and subdued *kluk* notes. **HABITAT & BEHAVIOUR** Deciduous forest, secondary growth, bamboo, sometimes open broadleaved evergreen forest; up to 1,525 m. Usually found in flocks, hunting at relatively low levels. Flies with a few flaps and a glide.

COMMON GREEN MAGPIE *Cissa chinensis* 37–40.5 cm

(8) **Adult** *chinensis*: Mostly bright green; largely reddish-chestnut wings, black band from lores to nape-sides, bright red bill, eyering, legs and feet. Prominent black and whitish markings on tertial tips, inner secondaries and outertail feathers, whitish-tipped central tail feathers. (9) **Adult**

(worn): May have strongly bluish plumage and browner wings. (10) **Juvenile**: Somewhat duller with paler lower breast to vent, smaller dark subterminal markings on tertials and inner secondaries, browner bill and duller eyering, legs and feet. **Other subspecies** *C.c.robinsoni* (extreme S). **VOICE** Piercing loud high-pitched notes (sometimes ending with a harsh note): *wi-chi-chi jao* or *wi-chi-chi jao wichitchit wi-chi-chi jao...* etc. Manic scolding *chakakakakakak* or *chakakak-wi* (*wi* higher) in alarm. Also a softer chattering *churrk chak-chak-chak* and high-pitched *weeer-wit* and rising *wieeee* etc. Complex high shrill whistles, combined with avian mimicry, probably constitute the song. **HABITAT & BEHAVIOUR** Broadleaved evergreen and mixed deciduous forest; up to 1,800 m. Often in small parties, regularly associating with bird-waves. Shy.

INDOCHINESE GREEN MAGPIE *Cissa hypoleuca* 31–35 cm

(11) **Adult** *hypoleuca*: Very similar to Common Green but tertials and inner secondaries appear mostly pale greenish (with no black or white), has strong lemon-yellow wash on underparts; upperside slightly darker than underside, tail shorter. Can also show strongly bluish plumage. **Juvenile**: Somewhat duller with paler vent, browner bill and duller eyering, legs and feet. **VOICE** Similar to Common Green and equally variable. Loud shrill whistled *peeeoo-peeeoo peeeoo-peeeoo...*, more clipped, shrill *peu-peu-peu* and clear whistles terminated by harsh note: *po-puueeee chuk* and rising *eeeoooeeep graak* etc. Also long piercing falling *peeeeeoo* and abrupt *weep* notes. When agitated, utters very noisy, harsh, high-pitched, scolding chatters. **HABITAT** Broadleaved evergreen and semi-evergreen forest, bamboo; 200–1,500 m.

RUFOUS TREEPIE *Dendrocitta vagabunda* 46–50 cm (including tail up to 30 cm)

(12) **Adult** *kinneari*: Deep buff below, contrasting blackish-grey hood and upper breast. Large pale grey area across wing-coverts, tertials and secondaries, black-tipped pale grey uppertail. (13) **Juvenile**: Paler/browner hood, paler buff below, buffish-tipped greater coverts, tertials and tail feathers. **Other subspecies** *D.v.saturatior* (W), *sakerensis* (NE,SE): Both darker-hooded. **VOICE** Loud metallic *koku-lii*. Pairs utter loud *kuki-uii*, *akuak* and *ekhekbekh* etc. Harsh *herh-herh-herh hah-hah-hah herh-herh-herh...* in alarm. **HABITAT** Dry dipterocarp and mixed deciduous forest, secondary growth; up to 500 m.

GREY TREEPIE *Dendrocitta formosae* 36–40 cm (including tail up to 23 cm)

(14) **Adult** *assimilis*: Recalls Rufous but has paler grey hindcrown/nape, contrasting with blackish forecrown and face, blackish wings with white patch at base of primaries; dull greyish below with deep rufous undertail-coverts. Rump and uppertail-coverts pale grey, uppertail grey becoming blacker towards tip. (15) **Juvenile**: Less black on forecrown, paler hindcrown, nape, head-sides, lower throat and breast with warm buffish infusion and whiter belly; may show some rufous tips to wing-coverts and tertials. **VOICE** Repeated loud metallic comical *koh-kli-ka*, *koh-kli-koh-koh* and *kuh'kuh'kuh'-ki-kuh* etc. Scolding chatters in alarm. **HABITAT & BEHAVIOUR** Broadleaved evergreen forest, secondary growth; 800–1,800 m. Often in small noisy flocks.

PLATE 78 TREEPIES, BLACK-BILLED MAGPIE & ORIOLES

RACKET-TAILED TREEPIE *Crypsirina temia* 30.5–32.5 cm
(including tail up to 20 cm)

(1) **Adult**: Relatively small and slim with distinctive all-blackish plumage and long, straight, spatulate-tipped tail. Has dark bronze-green gloss on body plumage, blacker face and light bluish eyes. Could be confused with drongos when tail worn but note short thick bill and eye colour. (2) **Juvenile**: Head and body duller and browner, less contrasting dark face, brown eyes, narrower tail-tip. **VOICE** Short ringing *chu*, deep rasping *churg-churg*, harsh *chraak-chraak* or *chrrrk-chrrrk*, more rising, questioning *churrrk* and higher *grasp-grasp*. **HABITAT & BEHAVIOUR** Mixed deciduous woodland and open broadleaved evergreen and semi-evergreen forest (particularly near water), secondary growth, bamboo, mangroves, coastal scrub; up to 915 m. Often in pairs or small parties, working through vegetation.

RATCHET-TAILED TREEPIE *Temnurus temnurus* 32–35.5 cm (including tail up to 18 cm)

(3) **Adult**: Resembles Racket-tailed Treepie but has diagnostic broad tail with long spikes projecting from tips of outer webs of feathers. Overall greyish-black with black face and dark red to brown eyes. **First year**: Narrower tail feathers with blunter spikes, almost absent on outer feathers. **VOICE** Usually calls with ringing *clee-clee-clee*..., rhythmic grating *graak-graak-graak*... and squeaky rising *eeup-eeup-eeup*... Also, ringing *clipeeee* (*clip* stressed) and hollower starting *pupueeee* and short, rather high-pitched rasping, rippling *rrrrrrrr*. **HABITAT** Broadleaved evergreen forest, bamboo, secondary growth; 700–1,500 m.

BLACK-BILLED MAGPIE *Pica pica* 43–48 cm (including tail up to 26 cm)

(4) **Adult** *sericea*: Slim build, long tail, mostly black plumage with white scapulars and belly. Purplish-blue and green gloss on wings, green, purple and blue gloss on tail, and narrow white rump-band (sometimes indistinct). In flight shows largely white primaries. **Juvenile**: Dark body plumage duller and browner. **VOICE** Call is a harsh 4–12 note *chak-chak-chak-chak-chak*... Also an enquiring *ch'chack* and more squealing *keee-uck*. **HABITAT** Forest edge, vegetated waterways, cultivation, plantations; up to 1,500 m.

DARK-THROATED ORIOLE *Oriolus xanthonotus* 20–20.5 cm

(5) **Male** *xanthonotus*: Small size, black hood and wings, white lower breast/belly with prominent black streaks. Upperparts and tail-coverts yellow, tail mostly black, some narrow yellow and whitish fringing on flight feathers. (6) **Female**: Olive-green above with brighter lower rump/uppertail-coverts and darker, greyer crown/head-sides, whitish below with bold blackish streaks and yellow undertail-coverts. Could be confused with juvenile Black-naped but much smaller, bill plain fleshy-orange, crown and head-sides darker, more boldly patterned below. (7) **Immature male**: Like female but yellower-green above, sooty crown and nape and greyish wash on throat. **Juvenile**: Like female but bill duller; appears to have rufous fringes/tips to wing-coverts and sometimes also narrow tips to

outer wing feathers. **VOICE** Sings with repeated fluty *phu phi-uu*, *phu-phu-phu wo*, *phu'phu-wiu-uu* and *phu-pui* etc. Call is a high-pitched piping *kyew*, *pheeu* or *ti-u*, less harsh than other orioles. **HABITAT** Canopy of broadleaved evergreen forest; up to 300 m.

BLACK-NAPED ORIOLE *Oriolus chinensis* 24.5–27.5 cm

(8) **Male** *diffusus*: Relatively large; golden-yellow body and wing-coverts, broad black band from lores to hindcrown and nape. Rest of wings and tail patterned black and yellow, bill thick and fleshy-orange. (9) **Female**: Upperparts and wing-coverts mostly olive-yellow. (10) **Juvenile**: Much duller than female, lacking black head-band. Crown and upperparts yellowish-olive, sides of head yellow with faint dark eyestripe, underparts creamy to yellowish-white with narrow blackish streaks, yellow-washed flanks and plain yellow vent, wings mostly yellowish-green, tail greener, bill mostly blackish. Possibly not separable in field from Slender-billed, except by thicker, slightly shorter bill. (11) **Immature**: Gradually attains dark head-band. **VOICE** Sings with repeated loud fluty phrases: *kwia-lu*, *u-dli-u*, *u-li-u* and *u-liu* etc. Call is a harsh nasal *kyehhr*. **HABITAT** Open broadleaved evergreen and deciduous forest, open areas with scattered trees, parks, gardens, mangroves; up to 1,525 m.

SLENDER-BILLED ORIOLE *Oriolus tenuirostris* 23–26 cm

(12) **Male** *tenuirostris*: Very similar to female Black-naped but bill slightly longer and considerably thinner, black nape-band narrower, roughly equal to width of black surrounding eye (obviously broader on Black-naped). (13) **Female**: Like male but yellow of plumage tinged greener, has some indistinct, narrow darker streaks below. (14) **Juvenile**: Difficult to separate from Black-naped, except by longer, thinner bill. (15) **Immature**: As juvenile. **VOICE** Song is a repeated loud fluty *wip-wi'u'wow'wow* or *wi wi'u-wu-wu* and variants (more hurried than Black-naped). Also a single fluty *tchew* or *tchi'u*. Alarm call is a harsh, slightly nasal, grating *kyerrrrh* or *ey'errrrh*. **HABITAT** Open broadleaved evergreen forest, clearings with scattered trees; breeds in open pine, sometimes mixed pine/oak forest; 600–1,500 m (breeds above c. 1,300 m).

BLACK-HOODED ORIOLE *Oriolus xanthornus* 22–25 cm

(16) **Male** *xanthornus*: Uniform golden-yellow body and wing-coverts and contrasting black hood diagnostic. Rest of wings black with extensive yellow, bill fleshy-orange. (17) **Female**: Lower mantle to rump washed olive, underparts and wing markings slightly paler and less rich yellow, wing markings slightly smaller. (18) **Juvenile**: Similar to female but black of plumage duller, crown often streaked olive, has yellowish forehead with blackish streaks, yellowish-white eyering, whitish throat with blackish streaks (extending onto breast), less obvious wing markings (mostly fringing only) and blackish bill; shows some darker streaks on mantle. **VOICE** Song is a repeated, measured, clear fluty *h HWI'UU* and *h wu'CHI-WU* etc. Also loud mellow *tcheo* or *tchew* notes. Harsh *cheeeah* or *kwaaah* when alarmed. **HABITAT** More open dry dipterocarp, mixed deciduous and broadleaved semi-evergreen forest, forest edge, secondary growth, mangroves, freshwater swamp forest; up to 915 m.

1–3, 4 and 5–18 to different scales

PLATE 79 ORIOLES, CUCKOOSHRIKES & PIED TRILLER

MAROON ORIOLE *Oriolus traillii* 24–28 cm

(1) **Male** *traillii*: Dark maroon body, black hood and wings, pale dull maroon tail, grey bill, pale yellowish eyes. (2) **Female**: Crown, nape and sides of head blackish-brown, upperparts dark brown with variable maroon tinge and dark reddish-chestnut rump and uppertail-coverts, tail brownish-maroon (pale reddish-maroon below), underparts whitish with heavy dark streaks and pale reddish-maroon undertail-coverts. *O.t.nigellicauda* has reddish wash on mantle and back, distinctly deep reddish rump, tail-coverts and tail. (3) **Female variant**: Throat/upper breast darker and less distinctly streaked (sometimes mostly blackish). (4) **Juvenile**: Like paler-throated female but has pale streaks on forehead, rufescent tips to wing-coverts and scales on mantle, back and scapulars, dark streaks on rump, narrower dark streaks on underparts, washed-out undertail-coverts with dark streaks and browner eyes; often has pale rufous wash on lower throat and upper breast. (5) **Immature male**: Attains black hood and variable maroon wash on body while underparts still streaked. (6) **Male** *nigellicauda* (rare visitor SE): Much redder body and tail. **VOICE** Song is a fluty ***pi-loi-lo*** or ***pi-oho-uu*** etc. Call is a long nasal ***hwyerrrh***. **HABITAT & BEHAVIOUR** Broadleaved evergreen and sometimes deciduous forest; 800–2,100 m. Usually in upper storey; often joins bird-waves.

SILVER ORIOLE *Oriolus mellianus* 28 cm

(7) **Male**: Silvery-whitish body plumage, contrasting black hood and wings and dull maroon tail diagnostic. Has dull maroon centres to body feathers (hard to see in field), dull maroon undertail-coverts with narrow silvery-whitish fringes and silvery-whitish outer edges of tail feathers. Bill, legs and feet bluish-grey. (8) **Female**: Similar to Maroon Oriole but has mostly greyish mantle to rump and paler pinkish-maroon undertail-coverts with whitish fringes; tends to have narrower dark streaks on underparts. **Juvenile**: Little information. **HABITAT** Broadleaved evergreen and semi-evergreen forest; up to 800 m.

INDOCHINESE CUCKOOSHRIKE *Coracina polioptera* 21.5–22 cm

(9) **Male** *indochinensis*: From Black-winged by more pronounced pale fringing to wing feathers, tail less graduated (central feathers less than 25 mm longer than outer ones), greyer above and with somewhat broader white tips below (typically look barely separated); whitish area on underside of primaries. (10,11) **Female**: Dark and pale bars/scales on head-sides and underparts; indistinct pale supercilium, broken whitish eyering. Usually more contrastingly barred below than Black-winged; in flight shows larger whitish area on underside of primaries. Also differs by tail shape and pattern (as male). **Juvenile**: Best separated from Black-winged by tail shape and pattern and larger whitish patch on underside of primaries. **Other subspecies** *C.p.polioptera* (W): A shade paler. Paler, with paler wing fringing, than any subspecies of Black-winged. **VOICE** Sings with 5–7 generally descending loud whistles: ***wi-wi-wi-wi-wu*** and ***wi-wi-wi-wi-wiu-wu*** etc. (delivery quicker than Black-winged). Also, nasal chuntering ***uh'uh'uh'uh-ik*** and ***uh'uh'uh'uh***... **HABITAT & BEHAVIOUR** Deciduous, semi-deciduous and pine forest; up to 1,000 m. Relatively slow and deliberate feeder in middle/upper forest storey. May join bird-waves.

BLACK-WINGED CUCKOOSHRIKE *Coracina melaschistos* 21.5–25.5 cm

(12) **Male** *avensis*: Like Indochinese but wings uniformly blackish, tail more graduated (central feathers always more than 25 mm longer than outer ones), blackish above and with somewhat narrower white tips below (usually look well separated). In flight lacks or shows only small whitish area on underside of mid-primaries. (13,14) **Female**: Slightly paler; vaguely paler supercilium (before eye) and ear-coverts, faint darker/paler bars/scales below, blackish bars/scales on whitish undertail-coverts, some pale wing-fringing. Throat to belly typically more uniform than Indochinese; usually less obvious pale fringing on wings and less grey on upperside of central tail feathers; in flight shows much smaller (or no) whitish area on underwing. Also differs by tail shape and pattern (as male). (15) **Juvenile**: Paler; heavily barred/scaled buffish to whitish and dark sooty-brownish, whitish/buffish-white tips to wing feathers. (16) **Male** *melaschistos* (recorded in winter NW): Darker. (17) **Male** *saturata* (recorded in winter NW): Much darker, with little contrast between mantle and wings. **Immature**: Similar to female but shows scaling/barring on rump and uppertail-coverts and more prominently barred underparts. Best separated from Indochinese by tail shape and pattern; whitish patch on underside of primaries smaller or absent. **Other subspecies** *C.m.intermedia* (visitor W,C,NE,SE). **VOICE** Series of 3–4 clear, well-spaced, high-pitched whistles: ***wii-wii-jeeu-jeeu***, ***wi'i-wii-wii-juu*** and ***witi-jeeu-jeeu-jeeu*** etc.; slower and more measured than Indochinese. **HABITAT & BEHAVIOUR** Broadleaved evergreen forest; 1,000–1,920 m. In winter, also lowland gardens and more open areas, sometimes deciduous forest.

LESSER CUCKOOSHRIKE *Coracina fimbriata* 19–20.5 cm

(18) **Male** *neglecta*: Very similar to Black-winged but smaller with smaller white tips to undertail, tail less graduated, with central feathers less than 25 mm longer than outer ones. (19) **Female**: Like Indochinese but more uniformly barred below, tends to show more obvious pale supercilium and ear-covert streaks and dark eyestripe, smaller white tail-tips, usually no whitish area on underwing. **Juvenile**: Best separated from Indochinese by range, size and tail shape/pattern. **Other subspecies** *C.f.culminata* (extreme S). **VOICE** Sings with repeated loud clear ***whit-it-it-chui-choi*** etc. Squeaky nasal ***wherrrh-wherrrh-wherrrh***... and high ***whit-weei*** in alarm. **HABITAT** Broadleaved evergreen forest, secondary growth, plantations; up to 900 m.

PIED TRILLER *Lalage nigra* 17–18 cm

(20) **Male** *nigra*: Recalls Bar-winged Flycatchershrike but has whitish supercilium, black eyestripe and grey back to uppertail-coverts; underparts white with grey wash on breast. (21) **Female**: Dark parts of plumage greyish-brown, underparts tinged buffish (browner on breast and flanks) with extensive but indistinct dark scales/bars, patch on wing-coverts restricted to broad bars. (22) **Juvenile**: Paler and browner above than female with pale buff bars/scales, underparts paler with dark brown streaks on lower throat and breast (sometimes all underparts), wing-fringes and tips tinged buff. **VOICE** Disyllabic whistle (second note lower). Descending nasal ***chack*** notes. **HABITAT** Coastal scrub, lowland plantations, gardens.

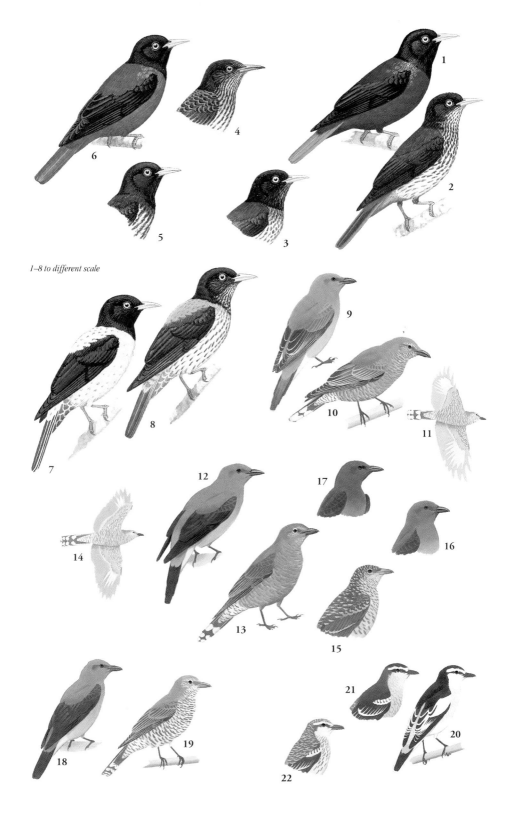

1–8 to different scale

PLATE 80 CUCKOOSHRIKES & MINIVETS

LARGE CUCKOOSHRIKE *Coracina macei* 27–30.5 cm

(1) **Male** *siamensis*: Relatively large; thick bill, mostly rather pale grey, with blackish lores, dark grey ear-coverts and whitish vent. Primaries blackish with pale grey to whitish outer fringes, tail grey to blackish with white tip, eyes reddish-brown. In flight, shows broad rounded wings, whitish underwing-coverts with a little dark barring. (2) **Female**: Paler, with pale lores and ear-coverts, whiter breast and belly with variable grey barring, variable pale barring on rump and uppertail-coverts and more dark bars on underwing-coverts. (3) **Juvenile**: Heavy buffy-whitish and dusky-brownish bars/scales on head, upperparts and breast, whitish rump; broad whitish fringing to wing-coverts, tertials and secondaries, blackish and whitish subterminal tertial markings, browner eyes. **Immature**: Like female but retains some juvenile wing-coverts and tertials; possibly more distinct barring below. **voice** Loud shrill *kle-eep*. Variable chuckling. **HABITAT & BEHAVIOUR** Open broadleaved evergreen and mixed deciduous forest, pine forest, open areas with scattered trees; up to 1,800 m. Usually high in trees or flying over forest. Alternately flicks up wings when perched.

JAVAN CUCKOOSHRIKE *Coracina javensis* 27.5–29 cm

(4) **Male** *larutensis*: Very similar to Large but darker grey, primaries and primary coverts blacker and more uniform, has less white on tail-tip, grey underwing-coverts. (5) **Female**: Differs from Large in same way as male. **Juvenile**: Probably similar to Large. **voice** Loud thin nasal *yiee*, *yi'ik* or *yi'ee* and lower, scratchier nasal *yerrk yerrk*... and *yer-err'erk* etc. **HABITAT & BEHAVIOUR** Broadleaved evergreen forest; above 1,000 m. Usually in tree-tops.

BAR-BELLIED CUCKOOSHRIKE *Coracina striata* 27.5–30 cm

(6) **Male** *sumatrensis*: Whitish/yellowish-white eyes, rather plain head (slightly darker lores), pale and some dark bars on rump and uppertail-coverts, faint grey bars on vent. Blackish-barred underwing-coverts in flight. (7) **Female**: Rump, uppertail-coverts and lower breast to undertail-coverts broadly barred blackish and whitish. (8) **Juvenile**: Head and body heavily scaled whitish, blackish and dusky-brownish, has whiter fringes to wing feathers, blackish and whitish subterminal markings on tertials, and brownish eyes. **voice** Loud shrill *krieu* notes. **HABITAT** Broadleaved evergreen and swamp forest, rarely mangroves; lowlands.

ROSY MINIVET *Pericrocotus roseus* 18–19.5 cm

(9) **Male** *roseus*: Brownish-grey above with greyer crown, reddish rump and red uppertail-coverts, rosy-pink below with whitish throat. Broad red wing-patch, red lines on tertials and primaries. (10) **Female**: Told by isolated yellow wing markings, pale yellowish-white throat and washed-out pale yellow underparts (breast/flanks often duller-tinged). Variable yellowish-olive wash on rump/uppertail-coverts. (11) **Male** *'stanfordi'* (recorded NE): Forecrown pale pinkish; can have pinkish/reddish on outertail feathers and wing-patch (latter sometimes larger), pinkish-/reddish-tinged rump/uppertail-coverts and pink tinge below. (12) **Female**: Resembles Swinhoe's but has prominent yellow wing markings, yellow on tail, yellowish tinge to uppertail-coverts. **Juvenile**: As female but yellowish-

white/whitish and dark scales/bars above, wing-coverts/tertials tipped same colour, obscure scales/mottling on breast. **Immature male**: Like female but has some orange to flame-red on uppertail-coverts and tail fringes, some orange on wing markings and variable pink suffusion on underparts. **voice** Whirring trill, similar to Ashy. **HABITAT** Deciduous, semi-deciduous and sometimes open broadleaved evergreen forest; up to 1,525 m.

SWINHOE'S MINIVET *Pericrocotus cantonensis* 19 cm

(13) **Male**: From Ashy by grey hindcrown/nape, white forehead-patch extending in short eyebrow to just behind eye, brown-tinged upperside (mainly greater coverts and tertials), pale vinous-brownish wash on breast/belly; rump and particularly uppertail-coverts pale brownish, clearly paler than rest of upperparts; wing-patch (if present) tinged very pale yellowish-buff (rather than whitish). (14) **Female**: Paler above, rump/uppertail-coverts less sharply contrasting, wing-patch (if present) may be yellower-tinged. From Ashy by paler rump/uppertail-coverts, slightly browner upperparts, lack of dark band across extreme forehead, usually more extensively pale forehead, extending in line to just behind eye; breast and belly typically dirtier. **First winter**: Shows similar characters to Ashy. Males have breast and belly recalling adult and a hint of adult head pattern. **HABITAT** Broadleaved evergreen, semi-evergreen and deciduous forest, forest edge; up to 1,200 m.

ASHY MINIVET *Pericrocotus divaricatus* 18.5–20 cm

(15) **Male** *divaricatus*: Black lores, crown and nape, all-grey mantle to uppertail-coverts, white forecrown and underparts; indistinct whitish wing markings (or almost lacking). Whitish band at base of flight feathers in flight. (16) **Female**: Crown and upperparts pale grey (a little darker on crown); has whitish band across forehead to eye, and blackish loral stripe extending narrowly across extreme forehead. **First winter**: Like female but shows white fringing and blackish subterminal markings on tertials, and white tips to greater coverts. **voice** Metallic jingling trill. Flight call rather unmelodious, a slightly hesitant ascending *tchu-de tchu-dee-dee tchu-dee-dee*. **HABITAT & BEHAVIOUR** Open forest, areas with scattered trees, mangroves, coastal vegetation, casuarinas, plantations; up to 1,000 m (mainly lowlands). Usually in small to quite large restless flocks.

SMALL MINIVET *Pericrocotus cinnamomeus* 14.5–16 cm

(17) **Male** *vividus*: Small size; grey head and upperparts with darker ear-coverts and cheeks (sometimes throat), reddish-orange rump, uppertail-coverts, breast and flanks, orange-yellow vent and orange and yellow wing-patch. (18) **Female**: Told by pale dull grey crown/upperparts, bright reddish-orange rump and uppertail-coverts (mixed yellowish on former), greyish-white throat and upper breast, pale yellow belly and vent. Wing-patch orange-yellow. **Juvenile**: As female, but pale yellowish-white to whitish bars/scales above, wing-coverts tipped and tertials fringed same colour, breast faintly mottled. **First-winter male**: As female but often some orange on flanks. **Other subspecies** *P.c.thai* (NW,NE). *P.c.separatus* (west S): Female less yellow below. **voice** Continuously repeated, very thin, high *twsee-eet* and *swee swee*... etc. **HABITAT & BEHAVIOUR** Deciduous forest, open areas with trees, parks, gardens; up to 1,000 m. In small flocks.

PLATE 81 MINIVETS & FLYCATCHER-SHRIKES

FIERY MINIVET *Pericrocotus igneus* 15–15.5 cm

(1) **Male** *igneus*: Like a miniature Scarlet but wing-patch orange/red-orange, no isolated markings on tertials/secondaries, underwing has orange (not red) coverts and band across base of flight feathers, has much more orange-coloured tail markings, and all-black central tail feathers; remaining red of plumage more orange-tinged. (2) **Female**: Told by size, orange-yellow forehead-band, bright red-orange rump/uppertail-coverts, all-yellow throat and underparts (tinged orange). Crown and upperparts slaty-grey, wing-patch pale orange to orange-yellow. (3) **Juvenile**: Browner above than female, with narrow whitish and dark fringing/barring, wing-coverts and tertials tipped/fringed paler, indistinct dark mottling on breast. Male attains patches of adult plumage during first winter. **VOICE** Call is a thin, rising *swee-eet*. **HABITAT** Broadleaved evergreen forest, forest edge; below 300 m.

GREY-CHINNED MINIVET *Pericrocotus solaris* 17–19 cm

(4) **Male** *rubrolimbatus*: From Long-tailed by dark grey head/mantle, with paler lower head-sides, pale grey to whitish chin, orange-yellow wash on lower throat; red plumage parts more orange, wing-patch lacks tertial line. (5) **Female**: Uniform grey forehead, crown, head-sides and mantle and greyish-white chin diagnostic. Rest of underparts and wing-patch yellow, rump and uppertail-coverts olive-yellow. (6) **Juvenile**: Similar to female (both sexes) but slightly darker above with pale yellow and blackish scales/bars; pale yellow wing-covert tips and tertial fringes, indistinct dark mottling/barring on sides of breast. **VOICE** Repeated thin *tswee-seet* and more slurred *swirrririt*. Also, soft *trip* notes and more sibilant *trii-ii*. **HABITAT & BEHAVIOUR** Broadleaved evergreen forest, sometimes pine forest; 1,000–1,800 m. Usually in small noisy parties; often joins bird-waves.

LONG-TAILED MINIVET *Pericrocotus ethologus* 17.5–20.5 cm

(7) **Male** *ethologus* (winter visitor NW,NE): Black with bright red lower back to uppertail-coverts, breast to vent and wing-patch. Outertail feathers extensively red, wing-patch has two spaced lines along tertials and primaries. (8) **Female**: Greyish-olive above, greyer crown, paler, yellow-tinged extreme forehead, pale grey lower head-sides (faintly washed olive-yellowish), yellowish olive-green lower back to uppertail-coverts; fairly bright yellow below (faintly washed olive) with paler lower throat, whitish upper throat. Yellow wing-patch lacks line on tertials. (9) **Juvenile**: Like female but yellowish-white and blackish scales/bars above, yellowish-white wing-covert tips; throat-sides, breast and flanks dark, spotted and/or barred and washed drab olive-greyish, less yellow below. (10) **First-summer male**: Typically has orange extreme forehead, darker crown to mantle (than female), deep orange to red-orange rump to uppertail-coverts and wing-patch, and extensive bright/deep orange on underparts. **Other subspecies** *P.e.ripponi* (resident NW; this race resident NE?): Female's mantle greyer, yellow of plumage deeper/brighter, forehead/cheeks/upper throat yellower. **VOICE** Sweet, rolling *prrr'wi*, *prrr'i-wi* and *prrr'i-prrr'i*, thin sibilant *swii-swii swii-swii-swii*... **HABITAT & BEHAVIOUR** Broadleaved evergreen forest, pines; 900–1,800 m. Sometimes in quite large flocks in winter.

SHORT-BILLED MINIVET *Pericrocotus brevirostris* 17.5–19.5 cm

(11) **Male** *neglectus*: Like Long-tailed but wing-patch has single red line on primaries, has more red on outertail (all red from below, or almost so), black of throat extends in semi-circle onto upper breast (not sharply cut off). (12) **Female**: Like Long-tailed (*P.e.ethologus*) but forehead tinged golden-yellow, forecrown washed yellow/golden-yellow, mantle greyer, throat always yellow; much more yellow on outertail feathers (similar pattern to male). **Juvenile**: From adult as Long-tailed. **VOICE** Call is a very thin whistled *tsuuuit tsuuuit tsuuuit*... Also dry *tup* notes. **HABITAT & BEHAVIOUR** Broadleaved evergreen forest, sometimes pine forest; 1,000–2,000 m. Usually in pairs.

SCARLET MINIVET *Pericrocotus flammeus* 17–21.5 cm

(13) **Male** *semiruber*: Larger and shorter-tailed than Long-tailed/Short-billed, more vivid red; isolated red markings on tertials and inner secondaries, mostly flame-red tail (outer webs of central tail feathers usually red). (14) **Female**: Yellow forehead, yellow-washed forecrown, slaty-grey hindcrown to mantle, uniform yellow throat and underparts, distinctive wing pattern (like male but yellow). (15) **Juvenile**: Recalls Long-tailed/Short-billed but yellower below, suggestion of adult tertial/secondary pattern. **Immature male**: Differs from female in similar way to Long-tailed. **Other subspecies** *P.f.elegans* (recorded in winter NW): Larger, with mostly black central tail feathers. *P.f.flammifer* (W,S): Smaller (within size range given). **VOICE** Loud, piercing whistles: *sweeep-sweeep-sweeep*... and *weeep-weeep-weeep-wit-wip* etc. **HABITAT & BEHAVIOUR** Various broadleaved forests; up to 1,700 m. Gregarious; regularly joins bird-waves.

BAR-WINGED FLYCATCHER-SHRIKE *Hemipus picatus* 12.5–14.5 cm

(16) **Male** *picatus*: Black above, whitish below, prominent long white wing-patch. Lower throat to belly dusky-washed (more vinous on breast), has white rump-band and prominent white on outertail feathers. (17) **Female**: Similar to male but black of upperside replaced by brown, underparts somewhat paler. (18) **Juvenile**: Like female but barred/scaled buff above, wing-patch buffish with dark bars/scales, underparts whiter with brown wash across breast. (19) **Male** *capitalis* (NW): Dark brown mantle, back and scapulars. **Other subspecies** *H.p.intermedius* (S): Female is more blackish-brown above, darker below (more like male). **VOICE** Rapid, thin musical *swit'i'wit-swit'i'wit*..., *sitti-wittit* and *sittititit* etc. **HABITAT & BEHAVIOUR** Broadleaved evergreen, mixed deciduous and peatswamp forest; up to 1,830 m. Usually in small groups, often with bird-waves.

BLACK-WINGED FLYCATCHER-SHRIKE *Hemipus hirundinaceus* 13.5–14.5 cm

(20) **Male**: No wing-patch, tail almost all black, breast washed greyish. (21) **Female**: Upperside browner. (22) **Juvenile**: Paler/browner above than female with buff bars/scales, coverts mostly buffish, with dark brown markings, underparts whiter with browner wash across upper breast. **VOICE** Coarse *tu-tu-tu-tu hee-tee-tee-teet* and *hee-too-weet*, mixed with high *cheet-weet-weet-weet* etc. **HABITAT** Broadleaved evergreen and freshwater swamp forest; below 200 m.

PLATE 82 FANTAILS & IORAS

YELLOW-BELLIED FANTAIL *Rhipidura hypoxantha*
11.5–12.5 cm

(1) **Male**: Dull greenish above, long dark white-tipped graduated tail, blackish mask, yellow forehead, supercilium and underparts. Whitish tips to greater coverts, bill short and triangular when viewed from below. (2) **Female**: Mask same colour as crown. **Juvenile**: Like adult but upperparts duller, yellow parts paler, less yellow on forehead and in front of eye. **VOICE** Song is a series of thin, sweet *sewit, sweeit* and *tit* or *tsit* notes, followed by a high-pitched trill. **HABITAT & BEHAVIOUR** Broadleaved evergreen forest; 1,500–2,565 m. Fans tail and nervously twitches from side to side.

WHITE-THROATED FANTAIL *Rhipidura albicollis*
17.5–20.5 cm

(3) **Adult** *celsa*: Mostly dark greyish to blackish-slate plumage (crown blacker) with contrasting white supercilium and throat and fan-shaped white-tipped tail diagnostic. Chin blackish. (4) **Juvenile**: Browner above, scapulars to uppertail-coverts scaled/barred paler brown to warm brown, wing-coverts faintly tipped same colour; indistinct paler bars below; throat mostly dark, supercilium often buffish. **Other subspecies** *R.a.atrata* (S). **VOICE** Song is a series of 4–8 widely and unevenly spaced, clear, high-pitched whistled notes, in mostly descending sequence: *tsu sit tsu sit sit sit sit-tsu*. Call is a squeaky, harsh *jick* or *wick*. **HABITAT** Broadleaved evergreen forest, locally groves and bamboo in cultivated areas, parks, wooded gardens; 600–2,565 m.

WHITE-BROWED FANTAIL *Rhipidura aureola* 16–18.5 cm

(5) **Adult** *burmanica*: From other fantails by combination of long broad white supercilium (crossing forehead) and mostly whitish underparts. Upperside and breast-sides brownish-grey, crown and uppertail blacker, the latter broadly tipped and edged white, throat-centre greyish (feathers black, tipped/scaled white); has pale creamy-buffish wash on belly, flanks (fainter on breast), and small white spots on wing-covert tips. (6) **Juvenile**: Similar to adult but throat initially darker, upperparts browner with pale warm brown scales/bars, mainly on scapulars, back and rump, broad whitish to dull pale rufous tips to wing-coverts and fringes to tertials. **VOICE** Series of 6–7 well-spaced melodious whistles, usually with first few ascending, rest descending: *chee-chee-cheweechee-vi* etc. Call is a harsh *chuck*. **HABITAT** Dry dipterocarp and mixed deciduous forest; up to 1,065 m.

PIED FANTAIL *Rhipidura javanica* 17.5–19.5 cm

(7) **Adult** *longicauda*: From other fantails by pale underparts with contrasting blackish breast-band. Throat and lower breast white, rest of underparts pale creamy-buffish, upperparts dark brown to blackish-brown with blacker crown, only small amount of white above eye (may be concealed). **Juvenile**: Browner, more uniform upperparts, duller breast-band, dull rufescent scales/bars on upperparts (mainly scapulars and back to uppertail-coverts) and dull rufescent tips to wing-coverts and tips and narrow fringes to tertials. **VOICE** Squeaky, measured *chew-weet chew-weet chew-weet-chew*, last note falling. Various squeaky chattering and squawking calls:

chit, cheet etc. **HABITAT** Mangroves, freshwater and peatswamp forest, parks, gardens, plantations, secondary growth, scrub; usually near water; lowlands.

SPOTTED FANTAIL *Rhipidura perlata* 17–18 cm

(8) **Adult**: Easily identified from other fantails by uniform blackish-slate plumage, white vent and prominent white spots/streaks on throat and breast. Outertail feathers broadly tipped white, only small white eyebrow; usually shows small white spots on wing-covert tips. **Juvenile**: Browner above with warm brownish tips to wing-coverts. **VOICE** Melodious *chilip pechilip-chi*, second phrase rising sharply. **HABITAT** Broadleaved evergreen forest; up to 1,130 m.

COMMON IORA *Aegithina tiphia* 12–14.5 cm

(9) **Male non-breeding** *philipi*: Yellow head-sides and underparts, olive-washed flanks, rather deep olive-green upperparts, mostly black wings and tail with two pronounced white to yellowish-white wing-bars. (10) **Male breeding variant**: May show some black on mantle to rump; bright yellow head-sides/underparts. (11) **Female non-breeding**: Paler/duller body than male non-breeding, wings duller with less distinct bars. (12) **Male breeding** *horizoptera* (W,S): Often has black hindcrown/mantle (less often on rest of upperparts). **Male breeding**: Head-sides and underparts more vivid yellow than non-breeding, lacks olive flank-wash. **Female breeding**: Yellow of underparts darker/brighter. **Juvenile**: Body slightly paler than female non-breeding, upper wing-bar less distinct. **Other subspecies** *A.t.cambodiana* (SE): Breeding male may have black on crown/nape. **VOICE** Song is a long thin note descending abruptly to about an octave lower: *whiiiiii piu*. May start with several whistles. Also various short whistled phrases and subdued chattering. **HABITAT** Open forest, mangroves, swamp forest, parks, gardens, plantations; up to 1,500 m.

GREEN IORA *Aegithina viridissima* 12.5–14.5 cm

(13) **Male** *viridissima*: Like Common but body dark olive-green with paler belly and yellow vent; has dark lores and distinctive broad broken yellow eyering. (14) **Female**: Similar to Common but upperparts deeper green, breast and flanks darker and greener, rest of underparts more greenish-yellow, has greenish lores and indistinct broken eyering; wing-bars always yellow. **Juvenile**: Paler/duller than female. **VOICE** Song is a thin high *tsiiiu tsii-tu* (*tu* stressed) or *itsu tsi-tu tsi-tu* (*itsu* stressed). Chattering *tit-teeer*, subdued *chititititit*. **HABITAT** Broadleaved evergreen forest; up to 825 m.

GREAT IORA *Aegithina lafresnayei* 15.5–17 cm

(15) **Male** *innotata*: Told by size, big bill, plain wings. Upperparts/wing-coverts dark olive-green, rest of wings blackish with green fringing, bright rich yellow below. Female is slightly paler above and less vivid yellow below. (16) **Juvenile**: Like female but underparts duller and washed olive, particularly on flanks. (17) **Male** *lafresnayei* (S): Mostly glossy black above (apart from forehead). (18) **Male variant**: Individual with less black on upperparts. **VOICE** Song is a clear *chew chew chew chew*... or *tieu tieu tieu tieu*. **HABITAT** Broadleaved forests; up to 900 m.

BLACK-NAPED MONARCH *Hypothymis azurea* 16–17.5 cm

(1) **Male** *styani*: Blue, with whitish belly/vent; black nuchal tuft, breast-band, extreme forehead and upper chin. (2) **Female**: Blue duller (mainly on head), no nuchal tuft or breast-band, greyish-brown above, greyish breast. **Juvenile**: Like female. **Other subspecies** *H.a.montana* (W,NW,NE), *galerita* (W[south],SE). VOICE Song is a ringing *wii'wii'wii'wii'wii'wii-i'wii*... (c.3 notes per s). Calls with harsh *shweh-shweh* or *chwe-wi* and *chit-whit-whit*... and high metallic rasping *tswit* and *tswit-wit*. HABITAT & BEHAVIOUR Middle/lower storey of various broadleaved forests, secondary growth; up to 1,520 m. Holds tail stiffly, often slightly spread.

ASIAN PARADISE-FLYCATCHER *Terpsiphone paradisi* 19.5–23.5 cm (male tail to 27 cm more)

(3) **Male** *indochinensis*: Bright rufous-chestnut upperside and extremely long tail. Head/breast slaty-grey, crown and crest glossy bluish-/greenish-black, rest of underparts whitish; has stout blue bill and broad blue eyering. May lack long central tail feathers. Birds with all-black heads are probably immatures of the white 'morph'. (4) **Male white 'morph'**: All white, apart from glossy black head, black feather shafts and white-fringed black flight feathers. It is not clear whether this plumage is age-related. (5) **Female**: Like rufous male but lacks tail-streamers, crest shorter, eyering usually somewhat duller. (6) **Juvenile**: Paler/more rufous above than female (including crown/head-sides), underparts whitish, initially scaled/mottled dull rufous on breast, bill dark brownish with flesh-coloured base, no pronounced eyering. Male begins breeding in female-like plumage (before developing longer tail) and may only be separable by brighter blue eyering. (7) **Male** *incei* (visitor throughout): Head all black (contrasts with breast), much darker chestnut above (often violet-tinged). (8) **Female**: Throat obviously darker than breast. **Other subspecies** *T.p.saturatior* (winters S): Duller, paler, more rufous (less chestnut) above, buffish-tinged belly and particularly undertail-coverts. VOICE Song is a rolling *chu'wu'wu'wu'wu'wu*..., similar to Black-naped Monarch. Also a repeated harsh *whiwhi-chu-whiwhi-chu* and variants. Typical calls are repeated shrill rasping *whii*, *whi-whu* and *whi-whu'whu* etc. HABITAT Broadleaved evergreen forest, sometimes mangroves, island forest; also parks/wooded gardens on migration. Up to 1,500 m.

JAPANESE PARADISE-FLYCATCHER *Terpsiphone atrocaudata* 17.5–20.5 cm (male tail to 23 cm more)

(9) **Male** *atrocaudata*: Plumage all black, apart from glossy dark purple mantle to rump and whitish belly/vent. (10) **Female**: Crown duller and less contrasting than Asian (no obvious gloss), head-sides/throat, typically duller, darker and brownish-tinted, breast usually looks more sharply cut off from whitish belly; duller above, tail darker and browner, never bright rufous/chestnut. Some (possibly spring only) show more purplish-chestnut upperparts. **First winter**: Similar to female, possibly with browner tint to throat and breast. Male possibly shows blacker crown, slightly darker, warmer upperparts and darker throat and breast. HABITAT Broadleaved evergreen forest, also mangroves, parks and wooded gardens on migration; up to 1,200 m.

RUFOUS-WINGED PHILENTOMA *Philentoma pyrhopterum* 16.5–17 cm

(11) **Male typical morph** *pyrhopterum*: Rather stocky and stout; mostly dull blue head/body, buffy-whitish belly and vent, sharply contrasting reddish-chestnut greater coverts, tertials, secondaries and tail. Eyes red to dark red. (12) **Male blue morph**: Scarce. All dull blue, with greyish vent (mixed whitish). See Pale Blue Flycatcher. (13) **Female**: No blue; crown/head-sides dark greyish-brown (sometimes tinged blue), otherwise mid-brown above, buffy-whitish below (throat/breast more buffish), breast-sides (sometimes across breast) and flanks mid-brown. Shape, bill structure, reddish eyes and prominent reddish-chestnut of wings and tail eliminate flycatchers. **Juvenile**: Poorly documented. Sexes said to be separable soon after fledging. VOICE Song is a clear whistled *tu-tuuu* (*tuuu* slightly lower). Also harsh scolding notes. HABITAT Middle/lower storey of broadleaved evergreen forest; up to 915 m.

MAROON-BREASTED PHILENTOMA *P.velatum* 19–21 cm

(14) **Male** *caesium*: Dull blue; black forehead, upper throat and head-sides; dark maroon lower throat/breast. (15) **Female**: Duller/darker; dull blackish lores/cheeks, throat and upper breast. **Juvenile**: Poorly documented. Males show some chestnut-maroon on breast soon after fledging. VOICE Series of clear bell-like whistles: *phu phu phu phu phu phu*... Also rather powerful clear *chut-ut chut-ut chut-ut chut-ut*... HABITAT & BEHAVIOUR Middle/upper storey of broadleaved evergreen forest; up to 1,000 m. Very sluggish, often sits motionless.

LARGE WOODSHRIKE *Tephrodornis gularis* 18.5–22.5 cm

(16) **Male** *jugans*: Greyish crown/nape, pale greyish-brown rest of upperside, blackish mask, white rump-band. (17) **Female**: Crown duller and brown-streaked, mask and bill browner, wash on throat and breast more buffish. *T.g.fretensis* is somewhat darker on crown, throat and breast. (18) **Juvenile**: Browner above than female with whitish shafts and tips on crown, mantle and scapulars, and buffish and whitish bars on wing-coverts and tertials. (19) **Male** *fretensis* (south-east S): Smaller (within range given), quite uniform bluish-slate crown to scapulars. **Other subspecies** *T.g.annectens* (rest of S): More greyish-washed, less contrasting upperparts. *T.g.vernayi* (W), *mekongensis* (NE,SE). VOICE Song is a loud ringing *pi-pi-pi-pi-pi-pi*... Harsh *chreek chreek chreek*... call. HABITAT & BEHAVIOUR Broadleaved forest; up to 1,500 m. Usually in groups, often in bird-waves. Moves rather sluggishly, often high in trees.

COMMON WOODSHRIKE *T.pondicerianus* 14.5–17.5 cm

(20) **Adult** *pondicerianus*: Like Large but smaller, prominent broad dull whitish supercilium, whitish outertail feathers and smaller, less distinct whitish rump-band. See female Grey Bushchat. (21) **Juvenile**: Browner above and spotted whitish-buff (mainly crown/nape), broad whitish-buff wing-covert tips; pale and dark markings on tertials, dusky-brown speckles/mottling on throat-sides/breast. VOICE Song is an accelerating trill: *pi-pi-i-i-i-i-i*. Weak *tue* and *tee* contact notes, harsh, slightly ascending *wih-wih-whee-whee* etc. HABITAT Deciduous forests, open areas with scattered trees; up to 1,100 m. In small groups.

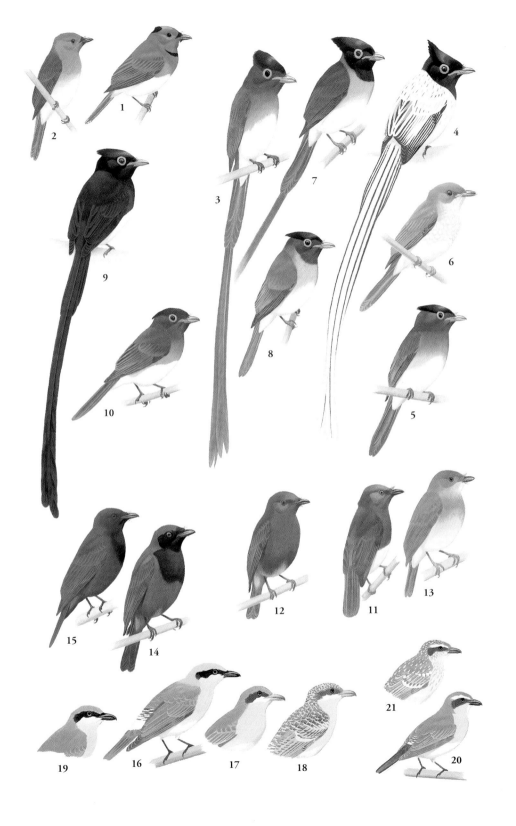

PLATE 84 ROCK THRUSHES, BLUE WHISTLING THRUSH & TYPICAL THRUSHES

WHITE-THROATED ROCK THRUSH *Monticola gularis* 18–19.5 cm

(1) **Male non-breeding**: Blue crown and nape, blue-black mantle, chestnut lores, rump and underparts, white wing-patch, white patch on throat and upper breast; greyish-white fringing above. (2) **Male breeding**: No fringing on head and upperparts. (3) **Female**: Greyish-brown above with black bars, heavy blackish scales below, white throat-patch. **First winter**: Like non-breeding adults. **VOICE** Sings with rather melancholy, long, flute-like, slightly rising whistles, mixed with 1–2 more complex phrases and short repeated *chat-at-at*. Calls with soft *queck-quack* mixed with sharp *tack-tack*; thin *tsip* in flight. **HABITAT** More open deciduous and broadleaved evergreen forest, plantations; up to 1,220 m.

CHESTNUT-BELLIED ROCK THRUSH *Monticola rufiventris* 22–24 cm

(4) **Male breeding**: Shining cobalt-blue above, dark blue face/throat, chestnut below. (5) **Female**: Buff to whitish submoustachial and dark malar stripes, buffish-white behind dark ear-coverts, pale eyering, buff to whitish below with blackish bars/scales (not throat). Some dark-and-pale bars/scales above. (6) **Juvenile female**: Sooty-blackish body/wing-coverts with pale buff/whitish spots, buff-fringed greater coverts, tertials and secondaries, dark rufous tips to uppertail-coverts, mostly whitish-buff throat with dark feather-tips. **Male non-breeding**: Duller above; pale fringing on mantle/scapulars (some on throat). **Juvenile male**: Like juvenile female but wings/tail mostly blue, rump/uppertail-coverts washed dull chestnut; warmer below. **First winter**: From non-breeding adults by juvenile greater coverts. **VOICE** Sings with warbling, whistled phrases: *twew-twi-er tre-twi teedle-desh* or *jero-terry-three fir-tar-ree*, sometimes *tewleedee-tweet-tew* or *til-tertew*. Calls with a sharp *quach*, thin *sit* and rasping *chhrrr*. **HABITAT** More open broadleaved evergreen and coniferous forest; 1,200–2,565 m.

BLUE ROCK THRUSH *Monticola solitarius* 21–23 cm

(7) **Male breeding** *pandoo*: Lacks scales on body, bluer overall than non-breeding. (8) **Male non-breeding**: Rather uniform grey-blue, whitish-and-blackish body-scales, unbarred browner crown. (9) **Female non-breeding**: More uniform than other rock thrush females. Even plainer above when breeding. (10) **Juvenile**: Like female but crown and mantle speckled dull pale buffish, underparts paler. (11) **Male non-breeding** *philippensis* (winter visitor throughout): From Chestnut-bellied by dense bars/scales on body, head may appear largely greyish, has less blue above and less chestnut below. (12) **Male breeding**: Cleaner; closer to Chestnut-bellied. **Juvenile**: Like female but crown/mantle speckled dull pale buffish, more diffusely marked below. **First winter**: As non-breeding adults. **Other subspecies** *M.s.madoci* (resident S). **VOICE** Sings with fluty *chu sree chur tee tee* and *wuchee-trr-trrt* etc. (some notes rather scratchy). Calls include a harsh *tak-tak*; low *tchuck* notes (may be mixed with high *tsee* or *tzick*); rapid *chakerackack* and *chack chack chack eritchouitchouitchouit tchoo tchoo* and harsh rattling *trrr*. **HABITAT** Rocky areas, roadsides, cultivation; residents frequent cliffs, sometimes urban buildings; up to 1,830 m (southern breeders mainly coastal).

BLUE WHISTLING THRUSH *Myophonus caeruleus* 30.5–35 cm

(13) **Adult** *eugenei*: Relatively large; dark purplish-blue with lighter blue spangling. Bill yellow. (14) **Juvenile**: Body mostly dark brown, bill duller. (15) **Adult** *caeruleus* (winter visitor throughout): Smaller all-blackish bill. (16) **Adult** *dicrorhynchus* (south-east S): Much duller and browner with dull whitish median covert tips and vague shiny bluish speckles/spots on mantle, scapulars, neck-side and throat. **Juvenile**: Mostly plain dark brown body, duller bill. **Other subspecies** *M.c.temminckii* (winters NW), *crassirostris* (SE,S). **VOICE** Song is a mix of mellow fluty and harsh scratchy notes. Calls with loud harsh *scree*, recalling White-crowned Forktail, and occasional shrill whistles. **HABITAT** Broadleaved forests, usually near rocky rivers/streams, waterfalls; up to 2,565 m.

DARK-THROATED THRUSH *Turdus ruficollis* 22.5–26 cm

(17) **Male breeding** *ruficollis* (NW): Rufous-red supercilium, throat and breast, largely reddish-rufous outertail. (18) **Female**: Black streaks on throat-sides/upper breast, less rufous-red on supercilium, throat and breast. (19) **First-winter female**: Little rufous-red; supercilium whitish, throat/breast whitish with blackish streaks, lower breast washed greyish, breast/flanks mottled/streaked warmish brown; some rufous on tail. (20) **Male breeding** *atrogularis* 'Black-throated Thrush' (NW): Black face, throat, upper breast; 23.5–27.5 cm. (21) **Female**: Whiter throat and submoustachial area, pale-scaled upper breast. (22) **First-winter female**: No rufous; darker mottling/streaks on breast/flanks (first-winter male differs in same way). **Male non-breeding**: Narrow whitish feather fringes on supercilium, throat and upper breast. *T.r.atrogularis* is similarly patterned but has black base colour to supercilium, throat and upper breast and lacks rufous-red in tail. Intergrades occur. **First-winter male**: Resembles adult female but has pale fringes and tips to greater coverts. **VOICE** Song is a rambling, cackling *chve-che-chve-che chvya-chya-chvya-chya...*; *chooee chooee whee-oo-ee oo* etc. *T.r.atrogularis* gives raucous, whistled *t'eeee t'yuyuu teeu-eet* etc. (first two phrases drawn out/falling, latter sharp/rising), sometimes preceded by slower *hweet* or *hweet-a*. Calls include soft *jak* or *chuck* notes, abrupt *chk* and single thin *seee* or *ziep* in flight. Contact calls include *qui-kwea*, rapid *het-etetet*, and hoarser *retet riep riep*. *T.r.ruficollis* also has softer chuckling *which-which-which*. **HABITAT** Open broadleaved evergreen forest, clearings, cultivation; 1,000–2,565 m.

DUSKY THRUSH *Turdus naumanni* 22.5–25 cm

(23) **Male** *eunomus*: Whitish supercilium, largely blackish white-scaled breast and flanks, rufous-chestnut wings. (24) **First-winter female**: Can resemble Dark-throated but darker, browner ear-coverts and upperparts (latter with darker feather-centres), rufescent wing-fringing, bolder dark markings on breast/flanks. **Female**: Usually duller; less black on ear-coverts, upperparts and breast. **First winter**: Like female or duller (can approach respective adults); less rufescent wing-fringing, pale-tipped tertials and some/all greater coverts (retained juvenile feathers). **VOICE** Sings with clear descending notes, then a brief twitter. Calls include a squawking *chuk-chuk*, clacking *chack-chack* and thinner *shrree* and *swic*. **HABITAT** Open broadleaved evergreen forest, cultivation; up to 2,565 m.

PLATE 85 TYPICAL THRUSHES

CHESTNUT-CAPPED THRUSH *Zoothera interpres* 17.5–18.5 cm

(1) **Adult** *interpres*: Chestnut crown and nape, black throat and breast, bold white markings on blackish head-sides and wings, and white remainder of underparts with black spots on lower breast and flanks. (2) **Juvenile**: Crown and mantle mostly dull chestnut with pale rufous streaks; head-sides, throat and breast rufous-buff (upper breast more rufescent) with two blackish bars on ear-coverts, and blackish malar line and breast-blotching; wing-patches smaller and tinged rufous-buff. **VOICE** Song is a series of rising fluty whistles, mixed with chirrups: *see-it-tu-tu-tyuu* etc., sometimes with some grating and higher-pitched notes. Calls include harsh, hard *tac* notes and a very thin high-pitched falling *tsi-i-i-i*. **HABITAT & BEHAVIOUR** Broadleaved evergreen forest; up to 760 m. Very secretive, usually near ground but often sings from quite high in trees.

ORANGE-HEADED THRUSH *Zoothera citrina* 20.5–23.5 cm

(3) **Male** *innotata* (breeds NW,NE; winters SE,S at least): Bright orange-rufous head and underparts (vent whitish) and bluish-grey upperparts and wings diagnostic. (4) **Female**: Upperparts and wings mostly greyish-olive; grey on back to upper-tail-coverts, duller orange-rufous head and underparts. *Z.c.gibsonhilli* has white-tipped median coverts. (5) **Juvenile**: Browner above than female, dark ear-covert bars and malar line, dark mottling/scales on breast and flanks; thin rufous-whitish streaks on crown, mantle and breast; may show rufous-tipped uppertail-coverts. (6) **Male** *gibsonhilli* (resident/breeds W; winters S): White-tipped median coverts. **VOICE** Sings with sweet rich musical phrases: *wheeper-pree-pree-teelee wheeeoo-peeerper-wheechee-leet-wheeechee-leet pir-whoo-peer-rte-rate*... etc. Often uses mimicry. Calls include a subdued low *tjuck*, loud screeching *teer-teer-teer* or *kreeee*... and thin *tsee* or *tzzeet*. **HABITAT & BEHAVIOUR** Broadleaved evergreen forest, secondary growth and thickets (particularly on migration); up to 1,525 m. Usually on ground but also feeds on fruit and sings from quite high in trees.

SIBERIAN THRUSH *Zoothera sibirica* 21.5–23.5 cm

(7) **Male** *sibirica*: Dark slaty; white supercilium, white belly-centre and vent (latter dark-scaled). Two broad whitish bands bordering dark band on underwing and whitish-tipped outertail feathers in all plumages. (8) **Female**: Bold buffish supercilium, dark eyestripe and scales/mottling below; plain above, narrow wing-bars. (9) **First-winter male**: Mixture of male and female features. **Other subspecies** *Z.s.davisoni* (recorded NW): More blackish and usually has all-dark belly. **VOICE** Languid song of rich 2–3 note phrases: *tvee-tring, tvee-tryu, tvee-kwi-tring* and *yui'i-tss* etc., punctuated by long pauses. Calls with thin *tsit*, stronger *tseee*, soft *tsip* and soft *tsss* or *chrsss* in alarm. **HABITAT & BEHAVIOUR** Broadleaved evergreen forest; up to 2,565 m (winters mainly in mountains). Very shy, visits fruiting trees.

BLACK-BREASTED THRUSH *Turdus dissimilis* 23–23.5 cm

(10) **Male**: Easily identified by black hood and upper breast, dark slaty upperside and orange-rufous lower breast and flanks. (11) **Female**: Told by combination of yellowish bill, plain brown head-sides and upperside, rather dull breast (mixed grey and pale rufous), blackish spots/blotches on throat and breast, and orange-rufous flanks. **VOICE** Sings with sweet mellow phrases of 3–8 notes: *tew-tew weet*; *pieu-pieu-pieu twi* and *wirriwi-wu iih* etc. Calls with resounding *tup* notes and thin *seee*. **HABITAT** Broadleaved evergreen forest; 1,000–2,500 m.

JAPANESE THRUSH *Turdus cardis* 22.5 cm

(12) **Male**: Black hood, dark slaty/blackish above, white below with dark-spotted lower breast/flanks; yellow bill. (13) **Female**: Recalls Black-breasted but little orange-rufous on flanks, dark spots on flanks (sometimes also belly), breast typically paler and less greyish, often shows some warm buff on throat and breast. (14) **First-winter male**: Paler and more uniformly slaty-greyish above than adult male; has whitish centre of throat with dark markings and grey breast with heavy blackish markings. **VOICE** Thin *tsweee* or *tsuuu*. **HABITAT** Broadleaved evergreen forest, secondary growth; up to 1,100 m.

CHESTNUT THRUSH *Turdus rubrocanus* 24–26.5 cm

(15) **Male** *gouldi*: Chestnut body, dark greyish hood, blacker wings/tail. Whitish tips to blackish undertail-coverts. (16) **Female**: Similar to male but body somewhat paler and more rufous (browner on mantle and scapulars), wings and tail browner. **VOICE** Song is a series of short phrases, each repeated 3–8 times: *yee-bre yee-bre yee-bre-diddyit diddyit-yip bru yipbru-yip-bru*. Calls with deep *chuk-chuk*... and faster *kwik-kwik* when alarmed. **HABITAT** Broadleaved evergreen forest; 900–2,565 m, rarely down to 200 m.

GREY-SIDED THRUSH *Turdus feae* 23.5 cm

(17) **Male**: Usually warmer above than female Eye-browed (particularly crown); grey below with white chin, belly-centre and vent. (18) **First winter**: From female by warmer breast/flanks, darker-streaked throat-sides, buffish greater covert tips. **Female**: Breast and flanks less extensively pure grey, usually with less grey on throat; has slight dark spots/streaks on sides of throat and upper breast and warm brownish fringes to breast feathers. **VOICE** Call is slightly but distinctly thinner than that of Eye-browed: *zeeee* or *sieee*. **HABITAT** Broadleaved evergreen forest; 520–2,565 m.

EYEBROWED THRUSH *Turdus obscurus* 22.5–24.5 cm

(19) **Male**: Grey hood, white supercilium, cheek-bar and chin, olive-brown above, orange-rufous on breast/flanks. (20) **Female**: Head much browner, throat-centre and submoustachial line whitish, flanks more washed out. **First winter**: As adult female but buffish greater covert tips. Male often has greyer ear-coverts to upper breast, brighter flanks. **VOICE** 2–3 clear mournful phrases: *teveteu trrryutetyute trrryutetyutyu*..., followed by twittering and discordant warbling (may include mimicry). Thin *zieeh* or harsher *tseee* in flight. Also thin *sip-sip*, chuckling *tuck-tuck* and *tchup*. **HABITAT** Forest, plantations; mangroves and gardens on migration; up to 2,565 m.

PLATE 86 BROWN DIPPER, TYPICAL THRUSHES & COCHOAS

BROWN DIPPER *Cinclus pallasii* 21.5 cm

(1) **Adult** *dorjei*: Robust shape, stout bill, short tail (often cocked) and uniform dark brown plumage distinctive. (2) **Juvenile**: Paler and greyer-brown, with fine blackish scales on body plumage, pale greyish markings on throat and belly and whitish fringes to wing feathers. **VOICE** Song is a strong, rich and full warbling. Call is an abrupt shrill high-pitched rasping *dzzit* or *dzit-dzit*. **HABITAT** Rivers and streams; 200–1,000 m.

LONG-TAILED THRUSH *Zoothera dixoni* 25.5–27 cm

(3) **Adult**: Bold head pattern and buffy-white underparts with blackish scales/bars recall Scaly but has plain olive-brown upperparts and two distinct buffy-whitish bars on wing-coverts. Sides of head mostly whitish with dark patch on rear ear-coverts, has pale area behind eye (above ear-coverts) and contrasting darker bar from middle of inner primaries to base of secondaries. In flight shows prominent pale buffish bands on underwing. **VOICE** Song has fairly slow, rather dry *wu-ut-cheet-sher* or *wut-chet-shuur* phrases (last note slurred), mixed with twitters and *too-ee* or *ee-ee*. Rising *w'i-it* may also be incorporated or used as introductory note. **HABITAT & BEHAVIOUR** Broadleaved evergreen forest; 1,400–2,565 m. Often feeds along leafy tracks and roadsides.

SCALY THRUSH *Zoothera dauma* 27–30 cm

(4) **Adult** *dauma* (incl. *hancii, affinis*): Mostly warm olive-brown/buffish upperbody and whitish underbody with heavy blackish scales. Two buffy-white bands on underwing, white-tipped outertail feathers. **Juvenile**: Warmer above, more diffuse scaling; initially blackish breast-spots. **Other subspecies** *Z.d.aurea* (winters NW,NE): Larger; greyer above. **VOICE** Sings (Himalayas) with slow phrases *pur-loo-tree-lay, dur-lee-dur-lee* and *drr-drr-chew-you-we-eeee* etc., after long pauses. Long thin whistles: *huuwiieee, weeeooooooo*, or *pee-yuuuuu...* (*pee* higher) from *Z.d.aurea*. Calls include thin high *tzeep*. **HABITAT & BEHAVIOUR** Broadleaved evergreen and sometimes mixed deciduous forest; up to 2,565 m (breeds above 365 m). Very shy, often flushed from ground.

DARK-SIDED THRUSH *Zoothera marginata* 23.5–25.5 cm

(5) **Adult**: Noticeably long bill, robust shape, relatively short tail. Warm olive-brown above; head-sides and underparts resemble Long-tailed but flanks more uniform and dark olive-brown. Tail all dark. **Juvenile**: Similar to adult but rufous-buff streaks on crown, mantle and scapulars, rufous-buff triangular spots on tips of wing-coverts and tertials, more rufescent/buffish breast with darker scales/mottling. **VOICE** Song is a thin monotone whistle, softer and shorter (0.5 s) than that of Scaly (*Z.d.aurea*) and downward-inflected. Call is a soft deep *tchuck*. **HABITAT** Broadleaved evergreen forest, usually near streams or wet areas; 600–2,565 m.

GREY-WINGED BLACKBIRD *Turdus boulboul* 27.5–29 cm

(6) **Male**: Blackish with large pale greyish wing-patch. Bill orange. (7) **Female**: Rather plain, warm olive-brown with yellowish bill. Has similarly shaped wing-patch to male but colour only slightly paler (and warmer) brown than rest of wing. **VOICE** Rich and melodious song, usually with few repeated

phrases: *tweee-toooh tweee-toooh chuiyui-twit weear-twit weear-trtrtrtt-whih-whih-which wheeeyar-wheee-yar* and *chir-bles-we-bullie-dee we-put-kur-we-put-kur who-bori-chal-let-cha-he* etc. Low *chuck-chuck*, and emphasised *chook-chook* when alarmed. **HABITAT** Broadleaved evergreen forest, clearings; 1,000–2,565 m.

EURASIAN BLACKBIRD *Turdus merula* 28–29 cm

(8) **Male** *mandarinus*: Overall sooty-black plumage and yellow bill diagnostic. (9) **Female**: Very similar but a shade browner above and particularly below, throat often paler with narrow dark streaks. Similar to Grey-winged but darker, with darker bill and uniformly dark wings. **First winter**: Similar to respective adults but has mostly dark bill. **VOICE** Song is a beautiful, mellow, leisurely series of melodious warbling and flute-like notes, with little phrase repetition. Calls with explosive deep *chup-chup...*, higher *whiiik* and soft *p'soook*. **HABITAT & BEHAVIOUR** Open forest, secondary growth, clearings, cultivation; up to 950 m. Often in flocks.

PURPLE COCHOA *Cochoa purpurea* 26.5–28 cm

(10) **Male**: Brownish-purple with pale lavender-blue crown and black head-sides. Has broad pale lavender-purple band across base of black flight feathers, and lavender-purple tail with black tip (all blackish below). (11) **Female**: Similar pattern to male but throat, body and wing-coverts rufescent-brown (more buffish below). (12) **Juvenile male**: Bold white markings on blackish crown, dark tips and warm buff streaks/spots above, rich buff below with bold blackish bars, throat plainer with blackish malar line, ear-coverts with some white markings. **Juvenile female**: Differs from adult as juvenile male. **VOICE** Song recalls Green but deeper and clearer: *whiiii-ii*. Contact calls include very thin, rather thrush-like *sit* and *tssri* notes. **HABITAT & BEHAVIOUR** Broadleaved evergreen forest; 1,000–1,800 m, rarely down to 400 m. Forages on ground and visits fruiting trees.

GREEN COCHOA *Cochoa viridis* 27–29 cm

(13) **Male**: Green plumage (variably mixed blue on underparts), bright blue crown and nape, extensive silvery-blue markings on black wings and blue tail with broad black tip. (14) **Female**: Like male but brownish wash on secondaries, tertials and inner greater coverts, no blue below. (15) **Juvenile**: Crown blackish with bold white markings, rest of upperparts broadly fringed blackish and spotted buff, cheeks/ear-coverts largely whitish, wings like respective adults but with rich buff to rufescent spots on wing-covert tips, underparts rich buff with bold blackish scales; throat plainer with blackish malar line. Tail as adult. (16) **First-summer male**: Whitish stripe from chin to lower ear-coverts/neck-side, golden-buff wash below (also slightly above). **First summer female**: Differs from adult as juvenile male. **VOICE** Song is a series of loud pure monotone whistles: *hiiiiii*, lasting c. 2 s. **HABITAT** Broadleaved evergreen forest; 1,200–2,565 m, occasionally down to 400 m.

PLATE 87 MANGROVE WHISTLER & FLYCATCHERS

MANGROVE WHISTLER *Pachycephala grisola* 15.5–17 cm

(1) **Adult** *grisola* (west S) Drab brown above, rather slaty-grey crown, white below with duller throat and greyish-washed breast. Thick black bill, no obvious head/wing markings or rufous tones in plumage. **Juvenile**: Rufous secondary edges, pinkish/brown bill. **Other subspecies** *P.g.vandepolli* (S[east],C,SE): Slightly richer/browner above. **VOICE** Song of loud high-pitched phrases introduced by 2–4 short notes: ***tit tit phew-whiu-whit***; ***chi chi chi wit-phew-chew***; ***tit tit tit too-whit*** etc. Last note often more explosive. **HABITAT & BEHAVIOUR** Mangroves, adjacent coastal vegetation, island forest. Sits still for longish periods amongst foliage.

BROWN-CHESTED JUNGLE FLYCATCHER *Rhinomyias brunneata* 15 cm

(2) **Adult** *brunneata*: From other *Rhinomyias* flycatchers by rather long, stout bill with pale yellow lower mandible, faint dark mottling/flecking on whitish throat. Upper breast dull brownish. **First winter**: Dark tip to lower mandible, rufous-buff tips to greater coverts and tertials. **HABITAT** Broadleaved evergreen and mixed deciduous forest; up to 395 m.

FULVOUS-CHESTED JUNGLE FLYCATCHER *Rhinomyias olivacea* 15 cm

(3) **Adult** *olivacea*: From other *Rhinomyias* and female *Cyornis* by all-dark bill, pinkish legs/feet, plain whitish throat, warm buffish-brown upper breast and flank-wash. Warm-tinged uppertail-coverts and outertail-fringing. (4) **Juvenile**: Upperparts and wings warmer, upperpart feathers tipped blackish-brown and speckled buff, wing-coverts and tertials tipped rufous-buff, breast-band and flanks mottled buff and dark brown. **VOICE** Song recalls *Cyornis* flycatchers but phrases rather short (1–2 s) and slurred, including scratchy notes. Calls include drawn-out *churr* or *trrt* and a harsh *tac*. **HABITAT** Broadleaved evergreen forest; up to 885 m.

GREY-CHESTED JUNGLE FLYCATCHER *Rhinomyias umbratilis* 15 cm

(5) **Adult**: From other *Rhinomyias* by grey/olive-grey upper breast, contrasting with gleaming white throat and dark malar area. See Moustached Babbler. (6) **Juvenile**: Darker above than Fulvous-chested with bolder rich buff spots, breast-mottling washed greyish. **VOICE** Song has sweet, well-structured, slightly descending phrases: *si ti-tu-ti'tooee'u* (sharp second note); *sii tu'ee'oo* and *sii tee'oo'ee* etc. Richer/more varied than Fulvous-chested (recalls *Cyornis*). Alarm calls are a scolding *chrrr-chrrr-chrrr* and *trrrt'it'it'it* etc. **HABITAT** Broadleaved evergreen forest; up to 900 m.

DARK-SIDED FLYCATCHER *Muscicapa sibirica* 11.5–13 cm

(7) **Adult** *rothschildi* (NW,W,S at least): Small bill, grey-brown breast and flanks with smudgy darker streaks, dark-centred undertail-coverts; variable pale line down centre of abdomen; wing-tips nearer tail-tip than Asian Brown. (8) **Juvenile**: Blacker above with buff spots, blackish-marked throat to flanks; coverts tipped/fringed warm buff. (9) **Adult** *sibirica* (NW,C,SE,S at least): Whiter abdomen, clearer breast-streaks, fainter undertail-covert centres. (10) **Adult (worn)**: Spring. Less breast-streaking.

More similar to darker individuals of Asian Brown. **VOICE** Sings with weak sibilant *tsee* notes, followed by quite melodious trills or whistles. **HABITAT** Relatively open broadleaved forests, plantations, gardens, mangroves etc. on passage; up to 2,000 m.

ASIAN BROWN FLYCATCHER *Muscicapa dauurica* 12.5–13.5 cm

(11) **Adult** *dauurica*: Plain brownish-grey above, breast washed brownish-grey, usually lacking defined streaks; pale basal half of lower mandible, whitish eyering/loral stripe, pale greyish wing-covert/tertial fringes. (12) **Adult (worn)**: Greyer above and paler below. (13) **Adult** *siamensis* (resident): Browner above, duller/plainer below, mostly pale lower mandible, dull eyering. **Juvenile**: Whiter scapular/wing-covert markings than Dark-sided, fine breast-scaling. **First winter**: Paler greater covert tips/tertial fringes than adult. **VOICE** Sings with short trills and 2–3 note whistled phrases. Calls with thin *tse-ti-ti-ti-ti* and short *tzi*. **HABITAT** Open forest, parks, gardens, mangroves. Up to 1,500 m (breeds 600–1,400 m in open forest).

BROWN-STREAKED FLYCATCHER *Muscicapa williamsoni* 13 cm

(14) **Adult**: Warmer/browner above than *M.d. dauurica*, yellowish lower mandible (tip usually dark), duller and buffier submoustachial, buffier lores and wing-fringing, usually distinct brownish streaks on breast/flanks. (15) **Adult (worn)**: Breeders have vaguer underpart-streaking and plainer head and wing pattern. Apart from underparts, could be confused with resident subspecies of Asian Brown (*M.d.siamensis*). **Juvenile**: Like Asian Brown. **VOICE** Calls include sharp *tzi* and slurred *cheititit*. **HABITAT** Open broadleaved evergreen and semi-evergreen forest, clearings, parks and wooded gardens on migration; up to 1,295 m.

BROWN-BREASTED FLYCATCHER *Muscicapa muttui* 13–14 cm

(16) **Adult (fresh)**: Typical autumn/early winter bird. Larger and bigger-billed than Asian Brown, uniform pale yellowish lower mandible, colder greyish-brown crown/head-sides (greyer than illustrated) contrasting sharply with broad whitish eyering and loral patch, rufescent-tinge above, enclosed white submoustachial patch, warm greyish breast and flanks, deep buff fringes to greater coverts, tertials and secondaries. Duller when worn. **VOICE** Song is said to be pleasant but feeble. Typical call is a thin *sit*. **HABITAT** Broadleaved evergreen forest; 1,220–1,645 m.

FERRUGINOUS FLYCATCHER *Muscicapa ferruginea* 12.5–13 cm

(17) **Adult (fresh)**: Autumn/winter bird. Recalls Dark-sided but slaty-grey cast to head, strongly rufescent rump, uppertail-coverts and tail, rusty-rufous fringes to greater coverts and tertials and rusty-buff breast and flanks (former mixed with brown). Duller/greyer on breast/flanks when worn, plainer-winged, lores/eyering possibly whiter. **VOICE** Probable song consists of very high-pitched silvery notes introduced by a short sharp harsher note: *tsit-tittu-tittu* and *tsit tittu-tittu tsit tittu-tittu* etc. Calls include a short sharp high-pitched *tssit-tssit* and *tssit tssit tssit...* **HABITAT** Broadleaved evergreen forest; up to 2,000 m.

PLATE 88 FLYCATCHERS

YELLOW-RUMPED FLYCATCHER *Ficedula zanthopygia*
13–13.5 cm

(1) **Male (winter)**: Vivid yellow rump and underparts, white supercilium, long wing-patch and undertail-coverts. (2) **Male (spring)**: Orange flush on throat and breast. (3) **Female**: Dull greyish-olive above, yellow rump, white wing-patch (often less white on greater coverts than male). Buffy-/yellowish-white loral stripe and underparts, faint brownish scales/mottling on throat and breast. **First-winter male** Like female but largely blackish uppertail-coverts, white on wing restricted to bar on inner greater coverts. **VOICE** Dry, rattled *tr'r'r't*. **HABITAT** Broadleaved forests, parks, gardens, mangroves; up to 950 m.

NARCISSUS FLYCATCHER *Ficedula narcissina* 13–13.5 cm

(4) **Male** *narcissina*: From spring Yellow-rumped by yellow supercilium, whiter belly, no white on tertials. (5) **Female**: Like Green-backed but much browner above (olive-tinged on lower back/rump) and whitish underparts with variable dark scales/mottling on throat-sides and breast, greyish/brownish wash on breast and flanks, and sometimes a faint yellowish tinge on belly. **First-winter male** Like adult female. **HABITAT** Recorded in lowland dry mixed deciduous woodland and scrub.

GREEN-BACKED FLYCATCHER *Ficedula elisae* 13–13.5 cm

(6) **Male**: Greyish olive-green above, wings and tail dark, has contrasting bright yellow loral stripe, eyering, rump and underparts and broad white wingpatch. (7) **Female**: Duller above, no yellow on rump or white on wing, subdued facial pattern, two faint narrow pale wing-bars, rufescent-tinged uppertail-coverts and tail; underparts duller but still quite bright yellow. **HABITAT** Broadleaved evergreen forest, forest edge, also plantations, parks and gardens on migration; lowlands. **NOTE** Often lumped in Narcissus Flycatcher.

MUGIMAKI FLYCATCHER *Ficedula mugimaki* 13–13.5 cm

(8) **Male**: Short white supercilium, large white wing-patch, rufous-orange throat/breast. White at base of outertail. (9) **Female**: Greyish-brown above (greyer in spring), throat/breast buffishorange, supercilium faint/lacking; usually no white on tail, one or two narrow buffish/whitish wingbars, faint pale edges to tertials. (10) **First-winter male**: Like female but lores and head-sides often greyer with slight dark moustachial line, has bolder supercilium, brighter throat/breast, mostly blackish uppertail-coverts, some whitish on base of outertail. **VOICE** Rattled *trrr'rr* or *trrrik*. **HABITAT** Middle storey and canopy of broadleaved evergreen forest; 800–1,800 m. Also lowland parks, gardens etc. on passage.

RUFOUS-GORGETED FLYCATCHER *Ficedula strophiata*
13–14.5 cm

(11) **Male** *strophiata*: Blackish-grey face/throat, whitish eyebrow, slaty-grey breast with orangerufous patch on upper centre (sometimes lacking), blackish tail with white-based outer feathers. Dark warmish brown above. (12) **Female**: Duller; paler grey throat and breast (no black), less distinct eyebrow, smaller gorget, buffish chin. (13) **Juvenile**: Warmer

above than female with blackish feather-tips, crown streaked rich buff, rest of upperparts and median coverts spotted/streaked rich buff, throat to belly buff with heavy blackish scales/streaks. **VOICE** Thin *zwi chir rri* song. Low *tchuk* and harsh *trrt* calls. **HABITAT** Broadleaf evergreen forest; 900–2,565 m.

RED-THROATED FLYCATCHER *Ficedula parva* 13–13.5 cm

(14) **Male non-breeding/female** *albicilla*: Pale buffish-grey wash on breast, blackish tail with prominent white on base of outertail feathers (very obvious in flight); pale eyering, blackish bill. (15) **Male breeding**: Rufous-orange throat, surrounded by grey. **First winter**: Buffish greater covert/tertial tips. **VOICE** Song is a rhythmic *zri zri zri chee chee dee-cha dee-cha dee-cha chu chu chu tu tu tu tu too taa* (sharp then clear, descending). Rattling *trrrt* and clicking *tek* call notes. **HABITAT & BEHAVIOUR** Open woodland, plantations, parks, gardens; up to 2,000 m. Regularly cocks tail.

RUFOUS-CHESTED FLYCATCHER *Ficedula dumetoria*
11.5–12 cm

(16) **Male** *muelleri*: Smaller and shorter-winged/-tailed than Mugimaki; supercilium extends in front of eye, long white streak across wing-coverts, alldark tertials, pale buffy-rufous throat, paler orange-rufous breast. (17) **Female**: Pale throat contrasts with breast, buff loral line/eyering, rustybuffish wing-covert tips/tertial edges. **Juvenile**: Poorly documented but certainly speckled with warm buff. Male probably shows some adult characters at early age. **VOICE** Song phrases are very thin and wispy: *sii'wi-sii*, *si-wi-si-ii* and *si-wi-oo* etc. **HABITAT** Broadleaved evergreen forest; up to 825 m. Inhabits low vegetation, often near streams.

BLUE-AND-WHITE FLYCATCHER *Cyanoptila cyanomelana*
18 cm

(18) **Male** *cyanomelana*: Large; azure to cobaltblue above, blackish head-sides, throat, breast, otherwise white. (19) **Female**: Clear-cut white belly/vent, no blue, no white on outertail (patch at base on male); throat and breast rather uniform pale brownish, usually with buffish to whitish vertical or horizontal patch on lower throat. (20) **First-winter male**: As female but wings, tail, scapulars and back to uppertailcoverts similar to adult male. **Other subspecies** *C.c.cumatilis* (? widespread): More turquoise above, bluer/turquoise headsides, throat and upper breast. Perhaps not a valid subspecies. **VOICE** Low *tic* and *tac* notes. **HABITAT** Broadleaved evergreen forest, parks, woody gardens; up to 1,830 m.

WHITE-TAILED FLYCATCHER *Cyornis concretus* 19 cm

(21) **Male** *cyanea*: Relatively large; blue head and body, white belly and vent, white lines down outertail. (22) **Female**: White crescent/patch on uppermost breast, white tail-lines. Warmish brown upperparts and breast. (23) **Female** *concretus* (S): Brighter rufous-brown; warm buff throat and whiter, more demarcated belly. **Juvenile**: Large rufous-buff spots on upperparts and wing-coverts. **VOICE** Song is very variable, sometimes with skilled mimicry. Usually 3–7 rather piercing but tuneful notes: *pieu pieu pieu jee-oee*; *ti ti ti teu tear-tear* and *phi phi phi phi ju-rit* etc. Harsh *scree* call notes. **HABITAT** Broadleaved evergreen forest; 200–1,000 m.

PLATE 89 FLYCATCHERS

SLATY-BACKED FLYCATCHER *Ficedula hodgsonii* 13–13.5 cm

(1) **Male**: Told by combination of dark, dull bluish-slate upperside, blackish tail with white at base of outer feathers and orange-rufous underparts (fading on vent). Larger/longer-tailed than Snowy-browed, no white eyebrow. (2) **Female**: Nondescript; dull olive-brown above, dull greyish to buffish-grey throat/breast, rufescent uppertail-coverts, whitish eyering/loral line. Often has narrow buffish/buffish-white wing-bar, no white on tail. Most likely to be confused with Slaty-blue but no obvious buff below or rufous on tail; posture more vertical. See Narcissus. **First winter**: Like female but rather warmer brown above, wing-bar more prominent. VOICE Song is a rather short, meandering, generally descending ditty of slurred-together whistled notes. Typical call is a hard rattling *terrht* or *tchrt*. HABITAT More open broadleaved evergreen forest, forest edge, secondary growth; 900–2,565 m.

WHITE-GORGETED FLYCATCHER *Ficedula monileger* 12–13 cm

(3) **Adult** *leucops*: Small, robust; short tail, white throat bordered by black. Olive-brown above, greyer head-sides, broad whitish eyebrow, warm-tinged uppertail-coverts, tail and wings, buffish olive-brown breast and flanks. **Juvenile**: Warm buff streaks on darker upperparts, buff-tipped greater coverts; buffish below with diffuse dark streaks. Pinkish legs/feet like adult. VOICE Sings with very high-pitched, wispy, slurred scratchy phrases (sometimes a few well-structured ones). Metallic *tik* or *trik* calls, sometimes mixed with very thin, stressed *siii* or *siiu* notes. HABITAT & BEHAVIOUR Broadleaved evergreen forest, bamboo; 900–1,900 m. Skulks in low vegetation.

RUFOUS-BROWED FLYCATCHER *Ficedula solitaris* 12–13 cm

(4) **Adult** *submonileger*: Like White-gorgeted but usually lacks complete black throat border, has bright rufous lores, eyering and crown-sides; overall plumage tones considerably more rufescent. (5) **Adult** *malayana* (southern S): Richer, more rufous-chestnut brown parts of plumage, including lores. **Juvenile**: Presumably very similar to White-gorgeted. VOICE Like White-gorgeted. HABITAT & BEHAVIOUR Broadleaved evergreen forest, bamboo; 400–1,400 m. Behaves like White-gorgeted.

SNOWY-BROWED FLYCATCHER *Ficedula hyperythra* 11–13 cm

(6) **Male** *hyperythra*: Small and relatively short-tailed, with dark slaty-blue upperparts, orange-rufous throat and breast and distinctive white eyebrow and white patch at base of outertail feathers. Size, short tail and white eyebrow rules out Slaty-blue, Pygmy Blue and male *Cyornis* flycatchers. (7) **Female**: Small size, shortish tail, buffy loral stripe/eyering and underparts (paler throat and vent), rufescent-tinged wings, without obvious markings. Upperparts rather cold greyish olive-brown. See Lesser Shortwing. (8) **Juvenile female**: Darker above than adult with blackish fringing and warm buff streaks/speckles; throat and breast heavily streaked/scalloped blackish, fading on throat-centre, belly and vent. Male has slaty-blue tail. VOICE Song consists of fairly well-structured but subdued, thin, high-pitched, wheezy phrases: *tsit-sit-si-sii*, *tsi-sii-swrri* and *tsi sii'i* etc. Calls include thin *sip* notes. HABITAT Broadleaved evergreen forest; 800–2,565 m.

LITTLE PIED FLYCATCHER *Ficedula westermanni* 11–12.5 cm

(9) **Male** *australorientis*: Only black and white flycatcher in region. See Bar-winged Flycatcher-shrike. (10) **Female**: Greyish above with rufescent uppertail-coverts, white below, greyish wash on breast-sides/flanks. (11) **Juvenile female**: Darker above than adult with blackish fringes and buff spots, whitish below, lightly scaled. **Juvenile male**: Blacker wings/tail than juvenile female, with white markings recalling adult. **Other subspecies** *F.w.westermanni* (S): Female more slaty-grey above. VOICE Song is thin, sweet and high-pitched, often followed by a rattled call note. Calls with a sharp *swit*, then a rattling *trrrrt*. HABITAT Upper storey/canopy of broadleaved evergreen forest; 700–2,565 m.

ULTRAMARINE FLYCATCHER *Ficedula superciliaris* 12 cm

(12) **Male** *aestigma*: Deep blue above, broad dark blue lateral breast-patches, contrasting white underparts. (13) **Female**: Like Little Pied but larger, no rufous on uppertail-coverts, distinctly brownish-grey to grey sides of throat and breast (mirroring pattern of male); may show a little blue on uppertail-coverts and tail. (14) **First-winter male**: Resembles female but scapulars and back to uppertail-coverts mostly blue, has extensive blue on wings, tail and mantle, and broad buff greater covert bar and tertial fringes. VOICE Song is high-pitched, quite disjointed: *tseep-te-e-te-e-te-e te-tih tseep tse-e-ep*... etc. Calls with a low *trrrrt* (slower/deeper than Little Pied) and *chi trrrrt* (*chi* squeaky). HABITAT Open broadleaved forest, pines; 915–1,700 m.

SLATY-BLUE FLYCATCHER *Ficedula tricolor* 12.5–13 cm

(15) **Male** *diversa*: Pale blue forehead/eyebrow, blacker head-sides, blackish tail with white at base of outer feathers, whitish/buffy-white throat, buffy blue-grey breast-band; buffish/buffy-whitish belly and vent, greyish flank-wash. (16) **Female**: Like Slaty-backed but somewhat darker and warmer above, distinctly rufous-chestnut tail (browner at tip), strongly buffish narrow loral line, eyering and underparts (throat and sometimes belly-centre slightly paler). **First-winter male**: Like female. VOICE Sings with 3–4 high notes: *chreet-chrr-whit-it* (*chreet* long, *chrr* and stressed, *whit-it* low/more trilled) etc. Sharp *tic* and rolling *trrri trrri trrri*... calls. HABITAT & BEHAVIOUR Scrub, secondary growth, tall grass, bamboo; 1,200–2,565 m. Skulks in low vegetation. Posture distinctly horizontal; often cocks tail.

SAPPHIRE FLYCATCHER *Ficedula sapphira* 11–11.5 cm

(17) **Male breeding** *sapphira*: Like Ultramarine but much brighter blue, orange-rufous throat/breast-centre. (18) **Male non-breeding**: Like female but scapulars, back to uppertail-coverts, wings and tail as breeding male. (19) **Female**: Small size, shortish tail, warm brown above, rufescent uppertail-coverts, deep buffish-orange throat and upper breast. Eyering/loral stripe buff, belly/vent white, wings/tail unmarked. See female *Cyornis* flycatchers. **First-winter male**: Like non-breeding adult but has buff wing-bar and pale tertial tips. VOICE Call consists of short hard rattles, sometimes introduced by high thin note(s): *tssyi tchrrrt, tchrrrt tchrrrt tchrrrt*... etc. HABITAT & BEHAVIOUR More open broadleaved evergreen forest; 1,200–2,565 m. Usually rather high in trees.

PLATE 90 FLYCATCHERS

HAINAN BLUE FLYCATCHER *Cyornis hainanus* 13.5–14 cm

(1) **Male**: Dark blue throat/breast, pale bluish-grey belly grading to whiter vent. No white in tail, belly/vent often vaguely buffish-tinged. Duller than Small Niltava, no shining neck-patch or rump/uppertail-coverts, belly whiter. (2) **Male variant**: Often shows white triangle/patch on centre of lower throat and/or white breast-scaling. (3) **Female**: Like Blue-throated but usually duller and darker above, throat/breast duller buffy-rufous (browner at side), lores/eyering usually paler. From Hill Blue by usually paler throat than breast, paler lores/eyering, no orange-buff on flanks (may be washed light buff). **Juvenile**: Resembles female but upperpart feathers dark-tipped and spotted buff (crown-centre streaked), buff spots on wing-coverts, dark-scaled breast. Males show blue on wings and tail. **VOICE** Song weaker and typically simpler than Hill Blue, consisting of rather short hurried slurred phrases. Light *tic* call notes. **HABITAT** Broadleaved forest, bamboo; up to 800 m.

BLUE-THROATED FLYCATCHER *Cyornis rubeculoides* 14–15 cm

(4) **Male** Dark blue throat with orange-rufous triangle/wedge up to its centre. Upperside fairly deep blue. (5) **Female**: Like Hill Blue but throat and breast markedly paler and more rufous-buff, lores somewhat paler, crown and mantle usually paler and greyer with less rufescent forehead. Has strongly rufescent tail. (6) **Juvenile female**: Like Hill Blue but paler above, paler, more rufous tail, lighter breast-scaling. (7) **Male** *glaucicomans* (visitor C,NE,S): Deeper blue above than Hill Blue, with contrasting shining azure shoulder-patch and uppertail-coverts, more azure-blue forehead/eyebrow, dark blue chin, brown flank-wash. (8) **Female**: Deeper orange-rufous breast, contrasting pale buff throat, brown-washed flanks, darker/warmer above, duller tail. **VOICE** Trilled and slurred notes, mixed with fairly well-structured phrases: *tch'tch'tch-hiu'hiu'hiu'hiu*, *trrr-sweei-iu-iu* and *trr-trr-swiwiwiwi* etc. (*tit* and *trrt* notes often mixed in). Hard *tac* and *trrt* calls. *C.r.glaucicomans* has richer, more varied warbling song. **HABITAT** Broadleaved forests, bamboo, also gardens, mangroves on passage; up to 1,700 m, breeds below 1,350 m.

HILL BLUE FLYCATCHER *Cyornis banyumas* 14–15.5 cm

(9) **Male** *whitei*: Very like Tickell's Blue but orange-rufous of breast grades to white belly, orange-rufous often extends down flanks. Uppermost chin at base of bill dark or as rest of throat. (10) **Female**: Same gradation of orange-rufous to white below as male, warm-tinged olive-brown above, uppertail-coverts, tail and wing-fringing markedly rufescent. Almost uniform deep orange-rufous throat and breast. (11) **Juvenile female**: Darker tips and warm buff spots above (crown more streaked), warm buff spots on coverts; buffy below, deeper buff breast/upper belly/flanks with heavy dark scales. Male shows blue on wings/tail. **Other subspecies** *C.b.magnirostris* (visitor S), *lekahuni* (recorded NE), *deignani* (recorded SE): Big bills, males slightly deeper blue above; female *magnirostris* may have rufous throat/breast (throat may be slightly paler than breast). *C.b.coerulifrons* (resident S): Male slightly deeper blue above, possibly more rufous breast (may contrast slightly with throat). **VOICE** Sweet, high-pitched and melancholy song usually starts with thin *tsi* notes. Phrases longer, more complex and rapidly delivered than Tickell's Blue. Calls a hard *tac* and scolding *trrt-trrt-trrt*... **HABITAT** Broadleaved evergreen forest, also parks, gardens etc. on passage; 400–2,515 m.

MALAYSIAN BLUE FLYCATCHER *Cyornis turcosus* 14 cm

(12) **Male** *rupatensis*: Like Blue-throated (nominate) but throat bright deep blue, breast paler rufous-orange, upperparts somewhat deeper, brighter blue, with paler shining blue rump and uppertail-coverts. (13) **Female**: As male but throat pale warm buff (whiter on chin/sides), less deep blue above. From male Hill Blue and Tickell's Blue by paler blue upperparts, shining blue rump/uppertail-coverts, paler throat and breast. **VOICE** Song consists of relatively weak 5–6 note phrases. Female may give thin, strained *swii swii-swew*. **HABITAT** Broadleaved evergreen forest, near rivers and streams; up to 760 m.

TICKELL'S BLUE FLYCATCHER *Cyornis tickelliae* 13.5–15.5 cm

(14) **Male** *indochina*: Sharp demarcation between orange-rufous breast and white belly, rarely showing obvious orange-rufous on flanks. Upperparts rather uniform deep blue with paler blue forehead and sides of forecrown. (15) **Female**: Greyish/bluish-grey tinge above, demarcated colours below (as male); tail usually with some blue, throat usually paler/buffier than breast (contrasts sharply with head-sides). Lores broadly pale buff/buffy-whitish. (16) **Female** *sumatrensis* (S): Ranges from similar to much bluer on mantle and scapulars to uppertail. Males are slightly deeper blue above, throat usually paler/buffier than breast. **Juvenile**: Resembles Blue-throated and Hill Blue but base colour to upperparts greyish-tinged, lacks rufous on tail, has narrow pale buffish crown-streaking. **VOICE** Song consists of quite slowly delivered, sweet, high-pitched, slightly descending (or rising then descending) phrases: *tissis-swii'i'i'i-ui, sisis'itu'i-i'iiw, tis-swiu'iiu'iiu*. Typical calls are a hard *tac* and *trrt* notes. **HABITAT** Broadleaved evergreen, semi-evergreen and deciduous forest, bamboo; up to 600 m.

MANGROVE BLUE FLYCATCHER *Cyornis rufigastra* 14.5 cm

(17) **Male** *rufigastra*: Resembles Tickell's Blue and Hill Blue but somewhat darker/duller blue above, less obvious lighter forehead and eyebrow, dull deep orange-rufous below, with buffier vent and whiter belly-centre. (18) **Female**: Like male but shows distinctive whitish lores, cheek-spot and chin. **Juvenile**: Sooty-coloured above with darker feather tips and dull buff speckling (crown more streaked with plainer centre), dull buff spots on wing-coverts; pale buff below (breast deeper buff, vent whiter) with prominently dark-scaled throat-sides, breast and upper belly. **VOICE** Song is like Tickell's but slightly slower/deeper. **HABITAT** Mangroves.

PYGMY BLUE FLYCATCHER *Muscicapella hodgsoni* 9–9.5 cm

(19) **Male** *hodgsoni*: Upperparts rather deep dark blue, with lighter, brighter forecrown, underparts rather uniform buffy rufous-orange (vent may be slightly paler). (20) **Female**: Resembles Sapphire but smaller and shorter-tailed, upperparts warmer, particularly back to uppertail, underparts rather uniform pale rufescent-buff (sometimes whiter on vent). **VOICE** Song is a thin high-pitched *sii-su'u-siiii* (*siiii* quavering). Calls with weak *tup* or *tip* notes. **HABITAT & BEHAVIOUR** Middle/upper storey of broadleaved evergreen forest; 1,200–2,565 m. Often flicks wings and cocks tail.

PLATE 91 FLYCATCHERS

VERDITER FLYCATCHER *Eumyias thalassina* 15–17 cm
(1) **Male breeding** *thalassina*: Turquoise-tinged pale blue; black lores, dark undertail-coverts tipped whitish. (2) **Male non-breeding**: Duller and more turquoise. (3) **Female breeding**: Similar to male but duller and slightly greyish-tinged, with dusky lores. (4) **Female non-breeding**: Underparts duller and greyer. **Juvenile**: Recalls non-breeding female but head/body greyer with buff/whitish speckling, wing-coverts tipped buff/whitish, has dark tips/scales on throat and underparts. **Other subspecies** *E.t.thallasoides* (S): All plumages generally somewhat bluer, less turquoise. **VOICE** Song is a rather hurried series of high-pitched, undulating musical notes, gradually descending. **HABITAT** More open broadleaved evergreen forest, also wooded gardens and mangroves on migration; up to 2,565 m.

PALE BLUE FLYCATCHER *Cyornis unicolor* 16–17.5 cm
(5) **Male** *unicolor*: Recalls female Verditer but bill longer (less triangular from below), no turquoise in plumage, wings much duller, mid-blue above with contrasting shining blue forecrown and eyebrow, paler throat and breast grading to paler and greyer on belly and vent; lores blackish-blue. (6) **Female**: Told by grey-tinged crown/nape, rufescent uppertail-coverts/tail, brownish-grey underparts with whiter belly-centre. Upperparts brownish, chin and throat-centre often paler than breast, vent faintly buff-tinged. **Juvenile**: Similar to female but broad blackish tips and buff spots above, buff spots on wing-coverts, uniformly dark-scaled below. Males have blue on wings/tail. **Other subspecies** *C.u.harterti* (S): Rather more rufescent upperside, greyer crown, somewhat warmer brownish wash below. **VOICE** More melodious song than other *Cyornis*, phrases often start with shorter *chi* notes and end with buzzy *chizz* or *wheez*. **HABITAT** Middle/upper storey of broadleaved evergreen forest; up to 1,600 m.

LARGE NILTAVA *Niltava grandis* 20–21.5 cm
(7) **Male** *grandis*: Very dark blue, lighter and brighter crown, neck-sides, shoulder-patch and rump/uppertail-coverts; blackish head-sides, throat and upper breast, greyer vent. See Blue-fronted Robin. (8) **Female**: Light blue neck-patch, quite uniform dark brown below, with contrasting narrow buffish throat-patch, greyer abdomen-centre and no white gorget. Crown/nape greyish, undertail-coverts fringed buffish. (9) **Juvenile female**: Black tips and buff/rufous-buff spots above, rich buff below, paler throat-centre/vent, narrow blackish scales on throat-sides, breast and upper belly (fading to vent). Males have mostly blue wings/tail. (10) **Female** *decipiens* (S): Darker, warmer plumage, darker blue neck-patch, bluish-slate crown and nape. **VOICE** Usually 3–4 ascending soft whistles: *uu-uu-du-di* or *uu'uu'di* etc. Also rasping rattles and soft *chu-ii* (*ii* higher). **HABITAT & BEHAVIOUR** Broadleaved evergreen forest; 900–2,565 m. Usually in middle storey, sometimes drops to ground.

SMALL NILTAVA *Niltava macgrigoriae* 13.5–14 cm
(11) **Male** *signata*: Like a miniature Large but throat and upper breast blue-black, grading to much paler grey belly and whitish vent; shows brighter, lighter blue forehead and neck-patch (rest of crown like mantle). (12) **Female**: Also like miniature Large but has darker, less contrasting throat-centre, browner (less greyish) crown/nape, generally greyer underparts with whitish

centre to abdomen and buffy undertail-coverts. (13) **Juvenile female**: Small size, throat concolorous with breast, abdomen-centre/vent whitish. **VOICE** Song is a very thin, high-pitched, rising and falling *swii-swii-ii-swii*, level *tsii-sii* or descending *tsii-sii-swi*. Typical calls include harsh metallic churring and scolding notes. **HABITAT** Broadleaved evergreen forest; 900–2,565 m.

FUJIAN NILTAVA *Niltava davidi* 18 cm
(14) **Male**: As Rufous-bellied but only front/side of crown (to above eye) shining blue, hindcrown hardly brighter than mantle, no shoulder-patch, breast duller, darker and more rufous, usually contrasting with buffier belly/vent. (15) **Female**: Upperside a shade darker/colder than Rufous-bellied, no bright rufous on wings and tail; lower throat, upper breast and flanks usually slightly darker, making gorget (which may be larger) contrast more. **VOICE** Very thin, high *sssssew* or *siiiii*, repeated after shortish intervals. Sharp metallic *tit tit tit*... and *trrt trrt tit tit trrt trrt*... etc. **HABITAT** Broadleaved evergreen forest, also parks and gardens on passage; 900–1,700 m.

RUFOUS-BELLIED NILTAVA *Niltava sundara* 18 cm
(16) **Male** *denotata*: Very dark blue above, with paler shining blue crown (appears capped), neck, shoulder-patches, rump and uppertail-coverts; bluish-black head-sides and throat, rest of underparts dark orange-rufous. (17) **Female**: Told by very rufescent wings/tail (no white on latter), blue neck-patch, prominent whitish gorget on uppermost breast-centre (can be absent). Rest of underparts greyish-olive, with buff chin and paler buffy-grey to whitish belly-centre/undertail-coverts. Warm olive-brown above, greyer crown/nape; rufous-buff loral line/eyering. **VOICE** Thin *tsi tsi tsi tsi*..., hard *tic* and *trrt*, husky rattles. **HABITAT** Broadleaved evergreen forest; 900–2,565 m.

VIVID NILTAVA *Niltava vivida* 18.5–19 cm
(18) **Male** *oatesi*: Larger than Rufous-bellied, orange-rufous wedge/triangle on throat-centre (may almost reach chin); throat-sides bluer, crown, shoulder, rump and uppertail-coverts duller, no defined neck-patch. (19) **Female**: Lacks blue neck-patch. Otherwise like Large but somewhat paler/greyer below, belly-centre often paler still or buff-tinged, undertail-coverts pale buff, wings/tail a shade paler, less rufescent. Lacks white gorget. **VOICE** Sings with slow mellow whistles, usually mixed with scratchier notes: *heu wii riu chrt-trrt heu wii tiu-wii-u*... **HABITAT** Broadleaved evergreen forest; 750–2,565 m. Often in middle storey to canopy.

GREY-HEADED CANARY FLYCATCHER *Culicicapa ceylonensis* 11.5–13 cm
(20) **Adult** *calochrysea*: Head and breast grey, crown darker and tufted, upperside olive-green with yellower uppertail-coverts, rest of underparts bright yellowish with olive-washed flanks. (21) **Juvenile**: Similar to adult but head and breast duller/browner, upperparts duller, underparts paler yellow. **Other subspecies** *C.c.antioxantha* (south W,S): Darker hood, duller above/on belly. **VOICE** Sharp clear *wittu-wittu-wit*, *chuit-it-ui* or *witti-wuti* etc. Calls with sharp trills/twitters. **HABITAT & BEHAVIOUR** Broadleaved forest, also parks, gardens, mangroves on passage. Up to 2,565 m (mostly breeds above 650 m). Joins bird-waves.

PLATE 92 ROBINS

JAPANESE ROBIN *Erithacus akahige* 14–15 cm

(1) **Male** *akahige*: Rufous-orange forehead, head-sides, throat and upper breast. Rufescent-brown above with brighter tail; narrow blackish gorget, broadly greyish flanks. (2) **Female**: Lower breast and flanks browner, rufous-orange of head and breast duller, less extensive; no gorget. **VOICE** Song of simple spaced, mostly quavering phrases, with a brief introduction: *hi CH'H'H'H'H'H hi-tu CH'I'I'I'I hi CH'H'H'H'H'H ts-ti CH'U'U'U'U'U tsi CHUK'CHUK'CHUK*... etc. Metallic *tsip* call. **HABITAT & BEHAVIOUR** Broadleaved evergreen forest, sometimes parks, gardens; up to 1,525 m. Skulks on/near ground.

RUFOUS-TAILED ROBIN *Luscinia sibilans* 14 cm

(3) **Adult**: Like female Siberian Blue but has strongly rufescent uppertail-coverts/tail, no buff below, usually much more distinct brownish-grey scales/scalloping on throat, breast and upper flanks. Bill black. **VOICE** Song is an accelerating silvery trill, falling slightly in pitch towards end: *tiuuuuuuuu-uuwwww*. Calls with low *tuhk* or *tupp*, sometimes quickly repeated. **HABITAT & BEHAVIOUR** Broadleaved evergreen and semi-evergreen forest; up to 1,200 m. Skulking, on or near ground.

SIBERIAN RUBYTHROAT *Luscinia calliope* 15–16.5 cm

(4) **Male non-breeding**: Red throat, white supercilium/submoustachial stripe. Blackish lores and malar line, brownish-grey breast, paler-based lower mandible; blackish throat-border and extent of grey on breast varies. (5) **Female**: Throat white (may be pink) with no blackish border, supercilium and submoustachial stripes less distinct, lores paler, breast usually browner. **Male breeding**: Breast more solidly grey, bill all black. **First-winter**: As respective (non-breeding) adult but some buff-tipped tertials and greater coverts. Males usually show browner breast than adult, females rarely shows pink on throat. **VOICE** Song is a scratchy varied warble, with much mimicry. Calls include a clear *ee-uh* or *se-ic* and deep *tschuck*. **HABITAT & BEHAVIOUR** Grass, scrub, thickets, sometimes gardens; up to 1,800 m. Skulks in dense vegetation, runs along ground, often cocks tail.

WHITE-TAILED RUBYTHROAT *Luscinia pectoralis* 15–17 cm

(6) **Male breeding** *tschebaiewi*: Resembles Siberian Rubythroat but shows mostly black breast, slatier crown, head-sides and upperparts, and blackish tail with white on base and tips of outer feathers. (7) **Male non-breeding**: Has browner crown and upperparts and grey to whitish scaling on breast. (8) **Female**: From Siberian by white spots on outer-tail-tips, colder above, distinctly grey throat-sides/breast-band. **First-winter**: As female but buff greater covert/tertial tips. Male has white on outertail base; often darker head-sides, darker breast with some black. **VOICE** Sings with complex undulating trills/twitters. Deep *tchuk* and sparrow-like *tchink* calls. **HABITAT** Grass, scrub, often near water; up to 400 m.

BLUETHROAT *Luscinia svecica* 13.5–15 cm

(9) **Male non-breeding** *svecica*: Pale underparts with scaly blue, black and rufous-red breast-bands, broad whitish supercilium and extensively rusty-rufous basal half of outertail feathers (conspicuous in flight). (10) **Male breeding**: Blue throat/breast with red patch and black border, separate rufous-red

breast-band. (11) **Female**: Rufous on outertail feathers, prominent blackish malar stripe and markings across upper breast. Older birds can show blue on throat/breast and faint rufous-red breast-band (particularly in breeding plumage). **First winter**: As respective non-breeding adults but buffish greater covert tips. **VOICE** Song is a rapid varied series of fine ringing notes, mixed with calls and mimicry. Calls with twanging *dzink* and low *tuck* or *tchak* and *tsee-tchak-tchak* etc. **HABITAT & BEHAVIOUR** Grass, thickets, usually near water; up to 760 m. Skulking but ventures into open areas; cocks tail.

BLACKTHROAT *Luscinia obscura* 12.5–14.5 cm

(12) **Male**: All-black throat/upper breast, largely white basal two-thirds of outertail feathers. Legs and feet dark. (13) **Female**: Like Siberian Blue but no obvious scales below; pale buff undertail-coverts, rufous-tinged uppertail-coverts, warm-tinged brown tail, dark bill (lower mandible slightly paler), dark (brownish-plumbeous) legs/feet. **VOICE** Sings with rather shrill, laid-back, cheerful phrases, each repeated after shortish intervals: *whr'ri-whr'ri*, *chu'ti-chu'ti* (second note higher), alternated with purring trills, *hdrriiii-ju'ju* and *uu ji'uu* etc. Contact call is a series of soft, subdued *tup* notes. **HABITAT** Dense thickets, grass, scrub, bamboo; recorded at 395 m.

SIBERIAN BLUE ROBIN *Luscinia cyane* 13.5–14.5 cm

(14) **Male** *cyane*: Dull dark blue above, white below, broad black line from lores through cheeks to breast-side. (15) **Female**: Greyish-brown above, often some blue on rump/uppertail-coverts (sometimes tail), buffish-white throat, slightly deeper buff breast and usually flanks, darker scales/mottling on throat-side/breast. Legs pinkish. (16) **First-winter female**: Often no blue on rump to uppertail, outer greater coverts tipped rufous-buff. **First-winter male**: Resembles female but rump to uppertail dull blue, usually shows some blue on scapulars and wing-coverts (sometimes most of upper-parts and all wing-coverts), has rufous-buff tips to outer greater coverts. **VOICE** Song is a loud, rapid, rather explosive *tri-tri-tri-tri*, *tjuree-tiu-tiu-tiu-tiu* etc., usually introduced by fine, spaced *sit* notes. Calls with a subdued hard *tuk*, *tak* or *dak* and louder *se-ic*. **HABITAT & BEHAVIOUR** Broadleaved evergreen and mixed deciduous forest, bamboo; parks, gardens and mangroves on migration; up to 1,500 m. Skulks on or near ground, quivers tail.

ORIENTAL MAGPIE ROBIN *Copsychus saularis* 19–21 cm

(17) **Male** *erimelas*: Glossy blackish head, upper-side and upper breast, white belly, wing-stripe and outertail. (18) **Female**: Patterned like male but black body plumage replaced by dark grey. **Juvenile**: Duller above than female, flight feathers fringed brown, wing-stripe washed buff and scaled blackish on coverts; throat/breast paler and buffier with dark greyish scales. Males are darker above. **Other subspecies** *C.s.musicus* (S). **VOICE** Varied musical song, mixed with churrs and sliding whistles: upward-inflected *si-or* or *sui-i* and lower *su-u* etc. Clear rising whistle and rasping *che'e'e'h* in alarm. **HABITAT & BEHAVIOUR** Gardens, cultivated and urban areas, open woodland, mangroves; up to 1,830 m. Conspicuous and confiding. Cocks tail sharply.

PLATE 93 ROBINS, SHAMAS & REDSTARTS

ORANGE-FLANKED BUSH ROBIN *Tarsiger cyanurus* 14 cm

(1) **Male** *rufilatus*: Deep blue above and on throat/breast-side, white below with contrasting rufous-orange flanks. Supercilium shining pale blue, rump and uppertail-coverts shining deep blue. (2) **Female/first winter**: Brown above, blue rump to uppertail, white throat-patch, rufous-orange flanks. (3) **Male** *cyanurus* (recorded NW): Lighter, almost turquoise-tinged above, paler supercilium, duller below. **First-summer male**: May show blue on lesser coverts/scapulars. **VOICE** Song is clear *didiu-diu dew dew dew dew*. Deep nasal *agag* or *rug* and high *uist* calls. **HABITAT** Broadleaved evergreen forest; 1,200–2,565 m.

GOLDEN BUSH ROBIN *Tarsiger chrysaeus* 13–14 cm

(4) **Male** *chrysaeus*: Rufous-yellow supercilium, rump, uppertail-coverts and underparts, blackish head-sides, blackish tail with largely rufous-yellow basal half of outer feathers. (5) Crown, lower mantle and back rufescent-olive (sometimes blackish on lower mantle and back). (5) **Female**: Olive above, tail as male but browner; olive-yellow eyebrow and underparts, yellowish-white eyering. **VOICE** Song is a hurried wispy *tze'du'-tee'tse* etc., then a lower, rolling *tew'r'r'r*. Purring *trrr'rr* and harder *tcheck* calls. **HABITAT & BEHAVIOUR** Thickets, broadleaved evergreen forest; 1,900–2,565 m. Usually very skulking.

WHITE-RUMPED SHAMA *Copsychus malabaricus* 21.5–28 cm (male tail to 7 cm longer than female)

(6) **Male** *interpositus*: Blue-black hood and upperparts, orange-rufous below, white rump and uppertail-coverts, long tail with extensively white outer feathers (hidden on plate). (7) **Female**: Pattern similar to male but dark greyish not blue-black, duller, paler rufous below. (8) **Juvenile**: Dark brownish above with buff streaks/speckles, brownish fringing on rump and uppertail-coverts (initially no white), rich buff tips and fringing on wings, throat/breast initially buffish with dark mottling/scaling. **Other subspecies** *C.m.pellogynus* (S). **VOICE** Very varied, rich and melodious song, with skilled mimicry. Harsh *tschack* call. **HABITAT & BEHAVIOUR** Broadleaved evergreen and mixed deciduous forest, bamboo; up to 1,525 m. Rather skulking.

RUFOUS-TAILED SHAMA *Trichixos pyrropyga* 21–22.5 cm

(9) **Male**: Rufous rump/uppertail-coverts and most of tail (shorter than female White-rumped); white eyebrow. (10) **Female**: Head-sides/upperparts grey-brown, no eyebrow, throat and rump buffy-rufous, belly whitish. (11) **Juvenile**: Like female but heavy rich buff streaks above, uppertail-coverts and tail-base buffier, extreme tip rich buff; rich buff wing-covert tips and spots on tertial tips, head-sides and throat/breast buff with dark streaks. **VOICE** Sings with loud well-spaced whistles: *whi-ii* and *whi-uuu* etc. Harsh drawn-out *tcherrr* call. **HABITAT & BEHAVIOUR** Broadleaved evergreen and freshwater swamp forest; up to 915 m. Sits still for long periods; cocks tail.

BLACK REDSTART *Phoenicurus ochruros* 16 cm

(12) **Male non-breeding** *rufiventris*: Brownish-grey crown to back, some black on mantle, blackish head-sides to breast with brownish-grey scales, blackish wings with buff fringing; no white wing-patch. (13) **Male breeding**: Head, mantle, back, breast and wings more uniformly blackish.

(14) **Female/first-year male**: Like female Daurian but no wing-patch, duller below, less distinct pale eyering. **VOICE** Song is a scratchy trill followed by a short wheezy jingle. Calls include a high-pitched *tseep* or *tsip* (repeated when agitated), scolding *tak* or *tuc* and rapid rattling *tititik*. **HABITAT** Open country; lowlands.

DAURIAN REDSTART *Phoenicurus auroreus* 15 cm

(15) **Male non-breeding/first winter** *leucopterus*: Crown to upper mantle brownish-grey, brown fringing on lower mantle, pale greyish fringing on blackish throat/breast. Otherwise orange-rufous below. Rufous rump and uppertail-coverts, rufous tail with blackish central feathers. (16) **Male breeding**: Grey crown to upper mantle, black lower mantle and throat, white wing-patch. (17) **Female**: Mostly brown; paler/warmer below, white wing-patch, obvious pale buffish eyering. Tail as male. **VOICE** Song is a scratchy trill, then a short wheezy jingle. Calls include a high *tseep* or *tsip* (repeated when agitated), scolding *tak* or *tuc* notes and rattling *tititik*. **HABITAT** Open forest, forest edge, orchards, thickets; up to 2,565 m.

BLUE-FRONTED REDSTART *Phoenicurus frontalis* 16 cm

(18) **Male non-breeding/first winter**: Dark blue hood to back, with broad pale brown fringing, orange-rufous tail with blackish centre and tip. Brighter eyebrow, rufous rump, uppertail-coverts and rest of underparts. (19) **Male breeding**: Lacks pale brown fringing to blue of plumage, wings plainer. (20) **Female**: Told by tail pattern (as male), buffy tips to greater coverts and fringes to tertials; no wing-patch. **VOICE** Sings with 1–2 trilled warbles followed by short whistled phrases; repeated with some variation. Calls with thin *ee-tit* or *ee-tit-tit* and clicking *tik*. **HABITAT** Open forest, clearings, cultivation, thickets; 1,400–2,565 m.

WHITE-CAPPED WATER REDSTART *Chaimarrornis leucocephalus* 19 cm

(21) **Adult**: Black plumage, sharply contrasting white crown and nape and chestnut-red lower body and tail-base. (22) **Juvenile**: Head-sides and upperparts browner, faintly fringed brown on mantle and back, crown duller with blackish fringes, rump blackish-brown with dull rufous fringes, tail duller/darker, blackish-brown below with drab warmish brown scales; small drab warmish brown spots on wing-covert tips and tertials. **VOICE** Song is a weak drawn-out undulating *tieu-yieu-yieu-yieu*. Calls with a loud sharp upward-inflected *tseeit* or *peeeiii*. **HABITAT & BEHAVIOUR** Rocky rivers and streams, waterfalls; 300–2,565 m. Conspicuous, cocks tail.

PLUMBEOUS WATER REDSTART *Rhyacornis fuliginosus* 15 cm

(23) **Male** *fuliginosus*: Slaty-blue with chestnut tail-coverts and tail. (24) **Female**: Dark blue-grey above, scaled grey and whitish below, wings brown with two whitish bars on coverts; white uppertail-coverts and blackish-brown tail with white basal half of outer feathers. **Juvenile**: As female but buffish-white speckles/streaks on brown upperparts/wing-coverts, buffier below and more broadly mottled, vent paler. **First-year male**: Like female. **VOICE** Song is a rapidly repeated, insect-like *streee-treee-tree-treeeh*. Sharp *peet* call notes. **HABITAT** Vicinity of rocky rivers, streams, waterfalls; 600–2,285 m.

PLATE 94 SHORTWINGS, WHITE-BELLIED REDSTART & FORKTAILS

LESSER SHORTWING *Brachypteryx leucophrys* 11.5–12.5 cm
(1) **Adult** *carolinae*: Rather nondescript. Upperside warm dark brown, underside paler and buffier with whitish centre to throat and abdomen, whitish mottling on breast and whitish undertail-coverts. Short white eyebrow distinctive (when unconcealed). Can be confused with several species, including White-browed Shortwing (female-type plumages), Rufous-browed Flycatcher, female Snowy-browed Flycatcher and Buff-breasted Babbler. Note voice, habitat, small size, short tail, long pale legs, relatively strong blackish bill, restricted whitish areas on underparts and breast-mottling. (2) **Juvenile**: Ear-coverts and upperparts a little darker with rufous to rufous-chestnut streaks; initially lacks white eyebrow, underparts more uniform buff, deeper-coloured on breast and flanks where scaled/scalloped blackish-brown, wing-coverts tipped rufous-chestnut. Males of *B.l wrayi* apparently start to acquire adult plumage during first summer. (3) **Male** *wrayi* (extreme S): Slaty-blue head-sides and upperside, white eyebrow extending further forward, brown of underparts replaced by bluish-grey (paler than upperparts). **Other subspecies** *B.l.leucophrys* (most of S?). **VOICE** Song is brief, high-pitched and melodious, with pause after first note and ending with a rapid jumble. Typical calls are a subdued hard ***tack*** or ***tuck*** and thin high-pitched whistle. **HABITAT & BEHAVIOUR** Broadleaved evergreen forest; 1,000–2,000 m. Very skulking, on or near ground.

WHITE-BROWED SHORTWING *Brachypteryx montana* 12.5–13.5 cm
(4) **Male** *cruralis*: Uniform dull dark blue plumage with clear white supercilium (almost meets on forehead when flared). Bulkier and somewhat longer-tailed than Lesser. (5) **Female**: Rather uniform brown with distinctive rufous forehead, lores, orbital area and (short, slight) supercilium. See Rufous-browed and female Snowy-browed Flycatchers. (6) **Juvenile**: Very like Lesser. Best told by more uniformly dark throat and breast, darker legs and longer tail; breast is streaked buff and tends to appear less scalloped (may be similar). (7) **First-winter male**: Like female but has white supercilium (similar to adult male) and darker lores. **VOICE** Song is a complex monotone meandering warble, usually introduced by 1–3 ***wheez*** notes. Usual call is hard ***tack***. **HABITAT & BEHAVIOUR** Broadleaved evergreen forest; 1,400–2,565 m. Skulks on or near ground.

WHITE-BELLIED REDSTART *Hodgsonius phaenicuroides* 18–18.5 cm
(8) **Male** *ichangensis*: Dark slaty-blue plumage, white belly-centre, rather long graduated blackish tail with conspicuous orange-rufous on basal half of outer feathers. Two white markings near wing-bend. (9) **Female**: Nondescript brown with paler, buffier underparts and distinctive tail (browner than male but with similar but duller rufescent panel on outer feathers). **First-winter male**: Resembles female but has brighter tail-patches (similar to adult male); starts to turn blue during first summer. **VOICE** Song is a 3–4 whistle ***teuuh-tiyou-***

tuh etc., with second note rising and falling and last note lower-pitched. Calls include subdued, deep ***tuk*** and grating ***chack*** notes. **HABITAT & BEHAVIOUR** Scrub and grass, secondary growth, open broadleaved evergreen forest and edge, bamboo; 1,200–2,565 m. Very skulking, in low vegetation; usually adopts a very horizontal posture and often cocks tail.

CHESTNUT-NAPED FORKTAIL *Enicurus ruficapillus* 19.5–21 cm
(10) **Male**: From other forktails by chestnut crown to upper mantle and dark scales on white breast. See Chestnut-capped Thrush. (11) **Female**: Has dull chestnut extending from crown to back. (12) **Juvenile**: Duller above than male, has white submoustachial stripe and throat, black malar line and ill-defined breast markings. **VOICE** Calls with thin, shrill metallic whistles and high ***dir-tee***. **HABITAT** Rivers, streams, waterfalls; up to 915 m.

BLACK-BACKED FORKTAIL *Enicurus immaculatus* 20.5–23 cm.
(13) **Adult**: Like Slaty-backed but crown and mantle black. From White-crowned by white breast and black mid-crown. (14) **Juvenile**: Ear-coverts, crown and upperparts duller and browner; no white forehead-patch, throat white, breast with faint sooty scales. **VOICE** Short, high-pitched, whistled ***zeee*** (slightly higher-pitched than Slaty-backed); sometimes preceded by hollow ***buu***. **HABITAT** Rivers and streams, waterfalls; up to 760 m.

SLATY-BACKED FORKTAIL *Enicurus schistaceus* 22.5–24.5 cm
(15) **Adult**: Black and white plumage, long forked tail, slaty-grey crown, nape and mantle. Narrow band of white on forehead. (16) **Juvenile**: Grey of upperparts tinged brown, lacks white on forehead, has white throat with greyish flecks and extensive dull greyish scales/streaks on breast and upper belly. **VOICE** Usual call is a thin shrill sharp metallic whistle: ***teenk***. **HABITAT** Vicinity of rivers, streams and waterfalls; 400–1,800 m.

WHITE-CROWNED FORKTAIL *Enicurus leschenaulti* 28–28.5 cm
(17) **Adult** *indicus*: From other forktails by combination of large size (most of range), steep white forehead, black mantle and breast, all-white rump and white tips to tail feathers. (18) **Juvenile**: Black plumage parts tinged brown; initially lacks white on forehead and crown, shows indistinct white shaft-streaks on throat and breast. **Other subspecies** *E.l.frontalis* (S): Smaller (20.5 cm) and shorter-tailed; white extends slightly further back on crown, white wing-patch smaller. **VOICE** Song is an elaborate series of high-pitched whistles: ***tsswi'i'i-lli'i'i*** etc. Usual call is a harsh, shrill, whistled ***tssee*** or ***tssee chit-chit*** etc. **HABITAT** Rivers, streams and adjacent forest, swampy forest; up to 2,000 m (below 760 m in S).

PLATE 95 ROBINS & CHATS

WHITE-TAILED ROBIN *Myiomela leucura* 17.5–19.5 cm

(1) **Male** *leucura*: Blackish plumage (tinged blue above and on belly), paler shining blue forehead, supercilium and shoulder-patch, long white line on outertail feathers. White in tail often hard to see unless tail fanned. Also has distinctive white marking on neck-side (usually concealed). See White-tailed Flycatcher. (2) **Female**: Nondescript. Upperparts cold olive-brown, underparts paler and buffish-tinged with paler buffish patch on lower throat and buffy-whitish belly-centre; has dull rufescent fringes to wing feathers and distinctive white tail-lines (like male). Small white neck-patch always concealed. See White-tailed Flycatcher. (3) **Juvenile male**: Like juvenile female but somewhat darker brown; starts to attain adult plumage during first winter/spring. **Juvenile female**: Like adult (with similar tail) but ear-coverts and upperparts darker and warmer with dark feather-tips and warm buff streaks/spots; throat and breast (initially also belly and vent) warm buffish with heavy blackish-brown scales/streaks, wing-coverts tipped warm buff. **VOICE** Song is a short, rather hurried, clear, sweet, thin, quavering warble. Calls with thin whistles and low *tuc*. **HABITAT** Broadleaved evergreen forest, bamboo; 1,000–2,285 m, occasionally down to 400 m in winter.

BLUE-FRONTED ROBIN *Cinclidium frontale* 18–20 cm

(4) **Male** *orientale*: Like White-tailed but tail longer with no white, rather ashier-blue overall (never blackish on body). Distinct light shining blue shoulder-patch, no concealed white neck-patch (both sexes). See Large Niltava. (5) **Female**: Difficult to separate from White-tailed but tail longer with no white, upperparts somewhat deeper, richer brown, underparts deeper, more russet-brown. **Juvenile**: Best separated from White-tailed by lack of white in tail. Male starts to attain adult plumage during first winter/spring. **VOICE** Sings with short melodic phrases (clearer, less watery than White-tailed): *tuuee-be-tue* and *tuu-buudy-doo* etc. Harsh buzzy *zsh-wick* in alarm. **HABITAT** Bamboo, broadleaved evergreen forest; recorded at 2,000 m.

COMMON STONECHAT *Saxicola torquata* 14 cm

(6) **Male non-breeding/first winter** *stejnegeri*: Resembles female but black feather-bases visible on head-sides and throat, lores and chin often all black. (7) **Male breeding**: Black hood, blackish upperparts and wings, broad white patch on side of nape and neck, white wing-patch, whitish rump and uppertail-coverts and orange-rufous breast. (8) **Female non-breeding**: Fresh autumn bird. Warm sandy-brown above with dark streaks, warm buffish to rufous-buff rump, uppertail-coverts and tip to dark tail, unmarked buffish underparts with paler throat and vent, and more rufescent breast, white patch on inner wing-coverts (smaller than on male). (9) **Male breeding** *przewalskii* (resident form): Slightly larger, rufous-chestnut extends to belly. (10) **Juvenile**: Similar to non-breeding female but blackish-brown above, boldly streaked and spotted buff, ear-coverts boldly marked buff, more uniform buffish below with blackish-brown streaks/mottling on breast, tail broadly tipped warm brownish. **Female breeding**: Greyer above and paler below, particularly on belly, less rufescent rump and tail-tip. **VOICE** Sings with varied scratchy, twittering, warbling notes. Calls

with hard *chack* or *tsak* notes and thin *hweet*. **HABITAT** Grass, scrub, cultivation, open areas; up to 2,000 m (breeds above 1,600 m).

PIED BUSHCHAT *Saxicola caprata* 14 cm

(11) **Male non-breeding** *burmanica*: All blackish with white rump, vent and wing-streak. Blackish plumage parts prominently fringed brownish (less so on head), rump and uppertail-coverts tipped rufous. (12) **Male breeding**: Lacks brownish fringing on black of plumage. (13) **Female non-breeding**: Darker than Common Stonechat, dark streaks below, rusty uppertail-coverts and tinge to belly, no white wing-streak. Much plainer with less distinct body-streaks than breeding. (14) **Female breeding**: Much darker than Common Stonechat, upperparts broadly dark-streaked but less contrasting, broad dark mottling/streaks on underparts (except vent). **Juvenile**: Resembles non-breeding female but body speckled pale buffish. Male is darker with blacker wings and white wing-streak. **VOICE** Song is a series of brisk whistled phrases, with short-noted introduction: roughly *hiu-hiu-hiu u'wee'wipee'chiu* etc. Calls include a clear *chep* or *chep-hee*, *chek chek trweet* and clear whistled *hew*. **HABITAT** Open areas, cultivation, grass and scrub; up to 1,600 m.

JERDON'S BUSHCHAT *Saxicola jerdoni* 15 cm

(15) **Male**: Uniform glossy blackish above, all white below. (16) **Female**: Similar to non-breeding female Grey but lacks supercilium, tail longer, without dull chestnut fringing on outer feathers, centre of underparts and undertail-coverts usually whiter. **Juvenile**: Poorly documented but apparently spotted. **VOICE** Calls with a short clear whistle. **HABITAT & BEHAVIOUR** Tall grass, scrub, particularly bordering larger rivers and lakes, seasonally exposed bushland within river channels; up to 1,650 m. Relatively skulking.

GREY BUSHCHAT *Saxicola ferrea* 14–15.5 cm

(17) **Male non-breeding**: Late autumn/early winter bird. Slaty-grey above, with broad warmish brown fringing and dark streaks, dark brown head-sides contrasting with dull whitish supercilium and throat. Brownish breast/flanks, narrow whitish wing-patch. Greater/median covert fringes usually greyer than shown. (18) **Male breeding**: Cleaner grey above, black head-sides, white supercilium and throat, greyer breast/flanks. (19) **Female non-breeding**: Autumn bird. Warmer/browner above and on breast than breeding, fainter streaks. (20) **Female breeding**: Similar to non-breeding male but uppertail-coverts rufescent, outertail feathers edged dull chestnut; has fairly distinct dark streaks above, whitish throat contrasts with dull greyish-brown breast. No white wing-patch. **Juvenile**: Like non-breeding female but ear-coverts and upperparts darker with broad buff to rufous streaks and mottling, underparts buffish (whiter on throat) with blackish-brown scalloping on breast. **VOICE** Song is a brief repeated *tree-toooh tu-treeeh-t't't't-tuhr*, with more emphatic beginning and trilled ending. Calls include a soft *churr*, often followed by a clear *hew* and harsher *bzech*. **HABITAT** Open pine and broadleaved evergreen forest, thickets, cultivation; up to 2,565 m (breeds above 1,600 m).

PLATE 96 WOODSWALLOWS & STARLINGS

ASHY WOODSWALLOW *Artamus fuscus* 16–18 cm

(1,2) **Adult**: Reminiscent of some starlings at rest but bulky head, pale bluish bill, brownish-grey plumage with paler, browner lower breast and belly, and whitish undertail-coverts and band across uppertail-coverts. In flight shows broad-based pointed wings, rather short tail and mostly pale underwing. (3) **Juvenile**: Browner above with pale brownish-white to whitish feather-tips, uppertail-coverts duller with dark bars, lower throat to belly paler with vague darker vermiculations, bill duller. **VOICE** Song is a drawn-out twittering, interspersed with harsh chattering. Calls include a sharp nasal *ma-a-a ma-a-a*... and repeated shrill, nasal *chreenk* and *chek*. **HABITAT & BEHAVIOUR** Open areas with scattered trees, cultivation, sometimes over forest; up to 1,800 m. Gregarious, often found perched in huddled groups. Spends much time gliding and circling in search of food.

ASIAN GLOSSY STARLING *Aplonis panayensis* 19–21.5 cm

(4) **Adult** *strigata*: Glossy blackish-green plumage (sometimes slightly bluish-tinged), red eyes. (5) **Juvenile**: Greyish-brown above, whitish to dull buffish-white below with bold dark streaks; eyes often paler. **VOICE** Shrill sharp ringing whistles: *tieuu* or *tseu* etc. **HABITAT & BEHAVIOUR** Coastal scrub, secondary growth, cultivation, plantations, urban areas; lowlands. Gregarious.

ROSY STARLING *Sturnus roseus* 21–24 cm

(6) **Adult non-breeding**: Dull buffish-pink plumage with contrasting blackish hood, glossy greenish-black wings and blackish tail. Bill brownish-pink, vent scaled paler, has shaggy crest. (7) **Adult breeding**: Body plumage cleaner and pinker, hood glossy purplish-black, bill pink with black base. (8) **Juvenile**: Overall pale sandy greyish-brown with darker wings and tail and paler rump and underparts; bill yellowish. Similar to White-shouldered but has paler bill, legs and feet, paler wings, paler tail with no whitish tip and slight streaking on crown and breast. **VOICE** Song is a long series of bubbling, warbling and whistled phrases. Gives a loud, clear *ki-ki-ki*... in flight and harsh *shrr* and rattling *chik-ik-ik-ik*... when foraging. **HABITAT** Open areas, scrub; lowlands.

COMMON STARLING *Sturnus vulgaris* 20.5–23 cm

(9) **Adult non-breeding** *poltaratskyi*: Blackish plumage with extensive heavy buff speckling and spotting. Bill blackish. (10) **Adult breeding**: Plumage more uniform glossy purplish- and greenish-black with only sparse pale buffish speckling on mantle to uppertail-coverts, flanks, belly and vent (sometimes restricted to vent only); bill yellow. (11) **Juvenile/first winter (transitional)**: Like non-breeding adult but with dusky-brown hood. **Juvenile**: Rather uniform dusky-brown with paler throat and vent, indistinct dark streaking on underparts and buffish-fringed wing-feathers; bill and legs dark. **VOICE** Song is a complex mixture of chirps, twittering, clicks, drawn-out whistles and skilled mimicry. Calls include a soft *prurrp* in flight, short metallic *chip* in alarm and *scree* notes when foraging. **HABITAT & BEHAVIOUR** Open country, cultivation; lowlands. Gregarious, often in company with other starlings or mynas.

WHITE-CHEEKED STARLING *Sturnus cineraceus* 24 cm

(12,13) **Male**: Blackish head and breast with mostly white forehead and ear-coverts. Rest of plumage mostly dark with white band across uppertail-coverts, paler centre of abdomen and vent, whitish-fringed secondaries and whitish tail border; bill orange with dark tip. (14) **Female**: Upperparts somewhat paler, throat paler and mixed with whitish, base colour of breast and flanks paler and browner. (15,16) **Juvenile**: Paler and browner than female, greyish-brown overall with whitish ear-coverts and throat and submoustachial stripe; bill duller, lacking obvious dark tip. From other starlings by combination of bare-part colours, rather uniform plumage and contrasting whitish ear-coverts, uppertail-covert band and tail border. **VOICE** Monotonous creaking *chir-chir-chay-cheet-cheet*... **HABITAT** Open country; lowlands.

ASIAN PIED STARLING *Sturnus contra* 22–25 cm

(17,18) **Adult** *floweri*: Black and white with rather long, pointed, red-based yellowish bill. Head, upper breast, upperparts, wings and tail mostly blackish, forecrown heavily streaked white; has white ear-coverts, narrow scapular band, uppertail-coverts and lower breast to vent. (19) **Juvenile**: Black of plumage replaced by dark brown, including entire crown; centre or whole of throat paler to whitish, pale plumage parts duller, bill uniformly brownish. **VOICE** Song recalls Common Myna but more melodious. Calls include a myna-like *cheek-cheurk*, descending *treek-treek-treek* and variety of high-pitched musical liquid notes from flocks. **HABITAT** Open areas, particularly near water, cultivation, towns; lowlands.

BLACK-COLLARED STARLING *Sturnus nigricollis* 27–30.5 cm

(20) **Adult**: Relatively large; whitish head and underparts with broad blackish collar. Bill, legs and feet blackish, prominent facial skin yellowish; upperside blackish-brown with white band across rump and uppertail-coverts and prominent white wing markings and tail border. (21,22) **Juvenile**: Lacks black collar, head and breast dull brownish, white plumage parts duller. **VOICE** Loud, shrill, harsh *tcheeuw*, *tcheeuw-tchew* and *tcheeuw-tchew-trieuw* etc. **HABITAT** Open country, scrub, cultivation, urban areas; up to 1,525 m.

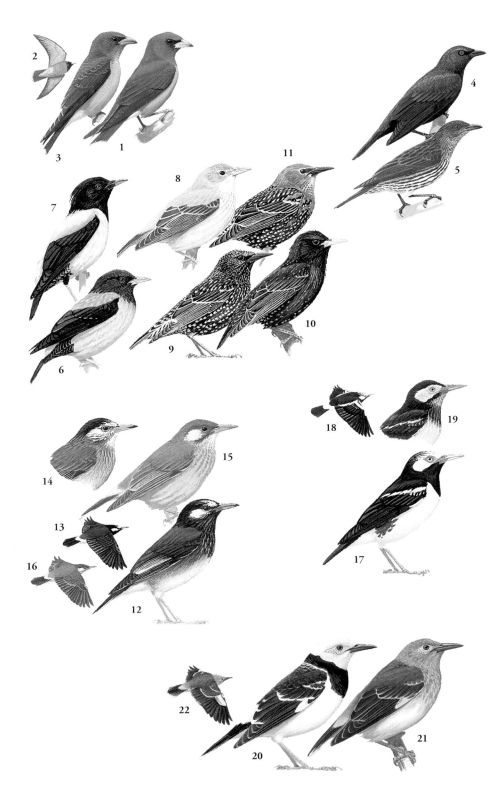

PLATE 97 STARLINGS

SPOT-WINGED STARLING *Saroglossa spiloptera* 19–20 cm

(1,2) **Male**: Greyish, dark-scaled upperparts, rufescent uppertail-coverts, breast and flanks, blackish ear-coverts, dark chestnut throat. Has pale yellow to whitish eyes and small white patch at base of primaries. (3,4) **Female**: From other starlings by slightly scaly brown upperparts, pale underparts with darker throat-streaking and breast-scaling, pale eyes and slender bill. In flight, upperparts and upperwing rather uniform, apart from small white wing-patch. **Juvenile**: Similar to female but underparts more streaked. **VOICE** Song is a continuous, harsh, unmusical jumble of dry discordant notes and some melodious warbling. Calls include a scolding ***kwerrh***, nasal ***schaik*** or ***chek*** notes and noisy chattering from flocks. **HABITAT & BEHAVIOUR** Open areas with scattered trees, open deciduous woodland, cultivation; lowlands. Gregarious; habitually feeds on nectar in flowering trees.

CHESTNUT-TAILED STARLING *Sturnus malabaricus* 18.5–20.5 cm

(5,6) **Adult** *nemoricola*: Blue-based yellowish bill, greyish-white hood, rufous-chestnut outertail feathers. Upperside greyish, with blacker primaries and primary coverts and small white area on wing-bend; rump and uppertail-coverts often tinged rufous-chestnut; underparts pale with variable amount of salmon-buff (usually restricted to belly and flanks). **Juvenile**: Similar to adult but has browner fringes to upperwing-coverts, tertials and secondaries and less rufous-chestnut on tail. **VOICE** Sharp disyllabic metallic notes and mild tremulous single whistles. **HABITAT & BEHAVIOUR** Open forest of various types, open country with scattered trees; up to 800 m. Gregarious; often feeds on nectar in flowering trees.

BRAHMINY STARLING *Sturnus pagodarum* 19–21 cm

(7) **Adult**: Blackish crown and nape, greyish upperparts, salmon-pinkish head-sides, breast and belly. Lighter breast-streaking, blue-based yellow bill. (8) **Juvenile**: Duller above, crown feathers duller, browner and shorter, underparts duller and paler with plainer breast, bill duller. **VOICE** Has short song, consisting of drawn-out gurgling sound followed by louder bubbling yodel: roughly ***gu-u-weerh-kwurti-kwee-ah***. **HABITAT & BEHAVIOUR** Dry open country; lowlands. May associate with other starlings.

PURPLE-BACKED STARLING *Sturnus sturninus* 17–19 cm

(9,10) **Male**: Pale greyish head and underparts, glossy dark purplish nape-patch and upperparts and glossy dark green upperwing, with whitish to pale buff scapular band and tips of median and greater coverts and tertials. Has blackish bill, legs and feet, pale buff uppertail-coverts and vent, glossy dark green tail, and buff fringing on flight feathers. (11,12) **Female**: Similarly patterned to male but glossy purple and green of plumage replaced with brown, crown duller and browner. **Juvenile**: Similar to female. **VOICE** Soft drawn-out ***chirrup*** or ***prrrp*** when flushed. **HABITAT & BEHAVIOUR** Secondary growth, forest edge, open areas, cultivation; lowlands. Highly gregarious, often associates with Asian Glossy.

WHITE-SHOULDERED STARLING *Sturnus sinensis* 18.5–20.5 cm

(13,14) **Male**: Mostly grey plumage, contrasting black wings (glossed dark green), blackish tail with white border, wholly white upperwing-coverts and scapulars. Has whiter rump and uppertail-coverts and mostly bluish-grey bill; whiter plumage parts occasionally washed salmon-buff. (15) **Female**: Wings almost glossless with smaller white patch, rump and uppertail-coverts duller. (16,17) **Juvenile**: Similar to female but initially lacks white wing-patch; upperparts, rump and uppertail-coverts more uniform, grey of plumage tinged brown, pale tail feather tips duller, bill duller. Combination of bare-part colour, all-dark upperwing and pale-bordered dark tail rules out similar starlings. **VOICE** Soft ***preep*** when flushed and harsh ***kaar*** when agitated. **HABITAT** Open areas with scattered trees, scrub, cultivation, coastal habitats; up to 700 m.

VINOUS-BREASTED STARLING *Sturnus burmannicus* 22–25.5 cm

(18) **Adult** *leucocephalus*: Pale grey to whitish head, narrow naked black mask, yellow to orange-yellow bill (some red at base), pale vinous-brownish underparts. Mantle, scapulars and back dark slate-grey, tail-coverts pale buffish, wings dark brownish with white patch on primary coverts and bases of primaries, tail dark with pale buffish-tipped outer feathers. (19,20) **Juvenile**: Browner overall with dull mask and bill and buffish-fringed wing feathers. Resembles Black-collared but has warmer-tinged plumage, slightly dark narrow mask and browner wings and tail. **VOICE** Similar to Black-collared. Loud, harsh ***tchew-ii***, ***tchew-tchieuw*** and ***tchew'iri-tchew'iri-tchieuw*** etc. **HABITAT** Semi-desert, dry open country, scrub, cultivation, large forest clearings; up to 1,500 m.

PLATE 98 MYNAS

COMMON MYNA *Acridotheres tristis* 24.5–27 cm

(1,2) **Adult** *tristis*: Brown plumage with greyish-black hood and whitish vent, yellow bill and facial skin. In flight, shows large white patch on primary coverts and bases of primaries, and distinctive white underwing-coverts. (3) **Juvenile**: Hood paler and more brownish-grey. Very similar to Jungle but upperparts, lower breast and belly warmer brown, shows some yellow facial skin, much larger white wing-patch and distinctive white underwing-coverts. **VOICE** Song consists of repetitive tuneless, whistled, chattering and gurgling notes: ***hee hee chirk-a chirk-a chirk-a*** and ***krr krr krr ci ri ci ri krrup krrup krrup chirri chirri chirri weeu weeu***... etc.; often combined with skilled mimicry. Typical calls include harsh, scolding ***chake-chake***... in alarm, and weak ***kwerrh*** when flushed. **HABITAT** Open areas, scrub, cultivation, urban areas; up to 1,525 m.

JUNGLE MYNA *Acridotheres fuscus* 24.5–25 cm

(4,5) **Adult** *fuscus*: Similar to White-vented but bill orange with deep bluish base, eyes yellow, crest very short; blackish head contrasts with greyer body plumage, which grades to dull whitish on undertail-coverts. In flight shows smaller white wing-patch (above and below) and mostly greyish underwing-coverts. (6) **Juvenile**: Browner overall, head less contrasting, centre of throat or whole throat slightly paler, no obvious crest, bill yellowish. From Common by greyer-brown upperparts, lower breast and belly, lack of yellow facial skin and, in flight, smaller white wing-patch and mostly dark underwing-coverts. **VOICE** Song is similar to Common. Typical calls include a repeated ***tiuck-tiuck-tiuck*** and high-pitched ***tchieu-tchieu***. **HABITAT** Open dry and grassy areas, often bordering wetlands and rivers, cultivation, roadsides; occasionally forest clearings, mangroves; up to 400 m.

WHITE-VENTED MYNA *Acridotheres grandis* 24.5–27.5 cm

(7,8) **Adult**: Yellow bill, long, floppy tufted crest, uniform slaty-black plumage with sharply contrasting white undertail-coverts. Eyes reddish-brown. In flight shows large white wing-patch (above and below), mostly blackish underwing-coverts and broadly white-tipped outertail feathers. (9) **Juvenile**: Somewhat browner overall, with no obvious crest, undertail-coverts dark brown with pale scaling, little or no white on tail-tip, bill duller. Very similar to Crested, differing primarily by yellower bill, legs and feet, somewhat paler undertail-coverts and

smaller white wing-patch. **VOICE** Song is a disjointed jumble of repeated tuneless phrases, very similar to Common but perhaps coarser and harsher. Typical calls include a high-pitched ***chuur-chuur***..., harsh ***kaar*** in alarm and soft ***piu*** when flushed. **HABITAT** Open country, cultivation, rice paddies, urban areas; lowlands.

CRESTED MYNA *Acridotheres cristatellus* 25.5–27.5 cm

(10,11) **Adult** *brevipennis*: Like White-vented but bill ivory-coloured with rosy-red flush at base of lower mandible, eyes pale orange, crest shorter and fuller, undertail-coverts black with narrow white fringes. In flight shows very large white wing-patches and narrow white tips to outertail feathers. (12) **Juvenile**: Very similar to White-vented but bill, legs and feet paler and duller, undertail-coverts darker, white wing-patch larger. **VOICE** Said to be similar to Common. **HABITAT** Open areas, scrub, cultivation, rice paddies, urban areas; lowlands.

GOLDEN-CRESTED MYNA *Ampeliceps coronatus* 22–24 cm

(13,14) **Male**: Glossy blackish plumage, yellow crown, lores, cheeks, throat and patch at base of primaries. Can be confused with Hill in flight but much smaller, wing-patch pale yellow (can appear white at distance). (15) **Female**: Yellow on head greatly reduced. (16) **Juvenile**: Duller and browner overall than female with no yellow on crown, yellowish-white lores, throat and wing-patch, and faint streaking on underparts. **VOICE** Somewhat higher-pitched and more metallic than Hill, including bell-like notes. **HABITAT & BEHAVIOUR** Broadleaved evergreen and mixed deciduous forest, forest edge and clearings; up to 800 m. Gregarious; often perches on exposed tops of tall trees.

HILL MYNA *Gracula religiosa* 27–31 cm

(17,18) **Adult** *intermedia*: Large size; glossy black plumage, heavy deep orange bill (often more yellowish at tip), connected yellow wattles on ear-coverts and nape, prominent white wing-patch. (19) **Adult** *religiosa* (S): Larger (29–34.5 cm) and thicker-billed, with separated head wattles (those on nape also longer). **Juvenile**: Duller and less glossy, shows naked pale yellow areas on head where wattles develop, bill duller. **VOICE** Extremely varied, including loud piercing whistles, screeches, croaks and wheezes. **HABITAT & BEHAVIOUR** Broadleaved evergreen and deciduous forest, forest edge and clearings; up to 1,300 m. Often seen in pairs; regularly perches in exposed tops of tall trees.

PLATE 99 NUTHATCHES, BROWN-THROATED TREECREEPER & TITS

CHESTNUT-VENTED NUTHATCH *Sitta nagaensis* 12.5–13.5 cm

(1) **Male** *montium*: From Chestnut-bellied by pale greyish-buff underparts (greyer when worn, after breeding), sharply contrasting with reddish-chestnut of lower flanks and vent. Undertail-coverts marked with white. **Female**: Lower flanks more rufous-chestnut, perhaps slightly duller buff and less grey below. **VOICE** Song is fast rattling *chichichichichi…* or *trr'r'r'r'r'r'r'ri…*; sometimes more spaced *chi-chi-chi-chi-chi…* or much slower *diu-diu-diu-diu-diu…* Calls with squeaky *sit* and drier *chit* note. Whining nasal *quir* or *kner* and hard *tsit* notes in alarm. **HABITAT & BEHAVIOUR** Broadleaved evergreen and pine forest; 1,300–2,100 m. Often in bird-waves.

CHESTNUT-BELLIED NUTHATCH *Sitta castanea* 13 cm

(2) **Male** *neglecta*: Pale buffish-chestnut below, white cheeks, white markings on mostly grey undertail-coverts. (3) **Female**: Pale, drab orange-buff below (cheeks whiter). (4) **Male** *tonkinensis* (NW; Doi Hua Mot): Darker above, deep dark reddish-chestnut below, sharply contrasting white cheeks (finely barred blackish); undertail-coverts blackish marked with white. (5) **Female**: Pale chestnut underparts with more contrasting white cheeks (more similar to male *neglecta*). **VOICE** Sings with repeated whistled *wheeu*, trilled *trilililili…* and slower *tutututu…* etc. Calls with sparrow-like *cheep-cheep-cheep…*, mellow *tui-tui-tui*, high *seet*, squeakier *vit*, full *chlip* or *chup* and rattled *sitit sidititit* (in bursts). **HABITAT & BEHAVIOUR** Dry dipterocarp and pine forest; 300–800 m (*tonkinensis* up to 1,400 m). Often in bird-waves.

VELVET-FRONTED NUTHATCH *Sitta frontalis* 12–13.5 cm

(6) **Male** *frontalis*: Red bill, violet-blue upperparts, black forehead and narrow post-ocular stripe, whitish throat and pale dull beige underparts (washed lavender on flanks, belly and vent). (7) **Female**: No black post-ocular line, slightly more cinnamon-tinged (less lilac) below, particularly breast/belly. (8) **Juvenile**: Mostly blackish bill, slightly duller above than adult, washed buffish below (no lilac), undertail-coverts pale pinkish-buff with fine dark cinnamon-brown bars. Males are slightly more orange-buff below. **Other subspecies** *S.f.saturatior* (S): Deeper cinnamon-/pinkish-buff below (washed lilac). **VOICE** Song is series of *sit* notes (lasting 1.5–2 s), sometimes running to fast rattle. Calls with stony *chit* and thinner *sit* notes, rattling *chit-it'it'it…* etc. **HABITAT & BEHAVIOUR** Various broadleaved forests; up to 1,800 m. Often associates with bird-waves.

GIANT NUTHATCH *Sitta magna* 19.5 cm

(9) **Male** *magna*: Resembles Chestnut-vented but much larger and bigger-billed, has much broader black head-bands, crown-centre paler grey than rest of upperparts; no chestnut on lower flanks, no buff wash on underparts. (10) **Female**: Underparts washed buff, head-bands duller, crown-centre less contrasting. **Juvenile**: Like female but crown mid-/drab grey with narrow dark fringing, greyer above, head-bands dark grey, tertials/greater coverts fringed warm brown. **VOICE** Calls with chuntering, rapidly repeated *gd-da-da* or *dig-er-up*; more melodic *kid-der-ku* or *ge-de-ku* (*ku* louder), or harsher *gu-drr gu-drr gu-drr*. Also, trumpet-like *naa*, and piping *kip* or *keep* notes.

HABITAT Open mature pine and mixed oak and pine forest; 1,200–1,830 m.

BEAUTIFUL NUTHATCH *Sitta formosa* 16.5 cm

(11) **Adult**: Large; black above, streaked bright blue to white on crown to mantle, broad blue band along scapulars to back/rump, black wings with two white bars, dull rufous-buff below with paler throat and head-sides. **Juvenile**: Very similar to adult but white streaks on upperparts may be bluer, underparts possibly paler and whiter, particularly breast. **VOICE** Rapid high shrill tremulous *chit'it'it'it'it'it'it'it…* (1–5 s in duration). Also a shorter, hesitant *chit-it chit-it chit-it…* and *chit'it-it*, *chirririt-it* etc. **HABITAT & BEHAVIOUR** Broadleaved evergreen forest; 1,800–2,285 m. Joins mixed-species feeding flocks.

BROWN-THROATED TREECREEPER *Certhia discolor* 15 cm

(12) **Adult** *shanensis*: Drab greyish throat and underparts, buffy vent and indistinct supercilium. **Juvenile**: Shows faint darker scaling on throat and breast. **VOICE** Song is a monotonous hesitant trotting rattle, *tchi-tchi tchi-tchi tchi-tchi tchi-tchi tchichip* etc. Calls with a loud, explosive *chit* or *tchip*, sometimes extended to a short, rattling *chi'r'r'it* and higher, thinner, softer *tsit* or *seep*. **HABITAT & BEHAVIOUR** Broadleaved evergreen forest; 1,370–2,440 m. Sometimes associates with bird-waves.

FIRE-CAPPED TIT *Cephalopyrus flammiceps* 10 cm

(13) **Male breeding** *olivaceus*: Tiny and warbler-like, yellowish-green above (yellower on rump), yellowish below, bright reddish-orange forehead-patch, faint reddish wash on chin and throat-centre. (14) **Female breeding**: Like breeding male but forehead-patch golden-olive, throat/breast dull olive-yellow. (15) **Adult non-breeding**: Like breeding female but throat whitish. Female generally rather duller than male. Recalls Yellow-browed Tit but no crest, greener above, yellowish-fringed wing-coverts/tertials, yellower below. (16) **Juvenile**: Underparts paler than non-breeding adult, rather uniform whitish, without yellow. **VOICE** Sings with 1–7 high-pitched notes: *pitsu-pitsu..*, hurried *pis-su-psisu-pissu-pissu…*, thin *tink-tink-tink-tink*, ringing *psing-psing-psing…* or sweet *tsui tsui-tsui…* Calls with high *tsit* notes and weak *whitoo-whitoo*. **HABITAT & BEHAVIOUR** Broadleaved evergreen forest, secondary growth; 1,400–2,135 m, rarely down to 400 m. Often in small flocks.

SULTAN TIT *Melanochlora sultanea* 20.5 cm

(17) **Male** *sultanea*: Large; longish tail, black with floppy-crested yellow crown and yellow lower breast to vent. (18) **Female**: Browner above (washed oily-green), head-sides/wings duller, throat/upper breast yellowish-olive. **Juvenile**: Like female but crest shorter, greater coverts finely tipped whitish, dark parts of plumage duller and glossless, throat and upper breast sooty olive-brown. **Other subspecies** *M.s.flavocristata* (W[south],NE[south-west],SE,S). **VOICE** Song is a clear mellow *piu-piu-piu-piu-piu…* Calls with stony, rattling *chi-dip* or *tji-jup* and shrill *tria-tria-tria*, *tcheery-tcheery-tcheery* and *squear-squear-squear* etc. **HABITAT & BEHAVIOUR** Various broadleaved forests; up to 1,000 m. Usually in small flocks, high in trees.

PLATE 100 TITS & MARTINS

GREAT TIT *Parus major* 14 cm

(1) **Male** *ambiguus*: Grey above, black head and ventral stripe, large white patch on head-side, small patch on nape and single broad wing-bar. Otherwise drab whitish below, pale flight-feather fringing, white on outertail. (2) **Juvenile**: Similar to female but dark parts of head duller and browner, upperparts tinged olive, head-sides and underparts may be very faintly tinged yellowish, ventral stripe much reduced. (3) **Male** *nubicolus* (NW): Yellowish-green on upper mantle, blue-grey flight feather fringes, more white on tail. **Female** Ventral stripe narrower, black of plumage may be duller. **Other subspecies** *P.m.templorum* (NE). **VOICE** Sings with combinations of 2–4 whistled notes: ***chew-a-ti chew-a-ti chew-a-ti…***, ***swee-pepe-ti swee-pepe-ti…***, ***wheat-ear wheat-ear…*** etc. Calls include metallic ***pink*** notes, thin ***tsee*** contact notes (each falling in pitch), lower ***pee*** and nasal ***tcha-tcha-tcha***, sometimes mixed with explosive ***psiu*** notes. When agitated, slowly repeated ***tsee-tsui***, rapid low ***chich-ich-ich-ich…*** and ***chur'r'r'r'rihihi***. **HABITAT** Dry dipterocarp forest, pines, mangroves, coastal scrub; 800–1,800 m (only coastal in S).

YELLOW-CHEEKED TIT *Parus spilonotus* 13.5–15.5 cm

(4) **Male** *subviridis*: Black crest (yellow at rear), yellow sides of head and underparts, black postocular stripe, bib and ventral stripe, broad whitish wing-bars. Yellowish-olive above with black scaling, flanks greyish-olive. (5) **Female**: Less black above (more uniform), bib and ventral stripe olive-yellow (sometimes absent). (6) **Juvenile male**: Crown/bib duller than adult, crest shorter, wing-bars washed yellow. Female differs similarly. **VOICE** Sings with rapidly repeated (2–6 times) ringing ***chee-chee-piu*** or ***dzi-dzi-pu*** etc. Calls with thin ***sit si-si-si***, lisping ***tsee-tsee-tsee*** and ***si-si-pudi-pudi*** and ***witch-a-witch-a-witch-a***, often combined with harsh ***chur-r'r'r'r'r***. **HABITAT & BEHAVIOUR** Broadleaved evergreen forest; 900–2,565 m. Often joins bird-waves.

YELLOW-BROWED TIT *Sylviparus modestus* 9–10 cm

(7) **Adult** *modestus*: Small and short-tailed, greyish-olive to olive-green above, pale greyish-olive below, variably washed olive-yellow to pale buffish-yellow on vent. Slight tufted crest, narrow pale yellowish-olive eyering, narrow indistinct paler bar on greater coverts, short pale yellowish eyebrow (often concealed). Could be confused with some *Phylloscopus* warblers but lacks obvious head or wing markings, bill short and stubby. **VOICE** Ringing 1–5 note ***pli-pli-pli-pli…*** or ***pili-pili-pili…*** or mellower 1–6 note ***piu-piu-piu…*** or ***tiu-tiu-tiu-tiu…***; sometimes more rapidly repeated with up to 15 notes. Contact calls include thin emphatic ***psit*** or ***tis*** and fuller ***chip*** or ***tchup***, often irregularly mixed in series. Also gives a rapid trilling ***tszizizizi, tszizizi…*** or ***sisisisisi***. **HABITAT & BEHAVIOUR** Broadleaved evergreen forest; 1,700–2,565 m. Often associates with bird-waves.

BLACK-THROATED TIT *Aegithalos concinnus* 11–11.5 cm

(8) **Adult** *pulchellus*: Very small, long tail, long black mask, white bib/neck-side with isolated black central patch, rufous-chestnut breast-band extending narrowly along flanks. Grey above, paler, drab greyish crown, whitish centre of underparts and vent, yellowish-white eyes. (9) **Juvenile**: No

throat-patch (may be mottled), row of smudges across lower throat/upper breast, paler crown. **VOICE** Song is a repeated twittering ***tir-ir-ir-ir-ir***, interspersed with well-spaced single chirping notes, or a very high thin ***tur-r-r-tait-yeat-yeat-yeat***. Contact calls are a thin ***psip psip*** and sibilant ***si-si-si-si…*** or ***si-si-si-si-li-u***. Gives a fuller ***sup*** when agitated, extending to a short rattling ***churr trrrt trrrt***. **HABITAT & BEHAVIOUR** Broadleaved evergreen forest, forest edge, secondary growth; 1,500–2,100 m. Usually in small fast-moving parties, sometimes joins bird-waves.

WHITE-EYED RIVER MARTIN *Pseudochelidon sirintarae* 15 (tail-streamers up to 9 cm more)

(10) **Adult**: Robust and big-headed with stout yellow bill, white eyes and broad eyering, all-dark underparts and white rump-band. Has long narrow streamers extending from central tail feathers. (11) **Juvenile**: Head and underparts browner with paler throat; lacks tail-streamers. **VOICE** Unknown. **HABITAT** Found in lakeside reeds during night (where possibly roosting); lowlands. Only recorded in winter at Bung Boraphet (last definite record 1980); possibly extinct.

NORTHERN HOUSE MARTIN *Delichon urbica* 13–14 cm

(12,13) **Adult** *lagopoda*: Like Asian but rump-patch whiter and larger (extends to uppertail-coverts), underparts whiter overall, has greyish-white underwing-coverts (often hard to discern in field) and more strongly forked tail. (14) **Juvenile**: Upperparts browner with pale-tipped tertials, underparts variably washed pale brownish-grey, often with duller breast-sides; shows some dark feather-centres on vent and tail-coverts. **VOICE** Sings with unstructured, chirpy twittering. Calls include a sharp ***d-gitt***, scratchy, dry twittering ***prrit*** notes and emphatic, drawn-out ***chierr*** when agitated. **HABITAT** Over forests and open areas; up to 2,565 m.

ASIAN HOUSE MARTIN *Delichon dasypus* 12–13 cm

(15,16) **Adult** *dasypus*: Very similar to Northern but uppertail-coverts and upper chin blackish, underparts sullied greyish-brown, undertail-coverts darker than belly, underwing-coverts blackish, tail less forked (often looks almost square when spread). (17) **Juvenile**: Upperparts browner, tertials tipped whitish, tail less deeply forked. **Other subspecies** *D.d.cashmiriensis* (recorded NW). **VOICE** Song is similar to Northern. Calls include a reedy ***screeeel***. **HABITAT** Over forests and open areas; up to 2,565 m.

NEPAL HOUSE MARTIN *Delichon nipalensis* 11.5–12.5 cm

(18,19) **Adult** *nipalensis*: Like Asian but somewhat smaller and more compact with almost square-cut tail, mostly dark throat (sometimes only chin), black undertail-coverts and narrower white rump-band. (20) **Juvenile**: Upperparts browner, throat and undertail-coverts mixed with whitish, breast greyish. **VOICE** Calls with high-pitched ***chi-i***. **HABITAT** Over forested and open areas, often near cliffs; recorded at c.1,400 m (could occur to highest levels).

10–20 to different scale

PLATE 101 MARTINS & SWALLOWS

SAND MARTIN *Riparia riparia* 11.5–13 cm

(1) **Adult** *ijimae*: Larger and stockier than similar Plain, underparts whitish with sharply contrasting broad brown breast-band, upperparts somewhat darker brown, tail somewhat more deeply forked. (2) **Juvenile**: Feathers of upperparts and wings fringed pale buffish to whitish (often most obvious on uppertail-coverts and tertials), throat tinged buff, rest of underparts may be less white. **VOICE** Dry rasping *trrrsh* and higher *chiir* in alarm. Probable song is harsh twittering *trrrsh trre-trre-trre-rrerrerre*... etc. **HABITAT & BEHAVIOUR** Lakes, rivers, marshes, sometimes open areas away from water; up to 800 m. Gregarious, often associates with other swallows and martins.

PLAIN MARTIN *Riparia paludicola* 10.5–12 cm

(3,4) **Adult** *chinensis*: Similar to Sand but smaller and daintier, with shallower tail-fork, no breast-band, throat and breast sullied greyish-brown, rump and uppertail-coverts noticeably paler than rest of upperparts. Throat often slightly paler than breast. **Juvenile**: Feathers of upperparts (except crown) and wings fringed warm buffish, throat and breast buffier. **VOICE** Song is a weak, high-pitched twitter. Usual calls are a subdued spluttering *chrr'r* and short, spaced, slightly explosive *chit* or *chut* notes. **HABITAT & BEHAVIOUR** Large rivers, lakes; up to 400 m. Gregarious.

DUSKY CRAG MARTIN *Hirundo concolor* 13–14 cm

(5,6) **Adult**: Uniform dark brown plumage. Throat and breast slightly paler with thin dark streaks on former, tail barely forked and with row of whitish spots (apparent when tail spread). **Juvenile**: Feathers of upperparts and wings narrowly fringed rufous-grey, throat paler with no streaks. **VOICE** Song consists of soft twittering sounds. Usually calls with soft *chit* notes. **HABITAT & BEHAVIOUR** Various habitats, normally in vicinity of cliffs, caves or buildings; up to 2,000 m. Often found in association with other swallows and martins.

BARN SWALLOW *Hirundo rustica* 15 cm (outertail feathers up to 5 cm more)

(7,8) **Adult breeding** *gutturalis*: Glossy blue-black upperside, chestnut-red forehead and throat, blue-black breast-band, all-whitish remainder of underparts and underwing-coverts, deeply forked tail. Row of whitish spots/streaks across tail, outertail feathers extend to long narrow streamers. Non-breeders lack tail-streamers, and moulting birds may be similar to juvenile. (9) **Juvenile**: As non-breeding adult but forehead and throat dull orange-buff, browner upperparts/breast-band. (10) **Adult non-breeding** *tytleri* (recorded C,SE): Pale rufous underparts and underwing-coverts. **Other subspecies** *H.r.mandschurica* (recorded NW). **VOICE** Sings with rapid twittering, mixed with croaking sound that extends to a dry rattle. Typical calls are a high-pitched sharp *vit* (often repeated), and louder, anxious *vheet vheet*... or *flitt-flitt* when agitated. **HABITAT & BEHAVIOUR** Open areas, often near water and habitation; up to 2,000 m. Often roosts in very large numbers.

PACIFIC SWALLOW *Hirundo tahitica* 13–14 cm

(11,12) **Adult** *abbotti*: Like Barn but chestnut-red of forehead more extensive, upper breast chestnut-red (without blue-black band), breast and flanks dirty greyish-brown, centres to undertail-coverts dark brown, underwing-coverts dusky brownish, tail less forked (without streamers). (13) **Juvenile**: Browner above than adult with less chestnut-red on forehead, paler throat and upper breast. **VOICE** Short, high-pitched, slightly explosive *swi* or *tswi*, sometimes in series: *tswi-tswi-tswi* etc. Also a lower *swoo*. **HABITAT** Coastal areas, often near settlements.

WIRE-TAILED SWALLOW *Hirundo smithii* 13–14 cm (tail-streamers up to 12.5 cm more)

(14) **Adult** *filifera*: Recalls Barn but has chestnut crown and completely snowy-white underparts (including throat) and underwing-coverts. Upperparts also bluer and tail square-cut, with much longer wire-like streamers. (15) **Juvenile**: Upperparts browner, crown duller and paler, throat faintly washed warm buffish. **VOICE** Has twittering song. Typical calls include *chit-chit*, and *chirrik-weet chirrik-weet*... and *chichip chichip*... in alarm. **HABITAT** Large rivers, lakes and nearby areas; up to 400 m.

RED-RUMPED SWALLOW *Hirundo daurica* 16–17 cm (tail-streamers up to 3 cm more)

(16,17) **Adult** *japonica*: Easily told from Barn by orange-rufous neck-sides and rump and dark-streaked whitish underparts (including throat). Difficult to separate from Striated (particularly *mayri*) but slightly smaller, with almost complete orange-rufous nuchal collar (narrowly interrupted on centre of nape) and somewhat narrower dark streaks on rump and underparts. Breast-streaks possibly tend to be slightly heavier than belly streaks. **Juvenile**: Duller; nuchal collar, rump and underparts paler, tertials browner and pale-tipped, tail-streamers short. **VOICE** Song is similar to Barn, but twittering lower-pitched, harsher, slower and shorter. Calls include a short nasal *djuit* or *tveyk* and sharp *kiir* notes in alarm. **HABITAT** Open areas, often near water; up to 800 m.

STRIATED SWALLOW *Hirundo striolata* 18–19 cm (tail-streamers up to 3 cm more)

(18) **Adult** *stanfordi* (resident NW,NE): Like Red-rumped but slightly larger, lacks orange-rufous nuchal collar, has much broader dark streaks on rump and underparts. Shows only a little reddish-rufous behind ear-coverts. (19) **Juvenile**: Duller above, rump paler, tertials browner and pale-tipped, tail-streamers shorter. (20) **Adult** *mayri* (winters NW): Narrower streaks on rump/underparts (only slightly broader than Red-rumped). (21) **Adult** *badia* (resident S): Larger with deep rufous-chestnut underparts and underwing-coverts. **Other subspecies** *H.s.vernayi* (resident W): Like *stanfordi* but base colour of lores, ear-coverts, upper breast, flanks and undertail-coverts reddish-rufous (rest of underparts with paler reddish-rufous wash), underpart-streaks shorter (more like spot-streaks on throat/breast). **VOICE** Sings with soft twittering notes. Calls include a loud metallic *cheenk*, long drawn-out *quitsch*, short *pin* and repeated *chi-chi-chi* in alarm. **HABITAT** Open areas (often near water), cliffs; up to 2,565 m.

PLATE 102 BULBULS

CRESTED FINCHBILL *Spizixos canifrons* 21.5 cm

(1) **Adult** *ingrami*: Relatively large, greenish above, yellowish-green below, thick pale bill and erect pointed crest. (2) **Juvenile**: Crown and crest paler, throat greener. **VOICE** Long bubbling trilled *purr-purr-prruit-prruit-prruit*... and gentle scolding bubbling *pri pri-pri prrrrrr* and *pri-pri* etc. in alarm. **HABITAT** Secondary growth, scrub and grass; 1,065–2,285 m.

STRAW-HEADED BULBUL *Pycnonotus zeylanicus* 29 cm

(3) **Adult**: Large; golden-yellowish crown and cheeks, blackish eye- and submoustachial stripes. **Juvenile**: Head duller and browner. **VOICE** Song consists of bursts of extended loud, rich and very melodious warbling. **HABITAT** Broadleaved evergreen forest, secondary growth, scrub, plantations and cultivation, sometimes mangroves; almost exclusively along banks of larger rivers and streams. Up to 245 m.

STRIATED BULBUL *Pycnonotus striatus* 23 cm

(4) **Adult** *paulus*: Yellowish-white streaking on head and body, prominent crest, yellow undertail-coverts. **VOICE** Loud repeated short jolly phrases: *chu-wip*, *chi'pi-wi* and *chit-wrrri* (slurred second note) etc. Also a harsh slurred *djrrri* or *rrri*. **HABITAT** Broadleaved evergreen forest, forest edge, secondary growth; 1,200–2,440 m.

BLACK-AND-WHITE BULBUL *Pycnonotus melanoleucus* 18 cm

(5) **Male**: Blackish-brown with mostly white wing-coverts. (6) **Juvenile**: Cold brownish plumage, darker-centred upperpart feathers and dark streaks on breast. **VOICE** Usual call is a tuneless *pet-it*. **HABITAT & BEHAVIOUR** Broadleaved evergreen forest, forest edge; up to 1,830 m. Nomadic; often frequents canopy.

BLACK-HEADED BULBUL *Pycnonotus atriceps* 18 cm

(7) **Adult**: Mostly yellowish-green, with glossy black head, blackish primaries and broad black subterminal tail-band. (8) **Adult**: Greener variant. (9) **Adult grey morph**: Neck, breast and belly grey. (10) **Juvenile**: Generally duller, head largely dull greenish. **VOICE** Song is a series of short, spaced, tuneless whistles. Calls with distinctive repeated loud chipping *chew* or *chiw*. **HABITAT** Broadleaved evergreen forest, mixed deciduous and evergreen forest, forest edge, secondary growth; up to 1,600 m.

BLACK-CRESTED BULBUL *Pycnonotus melanicterus* 18.5–19.5 cm

(11) **Adult** *caecilii* (S): Bright yellow below, glossy black head and tall crest; greenish-olive above. (12) **Juvenile**: Head duller and browner, throat mixed with olive-yellow, crest short. (13) **Adult** *johnsoni* (C,NE,SE): Deeper yellow below with red throat. **Other subspecies** *P.m.vantynei* (north NW, north-east NE), *xanthops* (north W, south NW), *auratus* (north NE), *elbeli* (islands off SE), *negatus* (south W). **VOICE** Song is a cheerful quick *whitu-whirru-wheet*, *whit-whaet-ti-whaet* and *whi-wiu* etc. **HABITAT** Broadleaved ever-

green and mixed deciduous forest, forest edge, secondary growth; up to 2,565 m.

SCALY-BREASTED BULBUL *Pycnonotus squamatus* 14–16 cm

(14) **Adult** *weberi*: Black head, white throat, white-scaled black breast and flanks, yellow undertail-coverts. **VOICE** Calls with a series of sharp, high-pitched, chinking *wit* or *tit* notes. **HABITAT & BEHAVIOUR** Broadleaved evergreen forest; up to 1,000 m. Often frequents canopy.

GREY-BELLIED BULBUL *Pycnonotus cyaniventris* 16.5 cm

(15) **Adult** *cyaniventris*: Grey head and underparts, yellow undertail-coverts, upperparts and tail olive-green. **VOICE** Clear minivet-like *pi-pi-pwi*..., *pi-pi-pwi-pwi*... etc. and subdued *wit wit wit*... contact calls. Also a slightly descending, bubbling, trilled whistle, *pi-pi-pi-pi-pi-pi-pi*. **HABITAT** Broadleaved evergreen forest, forest edge; up to 1,000 m.

RED-WHISKERED BULBUL *Pycnonotus jocosus* 18–20.5 cm

(16) **Adult** *pattani*: Tall black crest, whitish ear-coverts and underparts, red ear-patch and undertail-coverts. (17) **Juvenile**: Browner-tinged overall, crest shorter, no red ear-patch. **Other subspecies** *P.j.emeria* (W) has larger red ear-patch. **VOICE** Song is varied, lively, musical *wit-ti-waet*, *queep kwil-ya*, *queek-kay* etc. Call is a rolling *prroop*. **HABITAT** Secondary growth, scrub, cultivation; up to 1,800 m.

BROWN-BREASTED BULBUL *Pycnonotus xanthorrhous* 20 cm

(18) **Adult** *xanthorrhous*: Like Sooty-headed but browner above, brown ear-coverts and breast, little white on tail. (19) **Juvenile**: Browner and less distinctly marked. **VOICE** Song is a repeated quick simple *chirriwu'i whi'chu whirri'ui* etc. Calls with harsh *chee* notes and thinner *ti-whi*. **HABITAT** Secondary growth, scrub and grass, clearings; 1,020–2,290 m; sometimes down to 610 m.

LIGHT-VENTED BULBUL *Pycnonotus sinensis* 19 cm

(20) **Adult** *sinensis*: Undertail-coverts whitish, breast-band yellowish-grey, broad white patch from eye to nape. (21) **Juvenile**: Paler above, largely greyish-brown head, breast-band less distinct. **VOICE** Calls with short *jhieu* and *jhoit* notes (latter often doubled). **HABITAT & BEHAVIOUR** Cultivation, scrub, open woodland; up to 500 m. Often in large flocks in winter.

SOOTY-HEADED BULBUL *Pycnonotus aurigaster* 19–21 cm

(22) **Adult** *klossi*: Black cap and cheeks, whitish rump, greyish underparts and red undertail-coverts. (23) **Adult** *thais* (south C, south-west NE, SE)/*germani* (NE): Yellow undertail-coverts (red on some *thais*). **Juvenile**: Crown browner, cheeks and vent colour paler. **Other subspecies** *P.a.latouchei* (north NW), *schauenseei* (W). **VOICE** Song is a chatty *whi wi-wiwi-wiwi* (with stressed *whi*). Also, repeated clear, shrill whistled *u'whi'bi'bu* or *wh'i-i-wi* (with stressed *wh*). **HABITAT** Secondary growth, scrub, grass, forest clearings, cultivation; up to 1,830 m.

PLATE 103 BULBULS

PUFF-BACKED BULBUL *Pycnonotus eutilotus* 23 cm

(1) **Adult**: Brown above, whitish throat and under-parts, short crest. **VOICE** Song is a loud, rather high-pitched, cheerful, slurred, quavering warble: ***tchui'uui tch'i-iwi'iwi, iwu'iwi i'wu-u*** and ***tch'uwi'i'iwi*** etc. **HABITAT** Broadleaved evergreen forest, forest edge; up to 210 m. Usually frequents middle to upper storey of forest.

STRIPE-THROATED BULBUL *Pycnonotus finlaysoni* 19–20 cm

(2) **Adult** *eous*: Yellow streaks on forecrown, ear-coverts, throat and upper breast, yellow vent. (3) **Juvenile**: Crown and upperparts browner, little yellow streaking. **Other subspecies** *P.f.fin-laysoni* (S). **VOICE** Song is a throaty, measured ***whit-chu whic-ic*** and ***whit whit-tu-iwhit-whitu'tu*** etc. **HABITAT** Secondary growth, scrub, more open areas and clearings in broadleaved evergreen and mixed decid-uous and evergreen forest, forest edge; up to 1,300 m.

FLAVESCENT BULBUL *Pycnonotus flavescens* 21.5–22 cm

(4) **Adult** *vividus*: Yellowish below, greyish head, blackish crown and lores, whitish pre-ocular supercilium. (5) **Juvenile**: Browner and plainer on head and upperparts, bill paler. **VOICE** Song con-sists of jolly, rather quickly delivered 3–6 note phrases: ***joi whiti-whiti-wit, ti-chi whiti-whiti-whit-tu, chi whiti-whiti-whi-tu chitiwit*** and ***brr whiti-chu*** etc. Alarm call is a harsh rapid buzzing ***djo djo drrrrt, dreet dreet drrrr dreet-dreet***... etc. **HABITAT** Clear-ings in broadleaved evergreen forest, forest edge, secondary growth, scrub and grass; 900–2,590 m.

YELLOW-VENTED BULBUL *Pycnonotus goiavier* 20–20.5 cm

(6) **Adult** *personatus*: White supercilium and throat, dark crown, lores and bill, yellow vent. (7) **Juvenile**: Supercilium weaker, crown and bill paler. **Other subspecies** *P.g.jambu* (C,SE). **VOICE** Bubbling ***chic-chic-chic***... and ***tiddloo-tid-dloo-tiddloo***...., sharp harsh ***chwich-chwich***. **HABITAT** Coastal scrub, mangroves, secondary growth, planta-tions, cultivation; lowlands.

OLIVE-WINGED BULBUL *Pycnonotus plumosus* 20–20.5 cm

(8) **Adult** *plumosus*: Like Streak-eared but ear-streaks weaker, eyes red, bill dark; yellowish-green wing-fringes. (9) **Juvenile**: Browner overall. **VOICE** Song is a simple repeated chirruping ***whip wi-wiu wu-wurri'i*** etc. Calls include a throaty ***whip-whip***... and ***wrrh wrrh wrrh***... **HABITAT** Secondary growth, coastal scrub, mangroves; up to 610 m.

STREAK-EARED BULBUL *Pycnonotus blanfordi* 17.5–19.5 cm

(10) **Adult** *conradi*: Brownish; paler throat and belly, yellowish vent, whitish-streaked ear-coverts, pale eyes. (11) **Juvenile**: Less distinctively marked. **VOICE** Calls with harsh, rasping ***which-which-which***... and piping ***brink-brink-brink***... **HABI-TAT** Semi-desert, scrub, cultivation, gardens, urban areas, open mixed deciduous forest; up to 915 m.

CREAM-VENTED BULBUL *Pycnonotus simplex* 18 cm

(12) **Adult** *simplex*: Nondescript with whitish eyes. (13) **Juvenile**: Eyes pale brown, crown and upperparts warmer than adult. **VOICE** Subdued qua-vering ***whi-whi-whi-whi-whi***... interspersed with low ***pru-pru***, ***prrr*** and ***prr-pru***. **HABITAT** Broadleaved evergreen forest, forest edge, second-ary growth; up to 1,220 m.

RED-EYED BULBUL *Pycnonotus brunneus* 19 cm

(14) **Adult** *brunneus*: Nondescript with red eyes. (15) **Juvenile**: Eyes brownish, upperparts warmer than adult, bill paler. **VOICE** Series of high-pitched bubbling notes, the last ones rising sharply: ***pri-pri-pri-pri-pri-pit-pit***. **HABITAT** Broadleaved evergreen forest, forest edge, secondary growth; up to 1,000 m.

SPECTACLED BULBUL *Pycnonotus erythropthalmos* 16–18 cm

(16) **Adult** *erythropthalmos*: Very like Red-eyed but has orange to yellow-orange eyering, paler throat and vent. (17) **Juvenile**: Eyering duller, upperparts warmer brown. **VOICE** Distinctive, repeated, rather high-pitched mechanical ***wip-wip-wi'i'i'i***. **HABITAT** Broadleaved evergreen forest, forest edge, secondary growth; up to 900 m.

OLIVE BULBUL *Iole virescens* 19 cm

(18) **Adult** *virescens*: From Grey-eyed by dark reddish to brown eyes, typically stronger olive above, yellower below. **Juvenile**: Upperparts and wings more rufescent, undertail-coverts paler. **VOICE** Calls with a musical ***whe-ic***, like Buff-vented but less nasal than Grey-eyed. **HABITAT** Broadleaved evergreen and semi-evergreen forest; up to 915 m.

GREY-EYED BULBUL *Iole propinqua* 19–19.5 cm

(19) **Adult** *propinqua*: Small and slim; pale supercilium, yellowish below with rufous-buffish undertail-coverts. (20) **Adult** *cinnamomeoven-tris* (S): Smaller (17–18.5 cm), browner above, less yellow below (mainly on centre of abdomen). Less yellow below than Olive, darker-vented than Buff-vented. **Other subspecies** *I.p.simulator* (SE). *I.p.lekha-kuni* (W): Rather intermediate between nominate and *cin-namomeoventris* (closer to latter). **VOICE** Distinctive, loud, very nasal ***uuu-wit***, with stressed second note. *I.p.cinnamo-meoventris* is said to give a much less nasal ***prrrit***. **HABITAT** Broadleaved evergreen forest, forest edge, secondary growth; up to 1,500 m.

BUFF-VENTED BULBUL *Iole olivacea* 20–20.5 cm

(21) **Adult** *cryptus*: From Grey-eyed by browner wings, greyer underparts and buffish undertail-coverts. **VOICE** Call is a musical ***er-whit*** or ***wher-it*** with a sharper, more metallic second note, sim-ilar to Olive Bulbul but thinner, higher-pitched and less nasal than Grey-eyed. Also gives a flatter ***whirr***. **HABITAT** Broadleaved evergreen forest, secondary growth; up to 825 m.

PLATE 104 BULBULS

FINCH'S BULBUL *Alophoixus finschii* 16.5–17 cm

(1) **Adult**: Small; brownish-olive with shortish dark bill and yellow throat and vent. **Juvenile**: Very similar to adult. **VOICE** Call consists of harsh grating *scree* notes. **HABITAT** Broadleaved evergreen forest; up to 760 m.

WHITE-THROATED BULBUL *Alophoixus flaveolus* 21.5–22 cm

(2) **Adult** *burmanicus*: From Puff-throated by all-yellow breast to vent, whitish-grey lores/ear-coverts, longer crest. (3) **Juvenile**: Crown and upperparts brown, throat whitish, rest of underparts suffused brown. **VOICE** Calls similar to Puff-throated but sharper and higher-pitched: *chi-chack chi-chack chi-chack* and nasal *cheer* etc. **HABITAT & BEHAVIOUR** Broadleaved evergreen forest; up to 1,525 m. Often in small groups in middle storey of forest.

PUFF-THROATED BULBUL *Alophoixus pallidus* 22–25 cm

(4) **Adult** *henrici*: Browner below than White-throated, buffier vent, darker head-sides; darker below than Ochraceous, strong greenish-olive tinge above. **Other subspecies** *A.p.isani* (north-west NE). **VOICE** Harsh raucous abrupt *churt churt churt*..., *chutt-chutt-chutt*... and *chutt chutt chick-it chick-it*... etc. **HABITAT** Broadleaved evergreen forest; up to 1,450 m.

OCHRACEOUS BULBUL *Alophoixus ochraceus* 19–22 cm

(5) **Adult** *sacculatus*: Like Puff-throated but slightly smaller and shorter-crested, browner above, no yellow below. **Juvenile**: Wings/tail more rufescent. **Other subspecies** *A.o.cambodianus* (SE), *ochraceus* (south W), *sordidus* (S). **VOICE** Raucous *chrrt chrrt chrrt*..., *chik-chik-chik-chik* and *chit'it-chit'it-chit'it-it* (higher *it* notes), often preceded by distinctive nasal *eeyi* and *iiwu*. **HABITAT** Middle storey of broadleaved evergreen forest; up to 1,525 m.

GREY-CHEEKED BULBUL *Alophoixus bres* 21.5–22 cm

(6) **Adult** *tephrogenys*: No obvious crest, grey head-sides, olive wash across breast. **Juvenile**: Wings more rufescent-tinged, head-sides brown-tinged. **VOICE** Variable. Sings with well-structured mournful phrases: *whi'u wiu iwi* and *iiu you yuwi* etc., regularly followed by shriller, high-pitched, discordant *ii-wi tchiu-tchiu*, *whii wi witchi-witchi-witchi* and *iiu witchu witchu* etc. Also utters a clear *prii chiu chew chew* and longer *uu-ii-chewi-chew-chew-chew*, interspersed with rattled *trrit* notes. **HABITAT** Broadleaved evergreen forest; up to 915 m.

YELLOW-BELLIED BULBUL *Alophoixus phaeocephalus* 20–20.5 cm

(7) **Adult** *phaeocephalus*: Bluish-grey head, whitish-grey lores, white throat and bright yellow underparts. **VOICE** Calls with subdued, harsh, slightly buzzy *whi'ee whi'ee whi'ee*... **HABITAT** Broadleaved evergreen forest; up to 915 m. Usually frequents lower storey of forest.

HAIRY-BACKED BULBUL *Tricholestes criniger* 16.5–17 cm

(8) **Adult** *criniger*: Relatively small; broad yellowish orbital area, breast mottled greyish-olive, vent yellow. **VOICE** Presumed song consists of scratchy, chattering warbled phrases, interspersed with a quavering *whirrrh*. Also utters a long, fairly high-pitched, husky, rising whistle: *whiiii* (repeated at longish intervals). **HABITAT** Broadleaved evergreen forest; up to 915 m. Usually in lower to mid-storey of forest.

STREAKED BULBUL *Ixos malaccensis* 23 cm

(9) **Adult**: Olive upperparts, greyish throat and breast with narrow whitish streaks, white vent. (10) **Juvenile**: Upperparts warm rufescent-brown, breast less distinctly streaked. **VOICE** Sings with simple, short, rather high-pitched, slightly descending phrases: *chiri-chiri-chu* and *chiru-chiru* etc. Call is a loud, harsh rattle. **HABITAT** Broadleaved evergreen forest; up to 915 m. Usually in canopy.

ASHY BULBUL *Hemixos flavala* 20.5–21 cm

(11) **Adult** *hildebrandi*: Black crown/face, brown ear-coverts, grey above, yellowish wing-panel, grey-washed breast. (12) **Adult** *cinereus* (S): Plainer and browner above, black patch on lores/cheeks, plain wings. **Juvenile**: Browner above. **Other subspecies** *H.f.davisoni* (W) is browner above; *bourdellei* (NE) has blacker crown. **VOICE** Sings with rather high *ii-wit'ti-ui* etc. (second note higher). Calls with ringing nasal *tree-tree-tree*... **HABITAT** Upper middle storey and canopy of broadleaved evergreen forest, forest edge; up to 2,100 m (mostly above 600 m).

MOUNTAIN BULBUL *Hypsipetes mcclellandii* 21–24 cm

(13) **Adult** *tickelli*: Greenish-olive above, whitish streaks on shaggy crown, throat and upper breast, yellow vent. **Juvenile**: Browner above, wings duller and browner; crown less shaggy. **Other subspecies** *H.m.loquax* (east NW, north-west NE), *peracensis* (S). **VOICE** Calls with a repeated shrill, squawking *cheu* or *tscheu* and *tchi-chitu*. **HABITAT & BEHAVIOUR** Broadleaved evergreen forest; 800–2,590 m. Puffs out throat.

BLACK BULBUL *Hypsipetes leucocephalus* 23.5–26.5 cm

(14) **Adult** *concolor* (resident): Blackish-grey (greyer below), red bill and legs. (15) **Juvenile**: Browner overall. (16) **Adult** *stresemanni* (visitor NW,NE): All-white head. (17) **Adult** *leucothorax* (visitor NW,NE): All-white head and breast. **Other subspecies** *H.l.sinensis* (visitor NE): Blacker (often all black); greyer breast to vent sometimes as grey. **VOICE** Sings with rather discordant 4–5 note *trip wi tit-i-whi* etc (*wi/whi* notes higher). Calls include mewing whistled *hwieeer*. **HABITAT & BEHAVIOUR** Broadleaved evergreen and mixed deciduous forests; 500–2,565 m, down to 120 m in winter. Often in large flocks.

WHITE-HEADED BULBUL *Hypsipetes thompsoni* 20 cm

(18) **Adult**: Body paler grey than any race of Black, undertail-coverts rufous-chestnut, lores black. (19) **Juvenile**: Browner overall, head brownish-grey. **VOICE** Sings with squeaky rhythmic *chit-chiriu chit-chiriu*... etc. **HABITAT** Secondary forest, scrub and grass with scattered trees, edge of broadleaved evergreen forest; 900–2,135 m.

PLATE 105 GOLDEN-BELLIED GERYGONE, CISTICOLAS, PRINIAS, GRASSBIRDS & LESSER WHITETHROAT

GOLDEN-BELLIED GERYGONE *Gerygone sulphurea*
10–10.5 cm

(1) **Adult** Most likely to be confused with certain warblers and female sunbirds. Told by rather short straight blackish bill, plain greyish-brown upperparts, pale yellow underparts and whitish lores and subterminal spots on tail feathers. Darker cheeks/head-sides contrast sharply with yellow throat. (2) **Juvenile**: Narrow whitish eyering, plain greyish-brown head-sides, slightly paler below, pinkish bill-base. **VOICE** Song consists of up to ten high-pitched musical, wheezy, glissading, rising or descending whistles: *zweee*, *zrriii* and *zriii'i'i'i'uu* etc. Call is a musical, rising *chu-whee*. **HABITAT** Mangroves, coastal scrub, also inland in plantations (particularly rubber), swamp forest, sometimes other types of forest, secondary growth; lowlands.

ZITTING CISTICOLA *Cisticola juncidis* 10.5–12 cm

(3) **Adult non-breeding** *malaya*: Buffish-brown above with blackish streaks, rufescent rump, blackish subterminal markings and broad white tips on tail; whitish below, buff-washed breast/flanks. Supercilium whiter than non-breeding Bright-headed, nape duller, tail-tips whiter. Much smaller than Rusty-rumped Warbler, finer-billed. (4) **Adult breeding**: Crown/mantle quite uniform with broader dark streaks, tail paler/warmer, slightly shorter. (5) **Juvenile**: Upperparts intermediate between non-breeding and breeding adult, underparts washed light yellow. **VOICE** Monotonous clicking *dzip dzip dzip dzip*... or *pip pip pip*... song. Calls are *chipp* or *plit* notes. **HABITAT & BEHAVIOUR** Rice fields, marshes, grassland; lowlands. Skulks but has weak undulating, often wide-circling song-flight.

BRIGHT-HEADED CISTICOLA *Cisticola exilis* 9.5–11.5 cm

(6) **Male breeding** *equicaudata*: Unstreaked golden-rufous crown and rich buff breast; tail much shorter. (7) **Female breeding**: Like non-breeding but rump and uppertail-coverts plainer. (8) **Juvenile**: Like non-breeding female but upperparts and wing-feather fringes somewhat browner, underparts distinctly pale yellow, washed buff on flanks. **Non-breeding**: Male has longer tail than female. Hard to separate from Zitting but shows distinctive rufescent supercilium, nuchal collar and neck-sides, and duller brownish-white tail-tips. **VOICE** Song consists of one or two comical jolly doubled notes introduced by a long buzzy wheeze (often repeated on its own): *bzzzeeee joo-ee, bzzzeeee joo-ee di-di* and *bzzzeeee-dji-shiwi joo-ee* etc.; sometimes shorter *trrrt joo-ee*. **HABITAT & BEHAVIOUR** Tall vegetation in marshes, grassland with bushes, sometimes dry croplands; up to 800 m. Skulking. Has short song-flight but often sings from perch.

BROWN PRINIA *Prinia polychroa* 14.5–18 cm

(9) **Adult non-breeding** *cooki*: Resembles Plain but larger, with indistinct supercilium and dark streaks on crown and mantle. Bill brown. (10) **Adult breeding**: Greyer and less distinctly streaked above than non-breeding. Bill black (male only?). (11) **Juvenile**: Much more uniform above than adult breeding, very indistinct streaking above (restricted to forecrown or almost absent); upperparts, tail and wings warmer. Shows slight yellowish tinge to underparts. **VOICE** Sings with monotonous wheezy *ts'weu-ts'weu-ts'weu-*

ts'weu-ts'weu... or *tis'iyu-tis'iyu-tis'iyu*... Also, loud *chii* or *chiu* and *hu'ee* notes. **HABITAT** Grass and undergrowth in dry dipterocarp and pine forest; up to 800 m.

HILL PRINIA *Prinia atrogularis* 15–20.5 cm

(12) **Adult breeding** *erythropleura*: Relatively large, plain above, white supercilium, greyish head-sides, sparse dark breast-streaking, very long tail (longest late winter/spring, shortest when worn, during/after breeding). (13) **Adult non-breeding**: Breast more extensively and prominently streaked. **Juvenile**: Like non-breeding adult but upperparts, tail and wings warmer, breast-streaking diffuse and smudgy. **VOICE** Sings with a loud, clear *thew thew thew*..., faster *thew-thew-thew-thew-thew*... and *cher-cher-cher-cher-cher*... Also utters a higher-pitched *twi twi twi-chew twi twi-chew*... and *twi-twi-twi*... etc. **HABITAT & BEHAVIOUR** Grass and scrub, bracken-covered slopes, overgrown clearings; 900–2,565 m. Skulking.

STRIATED GRASSBIRD *Megalurus palustris* Male 25–28 cm, female 21.5–24 cm

(14) **Adult (female)** *toklao*: Told by size, long graduated pointed tail, buffish-brown upperside with heavy dark streaks, prominent white supercilium, largely whitish underparts with fine dark streaks on breast/flanks. (15) **Juvenile**: Supercilium and underparts washed yellow, streaking on breast and flanks fainter, bill paler. **VOICE** Song consists of loud, rich, fluty warbling notes. Call is an explosive *pwit*. **HABITAT & BEHAVIOUR** Marshlands with clumps of tall grass and reeds, scrub, sometimes in drier areas; up to 400 m. Often perches in open. Has high-soaring and parachuting song-flight.

RUFOUS-RUMPED GRASSBIRD *Graminicola bengalensis* 16–18 cm

(16) **Adult** *striata*: Resembles Rusty-rumped Warbler but larger, tail blackish with broad white crescent-shaped tips (prominent from below), undertail-coverts much shorter; broader blackish mantle-streaks, contrasting with plain rufous rump/uppertail-coverts, distinctive white streaks on neck/nape-side and relatively shorter, thicker bill. (17) **Juvenile**: Buff streaks on crown/mantle warmer and dark streaking above duller, paler rufous wing-fringing. **VOICE** Probable song is high *er-wi-wi-wi* or *bzz-wi-wi-wi you-wuoo yu-wuoo*, then call-notes or *er-wit-wit-wit*, ending with odd wheezy sounds. Calls with scolding *err-err-err-errrr* and *jjjerrreah* etc. **HABITAT & BEHAVIOUR** Tall vegetation in/by freshwater marshes/swamps or rivers; lowlands. Skulking; typically perches upright on grass-/reed-stems.

LESSER WHITETHROAT *Sylvia curruca* 14 cm

(18) **Adult** *blythi*: Rather dark grey crown, contrastingly darker lores and ear-coverts and rather square-ended tail with prominent white on outer feathers distinctive. Shows greyish-brown remainder of upperparts and whitish underparts, with greyish-brown wash on flanks. (19) **First winter**: As adult but crown sullied brownish, less blackish lores/ear-coverts, narrow pale supercilium. **VOICE** Song is a rather low-pitched scratchy warble often followed by a dry throbbing rattle. Calls with a fairly subdued dry *tett*, similar to Dusky Warbler. **HABITAT** Scrub and secondary growth in more open areas; up to 1,300 m.

216

PLATE 106 PRINIAS & TAILORBIRDS

RUFESCENT PRINIA *Prinia rufescens* 10.5–12.5 cm

(1) **Adult non-breeding** *beavani*: Small; plain rufescent mantle, strongly graduated tail with pale-tipped feathers. Bill slightly thicker than Grey-breasted, has buffier flanks and vent, longer supercilium. (2) **Adult breeding**: Head mostly slaty-grey. **Juvenile**: Crown more olive than non-breeding adult, yellow tinge below, warmer wing-fringing. **Other subspecies** *P.r.objurgans* (SE), *peninsularis* (S), *extrema* (extreme S): All darker above, slightly darker grey crown/nape. **VOICE** Rhythmic *ti'chew-ti'chew-ti'chew-ti'chew*... and rapid *chewp'chewp'chewp'chewp'*... Buzzing *peez-eez-eez-eez* and single *tchi* calls. **HABITAT & BEHAVIOUR** Undergrowth in open forests, grass, scrub; up to 1,600 m. In small parties.

GREY-BREASTED PRINIA *Prinia hodgsonii* 10–12 cm

(3) **Adult non-breeding** *erro*: Like Rufescent (which see for differences); often greyish on neck-sides/breast. (4) **Adult breeding**: Dark grey head and broad breast-band, whitish throat and belly. (5) **Juvenile**: Like non-breeding adult but more rufescent above, bill pale. **VOICE** Song is a repeated *ti swii-swii-swii-swii*, each *swii* louder than last. Also bouts of rapid scratchy warbling, mixed with thin *tee-tsi* and *tir tir tir*... Calls include a high-pitched *ti-chu* and laughing *bee-bee-bee-bee*. **HABITAT & BEHAVIOUR** Dry grassland, scrub, secondary growth; up to 1,525 m. Usually in small hyperactive flocks.

YELLOW-BELLIED PRINIA *Prinia flaviventris* 12–14.5 cm

(6) **Adult** *delacouri*: Greyish head, greenish mantle, whitish throat and breast, yellow belly and vent. (7) **Juvenile**: Plain rufescent olive-brown above, pale yellow below and on supercilium, buffier flanks. **Other subspecies** *P.f.rafflesi* (S). **VOICE** Song is a repetitive, rhythmic, descending, chuckling *didli-idli-u didli-idli-u didli-idli-u*... Call is a drawn-out mewing *pzeeew*. **HABITAT & BEHAVIOUR** Reeds and grass mainly in marshes, coastal scrub and landward edge of mangroves; up to 800 m. Skulks; makes curious snapping sound with wings.

PLAIN PRINIA *Prinia inornata* 13.5–15 cm

(8) **Adult** *herberti*: Long supercilium. Larger/longer-tailed than Rufescent, smaller/plainer above than Brown. (9) **Juvenile**: Like adult but warmer above, rufescent wing-fringing, faintly washed yellowish below. (10) **Adult non-breeding** *blanfordi* (NW): Rich buff below, warmer above, long tail (breeding as adult *herberti*). **VOICE** Song is a monotonous rattling buzzing *jit-it-it-it-it-it-it* or *jirt'jirt'jirt'jirt'jirt'jirt*... Calls include a clear *tee-tee-tee* and nasal *beep*. **HABITAT & BEHAVIOUR** Grass, reeds and scrub, usually in marshy areas, rice paddies, landward edge of mangroves; up to 800 m. Less skulking than most prinias; makes wing-snapping sounds.

MOUNTAIN TAILORBIRD *Orthotomus cuculatus* 11.5–12 cm

(11) **Adult** *coronatus*: Rufous forecrown, yellowish-white supercilium, dark eyestripe, yellow belly and vent. (12) **Juvenile**: Uniform dull green above, grey of hindcrown/nape duller, head-side pattern fainter with yellower supercilium, more uniform/duller yellow below. Lacks grey on crown of adult Yellow-bellied Warbler, bill longer. **Other subspecies**

O.c.thais (S). *O.c.malayanus* (probably this race extreme S): Rufous-chestnut on forecrown, more extensive darker grey on hindcrown and nape, deeper green above. **VOICE** Sings with 4–6 very high-pitched notes, glissading up and down the scale (usually introduced by 1–2 short notes). Gives thin *trrit* notes when agitated. **HABITAT** Undergrowth in broadleaved evergreen forest, bamboo, forest edge, scrub; 1,000–2,000 m.

COMMON TAILORBIRD *Orthotomus sutorius* 11–13 cm

(13) **Male breeding** *inexpectatus*: Rufescent forecrown, pale below (including vent), long bill and tail. (14) **Female**: Shorter tail (male non-breeding similar). (15) **Adult** *maculicollis* (southern S): Darker above, darker grey nape, ear-coverts and streaks on breast-sides. **Juvenile**: Crown initially all green. **VOICE** Explosive *chee-yup chee-yup chee-yup*..., *pitchik-pitchik-pitchik*... or *te-chi te-chi te-chi te-chi*... etc. Calls are repeated *pit-pit-pit*... and quick *cheep-cheep*... **HABITAT & BEHAVIOUR** Gardens, cultivation edge, open deciduous woodland, mangroves; up to 1,525 m. Cocks tail; quite skulking.

DARK-NECKED TAILORBIRD *Orthotomus atrogularis* 10.5–12 cm

(16) **Male breeding** *nitidus*: Lacks supercilium of Common, lower throat/upper breast solidly dark, vent and wing-bend yellow. (17) **Female**: Weak dark streaks on throat/breast (non-breeding male similar but throat-/breast-streaks stronger). (18) **Juvenile**: Duller above than female, rufous on crown initially lacking. **Other subspecies** *O.a.atrogularis* (S). **VOICE** Staccato nasal high *kri'i'i'i'i* and short *tew* notes. Staccato trilled *churrrit churrrit churrrit-churrrit* and *tittttrrrt tittttrrrt* etc.; ringing *prrrp-prrrp*. **HABITAT & BEHAVIOUR** Broadleaved forest, secondary growth/scrub, mangroves, rarely parks/gardens; up to 1,200 m. Behaves as Common.

RUFOUS-TAILED TAILORBIRD *Orthotomus sericeus* 12–13.5 cm

(19) **Adult** *hesperius*: Rufous-chestnut crown, dull rufous tail, grey upperparts, mostly whitish underside. (20) **Juvenile**: Little rufous-chestnut on crown, browner than adult above, tail paler. **VOICE** Song consists of rapidly repeated loud couplets with stressed first note: *chop-wir*, *chik-wir*, *tu-twik* and *prui-chir* etc. Partner joins in with monotonous *u'u'u'u'u'u*... Also a high-pitched wheezy *tzee-tzee-tzee*... **HABITAT** Forest edge, secondary growth, overgrown clearings, locally edge of cultivation and mangroves, dense gardens; up to 400 m.

ASHY TAILORBIRD *Orthotomus ruficeps* 11–12 cm

(21) **Male** *cineraceus*: Rufous 'face', dark grey throat, breast and flanks. (22) **Female**: Mostly whitish on centre of underparts. (23) **Juvenile**: Browner above without rufous, like female below but more washed out. **VOICE** Song is a repetitive *chip-wii-chip chip-wii-chip*... (first note brief, second stressed) and *chu-iip chu-iip chu-iip* (second note of couplet stressed). Calls with spluttering trilled *prrrrt*, rolling *prii'u* and harsh *thieu* notes etc. **HABITAT** Mangroves, coastal scrub, peatswamp forest, rarely inland forest; all habitats on certain islands. Lowlands.

PLATE 107 TESIAS, ASIAN STUBTAIL, BUSH WARBLERS & REED WARBLERS

CHESTNUT-HEADED TESIA *Tesia castaneocoronata* 9 cm

(1) **Adult** *castaneocoronata*: Almost tail-less; chestnut head, mostly yellow below, whitish patch behind eye. (2) **Juvenile**: Darker and browner above, dark rufous below. **VOICE** Sings with short phrases recalling Slaty-bellied but less hurried, more structured and without introductory notes: fairly quick *ti tisu-eei* and simpler *si tchui* etc. Calls with high shrill explosive *whit* (often doubled) and sharp stony *tit* notes. **HABITAT** Undergrowth in broadleaved evergreen forest, secondary growth, often near streams; 1,400–2,565 m.

SLATY-BELLIED TESIA *Tesia olivea* 9 cm

(3) **Adult**: Dark olive-green above, golden-yellow wash on crown, dark slaty-grey below, orange lower mandible. **Juvenile**: Said to be more uniform dull olive-green below than Grey-bellied. **VOICE** Song recalls Grey-bellied but phrases longer, more tuneless/jumbled, preceded by 4–11 irregular, more spaced introductory notes. Call is a spluttering: *trrrrt trrrrt trrrrt...* **HABITAT** Undergrowth in broadleaved evergreen forest, mainly near streams; 900–2,565 m.

GREY-BELLIED TESIA *Tesia cyaniventer* 8.5–10 cm

(4) **Adult**: Olive-green crown, yellowish supercilium, paler below than Slaty-bellied, dull yellowish lower mandible. (5) **Juvenile**: Dark brown above, supercilium and eyestripe duller, drab olive below. **VOICE** Song of loud rich slurred phrases, introduced by short spaced high notes: *ji ji ju ju ju-chewit* and *ji ji ji'wi-jui* etc. Rattling *trrrrrrk* call notes. **HABITAT** As Slaty-bellied; above 1,000 m (locally down to 500 m in winter).

ASIAN STUBTAIL *Urosphena squameiceps* 9.5–10 cm

(6) **Adult**: Very small, short-tailed; long buffy-whitish supercilium, black eyestripe, dark upperside, pale pinkish legs. **VOICE** Song is a repeated, extremely high-pitched, insect-like *si'i'i'i'i'i'i...* Also a slower *si-si-si-si-si-si-si...*, gradually rising in volume. Calls with sharp *sit* notes in alarm. **HABITAT & BEHAVIOUR** Undergrowth in broadleaved evergreen and mixed deciduous forest, bamboo; up to 2,000 m. Always on or close to ground; shy.

PALE-FOOTED BUSH WARBLER *Cettia pallidipes* 11–12 cm

(7) **Adult** *laurentei*: Striking pale supercilium and blackish eyestripe, cold olive-tinged upperparts, square-ended tail, whitish underparts, pale pinkish legs. **VOICE** Song is a sudden loud explosive jumbled series of chattering notes: roughly *wi wi-chi'ti'ti'chi* etc. Calls with short *chik* or *chip* notes. **HABITAT & BEHAVIOUR** Grass and scrub, sometimes in open broadleaved evergreen and pine forest, bracken-covered slopes; 1,200–1,800 m. Very skulking, in thick low vegetation.

CHESTNUT-CROWNED BUSH WARBLER *Cettia major* 13 cm

(8) **Adult**: Like Pale-footed but has rufescent-chestnut crown and nape, darker upperparts, breast and flanks. From smaller Grey-sided by rufescent lores, buffier supercilium, whiter underparts. **VOICE** Sings with rather hurried, shrill, slightly slurred *i i-wi-wi-wirri-wi*. Call is apparently very similar to Grey-sided. **HABITAT** Grass and scrub near wet areas, sometimes under open forest; 1,500–2,200 m; may occur lower.

ABERRANT BUSH WARBLER *Cettia flavolivacea* 12–13 cm

(9) **Adult** *intricata*: Relatively slim and long-tailed, slightly greenish-tinged olive-brown above, slightly paler warm olive rump and uppertail-coverts, faint yellowish wash on pale buffish supercilium and underparts. **VOICE** Song is a very distinctive thin wispy *it-it-uee'uee*, with rising *uee* notes. Calls with mixture of short, quickly repeated metallic *tit* and *trrt* notes. **HABITAT & BEHAVIOUR** Scrub and grass bordering broadleaved evergreen forest, overgrown clearings, sometimes undergrowth and bamboo inside forest; 1,200–2,565 m. Skulking. Flicks wings in alarm, flashing pale underwing-coverts.

BLACK-BROWED REED WARBLER *Acrocephalus bistrigiceps* 13.5–14 cm

(10) **Adult (worn)**: Paler and more greyish-olive than fresh adult. (11) **Adult (fresh)**: Long broad buffy-white supercilium, blackish lateral crown-stripe, warm olive-brown crown and upperparts, whitish below with warm buff breast-sides and flanks. **VOICE** Sings with quickly repeated short phrases, mixed with rasping and churring notes. Calls with clucking *chuc* notes. **HABITAT** Emergent vegetation and scrub in and around marshes, rice-paddy edges, sometimes drier areas on passage; up to 800 m.

PADDYFIELD WARBLER *Acrocephalus agricola* 13–14.5 cm

(12) **Adult (worn)**: Slightly greyer above and less rufescent on rump than fresh adult. (13) **Adult (fresh)**: Like Blunt-winged but supercilium extends further behind eye, and often bordered above by a faint dark line, bill shorter with dark tip to lower mandible, has longer primary projection. **VOICE** Sings with rich warbling, interspersed with squeakier higher-pitched notes; richer, more varied and slightly slower (less forced) than Black-browed. Calls with a soft *dzak* or *tack*, fairly gentle *trrrr* notes and rather harsh, nasal *cheeer*. **HABITAT** Reedbeds, emergent vegetation in freshwater marshes, lake borders; up to 400 m.

MANCHURIAN REED WARBLER *Acrocephalus tangorum* 13–14.5 cm

(14) **Adult (worn)**: Like Black-browed but bill longer, darker greyish-brown upperparts, thin dark line above supercilium. Darker above than Paddyfield, more prominent dark line above supercilium. (15) **Adult (fresh)**: Like Paddyfield but longer bill usually has completely dark lower mandible, has stronger blackish line on crown-side, usually more rufescent above. **VOICE** Similar to Paddyfield. **HABITAT** Reedbeds and emergent vegetation in freshwater marshes, lake borders; lowlands.

BLUNT-WINGED WARBLER *Acrocephalus concinens* 14–14.5 cm

(16) **Adult (worn)** *concinens*: Greyer above than fresh adult (rump warm-tinged). (17) **Adult (fresh)**: Relatively long bill with all-pale lower mandible, short supercilium, no dark line on crown-side, short primary projection. **VOICE** Song is relatively slow/deep (rhythm/quality may recall miniature Oriental Reed), broken into short repeated phrases and including some fairly deep churring notes. Calls are a short, quiet *tcheck* and soft drawn-out *churrr*. **HABITAT** Tall grass and reeds, usually near water; up to 800 m.

1–5 to different scale

PLATE 108 BUSH WARBLERS, *LOCUSTELLA* WARBLERS & REED WARBLERS

MANCHURIAN BUSH WARBLER *Cettia canturians*
Male 18 cm, female 15 cm

(1) **Male**: Large size, broad dark eyestripe and buffish-white supercilium (buffier in front of eye), rufous forecrown. Otherwise warm brown above, pale buffish below, greyer-washed ear-coverts and flanks, whiter throat and belly. (2) **Female**: Smaller; possibly buffier below. **VOICE** Song is a loud short fluty warble, usually introduced by a slurred liquid crescendo: ***wrrrrr-whuchiuchi*** etc. Calls with stony ***tchet tchet tchet***..., sometimes interspersed with short rattling ***trrrt*** notes. **HABITAT & BEHAVIOUR** Scrub, secondary growth, cultivation borders, bamboo, forest edge; up to 1,500 m. Fairly skulking.

SPOTTED BUSH WARBLER *Bradypterus thoracicus*
13–14 cm

(3) **Adult** *suschkini* (syn. *shanensis*): Cold dark brown upperside, dark speckles on lower throat and upper breast, contrasting white undertail-covert tips. (4) **Adult variant**: Weakly spotted individual. **VOICE** Song is a monotonous ***dzzzzr dzzzzr dzzzzr dzzzzr***... Calls with low ***tuk*** and ***rrtuk*** notes. **HABITAT & BEHAVIOUR** Tall grass, scrub and weeds in open areas (often near water); up to 1,400 m. Very skulking, on or close to ground.

CHINESE BUSH WARBLER *Bradypterus tacsanowskius*
14 cm

(5) **Adult**: Relatively long-tailed; greyish-olive upperparts, plain-looking undertail-coverts (faintly darker centres may be visible at close range), pale lower mandible, no speckling on throat or breast. (6) **First winter**: Supercilium and underparts washed yellow, often light speckling on throat/upper breast. **VOICE** Song is a monotonous, husky, crackling insect-like ***bhhhhht bhhhhht bhhhhht bhhhhhht***... **HABITAT** Tall grass, reeds and scrub, particularly in alluvial plains; up to 500 m.

BROWN BUSH WARBLER *Bradypterus luteoventris*
14–14.5 cm

(7) **Adult**: Dark rufescent above, buffy-rufous flanks, plain throat/breast and undertail-coverts, pale lower mandible. (8) **Juvenile**: Upperparts tinged more rufous-chestnut, pale areas of underparts washed yellow. **VOICE** Song is a prolonged sewingmachine-like repetition of rather quiet rapid short notes: ***tutututututututututut***... or ***hehehehehe-hehehe***... Calls with harsh deep ***thuck thuck thuck***.., sharp ***tink tink tink***... and harsh grating ***tchrrrk tchrrrrk***... **HABITAT** Low vegetation in clearings and along forest edge, grass and scrub; 800–2,565 m.

RUSSET BUSH WARBLER *Bradypterus mandelli* 13–14 cm

(9) **Adult** *mandelli*: Similar to Brown but dark brown undertail-coverts with broad whitish tips, all-blackish bill, usually speckled on throat/breast. More rufescent above and on flanks than Spotted. (10) **Adult variant**: Little or no throat/breast-spotting. (11) **Juvenile**: Like adult variant but tinged yellowish below. **VOICE** Song is a distinctive monotonous metallic buzzing ***zree-ut zree-ut zree-ut zree-ut***... Calls are very similar to Brown. **HABITAT** Low vegetation in clearings and along forest edge, grass and scrub; 1,200–1,830 m.

LANCEOLATED WARBLER *Locustella lanceolata* 12–13.5 cm

(12) **Adult (worn)**: Small, heavily streaked; streaked on rump, throat, breast, flanks and undertail-coverts. (13) **Adult (fresh)**: Upperparts and flanks rather warmer. **Juvenile**: Somewhat less heavily/boldly streaked, with looser, fluffier plumage. **VOICE** Song is a sustained shuttling trill: ***zizizizizi-izizizizi***... Calls include a rather subdued ***tack***, thin clicking ***chick*** or ***pit*** and trilled ***rit-tit-tit-tit***. **HABITAT & BEHAVIOUR** Grass, weeds and scrub, often in marshy areas, cultivation borders; up to 1,800 m. Very skulking, on or near ground, difficult to flush.

RUSTY-RUMPED WARBLER *Locustella certhiola* 14–15 cm

(14) **Adult** *certhiola*: Largish; dark rufescent above, whitish-tipped tail, rufescent rump, unstreaked below. (15) **Juvenile**: Like adult but washed yellowish below, with faint breast-streaks. (16) **Adult** *rubescens* (should occur NW at least): Upperside darker, less heavily and contrastingly streaked. **VOICE** Sings with rapid, well-structured musical warbling phrases: ***tri-tri-tri-tri***; ***prt-prt***; ***srrrrt***; ***sivih-sivih-sivih*** etc. Calls include metallic ***pit*** notes, clicking ***chick***, dry ***trrrrt*** and rattling ***rit-tit-tit-tit***... **HABITAT & BEHAVIOUR** Tall reeds/grass and other vegetation in freshwater wetlands, rice-paddy edges; up to 400 m. Rather less skulking than Lanceolated.

ORIENTAL REED WARBLER *Acrocephalus orientalis*
18–20 cm

(17) **Adult (worn)**: Greyish streaks on lower throat/upper breast more obvious than fresh adult, colder above. (18) **Adult (fresh)**: From Clamorous by somewhat stouter bill, more prominent supercilium (particularly behind eye), slightly longer primary projection, shorter tail with whitish tips; usually less buffish below. **VOICE** Sings with deep guttural churring and croaking notes mixed with repeated warbling phrases: ***kawa-kawa-kawa-gurk-gurk eek eek gurk kawa***... etc. Calls with loud ***chack*** and soft churring notes. **HABITAT** Emergent vegetation in marshes, rice paddies, cultivation borders, grass and scrub in less wet areas; up to 800 m.

CLAMOROUS REED WARBLER *Acrocephalus stentoreus*
18.5–20.5 cm

(19) **Adult (worn)** *brunnescens*: Very like Oriental but has narrower bill, shorter supercilium, slightly shorter primary projection and longer tail without whitish tips. (20) **First winter (fresh)**: Differs from Oriental as worn adult. **VOICE** Song more tentative and melodious than Oriental: ***track track track karra-kru-kih karra-kru-kih chivi tru chivi chih***... etc. Calls are deep ***track*** and hard ***trrrrr***. **HABITAT** Emergent vegetation in marshes; lowlands.

THICK-BILLED WARBLER *Acrocephalus aedon* 18.5–21 cm

(21) **Adult (worn)** *stegmanni*: Like Oriental/Clamorous but bill relatively short/stout, no supercilium or eyestripe. (22) **First winter (fresh)**: Rufescent tinge to upperparts, wings and flanks. **VOICE** Song is a fast loud stream of avian mimicry, interspersed with twittering and excitable sounds (many calls repeated 2–3 times). Calls include hard clicky ***teck*** notes and a harsh wheezy ***verrrh*** when agitated. **HABITAT** Scrub and grass in relatively dry areas, forest clearings and edge; up to 1,525 m.

PLATE 109 *PHYLLOSCOPUS* WARBLERS

DUSKY WARBLER *Phylloscopus fuscatus* 12–12.5 cm

(1) **Adult (fresh)** *fuscatus*: Smaller/slimmer than Radde's, bill finer (lower mandible typically dark-tipped), legs thinner, supercilium narrower, whiter and more sharply defined in front of eye, usually distinctly buffish behind. (2) **Adult (worn)**: Upperparts paler greyish-brown. (3) **Adult variant**: More olive-tinged individual. **VOICE** Song higher, slower, less varied than Radde's with fewer syllables per phrase, no strong rattling trills or *ty-ty* introductory notes; often begins with thin *tsir-it*. Call is a repeated hard *tett* or *tak*. **HABITAT** Low vegetation in open areas, mangroves; lowlands (up to 1,830 m on passage). More often in wet habitats than similar *Phylloscopus* warblers.

BUFF-THROATED WARBLER *Phylloscopus subaffinis* 11–11.5 cm

(4) **Adult (fresh)**: Yellowish-buff supercilium and underparts (including throat), no crown-stripes or wing-bars. **VOICE** Repeated, rather slow weak *whi-whi-whi-whi*, sometimes introduced by short, subdued *trr* or *trr-trr*. Call is a sibilant cricket-like *trrup* or *tripp*. **HABITAT & BEHAVIOUR** Scrub and low vegetation in open areas; 1,200–2,565 m. Typical leaf warbler; very active, usually in low vegetation and small trees etc.

YELLOW-STREAKED WARBLER *Phylloscopus armandii* 13–14 cm

(5) **Adult (fresh)**: From Radde's (close up) by finely yellow-streaked breast/belly, slightly more defined supercilium in front of eye; slightly smaller/proportionately smaller-headed, thinner bill/legs (slightly thicker than Dusky). (6) **Adult (worn)**: Yellow streaking less obvious. **First winter**: As fresh adult but buffish throat (paler than breast) has fine yellow streaks. **VOICE** Song of short rapid undulating/slurred phrases, after call notes. Call is a bunting-like *tzic*. **HABITAT & BEHAVIOUR** Low vegetation/small trees in clearings/edge of broadleaved and mixed broadleaved/pine forest; up to 1,500 m (sometimes 2,500 m).

RADDE'S WARBLER *Phylloscopus schwarzi* 13.5–14 cm

(7) **Adult (fresh)**: Very like Yellow-streaked (which see for differences). Larger than Dusky, more olive above, supercilium broader, often bordered darkish above, ill-defined/buffish in front of eye, undertail-coverts rusty-buff. (8) **Adult (worn)**: Lacks olive-tinge on upperparts. **VOICE** Sings with loud outbursts of fast trilling: *tydydydydydydyd ty-tytyrrrrrrrrrrrrrr ty-ty suisuisuisuisuisuisuisui tuee-tuee-tuee-tuee-tuee*... etc. Calls with low soft *tyt* or *tuc* notes, often in series. **HABITAT & BEHAVIOUR** Low vegetation in more open forest, clearings, forest edge; up to 2,000 m. Fairly skulking, near ground.

ARCTIC WARBLER *Phylloscopus borealis* 12.5–13 cm

(9) **Adult (fresh)** *borealis*: Slightly larger and longer-/heavier-billed than Greenish/Two-barred, supercilium falls short of bill-base, ear-coverts more obviously mottled, legs browner/yellower, breast-sides greyer/slightly streaked. (10) **Adult (worn)**: Duller, with narrower wing-bars. **VOICE** Song is a fast trilled *dyryryryryryryryryr*... or *der-*

erererererererererere... (pitch/speed varies). Loud sharp *dzip* or *dzrt* call. **HABITAT & BEHAVIOUR** Mixed deciduous and broadleaved evergreen forest, secondary growth, gardens, mangroves; lowlands (up to 1,800 m on passage). Sluggish/methodical compared to Greenish/Two-barred.

GREENISH WARBLER *Phylloscopus trochiloides* 12 cm

(11) **Adult (fresh)** *trochiloides*: Like Two-barred but usually only one narrow wing-bar on greater coverts. (12) **Adult (worn)**: Greyer above, wing-bar/s narrower. **Other subspecies** *P.t.obscuratus* (apparently recorded NW). **VOICE** Song is a simple hurried repetition of call or similar notes: *chiree-chiree-chiree-chiree-chee-chee witchu-witchu-witchu* etc. Calls with a fairly high-pitched, slurred, disyllabic *chiree* or *chir'ee*. **HABITAT** Broadleaved evergreen forest, secondary growth; up to 2,565 m (mainly in mountains).

TWO-BARRED WARBLER *Phylloscopus plumbeitarsus* 12 cm

(13) **Adult (fresh)**: Very like Greenish but shows two broader yellowish-white wing-bars. Can resemble Yellow-browed but larger and longer-billed, no whitish fringes to tertials. See Arctic for differences. (14) **Adult (worn)**: Often worn in winter, with narrower wing-bars (may lack shorter upper wing-bar). **VOICE** Song faster/more jumbled than Greenish. Usual call is a rather sparrow-like *chireewee* or *chir'ee'wee* (occasionally omits third syllable). **HABITAT & BEHAVIOUR** Mixed deciduous, semi-evergreen and sometimes broadleaved evergreen forest, bamboo, parks and gardens on migration; up to 800 m. Very active, working mid-storey foliage.

PALE-LEGGED LEAF WARBLER *Phylloscopus tenellipes* 12.5–13 cm

(15) **Adult** *tenellipes*: Resembles Arctic and Greenish Warblers but crown uniform dark greyish, rump paler olive-brown, legs pale greyish-pink; usually two narrow wing-bars. **VOICE** Song is similar to Arctic but faster, thinner and higher-pitched: *sresres-resresresre*... Call is a distinctive, very high-pitched, thin, metallic *tib* or *tip*. **HABITAT & BEHAVIOUR** Mixed deciduous, broadleaved evergreen and semi-evergreen forest, secondary growth, also mangroves and gardens on migration; up to 1,500 m (mainly winters below 1,000 m). Usually found close to ground, in undergrowth and understorey trees, rather secretive.

EASTERN CROWNED WARBLER *Phylloscopus coronatus* 12.5–13 cm

(16) **Adult**: Like Arctic but crown darker, with well defined pale median stripe, upperparts yellower-green, ear-coverts and underparts whiter, undertail-coverts pale yellow; lower mandible pale. **VOICE** Song is a repeated series of clear notes, terminating with a harsh squeaky drawn-out note: *tuweeu tuweeu tuweeu tuweeu tswi-tswi zueee* etc.; sometimes shorter *psit-su zueee*. Call is a harsh *zweet* (quieter than Arctic). **HABITAT & BEHAVIOUR** Broadleaved evergreen and mixed deciduous forest, also mangroves and gardens on migration; up to 1,830 m (mainly winters in lowlands). Shows strong preference for canopy of larger trees.

PLATE 110 *PHYLLOSCOPUS* WARBLERS

BUFF-BARRED WARBLER *Phylloscopus pulcher* 11–11.5 cm

(1) **Adult (fresh)** *pulcher*: Broad orange-buff wing-bar, yellowish rump, much white on outertail. (2) **Adult (worn)**: Wing-bar narrower, buffier. VOICE Song is a high-pitched twitter, either preceded by or ending with a drawn-out trill. Call is a sharp thin *swit* or *sit*, sharper and more strident than Ashy-throated. HABITAT Broadleaved evergreen forest; 1,500–2,565 m.

ASHY-THROATED WARBLER *P. maculipennis* 9–9.5 cm

(3) **Adult** *maculipennis*: Recalls Lemon-rumped, but supercilium white, throat/breast greyish, much white on tail. **Juvenile**: Said to have olive-washed crown and throat and brighter buffish-tinged wing-bars. VOICE Song recalls White-tailed Leaf Warbler but shorter, with repeated *sweechoo* and *sweeti* notes. Call is a thin sharp high-pitched *zip* or *zit*. HABITAT Broadleaved evergreen forest; 2,000–2,565 m.

PALLAS'S LEAF WARBLER *P. proregulus* 10 cm

(4) **Adult (fresh)**: As Lemon-rumped, but supercilium and crown-stripe much yellower, mantle greener. (5) **Adult (worn)**: Duller above, narrower wing-bars, less strongly yellow. VOICE Song is rich and varied, recalling Canary *Serinus canaria*. Calls with a subdued, squeaky *chuit* or *chui*. HABITAT Broadleaved evergreen forest; 1,600–1,800 m.

LEMON-RUMPED WARBLER *P. chloronotus* 10 cm

(6) **Adult** *chloronotus*: Tiny; small dark bill, pale yellow rump, supercilium, median crown-stripe and double wing-bar, no white on tail. From Pallas's by slightly duller head-stripes, wing-bars and mantle. VOICE Two songs: (1) rapid even-pitched notes, following long thin rattle: *tsirrrrrrrrr-tsi-tsi-tsi-tsi-tsi-tsi*...; (2) varied endless stuttering: *tsi tsi-tsi tsi-tsi tsu-tsu tsi-tsi tsu-tsu tsi-tsi tsi-tsi tsirrp tsi-tsi*... Call is a sharp sunbird-like *twit* or *tuit*. HABITAT Broadleaved evergreen/semi-evergreen forest, secondary growth; recorded at 1,685 m.

CHINESE LEAF WARBLER *P. sichuanensis* 10 cm

(7) **Adult**: Like Lemon-rumped but crown-sides slightly paler, median crown-stripe fainter, eyestripe slightly paler and fairly straight, no pale spot on ear-coverts; slightly larger, more elongated and longer-billed. VOICE Song is monotonous *tsiridi-tsiridi-tsiridi-tsiridi-tsiridi*... Calls with rather loud *tueet*, and (at least on breeding grounds) varied irregular loud scolding whistles *tueet-tueet-tueet tueet-tueet tueet-tueet-tueet tueet tUEE tuee-tuee-tuee-tuee-tuee*... etc., and hammering *tueet tuee-tee-tee-tee-tee-tee-tee*... HABITAT Broadleaved evergreen forest, secondary growth; 400–1,800 m.

YELLOW-BROWED WARBLER *P. inornatus* 11–11.5 cm

(8) **Adult (fresh)**: Broad supercilium/wing-bars, no median crown-stripe, rump-patch or white on tail. Smaller and shorter-tailed than Two-barred, tertials whitish-tipped, wing-bars broader, bill weaker (usually darker-tipped). (9) **Adult (worn)**: Narrower wing-bars. VOICE Song is a high-pitched *tsitsitsui itsui-it seee tsi tsi-u-eee* etc. Call is a distinctive high, slightly rising *tswee-eep*, *tsweet* or *wee-eest*. HABITAT Forest, secondary growth, parks, gardens, mangroves; up to 2,140 m.

HUME'S WARBLER *Phylloscopus humei* 11–11.5 cm

(10) **Adult (fresh)** *mandellii*: From Yellow-browed by grey wash on upperparts, rather darker lower mandible and legs; median covert bar usually slightly less distinct than greater covert bar and slightly duller throat and breast. (11) **Adult (worn)**: Greyer above, wing-bars weaker. Otherwise differs from Yellow-browed as fresh adult. VOICE Song is a thin falling *zweeeeeeeeeoooo*, preceded by repetition of call-notes. Call is a thin *we-soo* (often doubled) and *tschu'is*, *tschui* or *tschui* (first syllable stressed). HABITAT Forest, wooded areas, secondary growth; mostly mountains.

BLYTH'S LEAF WARBLER *P. reguloides* 11.5–12 cm

(12) **Adult** *assamensis*: From White-tailed by less yellow on supercilium and underparts, less white on tail. (13) **Juvenile**: Like adult but crown plainer (barely discernible median stripe), underparts duller. VOICE Sings with well-spaced strident, undulating, usually alternating phrases: *wit tissu-tissu-tissu wit tewi-tewi-tewi-wit chewi-chewi-chewi*..., *wit-chuit wit-chuit wit chuit...chi-tewsi chi-tewsi chi*... and *wit-chi wit-chi wit-chi-wit...wit-chi wit-chi wit-chi-wit*... etc. Calls with high *pit-chee* and *pit-chee wi'chit* (first note stressed). HABITAT & BEHAVIOUR Broadleaved evergreen forest; up to 2,565 m (mainly above 600 m). Breeds above 1,500 m. Clings nuthatch-like to tree-trunks and branches. Agitated birds on territory flick one wing at a time, relatively slowly, unlike White-tailed.

WHITE-TAILED LEAF WARBLER *P. davisoni* 11–11.5 cm

(14) **Adult** *davisoni*: Pattern like some smaller *Phylloscopus* warblers, but larger and longer-billed without pale rump and whitish tertial markings. From Blyth's by more white on outertail, yellower head markings. (15) **Adult** *klossi* (? this race in SE): Less white on tail (also yellow-tinged), brighter yellow above and below. VOICE Has higher-pitched, more quickly delivered/slurred song than Blyth's: *itsi-itsi-chee-wi itsi-itsi-chee-wi itsi-itsi-chee-wi*... and *seechewee-tis-seechewee-tiss seechewee-tisseechewee-tiss*... etc. Calls with quick high *ti'chee-wi* (first/second note stressed), or slower *wit-chee*. HABITAT Broadleaved evergreen and pine forest; 1,000–2,565 m.

YELLOW-VENTED WARBLER *P. cantator* 11 cm

(16) **Adult** *cantator*: Bright yellow on head, upper breast and vent, dark head-stripes, whitish lower breast to belly. VOICE Sings with quickly repeated, fast high-pitched phrases, introduced by a very short note and ending with a distinctive *si-chu* or *si-chu-chu*: roughly *sit siri'sii'sii si-chu*, *sit weet-'weet-weet'weet si-chu-chu* etc. HABITAT Mid/lower storey of broadleaved evergreen and semi-evergreen forest; 500–1,700 m.

SULPHUR-BREASTED WARBLER *P. ricketti* 11 cm

(17) **Adult**: Bright yellow on head and underparts, blackish eye- and median crown-stripes, narrow wing-bars. VOICE Song is a very high-pitched series of short notes, speeding up towards end: *sit'ti si-si-si-si'chu* and *sit si-si'si'si-chu* etc. HABITAT Broadleaved evergreen and mixed deciduous forest, rarely more open habitats on migration; up to 1,200 m.

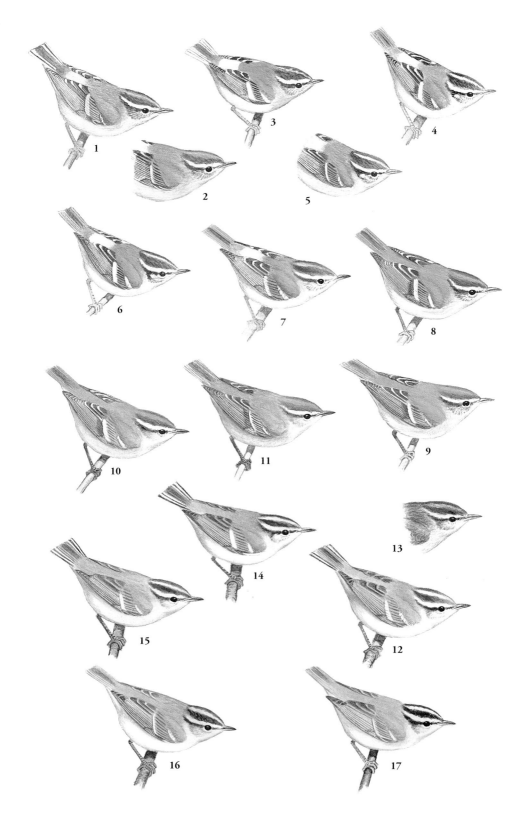

PLATE 111 WHITE-EYES & FLYCATCHER WARBLERS

CHESTNUT-FLANKED WHITE-EYE *Zosterops erythropleurus* 11–12 cm

(1) **Adult**: Chestnut flanks, green forehead. **VOICE** Similar to Japanese White-eye. **HABITAT & BEHAVIOUR** Broadleaved evergreen forest, secondary forest; up to 2,590 m, mostly above 800 m. Gregarious, often found in mixed flocks with Japanese.

ORIENTAL WHITE-EYE *Zosterops palpebrosus* 10.5–11 cm

(2) **Adult typical morph** *siamensis*: Yellowish-white ventral stripe, much yellow on forehead. (3) **Adult yellow morph**: All yellow below. (4) **Adult** *williamsoni* (coastal C,W,S[east]): Faint ventral stripe, paler yellow and grey below, duller above. (5) **Adult** *auriventer* (coastal west S): Clear yellow mid-ventral stripe, less yellow on forehead. **VOICE** Short thin wispy song made up of slurred call notes. Usual call is a repeated wispy sibilant *jeww* or *cheuw*. **HABITAT & BEHAVIOUR** Various broadleaved forests, secondary growth, mangroves, cultivated areas, parks, gardens. Up to 1,525 m, locally 1,830 m; mangroves and non-forest only in S. Highly gregarious.

JAPANESE WHITE-EYE *Zosterops japonicus* 10–11.5 cm

(6) **Adult** *simplex*: From Oriental by darker upperparts, no ventral stripe; defined yellow loral band. (7) **Juvenile**: Like adult but eyering greyer at first. **VOICE** Like Oriental. **HABITAT & BEHAVIOUR** Forest, secondary growth, cultivated areas, parks, gardens; up to 2,590 m (breeds in lowlands). Highly gregarious, often in large restless flocks in winter.

EVERETT'S WHITE-EYE *Zosterops everetti* 11–11.5 cm

(8) **Adult** *wetmorei*: Green forehead, deep grey sides, deep yellow throat and ventral stripe. **Juvenile**: Duller, with paler, less pronounced mid-ventral stripe and greener wing-feather fringes. **Other subspecies** *Z.e.tahanensis* (extreme S). **VOICE** Call notes are thinner and higher-pitched than Oriental: *tsieu* or *tschew*. **HABITAT & BEHAVIOUR** Broadleaved evergreen forest; up to 2,010 m. Highly gregarious.

GREY-CROWNED WARBLER *Seicercus tephrocephalus* 11–12 cm

(9) **Adult**: Greyish crown with black lateral stripes, yellow eyering, no wing-bar, much white on outer-tail. (10) **Juvenile**: Lateral crown-stripes weaker, upperparts slightly darker, underparts duller. **VOICE** Song differs from Plain-tailed and Bianchi's by presence of tremolos and trills. Also higher-pitched than Bianchi's, covering greater frequency range. Call is a short, rather faint *chup*, clear *chip* or double *chu'du*. **HABITAT & BEHAVIOUR** Broadleaved evergreen forest, secondary growth, bamboo; up to 2,565 m. Quite skulking, in low vegetation.

PLAIN-TAILED WARBLER *Seicercus soror* 10.5–11 cm

(11) **Adult**: Little white on outertail, forehead greenish, relatively short greyish-black lateral crown-stripes. **VOICE** Song is higher-pitched than Bianchi's and introduced by a soft *chip*; each series of notes covers a wider frequency range. Call is a short, rather high-pitched thin *tsrit* or *tsi-dit*. **HABITAT** Broadleaved evergreen forest, secondary growth; up to 1,200 m.

BIANCHI'S WARBLER *Seicercus valentini* 12 cm

(12) **Adult** *valentini*: As Plain-tailed but crown-stripes blacker/more extensive, more white on outertail, wing-bar usually distinct. **VOICE** Song is a series of short phrases, each with fewer than 10 short soft whistled notes, normally preceded by a short soft introductory *chu*; individual phrases often repeated either a few times or after some time. Call is a short, soft, deflected *tiu* or *heu* (may be doubled). **HABITAT** Broadleaved evergreen forest, secondary growth; recorded at 1,500–1,600 m.

GREY-CHEEKED WARBLER *Seicercus poliogenys* 9–10 cm

(13) **Adult**: Like White-spectacled but darker grey head, greyish-white chin and lores, broader eyering. **VOICE** Varied phrases of repeated thin notes (no tremolos or trills): ***titsi-titsi-chi***, ***chi-chi-chi-chi-chi***, ***titwi-titwi-titwi***, ***tewchi-chew-chi-chew*** and ***switu-switu-switu-switu*** etc. Calls with sibilant *tsew* and abrupt *twit* notes (may be mixed with song). **HABITAT** Broadleaved evergreen forest, secondary growth; 1,200–c.2,135 m.

CHESTNUT-CROWNED WARBLER *S.castaniceps* 9–10.5 cm

(14) **Adult** *collinsi*: Rufous crown with blackish lateral stripes, yellow rump, vent and wing-bars, grey throat/breast. (15) **Adult** *butleri* (presumably this in extreme S): Darker crown, dark grey below/on mantle, no yellow on rump. **Juvenile**: Crown duller/browner/brownish-grey, whitish patch on nape-side faint, throat/breast sullied yellowish-olive, paler yellow below. *S.c.butleri* apparently has ashy-grey lateral crown-stripes and eyestripe and pale grey supercilium. **Other subspecies** *S.c.youngi* (elsewhere S): As *butleri* but crown a little more rufous, more extensively grey above, rump paler (also without yellow), less yellow on flanks/vent; juvenile apparently has olive-rufous supercilium. **VOICE** Song is an extremely thin, high-pitched ***wi si'si'si-si'si'si*** etc. (*si* notes upward-inflected). Calls with soft *chit* notes. **HABITAT & BEHAVIOUR** Broadleaved evergreen forest; 1,200–2,200 m. Highly active, often in bird-waves.

RUFOUS-FACED WARBLER *Abroscopus albogularis* 9 cm

(16) **Adult** *hugonis*: Dull crown, rufous head-sides, dark throat, whitish below, yellow breast-band and vent. (17) **Juvenile**: Head-sides washed out, no lateral crown-stripes, throat-streaking less obvious. **VOICE** Sibilant, high-pitched, repetitive whistles: ***titiriiiii titiriiiii titiriiiii titiriii-ii***... **HABITAT** Broadleaved evergreen forest, bamboo, secondary growth; 800–1,400 m.

YELLOW-BELLIED WARBLER *A.superciliaris* 9.5–11.5 cm

(18) **Adult** *superciliaris*: Greyish head, whitish supercilium, greenish upperparts, whitish throat/breast, yellow belly. **Juvenile**: Paler yellow below. **Other subspecies** *A.s.bambusarum* (northern S); *sakaiorum* (southern S) shows white on centre of belly. **VOICE** Song thin, high-pitched and tinkling, with 3–6 notes per phrase: ***uu-uu-ti*** and ***uu-uu-ti-i*** etc., with higher *ti* notes. Occasionally gives a continuous, subdued thin twittering. **HABITAT** Bamboo in or near broadleaved evergreen, semi-evergreen and deciduous forest, secondary growth; up to 1,525 m.

PLATE 112 LAUGHINGTHRUSHES

WHITE-CRESTED LAUGHINGTHRUSH *Garrulax leucolophus* 26–31 cm

(1) **Adult** *diardi*: Broad whitish crest, black mask, white below with rufescent flanks/vent. **Juvenile**: Shorter crest, duller nape. **Other subspecies** *G.l. belangeri* (W): More chestnut mantle/flanks/vent. **VOICE** Loud outbursts of cackling, with rapid chattering and double-note phrases by different individuals in flock. **HABITAT & BEHAVIOUR** Various broadleaved forests, secondary growth, bamboo; up to 1,300 m. Always in flocks.

LESSER NECKLACED LAUGHINGTHRUSH *Garrulax monileger* 28.5–30.5 cm

(2) **Adult** *mouhoti* (NE[south],SE): Dark lores, broken moustachial, whitish throat/breast, pale primary coverts. (3) **Adult variant**: More black on ear-coverts. **Juvenile**: See Greater Necklaced. **Other subspecies** *G.m.schauenseei* (east NW, north-west NE). *G.m.stuarti* (W,NW) and *fuscatus* (south W): Buff/whitish rather than rufous/rufous-buff tail-tips, paler nuchal collar. **VOICE** Repeated mellow *u-wi-uu* and more quickly repeated *ui-ee-ee-wu* etc. Flocks give low calls, harsh and continuous in alarm. **HABITAT & BEHAVIOUR** Various broadleaved forests, secondary growth, bamboo; up to 1,200 m. Always in flocks.

GREATER NECKLACED LAUGHINGTHRUSH *Garrulax pectoralis* 31.5–33 cm

(4) **Adult** *subfusus*: Pale lores, black line under ear-coverts/cheeks, mostly buff throat/breast, dark primary coverts. **Juvenile**: Warmer above, less distinct gorget, smaller pale tail-tips. **VOICE** Mixed series of loud quavering nervous *wee'i'i*, *wee'u* and *wee'ee'u* phrases. Low gruff contact notes. **HABITAT & BEHAVIOUR** As Lesser Necklaced; up to 1,200 m.

BLACK LAUGHINGTHRUSH *Garrulax lugubris* 25.5–27 cm

(5) **Adult**: Blackish; naked bluish-white post-ocular patch, orange-red bill. **Juvenile**: Duller/browner (mainly mantle/wings). **VOICE** Song (typically by 2+ birds) is amazing loud hollow hooping *huup-huup-huup*... and rapid loud *okh-ohk-okh-okh-okh*..., mixed with harsh *awh* or *aak* notes. **HABITAT & BEHAVIOUR** Broadleaved evergreen forest, sometimes secondary growth; c.800–1,500 m. Quite shy, in pairs/small flocks.

WHITE-NECKED LAUGHINGTHRUSH *G.strepitans* 30 cm

(6) **Adult**: Brown crown, blackish-brown face to upper breast, rufous ear-coverts, white neck-patch; mostly brown. (7) **Adult variant**: Individual with browner upper breast. **VOICE** Like White-crested but faster, with longer, rapid rattles. Outbursts preceded by/mixed with clicking *tekh* notes (also used as contact calls). **HABITAT & BEHAVIOUR** Broadleaved evergreen forest; 500–1,800 m. Always in flocks. Shy.

BLACK-THROATED LAUGHINGTHRUSH *G.chinensis* 28 cm

(8) **Adult** *lochmius*: Slate-grey crown, black face to upper breast, white ear-coverts. **Other subspecies** *G.c.propinquus* (W): Rufescent-tinged body. **VOICE** Repetitive thrush-like song, including harsh *wraaah* notes and squeaky whistles. Calls include husky *how* notes. **HABITAT & BEHAVIOUR** Broadleaved forest, secondary growth, bamboo; up to 1,400 m.

CHESTNUT-CAPPED LAUGHINGTHRUSH *G.mitratus* 23 cm

(9) **Adult** *major*: Largely greyish; chestnut crown, broad white eyering, rufous-chestnut vent. **Juvenile**: Duller/browner; less forehead streaking. **VOICE** Sings with fairly clear 3–5 note phrases: *wi wu-wi-wu-wi* (first note stressed), *wiu-wu-wui-wi* (end sharper) etc. Calls with sibilant *ju-ju-ju-ju-ju* and cackling *wikakakaka*. **HABITAT** Broadleaved evergreen forest, forest edge; c.800–1,500 m.

SPOT-BREASTED LAUGHINGTHRUSH *G.merulinus* 26 cm

(10) **Adult** *laoensis*: Blackish spots on buffish-white throat/breast, thin buff supercilium. **Juvenile**: Upperside and flanks more rufescent. **VOICE** Song is melodious and thrush-like. Recalls Black-throated but richer and more varied, lacks harsh notes and squeaky whistles. **HABITAT & BEHAVIOUR** Edge of broadleaved evergreen forest, overgrown clearings, bamboo; 1,000–1,800 m. Usually in pairs; very skulking.

WHITE-BROWED LAUGHINGTHRUSH *G.sannio* 22–24 cm

(11) **Adult** *comis*: Buffish-white round front of eye (supercilium to cheek-patch), rufescent vent. **VOICE** Harsh emphatic *jhew* and *jhew-jhu*. Harsh buzzy *dzwee* notes when agitated. **HABITAT & BEHAVIOUR** Scrub and grass, secondary growth, bamboo, cultivation; 1,000–1,830 m, locally down to 600 m. In small noisy parties; not very shy.

CHESTNUT-CROWNED LAUGHINGTHRUSH *Garrulax erythrocephalus* 25.5–28.5 cm

(12) **Adult** *schistaceus* (NW; Doi Chiang Dao/Pha Hom Pok etc.): Rufous-chestnut crown, yellowish-olive wing/tail-fringing, mostly olive-greyish body, silvery-grey head-sides, chestnut throat/upper breast. (13) **Adult** *peninsulae* (S): Rufescent-brown, darker grey head-sides. **Other subspecies** *G.e.melanostigma* (NW; Doi Inthanon etc.) and *subconnectens* (east NW): Greyer, less chestnut on throat; latter has breast prominently scaled pale greyish. **VOICE** Song is a simple *weeoo-wip*, *wiu-wi* and *wu-eeoo* etc. (last/first note often stressed). Rattling *grrrrt-grrrrt-grrrrt*... in alarm. **HABITAT & BEHAVIOUR** Broadleaved evergreen and mixed broadleaved/conifer forest, secondary growth, bamboo; 1,300–2,565 m. Quite shy.

RED-TAILED LAUGHINGTHRUSH *G.milnei* 26–27 cm

(14) **Adult** *sharpei*: Bright rufous crown/nape and extensively red wings/tail. **VOICE** Sings with clear whistled phrases. Recalls *uuu-weeoo* or *eeoo-wee* etc. (rising at start) or *uuuu-hiu-hiu* and *uuuu-hiu-hiu-hiu* etc. (slightly rising introduction, faster soft laughter at end). **HABITAT & BEHAVIOUR** Broadleaved evergreen forest, bamboo, secondary growth; 1,800–2,200 m. Usually in pairs or small parties; shy.

RED-FACED LIOCICHLA *Liocichla phoenicea* 20.5–23.5 cm

(15) **Adult** *ripponi*: Striking red head-/throat-sides. **Juvenile**: Less red in plumage. **VOICE** Sings with clear 3-8 note (end usually rising) *chewi-ter-twi-twitoo* and *chi-cho-choee-wi-chu-chooee* etc. Call is a rasping *chrrrt-chrrrt* etc. **HABITAT & BEHAVIOUR** Secondary growth, broadleaved evergreen forest; 1,400–2,200 m. Skulking.

PLATE 113 JUNGLE BABBLERS & SCIMITAR BABBLERS

ABBOTT'S BABBLER *Malacocincla abbotti* 15–16.5 cm

(1) **Adult** *abbotti*: Short tail, largish bill, rufous-buff flanks/vent. From Horsfield's by paler, concolorous crown and upperparts, shaft-streaked on crown, less contrasting grey supercilium, lack of breast-streaking. (2) **Juvenile**: Crown and upperparts dark rufescent-brown (similar to adult Ferruginous Babbler). **Other subspecies** *M.a.williamsoni* (south-west NE), *obscurius* (coastal SE), *olivaceum* (extreme S). **VOICE** Song is a repeated jolly *chiu-woo-wooi*; *wiu-wuoo-wiu*; *wi-wu-yu-wi* etc. (may be 4/5 notes). Harsh *cheu* and high *wer* calls. **HABITAT & BEHAVIOUR** Broadleaved evergreen forest, secondary growth; up to 915 m. Close to ground.

HORSFIELD'S BABBLER *Malacocincla sepiarium* 14–15.5 cm

(3) **Adult** *tardinatum*: See under Abbott's Babbler above; crown darker than mantle, breast vaguely streaked. **Juvenile**: More rufescent above. **VOICE** Usual song is a strident, clearly spaced *wi-cho-teuu*, with first note high and sharp, second short, and third high and shrill. Variations occur, particularly when excited, and first note sometimes omitted. Call is a harsh explosive *whit-whit-whit*..., interspersed with quieter *wer* notes. **HABITAT & BEHAVIOUR** Broadleaved evergreen forest, often near water; up to 700 m. Usually fairly close to ground.

SHORT-TAILED BABBLER *Malacocincla malaccensis* 13.5–15.5 cm

(4) **Adult** *malaccensis*: From Abbott's and Horsfield's by smaller size, short tail, thinner bill, blackish moustachial line, grey ear-coverts, white throat. **Juvenile**: Paler crown, brown-tinged head-sides, rusty-fringed primaries. **VOICE** Song is a series of 6-7 loud rich whistled notes, descending in pitch, introduced by a dry trill: *pi'pi'pi'pi'pi pew pew pew pew pew pew*. Calls with low, harsh, crackling, rattling sounds and a harsh, mechanical *chutututututut*..., interspersed with soft *yer* notes etc. **HABITAT & BEHAVIOUR** Broadleaved evergreen forest, secondary forest; up to 915 m. Usually close to ground.

BUFF-BREASTED BABBLER *Pelorneum tickelli* 13.5–15.5 cm

(5) **Adult** *fulvum*: Longer-tailed and thinner-billed than Abbott's, upperparts paler and more olive-brown, head-sides tinged buffish, breast buff with faint streaks, flanks and vent paler. (6) **Juvenile**: Upperparts strongly rufescent. **Other subspecies** *P.t.tickelli* (W,S): More rufescent/slightly darker above. **VOICE** Song is a sharp, quickly repeated *wi-twee* or *wi-choo*, sometimes incessantly repeated: *witweewitweewitwee*... etc. Also high jolly laughing *swi-tit-tit-titchoo*. Calls with rattling *prrree* or *trrrit* notes, interspersed with higher *pieu* or explosive *whit* or *twit* notes. **HABITAT** Broadleaved evergreen forest, secondary growth, bamboo, sometimes mixed deciduous forest; up to 1,550 m.

SPOT-THROATED BABBLER *Pelorneum albiventre* 13–14.5 cm

(7) **Adult** *cinnamomeum*: Dark-spotted whitish throat. Resembles Buff-breasted but smaller, with shorter, rounded tail, shorter bill and greyish head-sides. **Juvenile**: More rufescent primary/secondary fringes. **VOICE** Surprisingly rich thrush-/chat-like song. Complex and quickly delivered with much repetition. Antiphonal fast high *tchu-tchu-tchu-tchu*... from females. Calls with harsh *chrrr* and rather explosive *tip* or *tchip* notes. **HABITAT & BEHAVIOUR** Open broadleaved evergreen forest, overgrown clearings, secondary growth, scrub and grass, bamboo; 1,100–2,100 m. Very skulking, in low undergrowth.

PUFF-THROATED BABBLER *Pelorneum ruficeps* 16–18 cm

(8) **Adult** *chthonium*: Rufescent crown, buffy-whitish supercilium, whitish below, dark breast-/flank-streaks. May show vague dark streaks on centre of upper mantle. (9) **Juvenile**: Upperparts (not crown) more rufescent, streaking below indistinct. (10) **Adult** *acrum* (W,S): Unstreaked upper mantle, neat light breast-streaks on buffier underparts. **Other subspecies** *P.r.indistinctum* (north NW), *elbeli* (north-west NE), *euroum* (east C,SE), *smithi* (islets off SE), *ubonense* (east NE). **VOICE** Loud *wi-chu* or *wi-ti-chu* and jolly descending *tuituititi-twititi-tititi*... etc. Rasping *rrrrrit* in alarm. **HABITAT & BEHAVIOUR** Broadleaved forests, secondary growth; up to 1,800 m. On or near ground.

BLACK-CAPPED BABBLER *Pelorneum capistratum* 17–18.5 cm

(11) **Adult** *nigrocapitatum*: Warm dark brown above, deep rufous below, black crown, nape and moustachial stripe, greyish-white supercilium and white throat. (12) **Juvenile**: Like adult but head pattern much less distinct, upperparts more rufescent. **VOICE** Sings with loud, high-pitched *teeu* (first syllable emphasised); repeated every few seconds. Calls include a subdued *bekbekbekbek*... and *yeryeryer*... and high nasal *nwit-nwit-nwit*... **HABITAT & BEHAVIOUR** Broadleaved evergreen forest; up to 760 m. Usually on or close to ground.

LARGE SCIMITAR BABBLER *Pomatorhinus hypoleucos* 25.5–28 cm

(13) **Adult** *tickelli*: Large; chestnut neck-patch, pale supercilium, grey sides with broad white streaks. (14) **Adult** *wrayi* (presumably this in extreme S): Colder and darker above, black and white supercilium. **Juvenile**: Breast-side/flank markings diffuse, very rufescent above. **VOICE** Usually 3 hollow piping notes (pairs duet): *wiu-pu-pu—wup-up-piu*; *wiu-pu-pu—wo-hu*; *whiu-pu-pu—whip-up-up* etc. Sometimes hurried *wiupupu*; *whipuwup* etc. Grating *whit-tchtchtchtch* and *bekbekbekbekbek*... in alarm. **HABITAT & BEHAVIOUR** Broadleaved evergreen and mixed deciduous forest, bamboo; up to 1,000 m (but montane in S?). Usually near ground.

RUSTY-CHEEKED SCIMITAR BABBLER *Pomatorhinus erythrogenys* 23.5–25 cm

(15) **Adult** *celatus*: Orange-rufous head-sides, flanks and vent, white throat, breast and belly. **Juvenile**: Rufous below, with white on centre of throat and narrowly down centre of abdomen. **VOICE** Commonly sings in pair-duet: loud fluty quick two-note phrase, either side of short sharp answering-note: *whi-u-ju-whi-u*...; *iu-chu-ip-iu-chu*...; *yu-u-yi-yu-u*... etc. Also a high *pu* or *ju*, and slightly rolling, spaced *jrr-jrr-jrr-jrr*... Rattling *whib-whibibibi* and harsh *whit-it* or *whoi-whititititit* in alarm (*whoi* is like sound of stone dropped in water; sometimes given singly). **HABITAT** Scrub and grass, open broadleaved evergreen forest; 1,200–2,000 m.

PLATE 114 SCIMITAR BABBLERS & WREN BABBLERS

WHITE-BROWED SCIMITAR BABBLER *Pomatorhinus schisticeps* 21–23 cm

(1) **Adult** *olivaceus* (W): Yellowish bill, drab olive-brown above, unmarked white throat, breast and belly-centre. (2) **Adult** *ripponi* (north NW): Duller/greyer above, broader rufous-chestnut nuchal collar, rufous-chestnut flanks. **Other subspecies** *P.s.difficilis* (west NW), *fastidiosus* (S), *humilis* (east NW,NE). *P.s.klossi* (SE): Darker above, has chestnut on flanks. **VOICE** 3-7 rather quick hollow piping notes: *hu-hu-hu-hu-hu*; *whu-wu-wu-pu*; *whi-hu-wi* etc. (sometimes abrupt first note/longer pause after first note). Also a fast *whuhuhuhuhuhu* or short *wu-hup*, *oo-hu* etc. Harsh *whihihihihi* etc. in alarm. **HABITAT** Broadleaved evergreen and deciduous forest, secondary growth, bamboo; up to 2,000 m.

CHESTNUT-BACKED SCIMITAR BABBLER *Pomatorhinus montanus* 19 cm

(3) **Adult** *occidentalis*: Like White-browed but has black crown and dark chestnut mantle to rump and flanks. **VOICE** Song is a clear loud resonant 2–3 note *whu-whoi*, *woi-woip* and *yu-hu-hu* etc. Duets include *whu-whi-whu-woi-whu-whi*... **HABITAT** Broadleaved evergreen forest; up to 1,370 m.

RED-BILLED SCIMITAR BABBLER *P.ochraceiceps* 22–24 cm

(4) **Adult** *ochraceiceps*: Long narrow red bill, rufescent crown and upperparts, white breast and belly-centre. **Other subspecies** *P.o.alius* (northwest NE). **VOICE** Song is a hurried hollow piping *wu-wu-wu*; *wu-wu-woi*; *wu-wu-whip*; *pu-pu* etc. Also, very rapid *wi-wuwu* and loud whistled *u-wip*, repeated after pauses. When alarmed, gives harsh scratchy *whi-chutututut*, *whi-trrrrrt whi-trrrrrt*... and *tchrrrtututut tchrrrt*... etc. Variable sounds when excited: purring *wrrrrrp*, clear *wuhu-wuhu*, nasal *woiee-woiee*, high *wheep* and *whi* etc. **HABITAT & BEHAVIOUR** Broadleaved evergreen forest, bamboo; 600–1,600 m. Often associates with bird-waves and particularly White-hooded Babbler.

CORAL-BILLED SCIMITAR BABBLER *P.ferruginosus* 22 cm

(5) **Adult** *albogularis*: Like Red-billed but thicker bill, black line above supercilium, broadly black head-sides. **Juvenile**: More rufescent. **VOICE** Various sounds (often by several birds): soft *whu* and *whoiee*, oriole-like *whheeeei* and yelping *yep-yep-yep*..., along with scolding *whit whit-tchrrrt; tchrrrt-tchrrrrt; whitchitit* etc. Also scratchy *weeitch-oo* and shrill *wheep-wheep*. Harsh dry *krururutt* and *krrrirrrurut* etc. in alarm, less scratchy than Red-billed. **HABITAT & BEHAVIOUR** Broadleaved evergreen forest, bamboo; 1,200–2,000 m. Sometimes in bird-waves.

STRIPED WREN BABBLER *Kenopia striata* 15 cm

(6) **Adult**: Bold white streaking on dark crown, mantle, wing-coverts and breast-sides, whitish head-sides, throat and underparts with buff lores and flanks. (7) **Juvenile**: Crown and breast-sides browner, streaks buffier, breast mottled, bill paler. **VOICE** Song is a clear whistled *chuuii* (every 1.5–2 s); sometimes *chiuuu* or *chi-uuu*, with very short space between notes. **HABITAT & BEHAVIOUR** Broadleaved evergreen forest; up to 1,050 m. Usually near ground.

LARGE WREN BABBLER *Napothera macrodactyla* 19–20.5 cm

(8) **Adult** *macrodactyla*: Black mask, black and white lores, white throat, blue orbital skin; faint-pattern below. (9) **Juvenile**: Plainer/more rufous above with buff streaks; rufescent-brown below, with whiter throat-/belly-centre. **VOICE** Clear whistled *chuu-chreeh*; *chu-chiii* etc., or descending/rising *phuu-wiii*; single *chuuu*, or longer *uuu-choriii*; *chuuu weearh-weearh*; *uuurr-wi'wi'wi'wi'wrriiu* etc. In duet, slow *pu-yu-yu*... answered by *chuuu* or *chuuu-chii*. **HABITAT & BEHAVIOUR** Broadleaved evergreen forest; below 200 m. On or near ground.

LIMESTONE WREN BABBLER *Napothera crispifrons* 18–20.5 cm

(10) **Adult** *crispifrons*: Larger than Streaked, longer tail, no covert-spots, bolder throat-streaks, whiter belly-centre. (11) **Adult white-throated morph**: White face and throat. (12) **Adult** *calcicola* (NE; Saraburi Province): Rufescent-brown below (except throat). **VOICE** Sudden loud rapid harsh slurred *chitu-wi-witchuwitchiwitchiwitchuwitchiu*, lasting 4–30 s; usually repeated after long intervals. Scolding *chrrr-chrrr-chrrr*... etc. in alarm. **HABITAT & BEHAVIOUR** Forest on limestone, limestone rocks and outcrops; up to 915 m. Usually in small parties, around rocks and tangled vegetation.

STREAKED WREN BABBLER *N.brevicaudata* 14–14.5 cm

(13) **Adult** *brevicaudata*: Whitish spots on some wing-feather tips, rufescent below, dark throat/breast-streaks. (14) **Juvenile**: Plain dark brown, paler chin/throat-centre, dull wing-spots, pale streaks on crown to upper back. (15) **Adult** *leucosticta* (S): Very broad sooty-brown streaks on throat and breast. **Other subspecies** *N.b.griseigularis* (SE): Duller/paler belly-centre, pale grey base colour to throat/upper breast. **VOICE** Repeated clear, ringing *peee-oo*; *pu-ee*; *chiu-ree*; *chewee-chui* etc. (sometimes single note). Alarm call is a rattling *chrrreerrrrt* etc. **HABITAT** Broadleaved evergreen forest, forest on limestone, limestone rocks/boulders; up to 1,620 m.

EYEBROWED WREN BABBLER *N. epilepidota* 10–11.5 cm

(16) **Adult** *davisoni*: Small; short tail, long buff supercilium, dark eyestripe, large whitish spots on wing-covert tips. (17) **Juvenile**: Plain warm dark brown above and dark rufous below, vague supercilium, buff wing-covert spots. **Other subspecies** *N.e.granti* (S): Paler breast-/abdomen-centre. **VOICE** Song is a repeated falling clear whistled *cheeeoo* or *piiiiiu*. Rattled *prrrt-prrrt-prrrt*, *wprrrt wprrrt wprrrt* and *chrrut-chrrut-chrrut* etc. in alarm. **HABITAT & BEHAVIOUR** Broadleaved evergreen forest; 1,000–2,135 m. On or close to ground.

PYGMY WREN BABBLER *Pnoepyga pusilla* 7.5–9.5 cm

(18) **Adult dark morph** *pusilla*: Small, tail-less, dark brown; indistinct scales/spots above, buff scales below. (19) **Adult pale morph**: Mostly white-scaled below. (20) **Juvenile**: Initially rather uniform dark brown, with paler throat. Only faintly scaled. **Other subspecies** *P.p.barterti* (S). **VOICE** Song is a high-pitched, well-spaced *ti-ti-tu* (c.4 s long), every 3–5 s. Call is a repeated sharp *tchit*. **HABITAT & BEHAVIOUR** Broadleaved evergreen forest; 1,200–2,565 m. On or near ground.

PLATE 115 JUNGLE BABBLERS, TIT BABBLERS & GRASS BABBLERS

WHITE-CHESTED BABBLER *Trichastoma rostratum* 15–16.5 cm

(1) **Adult** *rostratum*: Cold dark brown above, clean white below, light grey wash on breast-sides, rather slender bill. **Juvenile**: Similar to adult. **VOICE** Song is a repeated, quite high-pitched, clear *wi-ti-tiu*, *chui-chwi-chew* or *chwi-chi-cheei* etc., sometimes introduced with a short trill: *chr chr ooi-iwee* etc. Calls with harsh, scolding rattles. **HABITAT & BEHAVIOUR** Riversides and streams in broadleaved evergreen forest, secondary forest, freshwater swamp forest, mangroves; below 200 m. Usually on or close to ground.

FERRUGINOUS BABBLER *Trichastoma bicolor* 16–18.5 cm

(2) **Adult**: Bright rufescent above and rather clean creamy or buffy-whitish below. **Juvenile**: Brighter and more orange-rufous above. **VOICE** Sings with a repeated loud, clear, rather sharp *u-wit* or *u-wee* (second note higher). Also variable low jolly phrases: *wit wi-ti-tu-tu* etc. Calls are low, harsh, dry, rasping sounds and sharp, explosive *wit* notes etc. **HABITAT & BEHAVIOUR** Broadleaved evergreen forest, secondary forest; below 200 m. Usually fairly close to ground.

MOUSTACHED BABBLER *Malacopteron magnirostre* 16.5–18 cm

(3) **Adult** *magnirostre*: Greyish head-sides, dark moustachial stripe, whitish below with light greyish wash/streaks. (4) **Juvenile**: Moustachial stripe less distinct, lower mandible flesh-coloured, eyes greyish/brownish. **VOICE** Song usually 3–6 note (well-spaced), clear, sweet, whistled *tii-tu-ti-tu* or *ti-tiee-ti-ti-tu* etc. (lasts c.2–3 s; may descend slightly towards end). Call is repeated, quite explosive *whit*, mixed with buzzing *bzzii* notes. **HABITAT & BEHAVIOUR** Broadleaved evergreen forest; up to 900 m. Usually in pairs or small parties in middle storey.

SOOTY-CAPPED BABBLER *Malacopteron affine* 15–16.5 cm

(5) **Adult** *affine*: Like Moustached but smaller and more slender-billed, crown sooty, no moustachial stripe. (6) **Juvenile**: Crown paler, lower mandible dull flesh. **VOICE** Song usually 6–9 airy, rising/falling whistles: *phu-phi-phu-phoo-phu-phi-phu* etc. (lasts c.4–7 s). Also a variable *whi-whi-whui* and faster *chut-whi-whi-whi-whu-whi-whu* etc. Calls with a sharp *which-it* and harsh rattles. **HABITAT** Broadleaved evergreen forest (often near water), forest edge, freshwater swamp forest; below 200 m.

SCALY-CROWNED BABBLER *Malacopteron cinereum* 14–17 cm

(7) **Adult** *cinereum*: Smaller than Rufous-crowned, slenderer bill, lack of greyish streaks on breast, pinkish legs. (8) **Adult** *indochinense* (NE,SE): No blackish nape-patch, slightly paler above and buffier-tinged below. **VOICE** Song of four main parts (variously combined): (1) rapid *dit-dit-dit-dit-dit-dit*… etc.; (2) rapid *du-du-du-du-du-du*…(usually descends gradually); (3) more spaced, ascending *phu-phu-phu-phu*; *phu-pu-pi-pee* etc.; (4) rapid, high, even *wiwiwiwiwi-wi-wi-wi-wu*; *wi-wi-dududududu* etc. Sharp *chit*, *whit*, *tcheu* and *titu* calls. **HABITAT & BEHAVIOUR** Lower/middle storey of broadleaved evergreen forest; up to 800 m. Often in small parties.

RUFOUS-CROWNED BABBLER *M.magnum* 17.5–19.5 cm

(9) **Adult** *magnum*: Larger and bigger-billed than Scaly-crowned with greyish breast-streaks, greyish legs. **VOICE** Song has three main parts: (1) well-spaced clear *phu-phu-phi-phi* etc. (louder/more spaced than Scaly-crowned, usually not descending); (2) well-spaced *chuwee-chuwee-chuwee-chuwu-chuwu*; *chu-chi-chi-chi-chi-chu-chu-chu-chu-chu* etc. (may descend slightly/hurry towards end); (3) well-spaced, very even *chut-chut chut-chut-chut-chut-chut-chut* etc. **HABITAT** Broadleaved evergreen forest; below 200 m.

STRIPED TIT BABBLER *Macronous gularis* 12.5–14 cm

(10) **Adult** *sulphureus* (W[north],NW): Olive-brown above, rufous crown, yellow supercilium, narrow-streaked lower throat/breast. (11) **Juvenile**: More uniform above, paler below, supercilium narrower. (12) **Adult** *chersonesophilus* (S): Stronger throat-/breast-streaks, darker and more chestnut-tinged above. **Other subspecies** *M.g.saraburiensis* (south-west NE). *M.g.lutescens* (NW[north],NE): Much brighter below. *M.g.connectens* (south W, south C, south SE) and *inveteratus* (islands off SE): Roughly intermediate between *sulphureus* and *chersonesophilus*. **VOICE** Song is an even, well-spaced, 4–5 note *chut-chut-chut-chut-chut-chut*… or *chut chut-chut-chut-chut*… etc. Calls include harsh *chrrrt-chrr* and *titit-chrreeoo*. **HABITAT** Open broadleaved forests, peatswamp forest, mangroves, secondary growth, bamboo; up to 1,525 m.

FLUFFY-BACKED TIT BABBLER *Macronous ptilosus* 16.5 cm

(13) **Adult** *ptilosus*: Dark brown with rufous crown, black cheeks and throat and blue spectacles. **Juvenile**: Crown paler, mantle darker, throat less black, breast more rufous. **VOICE** Song is a low *puh puh-puh-puh* or *puh puh puh-puh-puh* or slower *wuh-wuh hu-wu hu-wu* etc., often mixed with a strange husky *hherrh herr hherr herr* or *iwit-cherrhh-iwit-cherrhh* etc. (female?). Also low frog-like creaking *aahk-eeah-oh* etc. **HABITAT** Edge of broadleaved evergreen forest, freshwater swamp forest, secondary forest, bamboo; below 200 m.

CHESTNUT-CAPPED BABBLER *Timalia pileata* 15.5–17 cm

(14) **Adult** *smithi*: Thick black bill, chestnut cap, black mask, white supercilium, cheeks, throat and upper breast. (15) **Juvenile**: Warmer brown above, head duller, lower mandible paler. **Other subspecies** *T.p.patriciae* (west C, south W): Greyer above (tinged warm buffish) and on flanks, duller below; *intermedia* (W) and *dictator* (NE,SE) roughly intermediate. **VOICE** Husky *wher-wher witch-it-it* etc. Also metallic *tzit* and harsh *chrrt*. **HABITAT & BEHAVIOUR** Grassland, thickets; up to 1,500 m. Often in small groups; skulking.

YELLOW-EYED BABBLER *Chrysomma sinense* 16.5–19.5 cm

(16) **Adult** *sinense*: Long tail, short black bill, white face to breast, orange-yellow eyes, orange eyering. **Juvenile**: Paler above, shorter-tailed, bill browner. **VOICE** Sings with variable clear high phrases: *wi-wu-chiu*, *wi-wu'chrieu*, *wi-wu-wi'tchu-it*, *wi-wi-chu*, *wi-wu'chrieu* and *wi-tchwi-wi-tchiwi* etc.; repeated after fairly short intervals. Calls include trilling *chrr-chrr-chrr*… and *chr'r'r'r'r'r*. **HABITAT & BEHAVIOUR** Grassland and scrub, secondary growth; up to 1,830 m. Skulking.

PLATE 116 TREE BABBLERS

RUFOUS-FRONTED BABBLER *Stachyris rufifrons* 12 cm

(1) **Adult** *rufifrons*: Rufous forehead to mid-crown, buffish underparts, pale greyish lores, eyebrow and eyering. (2) **Adult** *obscura*: Slightly darker, duller crown and upperparts, noticeably paler lower breast and belly. **Juvenile**: Crown and underparts paler. **Other subspecies** *S.r.adjuncta* (east NW). **VOICE** Song is a repeated, rather high piping 5–7 note *tuh tuh-tuh-tuh-tuh-tuh*, with brief pause after first note (sometimes more spaced or no pause); usually delivered quite quickly, lasting 1.25–1.75 s. Querulous rolling *wirrrri* in alarm. **HABITAT** Forest edge, secondary growth, grass, bamboo, broadleaved evergreen forest; up to 2,100 m.

GOLDEN BABBLER *Stachyris chrysaea* 10–12 cm

(3) **Adult** *assimilis*: Bright yellow forehead and underparts, black face and dark crown-streaking. Ear-coverts and nape yellowish-olive, upperparts and flanks greyish-olive. **Juvenile**: Washed below, yellowest on throat/upper breast, eyes brownish. **Other subspecies** *S.c.aurata* (north NW), *chrysops* (S). **VOICE** Song like Rufous-fronted but notes usually clearer (often sound more spaced), usually with more obvious pause (sometimes no pause) after first note: rapid *tu tu-tu-tu-tu-tu-tu* or slower *ti tu-tu-tu-tu-tu*. Usually 5–10 notes, lasting 1–1.25 s. Scolding *chrrrrr-rr-rr* and *chrirrrrr* etc. in alarm. **HABITAT & BEHAVIOUR** Broadleaved evergreen forest; 900–2,000 m. Often in bird-waves.

GREY-THROATED BABBLER *Stachyris nigriceps* 12.5–14 cm

(4) **Adult** *spadix*: Black and whitish crown-streaks, grey throat, white submoustachial patch, warm buffish below. (5) **Juvenile**: Upperparts washed chestnut, head-sides and underparts rufous-buff, hindcrown unstreaked. (6) **Adult** *dipora* (S)/*davisoni* (extreme S). Duller dark crown-streaks, narrower whitish streaks. **Other subspecies** *S.n.yunnanensis* (NW): Darker. **VOICE** Song is a high, quavering, rising *ti tsuuuuuuu-ueee* or *tsi tuuuuuuuuuiiii* etc.; sometimes spaced *si-si-sii-iiii-u* etc. Scolding *chrrrt* and *chrrrrrr-rrr-rrt* etc. in alarm. **HABITAT & BEHAVIOUR** Broadleaved evergreen forest, secondary growth; up to 1,830 m. Often in bird-waves.

GREY-HEADED BABBLER *Stachyris poliocephala* 14–15 cm

(7) **Adult**: Dark brown above, rufous-chestnut below, greyish head, whitish forehead-/throat-streaks and eyes. (8) **Juvenile**: Duller above, paler below, head-streaking less distinct, eyes browner. **VOICE** Song is a repeated clear, quite high-pitched *chit-tiwi-wioo-iwee* and *yit-uip-ui-wiee*, or higher, longer-spaced *chu-chi-chiee* and *chi-chu-chiee* etc. Other calls include a quiet descending *dji-dji-dji-du* and more even *dji-dji-dji-dji-dji*..., harsh scolding *chrrrttutut* and *chrrrrtut* in alarm, and very soft *tip-tip-tip*... contact calls. **HABITAT** Broadleaved evergreen forest, secondary growth; up to 700 m.

SPOT-NECKED BABBLER *Stachyris striolata* 16–16.5 cm

(9) **Adult** *guttata*: White throat, blackish malar streak, white-flecked supercilium and neck-/mantle-sides. **Other subspecies** *S.s.helenae* (east NW). *S.s.nigrescentior* (S): Deeper rufous-chestnut lower breast and belly. See Snowy-throated and Grey-throated Babblers. **VOICE** Song is a high, well-spaced

tuh tih tuh or *tuh tih*, repeated after longish intervals. May be accompanied by high rising note and hard rattle: *whiiii-titititi-titi* (from female?). Other calls are a scolding *tirrrrirrirr*; *tchrrrt-tchrrrt*... and short high *tip* notes. **HABITAT & BEHAVIOUR** Broadleaved evergreen forest, secondary growth, scrub and grass; 100–1,500 m. Often in small groups; joins bird-waves; skulking.

WHITE-NECKED BABBLER *Stachyris leucotis* 14–15 cm

(10) **Adult** *leucotis*: Like Black-throated but ear-coverts greyer bordered with bold white spots, wing-coverts and tertials tipped pale, no white cheek-patch or breast-line. (11) **Juvenile**: Dull chestnut above, neck-spots buffish, ear-coverts browner, throat to belly dark brown. **VOICE** Song is a repeated simple whistled *uu-wi-u-wi*, *uu-wi-u-wi-u* or *uui-wi-oi-wi* (second note lower-pitched). **HABITAT & BEHAVIOUR** Broadleaved evergreen forest; up to 800 m. Rather shy.

BLACK-THROATED BABBLER *Stachyris nigricollis* 15.5–16 cm

(12) **Adult**: Black face, throat and upper breast, white cheek-patch, forehead-streaks, eyebrow and breast-band. (13) **Juvenile**: Head and underside sooty-brownish but with white eyebrow and cheek-patch. **VOICE** Song is a repeated spaced, rather weak piping *pu-pu-pu-pu-pu-pu* or *too-too-too-too-too*... and faster *pupupupupupupupu*. Also a more convoluted, rapidly repeated hollow *puwut-puwut-puwut-puwut*; *pwut-pwut-pwut-pwut-pwut* and *chu-chuwu-chu-chu-chu-chu*... etc. Calls include a harsh slow rattled *tchrr-rrt* and *chrrrt-trrerrt-trrerrt*. **HABITAT** Broadleaved evergreen forest, freshwater swamp forest; lowlands.

CHESTNUT-RUMPED BABBLER *Stachyris maculata* 17–18.5 cm

(14) **Adult** *maculata*: Large, with black throat, broad blackish streaks on whitish lower throat to upper belly, and rufous-chestnut lower back to uppertail-coverts; whitish eyes, blue orbital skin. **Juvenile**: Throat/breast apparently pale grey, without black. **VOICE** Variable. Several birds often call together with combinations of: loud full *wup wup wup wup*...; *wu wup-wuhup-wup-wuhup*; *wuhup-wuhup* and *wuoo-wuoo-wuoo-wuoo*...; and tremulous *t'u'u'u'u'u'u* and *tik-tik-wrrrrrrr* etc. Often interspersed (by female?) with scratchy jumbled notes and quiet conversational notes: *jriii-jriii, tchup-tchup tchup, jrrt-jrrrt-jrr-jrr-jrr-jrr* and *ju-ju-ju-wiii* etc. **HABITAT & BEHAVIOUR** Broadleaved evergreen forest; below 200 m. Usually in small flocks.

CHESTNUT-WINGED BABBLER *Stachyris erythroptera* 12.5–13.5 cm

(15) **Adult** *erythroptera*: Drab brown above with rufous-chestnut on wings, mostly greyish head to upper belly with buffy vent, blue orbital skin. (16) **Juvenile**: Crown and upperparts more rufescent, grey much paler, orbital skin duller. **VOICE** Song is a soft, mellow, quite quick, piping 7–10 note *hu-hu-hu-hu-hu*, sometimes faster tremulous *hu hu'u'u'u'u'u'u'u* or slow *chu hu-hu-hu-hu*. Calls with harsh scolding *trrrrrt-trrrrrt*... and soft *wip* and *wit* contact notes. **HABITAT** Broadleaved evergreen forest, secondary forest; up to 800 m.

PLATE 117 SILVER-EARED MESIA, CUTIA, SHRIKE BABBLERS & MINLAS

SILVER-EARED MESIA *Leiothrix argentauris* 16.5–18 cm

(1) **Male** *galbana*: Yellow bill and forehead-patch, black head, silver-grey ear-coverts, orange-yellow throat/upper breast, red and orange-yellow wing pattern, orange-reddish tail-coverts. (2) **Female**: Duller/paler forehead, throat and breast, dull golden-olive nape, upper mantle and uppertail-coverts; pale yellowish-rufous undertail-coverts, duller wings. **Juvenile**: Duller than respective adults. **voice** Song is cheerful descending *che tchu-tchu che-rit* or *che chu chiwi chwu* etc. Calls include a flat piping *pe-pe-pe-pe-pe* and harsh chattering. **habitat & behaviour** Edge of broadleaved evergreen forest, secondary growth; 1,300–2,000 m. In small parties.

CUTIA *Cutia nipalensis* 17–19.5 cm

(3) **Male** *melanchima*: Black and bluish grey head/wings, rufous-chestnut above, whitish below, black flank-bars. (4) **Female**: Mantle, back and scapulars more olive-brown with broad blackish streaks, head-sides dark brown. **Juvenile**: Duller than respective adults, browner crown, fainter bars below. **voice** Repeated series (5–20) of loud, rather high notes: *yuip-yuip-yuip-yuip-yuip-yuip jiw-jiw-jiw-jiw yuip-yuip-yuip-yuip-yuip-yuip*… (or without faster high *jiw* notes) etc., or fairly slow to quick *ip-ip-ip-ip-ip-ip-ip*… or *jorrri-jorrri-jorrri-ip-ip-ip-ip*… etc. Calls include light *chick chick chick*…, sharper *chit*, and harsh low *jert jert*… **habitat & behaviour** Broadleaved evergreen forest; 1,200–2,100 m. Pairs or small parties, often in bird-waves; unobtrusive, often high in trees.

WHITE-BROWED SHRIKE BABBLER *Pteruthius flaviscapis* 16–17.5 cm

(5) **Male** *aeralatus*: Black head and wings/tail, white supercilium, grey above (may have black-mottled mantle), pale grey below with vinous-washed lower flanks. Black-tipped golden-rufous to chestnut tertials. (6) **Female**: Grey head, browner above, mostly golden-olive wings/tail; whitish to buff below. (7) **Juvenile male**: Like juvenile female but nape to uppertail-coverts more rufescent, has blackish head-sides, wings similar to adult male but with golden-olive fringing on median and greater coverts. (8) **Male** *ricketti*: (east NW): Darker above and below, black-mottled mantle and back, grey rear ear-coverts. (9) **Female**: Grey throat and upper breast. **Juvenile female**: Quite uniform grey-brown above with buffish-white streaks, whiter below. **Other subspecies** *P.f.schauenseei* (S): Female has browner crown, nape and head-sides, almost no chestnut on tertials. **voice** Repeated strident *ip ch-chu ch-chu* or *itu chi-chu chi-chu*. Calls with short *pink*, and grating churrs in alarm. **habitat** Broadleaved evergreen forest; 800–2,200 m.

BLACK-EARED SHRIKE BABBLER *P.melanotis* 11.5–12 cm

(10) **Male** *melanotis*: Like Chestnut-fronted but forehead yellowish, throat paler, nape grey, ear-coverts with broad black rear border, flight feathers with uniform slaty-grey fringes. (11) **Female**: From Chestnut-fronted by mostly greenish-olive forehead, grey nape, blackish rear ear-covert border, pale chestnut chin/malar area, yellower below, more greyish-olive wing-fringing. (12) **Juvenile**: Like female but head pattern duller, no grey on nape or chestnut on chin/malar area, whiter supercilium, much paler below, greener wing-fringing. *P.m.tahanensis* is

whiter below, malar area warm buff. (13) **Male** *tahanensis* (? extreme S): Less yellow forehead, paler below, only throat chestnut, greener wing-fringing. (14) **Female**: More whitish-yellow below with paler chestnut on chin/malar. **voice** Monotonous *twi-twi-twi-twi-twi*…, slower *dwit-dwit-dwit-dwit-dwit*… or rattling *dr'r'r'r'r'r'r'r'r*. Rapid *whiwhiwhiwhiwhi*… or *jujujujujuju*… from *P.m.tahanensis*. Short *chid-it* call. **habitat** Broadleaved evergreen forest; 1,600–2,200 m.

CHESTNUT-FRONTED SHRIKE BABBLER *Pteruthius aenobarbus* 11.5–12 cm

(15) **Male** *intermedius*: Small, robust; chestnut and yellow forehead, white eyering/wing-bars, pale grey supercilium, greenish-olive above, yellow below, dark chestnut throat-centre/breast-wash, greyish-white primary fringes. (16) **Female**: Rufous-chestnut forehead and throat-wash, yellowish-white below, rufescent wing-bars/primary edges. **voice** Sings with monotonous *chip-chip-chip-chip-chip*…, *wheet-wheet-wheet-wheet-wheet*…, and *wchip-wchip-wchip-wchip*… etc. Calls include buzzy *jer-jer-jer*… and *jwi-jwi-jwi*…, chattering *chr'r'r'r'uk* and sharp *pwit*. **habitat & behaviour** Broadleaved evergreen forest; 900–2,500 m. Often in bird-waves.

BLUE-WINGED MINLA *Minla cyanouroptera* 14–15.5 cm

(17) **Adult** *sordida*: Slim, long-tailed; dark violet-blue wing-/tail-fringing, dark violet-blue lateral crown-streak and faint forehead-streaks (may show some pale streaks), whitish supercilium, warm brown above, greyish-white below. **Other subspecies** *M.c.wingatei* (north-east NW): More blue/pale greyish streaks on forecrown, bluer crown-streaks and wing-/tail-fringes, whiter supercilium, warmer lower mantle to uppertail-coverts, greyer throat/breast/flanks. *M.c.sordidior* (S): Much plainer/browner above. *M.c.rufodorsalis* (presumably in SE): Distinctly chestnut above (rump/uppertail-coverts brighter), more intense blue on wings/tail. **voice** Song is a very thin, high *psii sii-suuu* (*suuu* rising) or rising and falling *tsuit-twoo* etc. **habitat & behaviour** Broadleaved evergreen forest, secondary growth; 900–2,000 m. Usually in small flocks.

CHESTNUT-TAILED MINLA *Minla strigula* 16–18.5 cm

(18) **Adult** *castanicauda*: Rufescent crown, broad black bars/scales on throat. Olive-greyish above, yellowish below, dull brownish-chestnut and black tail with whitish tip, black wings with orange-yellow and white markings. **Juvenile**: Hindcrown, nape and upperparts greyer, head-sides somewhat paler, throat-bars narrower and more broken, underparts more washed out. **voice** Sings with repeated, high-pitched, slightly quavering *tui-twi ti-tu*, *twi ti-u* or *twi-twi twi twi* with higher third note. **habitat** Broadleaved evergreen forest; 1,600–2,565 m.

STRIATED YUHINA *Yuhina castaniceps* 11.5–14 cm

(19) **Adult** *striata*: Short crest, graduated white-edged tail; thin greyish streaks above, pale brown ear-coverts. (20) **Adult** *torqueola* (east NW): Broad chestnut nuchal collar and ear-coverts with strong whitish streaks, greyer crown. **Juvenile**: Duller; crest shorter. **voice** Repeated high *tchu* or *tchi* (*torqueola* utters double *di-duit*). Endless chattering from flocks. **habitat & behaviour** Broadleaved evergreen forest, forest edge; 900–1,800 m. In restless flocks.

PLATE 118 FULVETTAS & YUHINAS

RUFOUS-WINGED FULVETTA *Alcippe castaneceps* 11 cm

(1) **Adult** *castaneceps*: Chestnut crown, black and white head-sides, blackish coverts, rufous wing-panel. **Other subspecies** *A.c.exul* (NW[east],NE): Darker crown and wings. *A.c.soror* (? extreme S): Darker, more chestnut on wing. **VOICE** Song is high undulating, slightly descending 4–8 note *si tju-tji-tju-tji-tju*. Calls with low harsh *tcht, tchit* and *tchrr* notes, thin *tsi-tsi-tsi-trrt* etc. **HABITAT & BEHAVIOUR** Middle/lower storey of broadleaved evergreen forest, secondary growth; 1,200–2,565 m. In small hyperactive flocks; clings to mossy trunks.

RUFOUS-THROATED FULVETTA *A.rufogularis* 12–14 cm

(2) **Adult** *major*: White supercilium, broad rufous-chestnut breast-band. **Other subspecies** *A.r. khmerensis* (SE): Darker above, more chestnut crown. **VOICE** Sings with loud, shrill phrases (first note usually high): *wi-chuw-i-chewi-cheeu, wi-ti-ti-tuee* and *chuu-chu-wichu-chi-chu* etc. Calls include worried low *wrrr-it wrrr wrrr wrrr-it…*, undulating *chrr-chrrr-chrr…* and explosive *whit whit-whit…* etc. **HABITAT** Understorey of broadleaved evergreen forest; up to 900 m.

RUSTY-CAPPED FULVETTA *Alcippe dubia* 13.5–15.5 cm

(3) **Adult** *dubia*: Black-scaled rufescent crown, buffy forehead-patch, white supercilium, buffy-brown breast/flanks. **VOICE** Song less shrill than Rufous-throated: *chu-witee-wee, chu-witchui-chu* and *wi-chi-chu-chiu* etc. Low grumbling *chrrr-rr…* and *chrrr-rrr-ritz* etc. in alarm. **HABITAT & BEHAVIOUR** Edge of broadleaved evergreen forest, secondary growth; recorded at 1,600 m. Close to ground; skulking.

BROWN FULVETTA *Alcippe brunneicauda* 14–15.5 cm

(4) **Adult** *brunneicauda*: Rather plain greyish head, whiter throat, dull below. **VOICE** Sings with measured, high-pitched, slightly undulating *hi-tu-tu hi-tu ti-tu* and *hi-tu hi-tu hi-tu* or descending *hi ti-tu ti ti-tu ti-tu* etc. Calls are stressed *whit* notes and short harsh rattles. **HABITAT** Middle to lower storey of broadleaved evergreen forest; up to 900 m.

BROWN-CHEEKED FULVETTA *A.poioicephala* 15.5–16.5 cm

(5) **Adult** *haringtoniae*: Plain greyish-buff head-sides, buff below, narrow crown-stripes, olive-brown above. (6) **Adult** *davisoni* (S): Crown browner, very faint crown-stripes, paler below (whiter throat/belly-centre). **Other subspecies** *A.p.alearis* (NW[east],NE): More olive above, duller below. **VOICE** Sings with pleasant phrases of spaced, fairly even notes (usually rising at end): *chu'uwi-uwi-uwee, i'chi-wi-uwi-uwee, yi'chiwi-wi-uwuuee* etc. Spluttering rattles when agitated: *witt-witt, witch-itititit* and higher *whi-sihihihi* etc. **HABITAT** Middle/lower storey of broadleaved forest, secondary growth, bamboo; up to 1,200 m (sometimes 1,520 m).

BLACK-BROWED FULVETTA *Alcippe grotei* 15.5–16.5 cm

(7) **Adult** *eremita*: Warm brown above, whitish below, brown-washed head-sides and flanks, no eyering. (8) **Juvenile**: Warmer above, grey duller and restricted to crown, head browner. **VOICE** Song similar to Brown-cheeked but rises less at end: *yu-chi-chiwi-chuwoo, yu-uwii-ii-uwoo* and *yi-*

yuii-yui-uwee-uwee etc. Spluttering *witchititit* and *err-rittirrirrrt* etc. in alarm. **HABITAT & BEHAVIOUR** Middle to lower storey of broadleaved evergreen forest, secondary growth, bamboo; up to 1,000 m. In small flocks, often with bird-waves.

MOUNTAIN FULVETTA *Alcippe peracensis* 14–15.5 cm

(9) **Adult** *peracensis*: Dull slate-grey crown, mid-grey head-sides, white eyering, whitish-centred throat/abdomen. **Juvenile**: Duller; crown contrasts less with upperparts, lateral crown-stripes faint/almost absent. **VOICE** Song recalls Grey-cheeked but somewhat faster and shorter, with no buzzy end-notes: *iti iwu-wi-wi* and *it iwu-u-wi* etc. Calls like Grey-cheeked. **HABITAT** Broadleaved evergreen forest (mostly lower storey), secondary growth, bamboo; above 900 m.

GREY-CHEEKED FULVETTA *Alcippe morrisonia* 13–15 cm

(10) **Adult** *fraterculus*: Distinctly buff below, black lateral crown-stripes, white eyering. **Juvenile**: More rufescent, crown tinged brown. **VOICE** Song of high-noted phrases: *it-chi wi-wi, ii chu chi-wi, ii yu yu-wi* and *ii yu yu-wi wi-you* etc. Song normally ends with 2–3 distinctive, curious buzzy *eerh* sounds. Calls with nervous *chrr'rr'r* and *chrr'rr'rrt* etc. and harsh *chittitit*. **HABITAT & BEHAVIOUR** Broadleaved evergreen forest (mostly lower storey), secondary growth, bamboo; 900–2,565 m. In small restless flocks; often with bird-waves.

WHISKERED YUHINA *Yuhina flavicollis* 12.5–13.5 cm

(11) **Adult** *rouxi*: Moustachial stripe, white eyering, golden-yellow nuchal collar, white-streaked olive-brown flanks. **Juvenile**: Browner above, duller/narrower moustachial stripe. **Other subspecies** *Y.f.rogersi* (east NW): Greyer above, considerably paler/duller nuchal collar, duller/browner flanks. **VOICE** Song is a repeated, shrill, high-pitched *tzii-jhu ziddi* (beginning stressed, end slightly undulating). Calls are a squeaky *swii swii-swii* and harsh nasal *jhoh*. **HABITAT & BEHAVIOUR** Broadleaved evergreen forest, secondary growth; 1,200–2,200 m. In small flocks, visits flowering trees.

BURMESE YUHINA *Yuhina humilis* 13 cm

(12) **Adult** *clarki*: Like Whiskered but has greyish-brown crown and ear-coverts, grey nuchal collar, grey base colour to flanks. **Other subspecies** *Y.h.humilis* (W). **VOICE** Undocumented. **HABITAT & BEHAVIOUR** Broadleaved evergreen forest, forest edge, secondary growth; 1,300–2,150 m. Often in small flocks, joins bird-waves (as Whiskered), visits flowering trees.

WHITE-BELLIED YUHINA *Y.zantholeuca* 12–13.5 cm

(13) **Adult** *zantholeuca*: Yellowish-green above, short crest, pale greyish below with whiter throat, yellow vent. (14) **Juvenile**: Crest shorter, unscaled. (15) **Adult** *tyrannula* (NW[east],NE) and *interposita* (S): Greener upperparts, darker grey underparts. (16) **Adult** *canescens* (SE): Pale grey wash above. **Other subspecies** *Y.x.sordida* (south-east NE): As *tyrannula* but underparts intermediate with *zantholeuca*. **VOICE** Song is a high-pitched descending trill: *si'i'i'i'i'i*. Calls with nasal tit-like *nher-nher* and *nhi* notes. **HABITAT & BEHAVIOUR** Broadleaved evergreen and mixed deciduous forest; up to 1,800 m. Often in small groups; joins bird-waves.

PLATE 119 WHITE-HOODED BABBLER, BARWINGS, SIBIAS & PARROTBILLS

WHITE-HOODED BABBLER *Gampsorhynchus rufulus* 22.5–26 cm

(1) **Adult** *torquatus*: White hood, rufescent-brown above, warm buff below, dark mark on neck-/breast-side. (2) **Juvenile**: Head rufous, throat buff-tinged white. (3) **Adult** *saturatior* (extreme S): Blackish collar (indistinct at rear, broken at front), more orange-buff below. **VOICE** Harsh hard stuttering rattle or cackle: *rrrrtchu-rrrrtchu-rrrrtchu, rrrrut-rrrrut* or *rrrt-rrrt-rrrt* etc. Also soft, very quiet *wit, wet* and *wyee* notes when foraging. **HABITAT** Bamboo in or near broadleaved evergreen and semi-evergreen forest; 500–1,480 m.

SPECTACLED BARWING *Actinodura ramsayi* 23.5–24.5 cm

(4) **Adult** *ramsayi*: Greyish-olive upperside, buffy-rufous forehead, white eyering, blackish lores, deep buff below. **VOICE** Song is a quite quickly repeated, rather mournful, high-pitched, bouncing, descending *iee-iee-iee-iuu*; sometimes accompanied (by female?) with high-pitched, even, forced 2–3 notes *ewh ewh ewh*. Calls include low harsh *baoh* or *berrh* notes. **HABITAT** Broadleaved evergreen forest, forest edge, secondary growth, scrub and grass; 1,200–2,100 m.

RUFOUS-BACKED SIBIA *Heterophasia annectens* 18.5–20 cm

(5) **Adult** *mixta* (north and east NW): Black head, rufous-chestnut back to uppertail-coverts, white to buff below. (6) **Adult** *saturata* (elsewhere NW): More black on mantle and scapulars, chestnut on rest of upperparts. (7) **Adult** *davisoni* (presumably this race in W): Almost completely black mantle and scapulars. **VOICE** Sings with loud strident jolly phrases, repeated every 5–11 s: *chwee-chwee-chui, wi-wi-chi-chui, wi-wi-chi-chi-chui, wi-chi-chew-chui* and *wi-chi-chew-chew* etc. Calls include harsh chattering in alarm. **HABITAT & BEHAVIOUR** Broadleaved evergreen forest; 1,000–2,000 m. Forages methodically in middle/upper storey; joins bird-waves.

DARK-BACKED SIBIA *Heterophasia melanoleuca* 21–23 cm

(8) **Adult** *radcliffei*: Blackish above, white below/on tail-tips. Mantle/scapulars to uppertail-coverts brownish-black. (9) **Adult** *melanoleuca* (presumably this race in W): Distinctly brown mantle and scapulars to uppertail-coverts. **VOICE** Sings with repeated loud high-pitched wavering whistle, dropping in pitch at end: *brrrr'rrr'r'r'i-u, brrrr'r'r'r'i-i* and *brrrr'r'r'i* etc. Calls include quite harsh *trr-trr-trr-trr* contact notes. **HABITAT & BEHAVIOUR** Broadleaved evergreen forest; 1,000–2,565 m. Often in small flocks.

LONG-TAILED SIBIA *Heterophasia picaoides* 28–34.5 cm

(10) **Adult** *cana*: All grey with very long whitish-tipped tail and long broad white wing-patch. **Juvenile**: Like adult but eyes grey. **VOICE** Thin, metallic high-pitched *tsittsit* and *tsic* notes, interspersed with a dry even-pitched rattling: *tsittsit-tsic-tsic-tsic-tsic chrrrrrrrt tsitsitsittsit-tsic-tsic-chrrrrrrrt*… etc. **HABITAT & BEHAVIOUR** Broadleaved evergreen forest, forest edge, secondary growth; 900–1,800 m. Usually in small flocks; regularly visits flowering trees.

GREY-HEADED PARROTBILL *Paradoxornis gularis* 17 cm

(11) **Adult** *transfluvialis*: Greyish head, white lores/eyering, black lateral crown-stripes and throat, pale buff below. **Other subspecies** *P.g.laotianus* (east NW): Paler grey on crown/nape, paler ear-coverts, whiter below. **Juvenile**: Warmer above, crown duller, black on throat less defined. **VOICE** Usually calls with short, quite harsh, rather slurred *jiow-jiow* or *jieu-jieu-jieu* and less harsh *djer* notes, sometimes interspersed with rapid low twittering, soft *chip* notes and a very soft short rattled *chrrrat*. **HABITAT & BEHAVIOUR** Broadleaved evergreen forest, secondary growth, scrub bordering forest, bamboo; 1,200–1,830 m. Often in small parties; joins bird-waves.

SPOT-BREASTED PARROTBILL *P.guttaticollis* 18–22 cm

(12) **Adult**: White head-sides with broad black patch, white throat/upper breast with pointed blackish spots. **Juvenile**: Crown paler, more rufescent above. **VOICE** Loud staccato series of usually 3–7 notes, repeated after 1.5–15 s: *whit-whit-whit-whit*…, jollier *wui-wui-wui-wui; whi-whi-whi-whi*… and *dri-dri-dri-dri-dri*… etc., or shorter strident *du-du-du*. Longer *ju-ju-jiu-witwitwitwit witwitwitwit witwit* or *ju-jujujuju witwitwitwitwit*… etc. when excited. Also, coarse *ee-cho-cho-cho-cho, chow-chow-chow-chow-chow, jieu-jieu-jieu-jieu* etc. Contact calls include low *ruk-ruk; rut-rut-rut-rut; chi-cho-cho* and sibilant *chu-chu* and *chut-chut-chut* etc. **HABITAT & BEHAVIOUR** Tall grass, scrub, secondary growth; 1,200–2,135 m. Often in small flocks.

BLACK-THROATED PARROTBILL *P.nipalensis* 11.5 cm

(13) **Adult** *feae*: Black lateral crown-stripes and throat, grey head-sides and breast, thin rufous supercilium. (14) **Adult** *beaulieui* (? NE): Short and broad crown-stripes, black ear-coverts, greyish and buff breast, white supercilium. **VOICE** Song is a thin, repeated, extremely high-pitched, steadily rising *ssu-ssu-si-si*. Also utters thin high-pitched undulating *srrt* and very soft *tit* notes. Flocks constantly utter thin sibilant short notes. **HABITAT & BEHAVIOUR** Bamboo, broadleaved evergreen forest, forest edge; 1,200–2,000 m. Usually in fast-moving flocks, sometimes quite large.

SHORT-TAILED PARROTBILL *P.davidianus* 10 cm

(15) **Adult** *thompsoni*: Short tail, thick bill, chestnut head, mostly black throat. **VOICE** Song is thin high-pitched rapid rising *ib'ib'ib'ib'ib'ib*. Calls with a subdued low twittering. **HABITAT & BEHAVIOUR** Bamboo in/near broadleaved evergreen forest, grass, scrub; c.600–1,200 m. Often in small flocks.

LESSER RUFOUS-HEADED PARROTBILL *Paradoxornis atrosuperciliaris* 15 cm

(16) **Adult** *atrosuperciliaris*: Buffy-rufous head, peaked crown, black eyebrow, buffish-white below. **VOICE** Sharp chipping notes, rapidly repeated at varying speeds: *tik-tik-tik-tik-tik-tik-tik*…, *tit-tit-tit-tit-tit-tit-tit-tit*…, *chit-chit-chit-chit-chit-chit*…, *tsu-tsu-tsu-tsu-tsu-tsu*… etc. Subdued rapid chattering from flocks, mixed with harsher *chut-chut-chut* or *chip-chip-chip*. Soft *wik-wik* and *tchip-tchip-tchip-tchip* contact calls. **HABITAT & BEHAVIOUR** Bamboo in/near broadleaved evergreen forest, forest edge; 700–2,000 m. In small active flocks.

PLATE 120 FLOWERPECKERS & PURPLE-NAPED SUNBIRD

YELLOW-BREASTED FLOWERPECKER *Prionochilus maculatus* 9.5–10 cm

(1) **Adult** *septentrionalis*: Distinctly greenish above, with orange crown-patch, thick dark bill; yellowish below with broad olive-green streaks. **VOICE** Repeated sibilant, high-pitched, silvery *tisi-sisit*. **HABITAT** Lower/middle storey of broadleaved evergreen forest, secondary growth; up to 1,600 m.

CRIMSON-BREASTED FLOWERPECKER *P.percussus* 10 cm

(2) **Male** *ignicapilla*: Slaty-blue above, yellow below, red crown- and breast-patches, white submoustachial stripe. (3) **Female**: Thick bill, orangey crown-patch, greyish-olive yellow-centred underparts, whitish submoustachial stripe. (4) **Juvenile**: Duller and more uniformly olive-coloured than female, bill mostly pinkish. **VOICE** Repeated sharp high-pitched *teez tit-tit*, with stressed first note, and buzzy *whit-whit* or *vit-vit*. **HABITAT** Broadleaved evergreen forest, forest edge; up to 1,200 m. Usually in tree-tops.

SCARLET-BREASTED FLOWERPECKER *P.thoracicus* 10 cm

(5) **Male**: Black head and breast, inset red crown-patch and large breast-patch, yellowish body, black wings and tail. (6) **Female**: Thick bill, greyish head, whitish throat and submoustachial stripe, and yellowish underparts with greyish-mottled reddish-orange wash on breast. (7) **Juvenile**: Duller and more greyish-olive below than female. **VOICE** Undocumented. **HABITAT** Broadleaved evergreen forest, swamp forest; up to 1,260 m (mainly lowlands). Usually in tree-tops.

THICK-BILLED FLOWERPECKER *Dicaeum agile* 10 cm

(8) **Adult** *modestum*: Thick bill, rather dull olive-green above, whitish below with rather faint greyish-olive streaks. **Juvenile**: Bill more pinkish, underpart-streaking less distinct. **VOICE** Unusual thin *pseeou* (particularly in flight). **HABITAT & BEHAVIOUR** Broadleaved evergreen, semi-evergreen and mixed deciduous forest, secondary growth; up to 1,500 m. Usually in tree-tops. Twists (wags) tail from side to side.

YELLOW-VENTED FLOWERPECKER *D.chrysorrheum* 10 cm

(9) **Adult** *chrysochlore*: Narrow, slightly downcurved bill, whitish loral stripe, white underparts with bold blackish streaks and yellow to orange-yellow undertail-coverts; yellowish-olive upperparts. **Other subspecies** *D.c.chrysorrheum* (S). **VOICE** Short harsh *dzeep*. **HABITAT** Broadleaved evergreen, semi-evergreen and mixed deciduous forest, forest edge, secondary growth, gardens; up to 1,100 m.

YELLOW-BELLIED FLOWERPECKER *Dicaeum melanoxanthum* 13 cm

(10) **Male**: Large; upper body black with white throat and centre of breast, rest of underparts yellow. (11) **Female**: Pattern as male but head dull olive-greyish, upperparts dull greyish-brown, belly duller/paler yellow. **Juvenile male**: As female but brighter yellow belly, blue-black cast to mantle/back. **VOICE** Agitated *zit* notes. **HABITAT & BEHAVIOUR** Broadleaved evergreen forest, forest edge; 1,300–2,500 m. Sits upright on exposed perch for long periods. Sallies for insects.

ORANGE-BELLIED FLOWERPECKER *D.trigonostigma* 9 cm

(12) **Male** *rubropygium*: Orange to yellowish mantle to uppertail-coverts and lower breast to vent, greyish throat. (13) **Female**: Slightly downcurved bill, orange-yellow rump, greyish throat/upper breast, yellowish belly-centre/vent. **Juvenile**: As female but throat/breast more olive-tinged. **Other subspecies** *D.t.trigonostigma* (southern S). **VOICE** Song is a high-pitched, slightly descending *tsi-si-si-si-sew*. Calls with harsh *dzip* notes. **HABITAT** Edge of broadleaved evergreen forest, secondary growth, gardens, cultivation; up to 900 m. Usually in tree-tops.

PLAIN FLOWERPECKER *Dicaeum concolor* 8-8.5 cm

(14) **Adult** *olivaceum*: Greenish-olive above and pale olive-greyish below, with cream belly-centre (sometimes throat), dark bill and relatively pale head-sides. (15) **Juvenile**: Bill pinkish with darker culmen. **VOICE** Sings with repeated, high-pitched *tsit tsi-si-si-si-si*. Also utters monotonous *tu-wit tu-wit tu-wit tu-wit*... **HABITAT** Open broadleaved evergreen, semi-evergreen and deciduous forest, secondary growth; up to 1,700 m. Usually in tree-tops.

FIRE-BREASTED FLOWERPECKER *D.ignipectus* 8–9 cm

(16) **Male** *ignipectus*: Glossy dark greenish-blue above, buffish below with red breast-patch and black line on belly-centre, black sides of head and breast. (17) **Female**: Dark bill, greenish-olive upperparts/head-sides, uniform buffish underside with olive-tinged flanks. (18) **Male** *cambodianum* (SE): No red breast-patch. **Juvenile**: As female but base of lower mandible paler, no buff below, greyish across breast, yellower belly-centre. From Plain by darker bill and head-sides. **Other subspecies** *D.i.dolichorhynchum* (S). **VOICE** Song is a high shrill *tissit tissit tissit*... or *titty-titty-titty*... Call is a sharp *dik* or *chip*. **HABITAT** Broadleaved evergreen forest, secondary growth; 600–2,565 m. Usually in tree-tops.

SCARLET-BACKED FLOWERPECKER *Dicaeum cruentatum* 8.5–9 cm

(19) **Male** *cruentatum*: Red crown and upperparts, blackish head- and breast-sides, glossy blue-blackish wings. (20) **Female**: Bright red rump and uppertail-coverts, pale underparts. (21) **Juvenile**: Like female but bill reddish-pink basally, upperparts uniform with orange-tinged uppertail-coverts. **VOICE** Song is a thin *tissit tissit tissit*... Call is a hard metallic *tip* (often quickly repeated) and thin metallic *tizz* and *tsi* notes (latter sometimes in long series). **HABITAT** Open forests, forest edge, secondary growth, parks, gardens; up to 1,220 m.

PURPLE-NAPED SUNBIRD *Hypogramma hypogrammicum* 14–15 cm

(22) **Male** *lisettae*: Olive above, shiny purple-blue nuchal band, rump and uppertail-coverts, bold streaks below. (23) **Female**: Lacks purple-blue markings. **Other subspecies** *H.h.nuchale* (S): Bluer nuchal band, rump and uppertail-coverts. **VOICE** Song is a repeated short rapid forced high tinkling trill, interspersed with short series of typical call notes. Calls with repeated high *chip* or *tchu* notes. **HABITAT & BEHAVIOUR** Lower storey of broadleaved evergreen forest; up to 900 m. Movements relatively slow for a sunbird.

PLATE 121 SUNBIRDS

PLAIN SUNBIRD *Anthreptes simplex* 13 cm

(1) **Male**: Olive-green above, pale greyish-olive below (greyer on throat and breast), browner tail, relatively short straight bill, no obvious yellow in plumage, dark iridescent blue-green forehead-patch. (2) **Female**: No forehead-patch. **VOICE** Inadequately documented. **HABITAT & BEHAVIOUR** Broadleaved evergreen forest, forest edge, occasionally coastal scrub; up to 915 m. Moves in slow methodical manner, reminiscent of Arctic Warbler.

BROWN-THROATED SUNBIRD *Anthreptes malacensis* 14 cm

(3) **Male** *malacensis*: Glossy dark green and purple above, dull brownish head-sides/throat, yellow breast to vent. (4) **Female**: Quite robust; straightish bill, all yellow below, broad yellowish eyering, no white on tail. **VOICE** Song is an irregular, tailorbird-like ***wrick-wrick-wrick wrah wrick-wrick-wrick wrick-wrick wrah***… Calls with a sharp ***too-wit*** (recalling Green Sandpiper). **HABITAT** Forest edge, mangroves, freshwater swamp forest, secondary growth, coastal scrub, plantations, gardens; lowlands.

RED-THROATED SUNBIRD *Anthreptes rhodolaema* 12.5–13 cm

(5) **Male**: From Brown-throated by pale brick-red throat, maroon-red head-sides and mostly chestnut-maroon wing-coverts, with only small metallic purple shoulder-patch. (6) **Female**: Plainer-faced than Brown-throated with greyish-tinged eyering, breast-sides tinged greenish, underparts less bright, sometimes orange-tinged on throat and breast. **VOICE** Rising high-pitched ***uu'is*** or ***tsuu'i***. **HABITAT** Broadleaved evergreen forest, forest edge; up to 790 m.

RUBY-CHEEKED SUNBIRD *Anthreptes singalensis* 10.5–11 cm

(7) **Male** *assamensis*: Iridescent dark green above, copper-red ear-coverts, pale orange-rufous throat and upper breast, and yellow belly and vent. (8) **Female**: Greenish-olive above, as male below. **Juvenile**: As female but mostly yellow below. **Other subspecies** *A.s.internotus* (south W, south C), *interpositus* (S). **VOICE** Song is a rapid, high-pitched ***switi-ti-chi-chu tusi-tit swit-swit switi-ti-chi-chu switi-ti-chi-chu***… Calls include a thin rising ***swiiii***, longer ***swit-si-swiiii***, thin ***tit-swit-swi*** and rising ***wee-eest*** (recalls Yellow-browed Warbler). **HABITAT** Various broadleaved forests, peatswamp forest, secondary growth, mangroves, occasionally gardens. Up to 1,370 m.

PURPLE-THROATED SUNBIRD *Nectarinia sperata* 10 cm

(9) **Male** *brasiliana*: Small and dark: iridescent green crown and purple throat, deep red belly. (10) **Female**: Small; dull olive above, plain head, dull yellow below with olive-washed throat and upper breast. **VOICE** Song is a discordant series of high ***swit*** or ***psweet***, ***psit-it*** and ***trr'rr*** notes. Also repeated, very thin ***tisisisit*** and ***si-si-si-si-si-si***… and high ***ti-swit titwitwitwitwitit***… **HABITAT** Open broadleaved evergreen forest, peatswamp forest, secondary growth, coastal scrub, gardens, cultivation, sometimes mangroves; up to 800 m.

COPPER-THROATED SUNBIRD *Nectarinia calcostetha* 14 cm

(11) **Male**: All dark and relatively long-tailed; iridescent green crown, shoulder-patch and upper-tail-coverts, iridescent copper-red throat and upper breast. (12) **Female**: Greyish crown and head-sides, white throat, mostly yellow below, longish tail with white outer tips. **VOICE** Poorly documented. **HABITAT** Mangroves, coastal scrub, rarely away from coast, in secondary growth/cultivation.

OLIVE-BACKED SUNBIRD *Nectarinia jugularis* 11.5 cm

(13) **Male** *flamaxillaris*: Plain above, blue-black forehead/throat/breast (latter with reddish band), white on tail. (14) **Male eclipse**: Blue-black stripe on central throat and breast. (15) **Female**: Downcurved bill, all-yellow underside and extensive white on tail. **VOICE** Sings with repeated varied rapid, alternating, high-pitched phrases, including ***tswi-tswit-titititi, tswi-switswitswitswitswit, tuittuittuittuit, tswit-tswit-tswit-tswit, tswi-tswi-tswi-tswi-tswi-tswi, tswitswitswi-trr-trr, tswi-tisisisisisisisis*** and ***tswit-tswittswittswittswittswit-tit-titchu-chi*** etc. Calls with a loud rising ***sweet***. **HABITAT** Deciduous woodland, open forest, swamp forest, mangroves, coastal scrub, gardens, cultivation; up to 915 m.

PURPLE SUNBIRD *Nectarinia asiatica* 10.5–11.5 cm

(16) **Male** *intermedia*: Uniformly dark: mostly iridescent dark bluish to purplish. (17) **Male eclipse**: Like Olive-backed but with mostly iridescent dark blue wing-coverts and darker wings. (18) **Female**: Like Olive-backed but pale yellow to whitish below, less white on tail-tips. **Juvenile**: All yellow below. **VOICE** Pleasant descending ***swee-swee-swee swit zizi-zizi***. Calls are a buzzing ***zit*** and upward-inflected ***swee*** or ***che-wee***. **HABITAT** Deciduous woodland, coastal scrub, gardens, cultivation; up to 800 m.

CRIMSON SUNBIRD *Aethopyga siparaja* 11–13.5 cm

(19) **Male** *seheriae*: Red head, mantle and upper breast, iridescent dark green crown and tail, greyish belly. (20) **Male eclipse**: Like female but throat and breast red. (21) **Female**: Overall dull olive, slightly yellower below. **Juvenile**: As female; male with red-washed throat/breast. **Other subspecies** *A.s.siparaja* (extreme S), *mangini* (south-east NE), *cara* (east NW,C,NE,SE), *trangensis* (south W,S). **VOICE** Rapid sharp ***tsip-it-sip-it-sit*** etc. Calls with sharp ***whit*** or ***tit*** notes. **HABITAT** Various broadleaved forests, secondary growth, gardens; up to 1,000 m (mostly lowlands).

TEMMINCK'S SUNBIRD *Aethopyga temminckii* 10–12.5 cm

(22) **Male** *temminckii*: Like Crimson but head-sides, nape, mantle, wing-coverts, throat, breast and tail all scarlet. (23) **Female**: Like Crimson but underparts yellowish-olive, wings and tail fringed reddish-rufous. **VOICE** Song is a monotonous rhythmic ***tit-it tit-it tit-it tit-it***… **HABITAT** Broadleaved evergreen forest, forest edge, secondary growth; up to 1,525 m.

PLATE 122 SUNBIRDS & SPIDERHUNTERS

MRS GOULD'S SUNBIRD *Aethopyga gouldiae* 11–16.5 cm

 (1) **Male** *dabryii*: Red upperparts and breast, yellow rump-band and belly. (2) **Female**: Yellow rump-band, yellow belly (both brighter than Black-throated). **Male eclipse**: Like female but retains red on breast and yellow belly. **Juvenile**: Like female. Male is yellower below. **VOICE** Calls include quickly repeated *tzip*, lisping *squeeeeee* (rising in middle) and *tshi-stshi-ti-ti-ti…* in alarm. **HABITAT** Broadleaved evergreen forest, forest edge, secondary growth; 1,200–2,565 m.

GREEN-TAILED SUNBIRD *Aethopyga nipalensis* 11–13.5 cm

 (3) **Male** *angkanensis*: Like Mrs Gould's but crown, throat and tail iridescent dark green, mantle dark red, breast yellow with defined scarlet-red patch. (4) **Female**: From Mrs Gould's and Black-throated by white-tipped graduated undertail, no clear-cut rump-band. From Crimson by yellower belly and tail. **Juvenile**: Apparently as female but tail squarer with less white on tips. Male may have orange wash on breast. **Other subspecies** *A.n.australis* (S): Breast yellow with slight red streaking. **VOICE** Sings with a monotonous high-pitched, metallic *wit-iritz wit-iri wit-iritz wit-iritz wit-iri wit-iritz…* and *tu-tsri tu-tsri tu-tsri tu-trsi* etc. Calls with loud, high-pitched *chit* notes. **HABITAT** Broadleaved evergreen forest, forest edge, secondary growth; 1,500–2,565 m (above 915 m in S).

BLACK-THROATED SUNBIRD *Aethopyga saturata* 11–15 cm

 (5) **Male** *petersi*: Black throat/upper breast, pale yellow lower breast, dull whitish-yellow belly and rump-band. (6) **Female**: Clear-cut pale yellow rump-band. Greyer than Mrs Gould's, paler, narrower rump-band, duller below. *A.s.anomala* is a little duller/greyer, with narrower rump-band. (7) **Male** *anomala* (S): More purplish on head/tail, darker maroon mantle, bluish-purple rump/uppertail-coverts (no yellow band), greyer belly/vent, orange-yellow narrowly across lower breast. **Other subspecies** *A.s.galenae* (southern NW). *A.s.wrayi* (? in extreme S): Roughly intermediate between *petersi* and *anomala* (has very narrow yellow rump-band) but more like latter below. **VOICE** Sings with sharp, high *swi*, *tis* and *tsi* tones, interspersed with rapid metallic trills: *swi'it'it'it'it'it* and *swi'i'i'i'i'i* etc. Calls with quick, high-pitched, thin *tit* and *tiss-it* etc. **HABITAT** Broadleaved evergreen forest, forest edge; 300–1,700 m.

FIRE-TAILED SUNBIRD *Aethopyga ignicauda* 11.5–19 cm

 (8) **Male** *ignicauda*: Uppertail-coverts and tail red, long tail-streamers. (9) **Female**: Rump yellower than Green-tailed, no white on squarer tail. Often some brownish-orange on tail-sides. **Male eclipse**: As female but with red on uppertail-coverts/tail-sides. **VOICE** Sings with short high-pitched *it'i'tit-tit'tut'tutututut* etc. **HABITAT** Open broadleaved evergreen forest, secondary growth; recorded at 2,075 m.

LITTLE SPIDERHUNTER *Arachnothera longirostra* 16.5 cm

 (10) **Adult** *longirostra*: Slaty-grey head, whitish lores/cheeks and throat, broken eyering, yellow belly, white tail-tip. **Juvenile**: Throat tinged yellowish-olive. **Other subspecies** *A.l.sordida* (east NW, north-west NE), *pallida* (SE), *cinereicollis* (S). **VOICE** Song is a monotonous *wit-wit-wit-*

wit-wit-wit… Calls with a loud abrasive *itch* or *chit*. **HABITAT & BEHAVIOUR** Broadleaved evergreen and semi-evergreen forest, forest edge, secondary growth, gardens; up to 1,300 m.

THICK-BILLED SPIDERHUNTER *Arachnothera crassirostris* 16.5–17 cm

 (11) **Adult**: Like Little but bill thicker, throat/breast greyish-olive, broad broken eyering yellowish, no white tail-tip. **Juvenile**: Greyer below. **VOICE** Song is a monotonous *whit whit whit whit whit…* or faster *whit-whit-whit-whit…* Calls include chattering *chit* notes and repeated worrisome, rather high *ut-u-it-it-it-it-it-it*. **HABITAT & BEHAVIOUR** Broadleaved evergreen forest, forest edge, clearings, banana groves; lowlands. Usually in canopy but descends to feed.

LONG-BILLED SPIDERHUNTER *A.robusta* 21.5–22 cm

 (12) **Adult** *robusta*: Very long, strongly downcurved bill, uniform head-sides, faintly dark-streaked yellowish-olive throat and breast, and yellow belly; outertail tipped white. **Juvenile**: Unstreaked. **VOICE** Loud *chit-chit-chit* in flight. **HABITAT** Broadleaved evergreen forest (usually in canopy), forest edge; up to 1,200 m.

SPECTACLED SPIDERHUNTER *A.flavigaster* 21.5–22 cm

 (13) **Adult**: Relatively large and robust; thick broad-based bill, broad yellow eyering, yellow patch on ear-coverts. **VOICE** Calls with a loud, rather deep *chit'it* or *chut'ut*, particularly in flight. **HABITAT** Broadleaved evergreen forest, forest edge, secondary growth; lowlands, occasionally up to 600 m.

YELLOW-EARED SPIDERHUNTER *A.chrysogenys* 18 cm

 (14) **Adult** *chrysogenys*: Like Spectacled but smaller with relatively thinner bill, narrower eyering, slightly larger yellow patch on ear-coverts. **Juvenile**: Duller, cheek/ear-covert patch smaller/almost absent. **VOICE** Call is a harsh *tchick*. **HABITAT** Broadleaved evergreen forest (mostly in canopy), forest edge, secondary growth, gardens; up to 900 m.

GREY-BREASTED SPIDERHUNTER *A.affinis* 18 cm

 (15) **Adult** *modesta*: Bright olive-green above, paler olive-greyish below, narrow dark streaks on throat and breast. **Juvenile**: Unstreaked below. **VOICE** Calls with (often quickly) repeated harsh *chititick*, sometimes extending to more chattering *tchitititew* and *tchew-tew-tew* when agitated. **HABITAT & BEHAVIOUR** Broadleaved evergreen forest, secondary growth, gardens, sometimes cultivation; up to 1,100 m. Often feeds in lower storey, particularly around banana plants.

STREAKED SPIDERHUNTER *A.magna* 17–20.5 cm

 (16) **Adult** *musarum*: Yellowish-olive above, whitish below, heavily streaked head and body, orange legs. **Juvenile**: Streaking somewhat less distinct. **Other subspecies** *A.m.pagodarum* (south W), *magna* (presumably this in S). **VOICE** Has strident chattering song. Calls with loud, strident *chit-ik*, particularly in flight. **HABITAT & BEHAVIOUR** Broadleaved evergreen and mixed deciduous forest, secondary growth; 300–1,800 m. Flight strongly undulating.

PLATE 123 FOREST WAGTAIL & PIPITS

FOREST WAGTAIL *Dendronanthus indicus* 17–18 cm

(1) **Adult**: Brownish-olive crown and upperparts, whitish underparts with double dark breast-band (lower one broken) and strongly contrasting blackish and whitish wing pattern. **VOICE** Song is an intense, repetitive see-sawing series of usually 3–6 notes: **dzi-chu dzi-chu dzi-chu dzi-chu**... Calls with subdued, metallic **pink** or **dzink-dzzt** (particularly in flight). **HABITAT & BEHAVIOUR** Open broadleaved evergreen and deciduous forest, forest tracks and trails, wooded cultivation, gardens, mangroves; up to 1,500 m. Often found walking on leafy ground, where well camouflaged. Roosts communally, locally in large numbers.

RICHARD'S PIPIT *Anthus richardi* 18–20.5 cm

(2) **Adult** *richardi*: From very similar Blyth's and Paddyfield by size, posture, subtle plumage details and voice. From Blyth's by slightly longer bill, legs and tail, slightly less contrastingly streaked upperparts, slightly more extensive white on outertail, more pointed and less clear-cut dark median covert centres; longer, straighter, less arched hindclaw. Much larger than Paddyfield, longer bill/tail, usually heavier/more extensive breast-streaking. (3) **Adult worn**: Greyer above with more pronounced dark streaking, paler below. (4) **First winter**: As adult but some whiter-fringed coverts; median covert fringes more even (very like Blyth's). **Other subspecies** *A.r.sinensis* (throughout[except SE]): Slightly smaller and less heavily streaked above (difficult to judge in field). **VOICE** Song is a simple grinding **tschivu-tschivu-tschivu-tschivu-tschivu**... (given in undulating song-flight). Loud, harsh **schree-ep** or **shreep** flight call, particularly when flushed. **HABITAT & BEHAVIOUR** Open country, grassy areas, cultivation; lowlands; up to 1,830 m. Frequently hovers before landing; typically adopts more upright posture than Blyth's.

PADDYFIELD PIPIT *Anthus rufulus* 15–16 cm

(5) **Adult** *rufulus*: Much smaller than Richard's, shorter bill/tail, usually more indistinct/restricted breast-streaks. (6) **Adult worn**: Differs as Richard's. (7) **Juvenile**: Upperparts appear more scalloped, has heavy dark spotting on breast. **Other subspecies** *A.r.malayensis* (S). **VOICE** Song is a simple repetitive **chew-ii chew-ii chew-ii chew-ii**..., sometimes also **chik-a-chik** in song-flight descent. Call is an explosive but relatively subdued **chip**, **chup** or **chwist**, usually in flight. **HABITAT & BEHAVIOUR** Open areas, drier cultivation; up to 800 m. Flight pattern typically weaker, more fluttering than Richard's; rarely hovers before landing. Undulating song-flight; also rises high in air and parachutes down.

BLYTH'S PIPIT *Anthus godlewskii* 17 cm

(8) **Adult**: See Richard's. Slightly shorter/more pointed bill, more square-cut/well-defined median covert centres; white on penultimate outertail feather usually in wedge on terminal third (usually mostly white on Richard's). (9) **First winter**: Not separable from Richard's by median coverts unless freshly moulted adult feathers present. **VOICE** Calls quieter, less rasping than Richard's. Short **tchu**, **dju**, **chep** or **tchupp** (may be doubled), softer **chewp** or **cheep**; slightly nasal **tchii** and shriller **psheet** or **pshreu** in alarm. **HABITAT & BEHAVIOUR** Open country, dry cultivation; lowlands. Rarely hovers before landing; posture often more horizontal (more wagtail-like) than Richard's.

OLIVE-BACKED PIPIT *Anthus hodgsoni* 16–17 cm

(10) **Adult** *yunnanensis*: Rather plain greenish-olive above, broad whitish supercilium (usually buffier in front of eye), whitish spot and blackish patch on rear ear-coverts (sometimes indistinct), prominent blackish streaking/spotting on buff breast and flanks. More greyish-olive above and somewhat whiter below when worn. (11) **Juvenile**: Initially differs from adult by browner, more boldly streaked upperparts. (12) **Adult** *hodgsoni* (recorded NW,NE): Heavier streaks above and on flanks, more streaks on lower underparts. **VOICE** Sings with rapid high sweet notes slurred together, mixed with shortish trills or rattles. Call is a thin hoarse **teez** or **spiz** in flight. Alarm call is a very quiet short **tsi tsi**... **HABITAT & BEHAVIOUR** Mostly open areas and tracks in forest, wooded cultivation; up to 2,565 m. Often walks amongst undergrowth and leaf-litter.

RED-THROATED PIPIT *Anthus cervinus* 15–16.5 cm

(13) **Adult**: Brick-/pinkish-red head-sides and throat/upper breast. Often no dark markings on head-sides/breast. (14) **Adult variant (dull female)**: Autumn/winter birds and females tend to have less reddish on head. (15) **First winter**: Lacks reddish coloration on head. Bold dark-streaks above (including rump), pronounced whitish to pale buff mantle 'braces', whitish wing-bars, bold blackish streaks on breast and flanks. **VOICE** Rhythmic ringing song of sharp drawn-out notes and dry buzzing sounds. Flight call is a long high **pseeoo** or **pssiih**. Also a short **chupp** in alarm. **HABITAT** Open areas, drier cultivation, often near water; up to 400 m.

ROSY PIPIT *Anthus roseatus* 16.5 cm

(16) **Adult non-breeding**: Like first-winter Red-throated but greyer-brown above (more olive when fresh), darker head-sides, prominent supercilium, faint/no mantle 'braces', more olive tertial/secondary fringes (mainly when fresh), quite plain rump/uppertail-coverts, darker bill. (17) **Adult breeding**: Loses dark malar and breast-streaks; vinous-pinkish supercilium, throat and breast. (18) **Juvenile**: Similar to non-breeding adult but browner above and less heavily streaked below. **VOICE** Sings in flight: twittering **tit-tit-tit-tit-tit teedle teedle** during ascent, and long fading **tsuli-tsuli-tsuli-tsuli**... or **sweet-sweet-sweet** during descent. Call is a thin **tsip tsip tsip**... or **seep-seep**... **HABITAT** Marshy areas, rice paddies, open short grassy areas and clearings; up to 1,300 m.

BUFF-BELLIED PIPIT *Anthus rubescens* 16.5 cm

(19) **Adult non-breeding** *japonicus*: Resembles Rosy but cold greyish-brown upperparts have only faint streaking and appear very plain at distance (a little more prominently streaked when worn), lores paler, base colour to underparts whitish to pale buffish. (20) **Adult breeding**: Greyer above, plainer/buffier below (breast warmer), fine dark streaks on breast only. **VOICE** Flight call is a thin high-pitched **tseep** or **zzeeep**, frequently repeated. **HABITAT** Marshy areas, wetland fringes, cultivation; lowlands.

PLATE 124 LARKS & WAGTAILS

AUSTRALASIAN BUSHLARK *Mirafra javanica* 14–15 cm

(1) **Adult** *williamsoni*: Weak streaks on strongly warm brown-washed breast, all-whitish outermost tail feathers. (2) **Juvenile**: Crown and mantle less clearly streaked, crown darker than mantle, with pale scaling, breast paler with more diffuse streaking, bill more uniformly pale. **VOICE** Sings with short varied strophes (often with mimicry); slower/less continuous than Oriental Skylark. Sharp rapid *pitsi pitsi pitsipipipipi* or *tsitsitsitsi* in alarm. **HABITAT & BEHAVIOUR** Short grassland with bushes, dry marsh edges, rice-field stubble; lowlands. Sings from perch or in towering song-flight, with flickering wings.

INDOCHINESE BUSHLARK *Mirafra marionae* 14–15 cm

(3) **Adult**: Relatively robust, stout-billed and broad-winged, no obvious crest. Extensively rufous-chestnut flight feathers in flight. Heavier-marked breast than Australasian, no white on outertail. (4) **Juvenile**: Scaled buff above, breast-streaking more diffuse, shows more obvious pale nuchal collar. **VOICE** Phrases of thin drawn-out notes, forming 2–8 s strophe: *tzu'eeez'eezu-eeez'eezu-eeez'eezu-eeez'eezu-eeez' eezu-eeez'eezu-eeez'eezu-eeez'-eeez'eez'piz'piz-eez' piz'piz-eeez'piz'piz-eeez'piz'piz-eeez'piz'piz-tzueeez' piz'piz-tzueeez'piz'piz-tzueeez'piz'piz-tzueeez pizeeeu-pizeeeu-pizeeeu-pizeeeu-pizeeeu*... Calls with a thin rattling *tirrrrrrrrrrrrrrrr*...; sometimes a hammering *tzet-tzet-tzet-tzet-tzet-tzet-tzet-tzet-tzet*... **HABITAT & BEHAVIOUR** More open, drier areas, open forest edge, cultivation; lowlands. Sings from ground, telephone wire, small tree etc., sometimes in short song-flight, ending in parachuting, with wings slightly raised, tail fanned, legs dangling.

ORIENTAL SKYLARK *Alauda gulgula* 16.5–18 cm

(5) **Adult** *herberti*: Slender bill, crest; dark-streaked above, pale buffy-whitish below, clear breast-streaking. Wings less rounded than bush-larks with thin paler sandy/rusty trailing edge and less rufous flight feathers. (6) **Juvenile**: Paler above with narrow whitish fringing, whitish wing-covert tips, more diffuse breast-streaking. **VOICE** Song is incessant, high-pitched and sweet. Calls with a dry twangy *chizz*, *baz baz* and *baz-terrr* etc. **HABITAT & BEHAVIOUR** Various open habitats, cultivation, larger forest clearings; lowlands. Flight stronger than bushlarks; has high soaring song-flight.

WHITE WAGTAIL *Motacilla alba* 19 cm

(7) **Male non-breeding** *leucopsis*: White head and underparts, black hindcrown, nape and isolated gorget, black upperside and wings with broad white fringes to wing-coverts and tertials, and white outertail feathers. (8) **Male breeding**: Black gorget extends up to lower throat and joins black of mantle. (9) **Female non-breeding**: Slaty-grey above, narrower gorget. (10) **Juvenile**: Like female but crown and nape grey, gorget more diffuse. (11) **Male non-breeding** *alboides* (NW): Black ear-coverts join broader gorget, less white on forecrown. (12) **Male breeding**: All-black throat. (13) **Female non-breeding**: Greyer above than male. (14) **Juvenile**: Appears more like very washed-out adult than

leucopsis. (15) **Male non-breeding** *baicalensis* (visitor NW,NE): Grey above, large gorget. Breeders have black lower throat/upper breast. (16) **Female non-breeding**: Crown duller than male, upperparts much paler grey than *leucopsis*. (17) **Male non-breeding** *ocularis* (visitor NW,NE,C): Like *baicalensis* but shows black eyestripe. (18) **Male breeding**: Black lower throat and upper breast. (19) **Female non-breeding**: Black of crown/nape greyer and less contrasting than male. (20) **Male non-breeding** *ssp./sp.* (Mekong R, south-east NE): Black forehead, broad white supercilium, white throat and patch on neck-side. **VOICE** Simple twittering, chattering song. Calls with clear harsh *tsli-vitt*. **HABITAT** Open habitats, often near water; up to 2,000 m.

CITRINE WAGTAIL *Motacilla citreola* 18–19 cm

(21) **Male breeding** *citreola*: All-yellow head and underparts, black nuchal band, grey mantle, back and rump. (22) **Male non-breeding/female**: Resembles female Yellow but shows distinctive yellow lores, supercilium, throat and breast, grey upperparts and whitish undertail-coverts; ear-coverts have dark border and paler centre (often washed yellow) and are encircled by yellow; usually shows prominent white wing-bars. (23) **First winter**: Usually purer grey above than Yellow, supercilium goes behind ear-coverts (or slightly broken), often a blackish lateral crown-line; buff-washed forehead, pale lores, all-dark bill, usually bolder wing-bars. **VOICE** Harsh *dzeep* or *brrzreep*. Song uses similar sounds. **HABITAT** Freshwater wetlands, wet farmland; up to 450 m.

YELLOW WAGTAIL *Motacilla flava* 18 cm

(24) **Male breeding** *thunbergi* (incl. *angarensis*, *plexa*): Olive-green above, blue-grey head, thin whitish supercilium, yellow below with whiter throat. Non-breeders have duller head, whiter below (races often inseparable). (25) **Female**: Dull greyish-/brownish-olive above, duller and less extensive yellow below. (26) **First winter**: Like female but upperparts tend to be greyer, underparts whiter. (27) **Male breeding** *macronyx* (widespread): Darker bluish-slate on head, no supercilium, yellow lower throat. (28) **Male breeding** *taivana* (recorded C,S): Olive-green crown and head-sides, broad yellow supercilium. (29) **Female**: Broad clear-cut yellowish supercilium. **VOICE** Long harsh *chrzeep*. Song of 2–3 scraping notes. **HABITAT & BEHAVIOUR** Open areas, mainly near water. Roosts communally.

GREY WAGTAIL *Motacilla cinerea* 19 cm

(30) **Male non-breeding/female** *cinerea*: Slaty-grey above and on ear-coverts, thin whitish supercilium, blackish wing-coverts, bright yellow rump, tail-coverts and vent. Females may show blackish throat-mottling in spring. (31) **Male breeding**: Underparts all yellow with black throat and upper breast. **Juvenile**: Browner above than non-breeding male/female, buff-tinged supercilium, dark-mottled breast-sides. **VOICE** Song is a short mechanical series of sharp notes: *ziss-ziss-ziss-ziss*..., often mixed with higher *si si si siu* etc. Loud *tittick* or *tzit-tzit* (higher than White). **HABITAT** Open areas/forest, often by flowing streams; up to 2,565 m.

1–6 to different scale

PLATE 125 SPARROWS, WEAVERS & PIN-TAILED PARROTFINCH

HOUSE SPARROW *Passer domesticus* 15 cm

(1) **Male breeding** *indicus*: Grey crown, whitish head-sides, broad black bib. Chestnut from eye to nape-side, blackish and pale brownish streaks on dull chestnut mantle, brownish-grey rump/upper-tail-coverts, black bill. (2) **Male non-breeding**: Browner crown, greyer mantle, pale tips on bib and crown-/nape-sides, pale bill. (3) **Female**: Rather nondescript with paler supercilium and underparts, blackish-brown streaks above, pale horn-coloured bill. Superficially resembles some weavers and buntings but lacks streaks on head and underparts. **Juvenile**: Initially paler above than female, plainer mantle/scapulars, often better-defined supercilium, paler bill. **VOICE** Sings in monotonous series of call notes: ***chirrup cheep chirp***... etc. Calls include ***chirrup***, ***chissick*** or ***tissip***, soft ***swee swee*** or ***dwee***, shrill ***chree*** and rolling ***chur-r-r-it-it-it*** in alarm. **HABITAT** Towns, villages, cultivation, scrub; lowlands.

RUSSET SPARROW *Passer rutilans* 13.5–14 cm

(4) **Male** *intensior*: Rufous-chestnut crown and upperparts, dingy pale yellowish head-sides and centre of abdomen, narrow black bib, prominent white wing-bar. Mantle streaked blackish, breast and flanks greyish. (5) **Female**: Resembles House but darker eyestripe, more contrasting supercilium, rufescent rump, whiter bar on median coverts, creamy-yellowish throat with dusky central stripe, creamy-yellowish belly-centre and vent. **Juvenile**: Like female but tinged warmer brown above, supercilium buffier, bill paler. **First-winter male**: Duller than adult, upperparts mixed with greyish-brown, bib dusky mixed with black. **VOICE** Song is similar to House: ***cheep-chirrup-cheweep*** or ***chwe-cha-cha*** etc., frequently repeated. Calls with ***cheeep*** or ***chilp*** notes, sweeter/more musical than House. Also ***swee swee***, in alarm. **HABITAT** Open forest, cultivation; up to 2,100 m (mainly in mountains).

PLAIN-BACKED SPARROW *Passer flaveolus* 13.5–15 cm

(6) **Male**: Unstreaked above, rufous-chestnut band from eye to nape-side, rufous-chestnut scapulars/lower mantle, yellowish lower head-sides and vent. Crown, upper mantle, back, rump and uppertail-coverts greenish-grey. (7) **Female**: Told from other sparrows by unstreaked upperparts and pale yellowish-tinged underparts (throat often buffish), with drab pale greyish wash across breast. **Juvenile**: Like female but crown and lower mantle slightly darker, throat duller. **VOICE** Loud clear ***filip*** or ***chirrup***, less harsh but more metallic than Eurasian Tree. Also ***chu-chu-weet*** in alarm. **HABITAT** Open woodland, coastal scrub, dry open areas and cultivation, margins of human habitation; up to 800 m.

EURASIAN TREE SPARROW *Passer montanus* 14–14.5 cm

(8) **Adult** *malaccensis*: Whitish head-sides with isolated blackish patch, dull chestnut crown and nape, small blackish bib. (9) **Juvenile**: Duller; crown paler brown with dark markings on forecrown, ear-covert patch and bib less defined, pale base to lower mandible. **VOICE** Song is a series of calls along with ***tsooit***, ***tsreet*** and ***tswee-ip*** notes. Harsh ***chip*** and ***chissip*** calls, sharp ***tet*** and ***tsooit*** and dry ***tet-tet-tet***... in flight. **HABITAT** Urban areas, human habitation, cultivation; up to 1,830 m.

STREAKED WEAVER *Ploceus manyar* 13.5 cm

(10) **Male breeding** *williamsoni*: Yellow crown, blackish streaks prominent on breast and narrow on flanks. (11) **Male non-breeding/female**: Well-defined (but often fine) blackish streaks on breast. Dark head-sides, with pronounced yellowish-white supercilium, submoustachial stripe and neck-patch; crown and upperparts boldly streaked buffish-brown and blackish. Resembles some buntings but much thicker-billed, tail shorter and more rounded, without white. Non-breeding male often with more distinct breast-streaking. **Juvenile**: Similar to female. **VOICE** Sings with soft continuous trill: ***see-see-see-see-see***... ending with ***o-chee***. Also ***tre tre cherrer cherrer***. Calls with loud ***chirt*** notes. **HABITAT & BEHAVIOUR** Grassland, reedbeds, marshes, cultivation, often near water; up to 915 m (mostly plains). Gregarious, often in mixed flocks with other weavers.

BAYA WEAVER *Ploceus philippinus* 15 cm

(12) **Male breeding** *angelorum*: Yellow crown and unstreaked warm buffish-brown breast. Rest of upperparts similar to Streaked; breast may appear faintly mottled or show faint dark streaks at sides. (13) **Male non-breeding/female**: Rather plain head-sides, quite plain warm brown breast, sometimes faintly dark-streaked at sides (no obvious streaks); whitish throat and vent. See Asian Golden. (14) **Juvenile**: Like female but breast and flanks rather deeper buff, crown-streaking broader and more broken. (15) **Male breeding** *infortunatus* (S): More rufescent base colour above, darker/more rufescent breast/flanks. **VOICE** Sings with chattering notes, then wheezy ***cher-wiu***. Calls with harsh ***chit*** notes. **HABITAT & BEHAVIOUR** Cultivation, grassland, open areas, secondary growth; up to 1,220 m (mostly lowlands). Roosts communally. Often associates with other weavers.

ASIAN GOLDEN WEAVER *Ploceus hypoxanthus* 15 cm

(16) **Male breeding** *hymenaicus*: Yellow head and body, black head-sides, throat and upperpart-streaking. (17) **Female**: Very like Baya but more conical bill (as deep as long), almost no obvious forehead, no mottling on breast, crown-streaks broader (more contrast with supercilium). **Male non-breeding**: Like female but often tinged yellow on supercilium and underparts (sometimes upperparts). **Juvenile**: Like female. **VOICE** Similar to Baya. **HABITAT** Marshes, grass and reeds, rice paddies, invariably close to water; lowlands.

PIN-TAILED PARROTFINCH *Erythrura prasina* 12.5–13 cm (male tail up to 3 cm more)

(18) **Male** *prasina*: Green above, blue face and throat, warm buff below, bright red lower rump, uppertail-coverts and long pointed tail. Often shows pale red patch on centre of abdomen and pale bluish wash on breast. (19) **Female**: Much shorter tail, often pale powder-blue on head-side but no blue face, washed-out buffish below. **Juvenile**: As female but lower rump to tail orange-/brownish-red, lower mandible mostly yellowish/pinkish. **VOICE** High ***zit***, ***tseet-tseet*** or ***tsit-tsit*** and sharp ***teger-teter-terge*** calls. **HABITAT & BEHAVIOUR** Bamboo, open forest; up to 1,500 m. Semi-nomadic, depending on seeding bamboo. Often in flocks, which can be quite large.

PLATE 126 RED AVADAVAT, MUNIAS, JAVA SPARROW, CHAFFINCH & BRAMBLING

RED AVADAVAT *Amandava amandava* 10 cm

(1) **Male breeding** *punicea*: Bright red with white spotting on scapulars, uppertail-coverts and underparts. (2) **Female**: Greyish-brown, paler below; red rump, uppertail-coverts and bill, small white spots on wing-coverts. (3) **Juvenile**: Like female but lacks red, wing-bars buff. **Male non-breeding**: As female but white-spotted uppertail-coverts, large wing-spots. **VOICE** Song is a very high feeble warble, mixed with sweeter twittering. Calls with thin *pseep*, *teei* or *tsi* (mainly in flight). **HABITAT & BEHAVIOUR** Grassland, marshes, secondary growth/scrub; up to 1,525 m (mainly lowlands). In small flocks; may be secretive.

WHITE-RUMPED MUNIA *Lonchura striata* 11–11.5 cm

(4) **Adult** *subsquamicollis*: Dark brownish plumage with contrasting whitish rump and belly. (5) **Juvenile**: Dark parts of plumage paler and browner, rump and belly tinged buffish. **Other subspecies** *L.s.acuticauda* (north NW). **VOICE** Song is a twittering *pit pit pit spee boyee* or *prt prt prt spee boyee*, with distinctly down-turned end-note. Calls with a tinkling metallic *prrrit*, *pirit* or *tr-tr-tr* etc., particularly when flying. **HABITAT & BEHAVIOUR** Clearings, secondary growth, scrub and grass, cultivation; up to 1,500 m. Usually in flocks.

SCALY-BREASTED MUNIA *Lonchura punctulata* 12–12.5 cm

(6) **Adult** *topela*: Drab above, yellowish-olive on rump/tail, chestnut-tinged head-sides, brown-scaled below. (7) **Juvenile**: Paler and plain above, slightly buffish drab brown below, lower mandible paler than upper. (8) **Adult** *fretensis* (southern S): Bolder scaling below, slightly paler/warmer above, greyer rump to uppertail. **VOICE** Song is a soft series of high flute-like whistles and low slurred notes. Calls include a sibilant piping *ki-dee ki-dee...* or *kitty-kitty-kitty* (mainly in flight), rapidly repeated harsh *chup* or *tret* notes and *kit-eeeeee* or *ki-ki-ki-ki-teeee* in alarm. **HABITAT & BEHAVIOUR** Cultivation, scrub, secondary growth; up to 1,500 m. In flocks.

WHITE-BELLIED MUNIA *Lonchura leucogastra* 11–11.5 cm

(9) **Adult** *leucogastra*: Very dark brown, olive-yellow tail-fringes, whitish belly, no whitish rump. **Juvenile**: Dark plumage parts browner, lacks shaft-streaks on upperparts, tail duller, belly buffier. **VOICE** Song is a rapidly repeated *di-di-ptcheee-pti-pti-pti-pteep*. Calls with a piping *prrip prrip...* and soft cheeping *chee-ee-ee*. **HABITAT & BEHAVIOUR** Open and secondary broadleaved evergreen forest, forest edge, scrub and cultivation near forest; up to 455 m. Often in small flocks.

BLACK-HEADED MUNIA *Lonchura malacca* 11–11.5 cm

(10) **Adult** *deignani*: Rufous-chestnut with black hood, blackish central belly and vent, blue-grey bill. (11) **Juvenile**: Plain brown above, buff below, bluish bill, crown darker than White-headed, underparts buffier. **Other subspecies** *L.m.sinensis* (south-west, S). **VOICE** Song is a very quiet series of bill-snapping notes followed by 'silent' singing (no sound

audible), ending with faint drawn-out whistled notes. Call is a weak reedy *pee pee...* (particularly in flight). **HABITAT & BEHAVIOUR** Grassland, marshes, scrub, cultivation, rice paddies; up to 400 m (mostly lowlands). Usually in flocks, sometimes very large.

WHITE-HEADED MUNIA *Lonchura maja* 11.5 cm

(12) **Adult** *maja*: White head, broad pale vinous-brown collar. (13) **Juvenile**: Like Black-headed but crown duller and paler, head-sides paler, underparts duller buff. **VOICE** Song involves bill-clicking followed by a high-pitched, tinkling *weeeeee heeheeheeheehee*, constantly repeated. Calls with a thin piping *puip*, *peekt* and *pee-eet* (mainly in flight); higher-pitched and less reedy than Black-headed. **HABITAT & BEHAVIOUR** Grassland, cultivation, rice paddies, scrub; up to 300 m. Usually in flocks, sometimes quite large.

JAVA SPARROW *Padda oryzivora* 16 cm

(14) **Adult**: Grey with black head and rump to tail, white ear-coverts, red bill and legs, pinkish belly. (15) **Juvenile**: Washed-out brownish; darker crown/tail, pale ear-coverts, dull buffish below, breast streaked. **VOICE** Sings with a series of soft bell-like notes, followed by trilling and clucking sounds and often ending with a whining, drawn-out, metallic *ti-tui*. Calls include a soft liquid *tup*, *t-luk* or *ch-luk* (particularly in flight) and sharp *tak*. **HABITAT** Cultivation, rice paddies, margins of human habitation; lowlands.

CHAFFINCH *Fringilla coelebs* 16 cm

(16) **Male non-breeding** *coelebs*?: Mostly blue-grey crown, vinous-pinkish face/underparts, grey-green rump. (17) **Male breeding**: Crown/nape smooth blue-grey, forehead black, more rufescent face/ear-coverts/underparts. (18) **Female**: Duller than Brambling; no orange, grey-buff to whitish below, vague head-bands; green-grey rump. **Juvenile**: Like female but nape and rump browner. **VOICE** Song is a bright, loud, almost rattling phrase, introduced by rapidly repeated sharp notes: *zitt-zitt-zitt-zitt-sett-sett-chatt-chiteriidia*. Call is a loud sharp *fink*, unobtrusive *yupp* in flight (softer than similar call of Brambling) and sharp fine *ziib* notes when agitated. **HABITAT** Open forest, secondary growth, cultivation; recorded at c.400 m.

BRAMBLING *Fringilla montifringilla* 15.5–16 cm

(19) **Male non-breeding**: Blackish head and mantle with heavy grey to brown scaling, pale orange throat, breast, flanks and scapulars, white rump. (20) **Male breeding**: Black and orange colours more solid, blackish bill. (21) **Female**: Like non-breeding male but crown and ear-coverts plainer greyish-brown. (22) **Juvenile**: Like female but head buffier. **VOICE** Song is a simple buzzing *rrrrhuh*. Calls include a hard nasal *te-ehp*, slightly nasal *yeck* in flight, sharp rasping *zwee* or *tsweek* and repeated silvery *slitt* notes when agitated. **HABITAT** Open forest, cultivation; recorded at c.1,500 m.

PLATE 127 BLACK-HEADED GREENFINCH, ROSEFINCHES, SCARLET FINCH & GROSBEAKS

BLACK-HEADED GREENFINCH *Carduelis ambigua* 13 cm

(1) **Male** *ambigua*: Largely olive-green, blackish crown/ear-coverts. Pale grey fringes and yellow slash on wing. (2) **Female**: Duller crown and ear-coverts, paler/more uniform throat, breast and flanks (latter tinged brown). (3) **Juvenile**: Duller above and paler below than female, with dark streaks; wing-bars buffier. **VOICE** Sings with long wheezes: *wheeeeeu* or *jiiiiii* etc., punctuated by call notes. Calls with jingling *titutitu* and *titu-titu titu-tittrititititit* etc., mixed with harder *jutututut*, quiet rising buzzy *jieuu* and soft *chu-chu* etc. **HABITAT & BEHAVIOUR** Open forest, secondary growth, cultivation; 1,200–2,565 m. In flocks, sometimes large.

DARK-BREASTED ROSEFINCH *Carpodacus nipalensis* 16–16.5 cm

(4) **Male** *intensicolor*: Dark brownish-red upperparts and breast, contrasting red forecrown, pinkish-red rear supercilium, lower ear-coverts, throat and belly. Lacks distinct pale wing markings. (5) **Female**: Unstreaked drab brown. Very vague darker mantle-streaking, warm buffish-brown wing-bars, slightly buffier-brown outer fringes to tertials; underparts paler and greyer than upperparts. **Juvenile**: Similar to female. **VOICE** Sings with series of chipping notes. Calls with clear double whistle, sparrow-like twittering and *cha'a'rrr* in alarm. **HABITAT** Underbrush in open broadleaved evergreen forest, forest edge, secondary growth, scrub, cultivation borders; 1,900–2,565 m.

COMMON ROSEFINCH *Carpodacus erythrinus* 16–16.5 cm

(6) **Male breeding** *roseatus*: Red head and body, with darker, vaguely streaked/mottled mantle, scapulars and uppertail-coverts; whitish vent. Dark brown wings with pale fringing and two red bars on coverts. (7) **Male non-breeding/Female**: Greyish-brown above, dull whitish below (duller on lower throat/breast); delicate darker streaking on crown, mantle, lower throat, breast, upper belly and flanks, two narrow buffy-whitish wing-bars. Rather plain head-sides (beady-eyed appearance), no pale supercilium. Resembles some buntings but plainer above and on head-sides, no white on tail, thicker bill. (8) **Juvenile**: Browner than female, stronger streaking above, broader, buffier wing-bars, pale buffish outer tertial fringes. (9) **Male breeding** *erythrinus* (visitor NW): Less vivid red, whiter belly/vent, greyer-brown above, duller wing-bars. **VOICE** Song is a slowly rising whistle: *weeeja-wu-weeeja* or *te-te-wee-chew*. Typically calls with a clear whistled *ooeet* or *too-ee* and sharp nasal *chay-eeee* in alarm. **HABITAT** Secondary growth and scrub, cultivation; up to 2,565 m.

PINK-RUMPED ROSEFINCH *Carpodacus eos* 15 cm

(10) **Male**: Pinkish-tinged greyish crown and upperparts with bold blackish streaking and contrasting, rather uniform, reddish-pink rump, supercilium, lower head-sides, throat and underparts. Face darker and redder. (11) **Female**: Resembles juvenile Common but has defined paler supercilium, greyer upperparts and whiter underparts, with denser, regular, darker streaking overall; wing-bars and tertial fringes indistinct, bill narrower. **VOICE** Calls with assertive *pink* or *tink* and bunting-like *tsip* or *tsick*. Also harsh *piprit* and

tinny *tvitt-itt-itt-itt*. **HABITAT** Forest edge, secondary growth and scrub, cultivation borders; recorded in lowlands.

SCARLET FINCH *Haematospiza sipahi* 19 cm

(12) **Male**: Uniform bright red head and body, pale yellowish bill. Wings and tail black with scarlet fringing. (13) **Female**: Rather uniform scaly brownish-olive, with paler underparts, distinctive pale bill and sharply defined bright yellow rump. See Yellow-rumped Honeyguide. (14) **First-year male**: Differs from female by orange-rufous tinge to head, upperparts and wing-feather fringes, more rufous-tinged throat and underparts, bright orange rump. **Juvenile**: Similar to female. **VOICE** Song is a clear liquid *par-ree-reeeeeee*. Calls with a loud clear *too-eee* or *pleeau* and *kwee'i'iu* or *chew'we'auh*. **HABITAT** More open broadleaved evergreen forest, forest edge, secondary growth; 1,200–2,100 m.

YELLOW-BILLED GROSBEAK *Eophona migratoria* 20.5 cm

(15) **Male** *migratoria*: Greyish-brown (darker mantle/back); bluish-black head and tail, bluish-black wings with white markings on tertials, flight-feather tips and primary coverts. Bill yellow with dark tip, base and cutting edge; rump and uppertail-coverts paler than rest of upperparts, flanks buffy-rufous, vent white. (16) **Female**: Head brownish-grey with darker face, less white on wings, more greyish below. **Juvenile**: Head and underparts initially buffier-brown than female with whitish throat, upperparts browner; shows two narrow, buffish wing-bars. **VOICE** Song consists of various whistles and trills. Call is a loud *tek-tek*. **HABITAT** Open woodland, secondary growth, scrub, cultivation, parks and gardens; recorded at 700–800 m.

COLLARED GROSBEAK *Mycerobas affinis* 24 cm

(17) **Male**: Black hood/wings/tail, yellow nape, back, rump and underparts, nape/rump washed orange-rufous. (18) **Female**: Head grey, upperparts pale greyish-green (greener on upper mantle, rump and uppertail-coverts), underparts plain yellowish-olive, wings similar to upperparts, primaries and tail blackish. (19) **Juvenile male**: As adult but olive-tinged yellow plumage, duller head, greyish-brown mottling on throat. **Juvenile female**: Paler chin/throat than adult, duller below, variable yellow on rump. **VOICE** Song is a loud piping 5–7 note *ti-di-li-ti-di-li-um* etc. Also loud creaky sounds, mixed with musical notes. Calls with rapid mellow *pip-pip-pip-pip-pip-pip-ugh*. Sharp *kurr* notes in alarm. **HABITAT** Broadleaved evergreen forest; recorded at c.2,565 m.

SPOT-WINGED GROSBEAK *Mycerobas melanozanthos* 23 cm

(20) **Male**: Black, with yellow breast to vent and whitish-tipped greater coverts, secondaries and tertials. (21) **Female**: Paler; yellow-streaked crown/mantle, streaky yellow supercilium/lower head-sides, all yellow below, with blackish malar line and streaking. Buffy-white wing-bars and tips to secondaries and tertials. (22) **Juvenile**: Dark plumage a shade paler than female, head-sides, throat, breast and flanks tinged buffish. **VOICE** Melodic *tew-tew-teeeu*, oriole-like *tyop-tiu* or *tyu-tio*, rising *ah*; rattled *krrr* or *charrarauk*. **HABITAT & BEHAVIOUR** Broadleaved evergreen forest, forest edge; 1,400–2,100 m. In flocks, often fairly large.

PLATE 128 BUNTINGS

CRESTED BUNTING *Melophus lathami* 16.5–17 cm

(1) **Male non-breeding**: Blackish with body feathers edged buffish-grey; chestnut wings/tail, long crest. (2) **Female non-breeding**: Less chestnut on wings and tail, short crest. Olive-brown above, with darker streaks; paler below with faint breast-streaks. Crest, largely chestnut wings/tail and lack of white on tail rule out other buntings. (3) **Juvenile**: Darker than breeding female, buffier below. Male develops black blotching on body plumage. **Male breeding**: Body blacker, without buffish-grey edgings. **Female breeding**: A little paler than non-breeding, mantle more boldly streaked. **VOICE** Song is brief, falling *tzit dzit dzit see-see-suee* or *tzit dzit tzit-tzitswe-e-ee-tiyuh* etc. (introductory notes hesitant and slightly grating). Call is a soft *tip* or *tup*. **HABITAT & BEHAVIOUR** Cultivation, scrub, tall grass; up to 2,565 m. Often roosts in sizeable numbers.

TRISTRAM'S BUNTING *Emberiza tristrami* 15 cm

(4) **Male non-breeding**: Duller head than breeding male, black feathers tipped paler, white feathers tinged buffish; larger buffish-white spot on ear-coverts. (5) **Male breeding**: Black head, white supercilium, median crown-/submoustachial stripes and ear-covert spot. (6) **Female**: Similar to non-breeding male but throat buffish-white, head-sides/lores pale brownish; breast/flanks streaked brown. From Little by whitish supercilium and median crown-stripe, duller ear-coverts, with bolder blackish border, unstreaked rufous-chestnut rump and uppertail-coverts, browner breast/flanks. **Juvenile**: Similar to female. **VOICE** Song is a simple *hsiee swee-swee swee-tsir-ririri* or *hsiee swiii chew-chew-chew* etc. (1–2 introductory notes). Explosive *tzick* call notes. **HABITAT** Underbrush in open forest, secondary growth; 1,500–2,565 m.

CHESTNUT-EARED BUNTING *Emberiza fucata* 15–16 cm

(7) **Male breeding** *fucata*: Dark-streaked grey crown/nape, chestnut ear-coverts, breast-gorget of black streaks. Otherwise mostly white below, with rufous-chestnut band across lowermost breast. Very little white on outertail. (8) **Female**: Similar to breeding male but duller crown/nape/underparts, less distinct gorget and breast-band. (9) **First-winter female**: Buffy crown, nape and breast/flanks. Dull birds (illustrated) have browner head-sides. **Male non-breeding/first-winter male**: As adult female but buffier supercilium, whitish base colour to throat and breast contrasts more with buffy flanks/upper belly. **VOICE** Sings with rapid twittering *zwee zwizwezwizizi trup-trup* or *zip zizewuziwiziriri chupee churupp* etc. Explosive *pzick* call. **HABITAT** Open country, cultivation; up to 1,300 m.

LITTLE BUNTING *Emberiza pusilla* 12–14 cm

10) **Adult non-breeding**: Small; fine dark streaks on breast/flanks, broad blackish (streaky) lateral crown-stripe, eyestripe and border to rufous-chestnut ear-coverts. Contrasting buffish median crown-stripe, supercilium, submoustachial stripe and ear-covert spot; rufescent lores and forehead, whitish eyering. (11) **Adult breeding**: Chestnut flush over most of head; lateral crown-stripes solid black. (12) **Juvenile**: Like non-breeding adult but weaker lateral crown-stripes, browner below with less neat streaking. **VOICE** Variable. Rather metallic *zree zree zree tsutsutsutsu tzriiitu* and *tzru tzru tzru zee-zee-*

zee-zee zriiiiiru etc. Call is a hard *tzik*. **HABITAT** Secondary growth, scrub and grass, cultivation, orchards; up to 2,000 m.

YELLOW-BREASTED BUNTING *Emberiza aureola* 15 cm

(13) **Male non-breeding** *ornata*: Yellow below, warm brown breast-band, white median/lesser coverts. Pale buffish supercilium and ear-coverts, the latter with broad dark border, indistinctly streaked above and on flanks. (14) **Male breeding**: Chestnut upperparts and breast-band, blackish forehead, face and upper throat. (15) **Female**: Duller than non-breeding male, no breast-band, paler below, darker streaks on breast-sides/flanks, duller/paler above, dark-streaked crown with paler median stripe. Often has paler mantle 'braces'. (16) **Juvenile**: Less yellow than female, fine breast-streaks/malar line. Pale brownish rump with darker streaks. **VOICE** Song is a fairly slow, high-pitched *djuu-djuu weee-weee ziii-zii* etc. Call is a short metallic *tic*. **HABITAT & BEHAVIOUR** Grass, scrub, cultivation, open areas, often near water; up to 800 m. Often roosts in large numbers, particularly in reedbeds.

CHESTNUT BUNTING *Emberiza rutila* 14–14.5 cm

(17) **Male non-breeding**: Duller than breeding male, with pale fringes to chestnut feathers. (18) **Male breeding**: Bright chestnut plumage with yellow breast and belly. (19) **Female**: Similar to juvenile Yellow-breasted but rufous-chestnut rump and uppertail-coverts, rather plain ear-coverts, no 'braces', almost no white on outertail. **Juvenile**: Resembles female. **VOICE** Song is a rather high *wiie-wiie-wiie tzrree-tzrree-tzrree zizizitt* etc. Call is a *zick* similar to Little. **HABITAT** Underbrush in open forest, scrub, grass, bamboo, cultivation; up to 2,500 m.

BLACK-HEADED BUNTING *Emberiza melanocephala* 16–18 cm

(20) **Male non-breeding**: Pattern as breeding but very washed out, pale fringes above, duller and buffier below. (21) **Male breeding**: Black crown and head-sides, rufous-chestnut nape and upperparts, all-yellow underparts. (22) **Female**: Large; washed-out look, no white on outertail, whitish wing-fringing, pale yellow undertail-coverts. (23) **First winter**: As female but streakier above, pinkish-buff breast-wash; may show sparse breast-/flank-streaks. **VOICE** Song is a melodious, quite harsh *zrt zrt preepree chu-chiwu-chiwu ze-treeurr*. Sparrow-like *chleep* or *chlip* calls, metallic *tzik* or *plutt*. Deep *tchup* in flight. **HABITAT** Open country, scrub, cultivation; lowlands.

BLACK-FACED BUNTING *Emberiza spodocephala* 14–15 cm

(24) **Male** *sordida*: Greenish-olive hood (may be paler-fringed on non-breeders), blackish face, yellow below. (25) **Female breeding**: No dark face, yellowish throat/breast, dark malar and streaks below. Dull birds (illustrated) resemble non-breeders, which are as first winter but with buffier-washed head and pale buffish-yellow wash below. (26) **First winter**: No obvious rufous or yellow in plumage, greyish ear-coverts/neck-side/lesser coverts, grey-brown rump, clear underpart-streaks, whitish submoustachial. Lores/neck-sides of some males resemble adult. **VOICE** Song is a variable, lively series of ringing chirps and trills: *chi-chi-chu chirri-chu chi-zeee-chu chi-chi* etc. Call is a sibilant sharp thin *tzii*. **HABITAT** Scrub and grass, cultivation, often near water; up to 400 m.

GLOSSARY

Axillaries: the feathers at the base of the underwing.

Bare parts: collective term for bill, legs and feet, eyering, exposed facial skin, etc.

Bird-wave: mixed species feeding flock.

Casque: an enlargement of the upper mandible, as in many hornbill species.

Cere: a fleshy structure at the base of the upper bill which contains the nostrils.

Comb: erect unfeathered fleshy growth, situated lengthwise on crown.

Crest: tuft of feathers on crown of head, sometimes erectile.

Distal: (of the part) farther from the body.

Eclipse: a dull short-term post-nuptial plumage.

Extirpated: locally or regionally (but not globally) extinct.

Face: informal term for the front part of the head, usually including the forehead, lores, cheeks and often the chin.

Flight feathers: in this work, a space-saving collective term for primaries and secondaries.

Fringe: complete feather margin.

Frugivorous: fruit-eating.

Graduated tail: tail on which each feather, starting outermost, is shorter than the adjacent inner feather.

Gregarious: living in flocks or communities.

Gular: pertaining to the throat.

Hackles: long, pointed neck feathers.

Hepatic: brownish-red (applied to the rufous morph of some cuckoos).

Knob: a fleshy protrusion on the upper mandible of the bill.

Lappet: a fold of skin (wattle) hanging or protruding from the head.

Lateral: on or along the side.

Leading edge: the front edge (usually of the forewing in flight).

Local: occurring or relatively common within a small or restricted area.

Mask: informal term for the area of the head around the eye, often extending back from the bill and covering (part of) the ear-coverts.

Mesial: down the middle (applied to streak on chin/throat, mostly of raptors); interchangeable with gular.

Morph: a permanent alternative plumage exhibited by a species, having no taxonomic standing and usually involving base colour, not pattern.

Nomadic: prone to wandering, or occurring erratically, with no fixed territory outside breeding season.

Nuchal: pertaining to the nape and hindneck.

Ocelli: eye-like spots, often iridescent.

Orbital: surrounding the eye.

Polyandrous: mating with more than one male (usually associated with sex-role reversal).

Post-ocular: behind the eye.

Pre-ocular: in front of the eye.

Race: see subspecies.

Rami: barbs of feathers.

Shaft-streak: a pale or dark line in the plumage produced by the feather shaft.

Subspecies: a geographical population whose members all show constant differences, in plumage and/or size etc., from those of other populations of the same species.

Subterminal: immediately before the tip.

Terminal: at the tip.

Terrestrial: living or occurring mainly on the ground.

Tibia: upper half of often visible avian leg (above the reverse 'knee').

Trailing edge: the rear edge (usually of the wing in flight).

Underparts: the lower parts of the body (loosely applied).

Underside: the entire lower surface of the body.

Upperparts: the upper parts of the body, usually excluding the head, tail and wings (loosely applied).

Upperside: the entire upper surface of the body, tail and wings.

Vagrant: a status for a species nationally or regionally when it is accidental (rare and irregular) in occurrence.

Vermiculated: marked with narrow wavy lines, often only visible at close range.

Web: a vane (to one side of the shaft) of a feather.

Wing-bar: a line across a closed wing formed by different-coloured tips to the greater or median coverts, or both.

Wing-panel: a lengthwise strip on closed wing formed by coloured fringes (usually on flight feathers).

SELECTED BIBLIOGRAPHY

Anon (1989) *Birds of Khao Yai National Park Check-list*. Bangkok: Conservation Data Centre, Mahidol University.

Anon (1989) *Birds of Doi Inthanon National Park: Check-list and Guide to Bird Finding*. Bangkok: Conservation Data Centre, Mahidol University.

Anon (1994) From the field. *Oriental Bird Club Bull.* 19: 65–7.

Bangs, O. (1921) The birds of the American Museum of Natural History's Asiatic zoological expedition of 1916-1917. *Bull. Amer. Mus. Nat. Hist.* 44: 575–612.

Boonsong Lekagul and Round, P.D. (1991) *A Guide to the Birds of Thailand*. Bangkok: Saha Karn Bhaet.

Crosby, M. (1995) From the field. *Oriental Bird Club Bull.* 21: 68–73.

Deignan, H.G. (1963) Checklist of the birds of Thailand. *U.S. Natn. Mus. Bull.* 226.

Gretton. A. (1990) Recent reports. *Oriental Bird Club Bull.* 11: 40–8.

Rasmussen, P.C. and Parry, S.J. (2001, in press) The taxonomic status of the 'Long-billed' Vulture *Gyps indicus. Vulture News*.

Robson, C. (1985–1999) Recent reports/From the field. *Oriental Bird Club Bull.* 1: 24–8; 2: 36–40; 4: 29–31; 5: 33–6; 7: 35–40; 8: 32–6; 9(10): 38–44; 10: 41–4; 12: 40–4; 13: 47–52; 14: 48–52: 15: 43–7; 16: 50–2; 17: 49–53; 18: 67–70; 20: 55–61; 22: 57–62; 23: 49–53; 24: 59–65; 25: 61–9; 26: 60–6; 27: 61–6; 28: 44–8; 29: 51–6.

Robson, C. (2000) *A Field Guide to the Birds of South-East Asia*. London: New Holland.

Round, P.D. (1988) *Resident forest birds in Thailand*. Cambridge, U.K.: International Council for Bird Preservation (Monogr. 2).

Round, P.D. (2000) *Field Check-list of Thai Birds*. Bangkok: Bird Conservation Society of Thailand.

Round, P.D. and Treesucon, U. (1997) *Birds of Khao Nor Chuchi: Check-list and Guide to Bird Finding*. Bangkok: Bird Conservation Society of Thailand.

Treesucon, U. and Round, P.D. (1991) *Birds of Khao Sam Roi Yot National Park: Check-list and Guide to Bird Finding*. Bangkok: Conservation Data Center, Mahidol University.

Treesucon, U. (2000) *Birds of Kaeng Krachan: Check-list and Guide to Birds Finding*. Bangkok: Bird Conservation Society of Thailand.

Wells, D.R. (1999) *The Birds of the Thai-Malay Peninsula*, 1. San Diego and London: Academic Press.

INDEX

267

ACKNOWLEDGEMENTS

I would like to take this opportunity to thank a number of people who greatly assisted me during the preparation of this work.

First of all, I would like to thank those artists who painted new figures and made amendments to some of the original ones.

During several visits to the bird collections at the Natural History Museum, Tring, I was greatly assisted, as usual, by the staff there (Mark Adams, Robert Prys-Jones, Frank Steinheimer, Michael Walters and F.E 'Effie' Warr).

I would like to extend a special thankyou to Philip Round, a world authority on Thai birds, who has constantly helped with important information during this and previous projects. Others who assisted me greatly in preparing the text were Pamela Rasmussen, Peter Davidson, Will Duckworth, Dave Farrow and Uthai Treesucon.

I am also very grateful to Nigel Collar for his painstaking work in editing the manuscript and the designer, David Price-Goodfellow, for his diligence, particularly during the creation of the plates and maps. Lorna Sharrock at New Holland was very supportive and showed a high level of commitment to the project.
Craig Robson

ARTWORK ACKNOWLEDGEMENTS

Richard Allen: Plates 1; 2 (except 12–15 (DC)); 4; 5; 6; 7; 21 (11–16); 22; 32; 33; 36 (13–18); 64; 65; 66; 67; 68; 69; 70; 71; 73 (except 1–10 (CB)); 74; 75 (except 18–19 (ME)); 76 (except 14–18 (ME)); 78 (except 1–4 (ME)); 79 (1–8); 82 (9–18); 99; 100; 101; 117; 118; 119; 120; 121; 122.

Tim Worfolk: Plates 8; 9; 10; 11; 12; 13 (except 11–20 (JW)); 23; 24 (except 17–20 (HB)); 26 (12–15); 27; 34; 35; 36 (except 13–18 (RA)); 37; 38; 39; 40; 41; 42; 43; 44; 45; 46; 47; 48; 49; 50; 51; 96; 97; 98; 102; 103; 104; 123; 124; 125; 126; 127; 128.

Stephen Message: Plates 52 (except 6–9 and 22–25 (AM) and 19–21 (IL)); 61; 107 (1–5); 111; 113; 114; 115; 116.

Jan Wilczur: Plates 13 (11–20); 14; 15; 16; 17; 79 (except 1–8 (RA)); 80; 81; 82 (except 9–18 (RA)); 83; 87 (1).

Clive Byers: Plates 72; 73 (1–10); 105 (18–19); 109; 110; 112.

Mike Langman: Plates 18; 19; 20; 21 (except 11–16 (RA)); 85 (6); 89 (15); 91 (10).

Ian Lewington: Plates 52 (19–21); 55; 56; 59; 62 (except 1–3 (AM)); 63.

Christopher Schmidt: Plates 84; 85 (except 6 (ML)); 86; 87 (except 1 (JW)); 88; 89 (except 15 (ML)); 90; 91 (except 10 (ML)); 105 (except 18–19 (CB)); 106; 107 (except 1–5 (SM)); 108.

Andrew Mackay: Plates 52 (6–9 and 22–25); 53; 54; 57; 58; 60; 62 (1–3).

John Cox: Plates 28; 29; 30; 31.

Anthony Disley: Plates 92; 93; 94; 95.

Hilary Burn: Plates 24 (17–20); 25; 26 (except 12–15 (TW)).

Daniel Cole: Plate 2 (12–15); 3.

Martin Elliott: Plates 75 (18–19); 76 (14–18); 77; 78 (1–4).

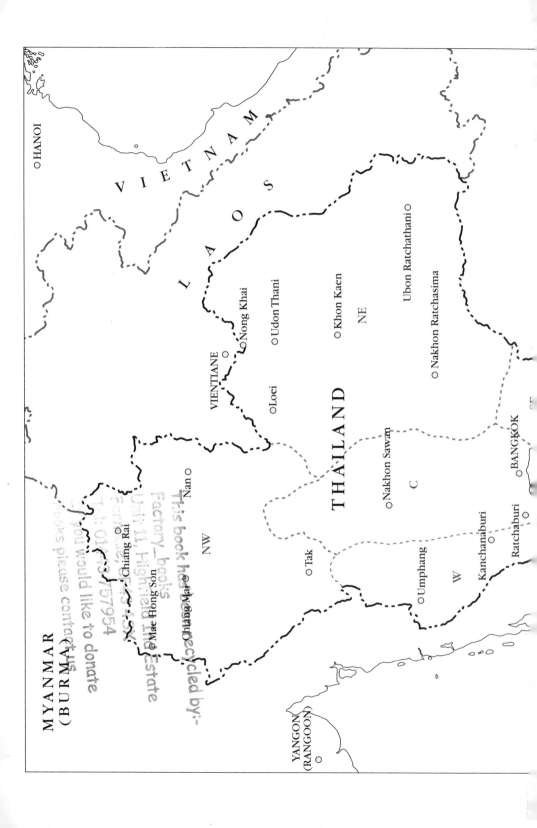